Clandestine Crossings

Clandestine Crossings

Migrants and Coyotes on the Texas-Mexico Border

David Spener

Cornell University Press
Ithaca and London

First published 2009 by Cornell University Press
First printing, Cornell Paperbacks, 2009

Printed in the United States of America

Library of Congress Cataloging-in-Publication Data

Spener, David, 1961–
  Clandestine crossings : migrants and coyotes on the Texas-Mexico border /
David Spener.
       p. cm.
  Includes bibliographical references and index.
    ISBN 978-0-8014-4749-5 (alk. paper) — ISBN 978-0-8014-7589-4 (pbk. : alk. paper)
  1. Human smuggling—Mexican-American Border Region.   2. Immigrants—
Mexican-American Border Region.   3. Illegal aliens—Mexican-American Border
Region.   4. Border crossing—Mexican-American Border Region.   5. Mexico—
Emigration and immigration—Social aspects.   6. United States—Emigration and
immigration—Social aspects.   7. Texas—Emigration and immigration—Social
aspects.   8. Mexican-American Border Region—Social conditions.   I. Title.

  JV6475.S64 2009
  304.8'73072—dc22   2009025029

Cornell University Press strives to use environmentally responsible suppliers and materials to the fullest extent possible in the publishing of its books. Such materials include vegetable-based, low-VOC inks and acid-free papers that are recycled, totally chlorine-free, or partly composed of nonwood fibers. For further information, visit our website at www.cornellpress.cornell.edu.

Cloth printing   10 9 8 7 6 5 4 3 2 1
Paperback printing   10 9 8 7 6 5 4 3 2 1

Contents

Acknowledgments

The research and writing that led to this book were generously supported by financial assistance from Trinity University and the John D. and Catherine T. MacArthur Foundation. In addition, many individuals were indispensable to the completion of this project.

David Kyle of the University of California, Davis was the person who initially convinced me to do field research on coyote-assisted border-crossings by Mexican migrants into South Texas. Robbie Greenblum, Robert Huesca, Olga Garza Kauffman, Rubén Hernández-León, Al Kauffman, Eleocadio Martínez, Monica Schurtman, and Víctor Zúñiga all pointed me to people I needed to talk to during the course of my research.

Rosie Rodríguez and her staff in the Clerk's Office of the U.S. court in Laredo, Texas, helped me find needed case files housed in the courthouse. Similarly, Jorge Saenz, Phil Reyna, and the staff of the Pretrial Services Office in the federal courthouse in San Antonio provided access to data on defendants.

The agents of U.S. Border Patrol in the Rio Grande Valley and Laredo sectors took me and my students on comprehensive tours of their facilities and operations on various occasions and graciously shared their views on a variety of issues.

Rodolfo Corona of the Colegio de la Frontera Norte and Luis Felipe Ramos Martínez of the Consejo Nacional de Población helped in interpreting the results I obtained from the Encuesta sobre Migración en la Frontera Norte de México.

I express my heartfelt appreciation to professors Fernando Pozos (of beloved memory) and Elena de la Paz Hernández Águila, who arranged for me to spend a delightful and productive semester as a visiting scholar at the Universidad de Guadalajara (UDG) while I was on leave from Trinity University in the spring of 2005. It was during my stay in Guadalajara that the main arguments of this book came into focus. In this regard, I especially thank the UDG's Jorge Durand and Ofelia Woo for their invaluable comments on earlier drafts of several chapters of this book. In addition, Professor Durand granted me generous access to data from the Mexican Migration Project (a joint project of the UDG and Princeton University), as well to as his extensive personal collection of migration-related books and documents. Also in Guadalajara, Melba Moeller produced detailed transcriptions of tapes of many of the Spanish-language interviews I conducted.

At Trinity University, Irma De León, Elizabeth Farfán, María McWilliams, Alfred Montoya, Carolina Palacios, and Joe Pierce all provided vital research and administrative assistance. I also thank John Donahue, Michael Kearl, Meredith McGuire, and Richard Reed for their steadfast support of my research and writing as chairs of Trinity's Department of Sociology and Anthropology.

Other friends and colleagues who gave helpful ideas, information, or advice include María Eugenia Anguiano, Patricia Arias, Randy Capps, Antonia Castañeda, Wayne Cornelius, Timothy Dunn, Karl Eschbach, Cynthia Gentry, Jacqueline Hagan, Josiah Heyman, Fernando Lozano, Arturo Madrid, Jennifer Mathews, Alida Metcalf, Joseph Nevins, Néstor Rodríguez, Efrén Sandoval, Michael Stone, Lee Terán, Gabino Torres (of beloved memory), and Gabrielle Winkler.

Special thanks go to *mi tocayo* David Peña-Alfaro for his careful review of my translations and use of Spanish terms throughout this book. Rosana Blanco-Cano, Jorge González, Hilda Peña-Alfaro, and Bladimir Ruiz also answered some of my frequent *preguntas lingüísticas*.

Peter Wissoker, my editor at Cornell University Press, has given significant support and encouragement from the beginning. In addition, I am grateful to the Press's anonymous reviewers, whose extensive comments were extremely helpful to me in preparing the final draft of my manuscript.

No one knows better than my family all the time and effort that went into the writing of this book. I am grateful to my wife, Marsha, and to my children, Benjamin and Nellie, for their love, support, and understanding during the many years I worked on this project. Finally, I express my deep admiration and gratitude to the migrants and their families who took the time to tell me about their border-crossing experiences. Their strength and accomplishments in the face of tremendous adversity have been an inspiration. They trusted me to tell readers their story. I have tried my best to tell it well.

David Spener

San Antonio, Texas

An earlier version of chapter 4 appeared in Spanish in Augustín Escobar Latapí, ed., *Pobreza y migración internacional* (Mexico City: Centro de Investigaciones y Estudios Superiores en Antropología Social, 2008). An earlier version of chapter 5 appeared in Spanish in Socorro Arzaluz Solano, ed., *La migración a Estados Unidos y la frontera noreste de México* (Mexico City: El Colegio de la Frontera Norte and Miguel Ángel Porrúa, 2007). They are used here with permission.

Terminology Used in This Book

The terminology used in the discourse about the movement of people across international boundaries carries with it important connotations, some intended, others not. In this book, I have tried to use terms that are faithful to the perspective of international migration as a form of resistance to the restrictions on human mobility imposed by nation-states. Because Mexicans who engage in this cross-border movement do not necessarily intend to settle permanently in the United States, I refer to them as *migrants* rather than *immigrants,* since the latter term implies a definitive move to the new country. Concomitantly, I refer to the process of cross-border movement as *migration,* rather than *immigration.*

A variety of terms are commonly used today to refer to persons who enter the United States to live and work without having received official permission from the U.S. government. *Illegal aliens* and *illegal immigrants* imply criminality and are often used by government officials and reporters in the United States.[1] *Undocumented immigrants* has come to be considered a less derogatory term, insofar as it highlights people's inability to obtain proper bureaucratic paperwork rather than their status as criminals. Today, however, this term is inaccurate, insofar as most such people do, in fact, possess documents that permit them to work in the United States. The problem is that these documents, such as Social Security cards and "green cards," have typically been purchased from third parties rather than issued officially by government agencies. In recognition of this situation, Durand and Massey (2003) have proposed referring to such persons as *clandestinos* (clandestine migrants), a term that emphasizes their intent to evade detection and deportation by government authorities. The word *clandestine,* however, itself carries the negative connotation of deception and illegality. In light of the disadvantages of each of the terms discussed here, and in keeping with the interpretive framework presented in the introduction, in most places I refer to persons whose cross-border movements are undertaken in spite of state efforts to exclude them as *autonomous migrants.* I reserve use of the adjective *clandestine* to describe the act of border-crossing itself, which is, in fact, typically secret, concealed, and surreptitious. By referring to such crossings as clandestine, I do not mean to imply anything about the character of the persons who engage in them.

Government officials and English-language journalists typically refer to the service providers hired by autonomous migrants as *alien smugglers* or *human traffickers.* In Spanish, a single term, *traficantes,* is used as an equivalent for both terms. *Smuggling* and *trafficking* are often used interchangeably in public discourse, in spite of their different definitions in international law. According to the 2000 United Nations Protocol to Prevent, Suppress, and Punish Trafficking, "human smuggling" refers to situations where migrants pay another party to help them gain illegal entry into a state in which they were neither a citizen nor a permanent resident (Laczko 2002). "Human trafficking" is similar, with the added ingredient of the "traffickers" taking control over the persons being trafficked in order to exploit them against their will (Laczko 2002). Although "smugglers" hired by Mexican migrants sometimes do turn out to be "traffickers" as defined by the UN Protocol, this is not so in the vast majority of cases. In addition, the use of the terms "trafficker" and "smuggler" by government officials and the press rhetorically links surreptitious border-crossing practices with drug trafficking and its attendant evils, even though the authorities have not proven any systematic connection between the two (see Chapter 4 for more discussion of this point). Although in previous publications I have used the terms *smugglers* and *smuggling* to refer to the guiding and transportation of autonomous migrants across the Northeast Mexico-South Texas border, I have abandoned their use in this book, because of their connotations with respect to drug smuggling and because they wrongly imply that migrants are inanimate objects that have border-crossing "done" to them rather than acknowledging that they set their own migratory agendas and actively pursue strategies, including the hiring of professional service providers, to carry out those agendas.

In Mexican Spanish, three colloquial terms—*patero, pollero,* and *coyote*—are commonly used to refer to the people hired by autonomous migrants to help them cross the border and reach their U.S. destinations. Historically, use of the first two terms has been regionally specific. On the South Texas-

Tamaulipas border, where the international boundary is formed by the river known in the United States as the Rio Grande and in Mexico as the Río Bravo del Norte, *patero* is commonly used. The term dates to the early twentieth century when men began to ferry migrants across the river in boats known as *patos* (ducks) (Ramos Aguirre 1994, 105). The term is still used today to refer to providers of this service, but it is seldom heard outside that part of the border region. The term *pollero* (chicken-man) derives from the colloquial use of the word *pollos* (chickens) to refer to the migrants they guide and transport. Its use formerly was restricted to the western stretch of the U.S.-Mexico border, but in recent years it has become more generalized. Increasingly, the Mexican press refers generically to the transporters of autonomous migrants as *polleros,* wherever they are found, including and especially in the interior of Mexico and on its southern border with Guatemala, where their clients are mainly Central Americans (see, e.g., El Sol de Irapuato 2005; Liñan 2003; and Romero 2004). Although the use of the term *pollero* in the discourse about border-crossing is growing, *coyote* remains the colloquial term most widely used in Mexico to refer to those who assist migrants in making clandestine border-crossings. Unlike *patero* and *pollero, coyote* is not specific to any particular stretch of the border or any single region in the Mexican interior. Although my field research for this book has focused on clandestine crossings of the South Texas-Northeast Mexico border where the term *patero* originates, nearly all of my Mexican migrant informants who crossed there spoke of *coyotes* rather than *pateros,* and few migrant informants referred to the guides and transporters of migrants as *polleros* unless prompted to do so during the interview. For this reason, and others having to do with cultural matters discussed in greater detail in chapter 3, I use the term *coyote* throughout the remainder of this book to refer to anyone hired by autonomous migrants to help them cross the border clandestinely. To avoid the connotations of smuggling mentioned above, I adopt the Mexican term *coyotaje* (pronounced *koh-yoh-TAH-hey*) to refer to the services that autonomous migrants contract with coyotes. The term *coyotaje* also captures a wider variety of border-crossing practices than smuggling normally does, a point to which I will return later in the book.

Until recently, the Immigration and Naturalization Service (INS) of the U.S. Department of Justice was the government agency charged with enforcing the nation's immigration laws, while the Customs Service of the U.S. Department of the Treasury was charged with enforcing the nation's laws with respect to the movement of merchandise in and out of the country. In March 2003, immigration and customs enforcement were integrated into the newly created Department of Homeland Security (DHS). The Border Patrol, the principal interdiction force on the border with Mexico away from legal ports of entry, was incorporated into the new DHS Customs and Border Protection (CPB) unit. Other immigration enforcement activities, including investigations and interior enforcement, were assigned to the new DHS Immigration and Customs Enforcement (ICE) unit. This change occurred during the course of my research for this book and I use the bureaucratic nomenclature that was in use at the time that a given observation was made. I also make occasional use of *la migra,* the colloquial term used by Mexican migrants to refer generically to all U.S. immigration enforcement agents and agencies. The official name of the McAllen sector of the U.S. Border Patrol was changed in March 2005 to the Rio Grande Valley sector. In order to avoid confusion, I refer to it as the Rio Grande Valley sector throughout the book.

Nearly all of the interviews I conducted with Mexican informants took place exclusively in Spanish. When I directly quote Mexican informants, I present only my English translation of their statements. In places where a translation may be ambiguous or where I wish to call attention to the use of specific Spanish words or expressions, I include the informant's original words in italics. I also use some Spanish words common among bilingual speakers in South Texas, such as the term *monte* to refer to the brush that covers much of the border region. In all cases, my goal is to most accurately convey to readers the intended meaning and flavor of statements made by my informants.

Clandestine Crossings

INTRODUCTION

Lives on the Line

This book documents and analyzes the experiences of Mexican men and women whose poverty and difficult circumstances at home obliged them to journey to the United States in search of work or to reunite with family members who had already done so. They would have liked to have had official permission from the U.S. government to do so, but they knew that such an invitation would not be forthcoming, so they crossed the border anyway, in spite of the risks involved. Mexicans have been crossing their country's border with the United States clandestinely since the early 1900s, and in large numbers. During the first half of the twentieth century, most of them swam across the Rio Grande into Texas. By the 1960s, more of them were headed to work in California, and so most began to cross on foot through Tijuana into neighboring San Diego. In the 1990s, the U.S. government cracked down on clandestine border-crossing by launching a series of paramilitary operations and building new walls and fences in the major urban corridors that Mexicans passed through as they headed north. These measures shifted an

The analysis presented in this book is based on scores of in-depth interviews with migrants and coyotes about their border-crossing experiences. These interviews were conducted between mid-1998 and early 2006. While many interview excerpts are included in these pages, space limitations preclude a complete retelling of individual informants' experiences. Readers who are interested in reviewing detailed accounts of the experiences of individual migrants and coyotes whom I interviewed should consult the website that accompanies this text. It can be accessed at http://www.trinity.edu/clandestinecrossings.

ever-growing proportion of the clandestine flow to the sparsely populated Arizona-Sonora Desert, where relatively few migrants had crossed in the past. This shift was dramatic and troubling insofar as the region was suddenly witness to thousands of migrants passing through on foot, with many dying en route in the unforgiving desert. Journalists, photographers, and film crews descended on the region to record the spectacle of an army of the poor marching north, "overrunning" small settlements and isolated ranches. Meanwhile, back in Texas, thousands of other Mexicans continued to cross the river into the United States as they had done for over a century, attracting major attention in the press only when a tragedy occurred.

Back in the 1960s, much of the fieldwork for the first major study of "illegal" immigration to the United States was conducted along the border between South Texas and Northeast Mexico. Directed by the pioneering Chicano sociologist Julián Samora, the findings were published in 1971 in *Los Mojados: The Wetback Story*. One of that book's major contributions was the vivid description of a clandestine crossing of the river made by Jorge Bustamante, then a young graduate research assistant working for Samora. Despite conditions having changed considerably, relatively little has been written by migration scholars about the experiences of Mexicans passing through the Northeast Mexico-South Texas corridor since Samora and his collaborators were in the field forty years ago, even though tens of thousands of migrants continue to cross this stretch of the border annually.[1] One of my specific goals in writing this book is to redress the relative inattention the region and its migrants have received from migration scholars in recent decades. Of perhaps greater significance in analytical terms, I attempt throughout to shed light on the more general social process by which migrants manage to enter the United States in spite of government efforts to interdict them at or near the international boundary. While most analyses of Mexican migration to the United States focus on the reasons migrants leave their homes or how they adapt to life and work in their destinations, my focus here is on migrants' experiences as they journey across the border, taking care to address both material and symbolic dimensions. I begin by presenting vignettes of three crossings of this stretch of the border in the first years of the twenty-first century.

Three Hitchhikers

I was driving home to San Antonio from Laredo on Interstate 35 one sunny Monday afternoon in October 2002 when I saw three men climb over a ranch fence and stagger up an embankment toward the shoulder of the access road that ran parallel to the highway. There were no houses or buildings nearby nor were there any cars or trucks parked alongside the road, just a great expanse of thorny brush beyond the fence. From the vantage point of my car zooming by a couple of hundred feet away on the interstate, I could see that each of the men was wearing a baseball cap and carried a small knapsack slung over his shoulder. I had been working on the border long enough to know who they were and what they were doing. I got off the highway at the next exit a mile or so up the road and then doubled back on the access road toward where I had seen them emerge from the brush. I found them standing on the embankment below the shoulder of the road and drove up to them slowly, wanting to get a better look before offering them a ride. I rolled down my window and asked them, "¿Necesitan alguna ayuda?" [Do you need any help?]. "¡Sí!," they answered in unison, looking grateful and relieved. "Súbanse," I told them, "Get in." One of the men opened the door and let his two companions crawl into the backseat of my old station wagon. When he started to get in back with them as well I motioned for him to sit in the empty front seat next to me.

As they got in the car, I could see that all three men were quite short and that their clothes were dirty and tattered. The face of the man who sat down next to me was broad and dark brown. In the rearview mirror, I could see that his companions' faces were like his. I thought to myself that they were probably *indígenas* from southern Mexico or Central America. When I asked them where they were from I learned that all three were from small rural villages in southern Mexico, one from the state of Veracruz, the other from Guerrero, and the third from Chiapas. They had met at the migrant shelter run by the Catholic Church across the river in Nuevo Laredo, Tamaulipas. Each was making his way across the border for the first time in hopes of finding work in the United States. They had no money, no guide, and no food or water left.

This was their second attempt in the last week to cross the border and walk out of South Texas toward San Antonio or Austin or Dallas or wherever they might be able to get a job. On their first try, they waded the Río Bravo del Norte, as the Rio Grande is known to Mexicans, only to be apprehended by the U.S. Border Patrol shortly after setting foot in Texas, who then immediately sent them back across the international bridge to Nuevo Laredo. Their second try was more "successful." They had evaded apprehension along the border itself and had begun the long hike through unknown brush country, hoping to get around the Border Patrol's immigration checkpoint located on the interstate north of Laredo. They walked day and night, stopping only to sleep fitfully on the bare ground beneath the stars. The thorns of *nopal* (prickly pear cactus), *maguey* (agave), and *mezquite* (mesquite) had pierced their skin and torn their clothes. They had stepped gingerly around several rattlesnakes poised to strike. Their food and water had run out two days into the trek. After that, they went hungry but had been able to drink the murky water from cattle troughs they found along the way. When I found them they had been wandering in the brush for *six days*. I had sized up their situation correctly when I first spotted them from the highway. They had decided that they had to get out to the highway to get some help, even if it meant getting picked up by the Border Patrol and sent back to Mexico again.

It was a good thing that the summer was over and that the weather had been overcast and relatively cool the last few days, with highs barely reaching the 80s. Had it been July, the temperatures would have been over 100° F in the shade, with little shade to be found. The three might never have made it out to the highway. With luck, their bodies would have been found, identified, and added to the mounting toll of deaths of migrants along the border. Over the preceding three years, the authorities had recovered the bodies of ninety people who had perished as they attempted to cross the border near Laredo.[2] It was equally possible that they would never have been found at all, and their families would never have known what happened to them. The men said that the lack of paying work in Mexico left them with little choice but to attempt the crossing. They had heard it would be difficult and dangerous, but they explained that they had to try, even if it cost them their lives. They had families to feed, clothe, and house and had no hope of adequately doing so if they stayed in their home villages. The dangers they might meet at the border had been abstract and hypothetical up to now, while the dangers they faced staying at home had been all too specific and concrete.

Aside from the Border Patrol agents that had apprehended them a week earlier, I was the first *gringo* they had met since entering the United States. They were surprised that I spoke Spanish. They wanted to know where I was from and what I did for a living. I explained that I was a college professor and was heading home to San Antonio after taking care of some business at the border. They had all heard of San Antonio and asked if I could take them there with me. I thought it over for a minute. We were past the immigration checkpoint, I reasoned, and as far as I knew it wasn't against the law to pick up hitchhikers, so I said I would be happy to. One of them asked how far San Antonio was from Dallas, where a cousin of his lived. I told him that Dallas was another four hours farther up the road from San Antonio. We agreed that I could leave them at the bus station in San Antonio and that he could try to call his cousin from there.

Almost immediately, I began to have second thoughts about having the men in the car with me. Although we were past the immigration checkpoint where Border Patrol agents searched vehicles, interrogated drivers and passengers, and inspected documents, I could still be pulled over by one of the many Border Patrol agents roving the interstate in their vehicles. I also remembered that the Border Patrol had opened a new state-of-the-art station a year or two earlier along the highway near Cotulla, which we had not yet passed. Moreover, if I were pulled over, I could hardly pretend that I didn't realize that my passengers were "illegal aliens." Some of the agents in the Laredo sector knew me because I had interviewed them in the past about their immigration-enforcement activities. In addition, they had taken my students and me on guided tours of Border Patrol operations in the area as part of a course on Mexico-U.S. border relations that I had been teaching for several years.

As I pulled off the interstate at the Encinal exit, I told my passengers that I had forgotten there was another Border Patrol station ahead of us and that I was sorry, but I wouldn't be able to drive them all the way to San Antonio after all. If they were perplexed or disappointed, they didn't show it. In fact, they hadn't had much time, only ten minutes or so, to get over the surprise of my stopping to pick them up in the first place. I handed one of them a twenty-dollar bill and let them off at a convenience store where they could buy something to eat and drink. I told them that there might be people in town who could help them get to San Antonio or even to Dallas. I gave them my card and told them to call me if they made it to San Antonio. They thanked me and then walked into the store. I quickly pulled away and left town. I never saw or heard from them again. Other migrants I subsequently interviewed told me how they had been able to get rides away from the border once they had made it past the immigration checkpoints. Maybe my three passengers had been able to do so as well, but I'll never know. For their sake and that of their families, I hope they made it.

The Victoria Tragedy

The following spring, on the night of May 13, 2003, somewhere between 75 and 100 people climbed into the back of a tractor-trailer rig in an isolated spot on the outskirts of Harlingen, Texas. They had come from Mexico, Honduras, El Salvador, and the Dominican Republic and were headed to Houston. They had all entered the United States clandestinely from Mexico, crossing the Rio Grande with the help of professional guides known as *coyotes*. These guides knew a twenty-six-year-old Honduran woman who lived in Harlingen and who had been able to arrange for their customers to be spirited away from the border in the back of this eighteen-wheeler. The Mexicans were paying $1,800 each to be taken to Houston, with half paid up front by relatives in the

United States who had wired the money to the coyotes. These relatives would be asked to pay the remainder when their family members arrived in Houston. The people from the other countries would be charged a bit more, but would pay on the same COD basis. Unlike the three men I had picked up along Interstate 35 north of Laredo, the people in this trailer would not have to make an arduous trek through the brush, facing all sorts of dangers, in order to get around the immigration checkpoints on the highways leading toward the Texas interior. Rather, they would go through the checkpoint hidden in the trailer, with their coyotes betting that the rig would not be inspected. The vast majority of vehicles were routinely waved through by the Border Patrol agents staffing the checkpoints.[3] Not only would they not have to walk at all, but this particular trailer was refrigerated, so it would be a relatively cool and comfortable two-hour ride to Robstown, Texas, just outside Corpus Christi, where the coyotes planned to unload the migrants from the trailer into cars and pickups to drive them the rest of the way to Houston.

Although it was dark and the temperature was only 75° F when the rig pulled out of Harlingen, the heat inside the trailer soon became unbearable. For reasons that have never been made clear, the rig's driver did not turn on the trailer's refrigeration unit. Although its normal temperature is 98.6° F, the human body radiates a great deal of additional heat through the process of respiration. Packing so many people inside the trailer with no ventilation was like closing the door on a wood stove filled with glowing embers. Within just a few minutes after leaving Harlingen, the temperature inside the trailer rose to 110° F. Within a half hour, men began to take off their shirts to try to stay cool. It became difficult to breathe. Two men punched out the trailer's turn signals in order to let in some air, but it was not enough to make much difference. People shouted and banged on the walls hoping to get the driver to stop and let them out of the trailer, but to no avail. Originally, the coyotes planned to use the trailer to transport the migrants only as far as Robstown, but en route one of the coyotes called the driver of the rig on his cell phone and offered him more money to drive them all the way to Houston instead. The driver said yes. Later, as he approached the town of Victoria, Texas, four hours after leaving Harlingen, the driver pulled into a gasoline station and convenience store. By this time, the temperature inside the trailer had risen to over 170° F. As he walked past the back of the trailer and the holes from which the tail lights dangled, the driver, who did not speak Spanish, heard people shouting and banging on the walls inside. He and a companion then went into the convenience store and bought twenty bottles of water. When they returned to the trailer and began passing water bottles into the trailer through one of the holes left by the broken tail lights, a man inside told them, in broken

English, that people were dying and they needed to open the trailer's doors to let them out.

When the driver opened the doors to the trailer, he saw a pile of people lying on the floor in the fetal position. Others jumped out of the trailer and stumbled dazedly off into the night. Seventeen people in the trailer were dead, including a five-year-old boy and his father. Two more died later in the hospital. It had been the single most lethal clandestine journey undertaken by migrants in the history of the United States.[4] But it would not be the last—330 more would die crossing the border in the coming year.[5]

Julián's Most Recent Journey

In August 2004, Julián Gómez headed back to work in Dallas, Texas, leaving behind his wife and three young children in Rancho San Nicolás, his home village in rural northern Guanajuato State.[6] It was his fourth clandestine crossing of the border. He had found a coyote in a neighboring village that had a good reputation for getting people across safely and agreed to pay him $1,400 when they arrived in Dallas. This amount was now the going rate, more than double what people had been paying the first time Julián traveled to Texas in 1993, owing to the greatly intensified patrolling of the border by U.S. authorities in the intervening years. He had never crossed with this particular coyote before, but other friends and relatives had and told him this one was reliable. Julián didn't have the $1,400 to pay the coyote, but a cousin in Dallas owed him some money for the pickup truck he had sold him before leaving for Guanajuato the previous year. The cousin agreed to cancel the debt by paying the coyote when he delivered Julián to him in Dallas.

The logistics of the trip would be the same as other times Julián had crossed with coyotes from his area. He would travel to the border at Nuevo Laredo in a bus with the coyote and several other migrants. From there they would go a certain distance up or downstream, where they would cross the Río Bravo with the assistance of a boatman known as a *patero*. Next came the hard part. They would have to walk through the rugged South Texas brush country for several days to get around the immigration checkpoint operated by the Border Patrol on Interstate Highway 35, which was located about fifteen miles north of Laredo. Once they trekked around the checkpoint, one of the coyote's accomplices would pick the group up in a car and drive them to San Antonio.

Everything went pretty much according to plan on this trip, with a couple of exceptions. They walked four days through the brush. As far as Julián was concerned, this wasn't as bad as it sounded. Except for the last day, they walked mainly at night, when it was cooler. They didn't walk continuously, but made many stops along the way. He had been playing on a baseball team in his hometown and was in good shape, so he didn't find the walking as hard as it had been for him on his earlier crossings. Nonetheless, a man on the trip, who was about forty years old and traveling with one of his sons, almost didn't make it because of the heat, lack of sufficient water, and the rough conditions on the trail. The man's feet became severely blistered by the third day, making it extremely painful for him to walk. After the jugs of water they were carrying were used up, the group had been forced to drink water from cattle troughs and puddles they found along the trail. This had made the man ill, and on the morning of the fourth day on the trail he could no longer keep down the water he was drinking and vomited several times. The man's son and the others in the group tried to encourage him to keep going, since they were almost at the point where the coyote's accomplice would pick them up. The coyote instructed the man to eat some more food and not drink so much water, hoping that would settle his stomach, but it didn't help much. Other members of the group carried the man's knapsack for him and they stopped more frequently to rest. The coyote was worried that the group was going to miss its ride, since he had arranged for them to be picked up at a certain time on the fourth day and they were running late. Fortunately, they were able to keep the sick man walking long enough to make it to the pickup point, just a few minutes before their ride arrived. If they had left the man behind, Julián thought he surely would have died, since they were walking through dense brush, far from any major thoroughfare.

The driver took Julián's group to a house in San Antonio. Some of the migrants were only going that far, while others, like Julián, were continuing on to Dallas. Julián called his cousin from the house in San Antonio to verify that he had the money ready to pay the coyote and found, much to his consternation, that the cousin was several hundred dollars short. Fortunately, the coyote was willing to negotiate a deal with Julián whereby the coyote paid his accomplices with what Julián could give him immediately and Julián would pay off the coyote by sending money home to his family in Rancho San Nicolás after he started working. Julián's wife would get the money to the coyote. At that point, the coyote called another accomplice in Dallas to drive to San Antonio to get Julián. The second driver took Julián to a place in Dallas that both his cousin and he knew how to find. They arrived around midnight. The cousin paid the driver the money he had been able to get together. The driver left Julián with his cousin and drove away into the night.

Julián went to work the next day as a "yard man," cutting grass, blowing leaves, trimming bushes, and weeding gardens. A couple of months later he got a construction job that paid ten dollars an hour. He started sending money home to his family in Rancho San Nicolás. The debt to the coyote was quickly repaid. All the money Julián sent after that went directly to supporting his wife and children. He was one of the millions of Mexicans working in the United States who sent a total of $16.6 billion home to their families in 2004.[7] Julián would not see his family again until the end of the following year, when he would return home for Christmas. He would stay with them in Guanajuato as long as he could, until money ran out, and he had to head north once more. By then, the crossing would be still more difficult.

No Legal Path into the United States for Mexican Migrants

At the beginning of the twenty-first century, about six hundred thousand Mexican migrants crossed the border into the United States each year in search of a better life. The vast majority of these migrants came without an official invitation from the U.S. government. A quarter to a third of them came across the Northeast Mexico-South Texas stretch of the border that is the focus of this book.[8] In other words, they crossed the Rio Grande some-where between the bridge connecting Ciudad Acuña, Coahuila, with Del Rio, Texas, and the mouth of the river at the Gulf of Mexico, around six hundred miles downstream. The basic conditions that motivated the migration of so many people were the same as they had been since the end of the nineteenth century when mass Mexican migration to the United States first began—lack of sufficient jobs with adequate pay in Mexican territory and a strong demand for low-wage manual labor in U.S. territory. The reason why a majority of these migrants came to the United States *sin papeles*—without papers—was that U.S. immigration policies made it nearly impossible for Mexican workers and peasants to get them. It was for this reason that so many border-crossings of the types described in the preceding pages took place.

In Mexico, major currency devaluations in the late 1980s and again in the mid-1990s, coupled with market restructuring brought about by implementa-tion of the North American Free Trade Agreement (NAFTA) in the late 1990s, intensified conditions that propelled Mexicans to the United States in search of work. At the same time, the economic boom experienced by the United States from 1992 to 2000 created a strong demand for manual workers north of the border, much of which was met by Mexican migrants. From 1990 to 1999, 4.4 million Mexican immigrants settled in the United States, 3.3 million or 76 percent of whom were undocumented. As the U.S. economy recovered from the one-two punch of the high-tech bust of 2000 and the terrorist attacks of 2001, Mexicans continued to move to the United States in large numbers: From 2000 to 2004 another 2.4 million settled, 85 percent of whom were undocumented (Passell 2005, 8, fig. 4). By 2005, 6.2 million undocumented Mexicans were living in the United States, amounting to 56 percent of the total U.S. undocumented population (Passell 2006, 5, fig. 4). Texas was the destination for a large proportion of the new Mexican immigrants to the United States, with its Mexican-born population growing from 907,432 in 1990 to 1,879,369 in 2000 (Grieco 2003). By 2005, Texas was home to between 1.4 and 1.6 million undocumented immigrants (Pew Hispanic Center 2006), most of whom were Mexican. Nationwide, the undocumented made up about 5 percent of workers in 2005, but they were especially concentrated in just a few occupations. Undocumented immigrants were 24 percent of workers engaged in farming, 17 percent of all cleaning-services workers, 14 percent of all construction workers, 12 percent of food-preparation workers, and 9 percent of manufacturing workers (Passel 2006, 11, fig. 10).

Today, most prospective Mexican migrants from working-class and peasant backgrounds have virtually no hope of fulfilling the bureaucratic requirements imposed by the U.S. government in order to migrate north legally. Annually, the United States makes available no more than about 26,500 immigrant visas to Mexicans who have no relatives to sponsor them who are either legal permanent residents or U.S. citizens (Ngai 2007; Preston 2006).[9] Although the U.S. State Department issues 140,000 visas worldwide annually to persons who wish to enter the country sponsored by an employer, only 5,000 of these are available to "unskilled" workers. In 2005, only two (not a misprint) Mexicans received such employment-based immigrant visas as unskilled workers (San Antonio Express-News 2006).[10] This raises the question of how we are to understand a situation in which key industries in the United States are dependent on manual workers from Mexico while the U.S. government issues only a tiny fraction of the immigrant visas that would be expected for a neighboring country of more than one hundred million residents with a century-old tradition of labor migration to the United States.

Interpretive Framework

Over the course of many years of study of migration across the Northeast Mexico-South Texas stretch of the international boundary, I have reflected extensively on how best to interpret the "facts on the ground" that I have observed in light of a variety of theoretical approaches and concepts developed by others who study migration, social inequality, and human rights.

To interpret the observations I made and the experiences related to me by my informants, I have synthesized a variety of approaches and concepts into a framework whose principal elements I outline here. These elements include the concepts of global apartheid, structural and cultural violence, autonomous international migration, everyday resistance, social capital, and funds of knowledge. Integrated into a common framework, these concepts permit me to present my findings in a coherent and analytically consistent manner that, I believe, offers a compelling alternative to the interpretations of clandestine border-crossing that are usually offered by participants in public debates surrounding international migration. I present this framework not as a theory or set of hypotheses to be tested but as a heuristic device whose intent is to promote a humane and comprehensive way of understanding an unresolved social problem that affects millions of people.

Global Apartheid and the Mexico-U.S. Border

Today all nation-states, including both Mexico and the United States, assert the sovereign right to restrict the entry of foreign nationals into their territories. Nevertheless, the context in which such restrictions are exerted and the ways in which they are imposed matter greatly. At the increasingly militarized border between the United States and Mexico, it is clear to whom such restrictions are mainly applied—dark-skinned working-class Mexicans. This has been clear to me since the early 1990s, when I first began to walk across the international bridges from Mexico into Texas. As a light-skinned, blue-eyed middle-class Anglo, I would routinely be waived through the ports of entry by border guards without being required to present any identification, while dark-skinned Latinos were routinely stopped, questioned, and required to produce passes that allowed them to enter the United States. I remember thinking at the time, "So, this is what apartheid looks like." It was not until a decade later that I discovered that other scholars had come to this same realization and had developed it as a conceptual framework for understanding world affairs.

A growing number of analysts and activists has begun to use the term *global apartheid* to refer to reliance on the principle of national sovereignty as a pretext for grossly unequal distribution of wealth, power, and well-being among nation-states in a way that mirrors the operation of the domestic regime of white supremacy in South Africa from 1948 to 1994 (see, for example, Alexander 1996; Booker and Minter 2001; Nevins 2008; Richmond 1994; and Sharma 2006). According to Alexander (1996, 171–72), the "legal structure of apartheid" in South Africa was a "thicket of laws which secured white superiority in every sphere of life." The mechanisms used by the South African apartheid system to secure white superiority included, among other things, the classification of the population into racial groups; the restriction of full citizenship and political rights to white people; "pass laws" and "influx controls" that limited the freedom of movement of nonwhites within South African territory; the racial differentiation of rights in "employment, enterprise, and economic participation"; and what in the United States used to be termed *segregation*, that is, the separation of the races in the areas of housing, education, medical care, and public accommodations.

Thirty years ago, Gernot Kohler, then a postdoctoral fellow at Princeton University's Center of International Studies, published a paper in which he noted that the condemnation of South African apartheid by the international community was "almost universal," given the ways in which apartheid "flagrantly violate[d] the aspirations of a majority of humanity for liberation from dominance" and "because apartheid constitute[d] the most repugnant form of human rights violation" (Kohler 1978, 2). He went on to point out how ironic this was, given that the contours of the emerging postcolonial world order so closely resembled the racial stratification of South African society. Kohler appears to have been the first scholar to give the name "global apartheid" to this "appalling" resemblance:

> Global apartheid is a structure of world society which combines socioeconomic and racial antagonisms and in which (i) a minority of whites occupies the pole of affluence, while a majority composed of other races occupies the pole of poverty; (ii) social integration of the two groups is made extremely difficult by barriers of complexion, economic position, political boundaries, and other factors; (iii) economic development of the two groups is interdependent; (iv) the affluent white minority possesses a disproportionately large share of world society's political, economic, and military power. Global apartheid is thus a structure of extreme inequality in cultural, racial, social, political, economic, military, and legal terms, as is South African apartheid. (Kohler 1978, 4)

In a follow-up essay published some years later, Kohler highlighted the importance of national boundary enforcement to the operation of apartheid on a world scale:

> The role of national boundaries is an important issue raised by global apartheid theory. In the global apartheid perspective, nation-states are compared to South African homelands; that is, territories reserved for nonwhites. National boundaries, passports, border patrols and fortifications function as

reinforcements of racial segregation at the world level, since they provide effective control mechanisms for keeping nonwhites (of the South) out of white areas (of the North) of the world, if so desired. (Kohler 1995, 405)

Other authors (Alexander 1996; Booker and Minter 2001; Richmond 1994; and Sharma 2006) have similarly highlighted how the restriction of the movement of the nonwhite poor across national boundaries separating the Global South from the capitalist core countries of the world-system is one of the main pillars of global apartheid. Unlike Kohler, who continued to place race at the root of the system of apartheid, whether practiced nationally or globally, these authors have argued that racial divisions are only one of the bases on which an apartheid regime may rest.[11] As Booker and Minter (2001, 15) have noted, even the "old apartheid was…not just 'about race'" but was also "an extreme mode of controlling labor by managing differential access to territorial movement and political rights." Similarly, Alexander (1996, 172) observed that the international system does not depend primarily on "race classification" to exclude the majority of the world's population from enjoying the fruits of capitalist production. Rather, "the laws of sovereignty, nationality, and property [are] sufficient to protect minority rule" over the global system. Sharma (2006), however, points out that contemporary border and migration controls retain a strong racial component, in spite of the lack of any specific reference to racial criteria in their legal rationale, insofar as they rest on historical foundations that were profoundly and often quite explicitly racial. Regardless of the extent to which global apartheid today rests on racist or nationalist foundations, it represents a form of what Galtung (1969, 168–71) called *structural violence,* that is, a structure of world society in which a substantial portion of the population is systematically deprived of things vital to their health and development.

An important component of the global apartheid system is the way that modern states have "expropriated the legitimate means of movement" and "monopolized the authority to determine who may circulate within and across their borders" (Torpey 1998, 239; Torpey 2000, 118–20). Crucial to this endeavor has been states' establishment of a "regime of identification" and "the construction of bureaucracies…to scrutinize persons and documents in order to verify identities," as well as "the creation of a body of legal norms designed to adjudicate claims by individuals to entry into particular spaces and territories" (Torpey 1998, 241). This "regime of identification," and the bureaucratic capacity to implement it, developed gradually over the course of several centuries. It did not become uniform as an international system governing movement between national territories until the outbreak of World War I in the second decade of the twentieth century (Torpey 2000, 93–121).

Turning our attention to the U.S.-Mexico border, Nevins (2005) reminds us that the state's prerogative with regard to restricting the movement of persons across its frontiers has been normalized to the point that today it is conceded to be legitimate by nearly everyone on both sides of the border, even by those who are strongly critical of U.S. immigration and border-control policies. Very few analysts today argue that nation-states do *not* have a legitimate sovereign right to regulate who may and may not enter their territories, despite the historical recency of states' assertion of this right.[12] Border enforcement has come to be seen as an essential element of the "rule of law" that maintains not only societal safety and order but also sacrosanct principles of justice. Here, however, we must not forget that the boundary in question was established not democratically but rather by a war of imperial conquest and that the manner in which it is enforced today has produced chaos, suffering, and injustice for those to whom the law is mainly applied, who were not party to the negotiations that produced it. Moreover, U.S. immigration policy as applied at the border with Mexico has closely resembled the kind of pass-law system that was in place under the apartheid regime of South Africa, in which the documents of nonwhites were closely scrutinized by agents of the apartheid state to determine whether or not given individuals were authorized to leave their "homelands" to enter white areas and, if they were authorized to enter, what types of activities they would be allowed to undertake and for what period of time.[13] Today, of course, this type of restriction of movement of persons *within* any given nation-state is widely condemned (Torpey 1998, 254). That the enforcement of apartheid-like pass-law controls is characteristic of many, if not most, international boundaries around the world—especially vigorous at the boundaries between affluent and poor/light-skinned and dark-skinned regions of the global system—makes it no less morally problematic. Brubaker (1994, 230) highlights that in the contemporary world-system the "tying of particular persons to particular states" by virtue of "morally arbitrary accidents of birth" results in the "profoundly illiberal" determination of their life chances. Moreover, he reminds us that "the prosperous and peaceful states of the world remain powerfully exclusionary." Sharma (2006), for her part, explicitly links the rise of this "passport culture" with the practice of global apartheid, insofar as "one's nationality is seen as a legitimate instrument of discrimination."

Torpey's (1998) conceptualization of the state's monopoly over the legitimate means of movement corresponds to Heyman's (1999b, 619) concept of *interdiction,* that is, the state's efforts "to stop flows of goods or people by intercepting them in movement, often at or near international boundaries." Interdiction thus represents the state's monopoly over legitimate movement and depends on state infrastructural capacity to identify and prevent movement regarded as illegitimate. As states have consolidated over the last several centuries, interdiction became an essential element in "the generally acknowledged ideal of a modern border" (Heyman 1999b, 620). Moreover, a great deal of a state's credibility depends on its ability to appear effective in carrying out interdiction activities (Heyman 1999a, 290). Although he does not use the terminology of apartheid to explicate the functional operation of border interdiction with respect to persons, Heyman (1999b, 621) summarizes how it works on the Mexico-U.S. border in a way consistent with the concept of global apartheid:

> In this and related instances, immigration interdiction: a) maintains the distinction between the two polities that undergirds their different social wages; b) restricts the free market movement of labour relative to those social wages; while c) facilitating the transfer of commodities produced in Mexico to U.S. consumers whose purchasing power reflects their higher social wage; and d) enabling the investment of capital in this process and the recovery of profit from it.

A corollary to this formulation is that labor migrants who manage to avoid interdiction at the border can "realize value" by doing so, as they avail themselves to some extent of the higher social wage offered in the United States, that is, as they partially reconfigure their productive relations vis-à-vis capital (Heyman 1999b, 619; Sharma 2006).

We see the effects of interdiction as part of an apartheid system insofar as the border divides North American territory into spaces characterized by vastly different levels of social well-being, even as it permits the operation of a highly integrated regional economy. The creation of the North American Free Trade Area in 1994 marked the culmination of a process of negotiated economic integration between the United States and Mexico that began in the early 1980s. By the early years of the new century, that integration had deepened considerably. In 2006, U.S. foreign direct investment in Mexico totaled $84 billion, and 2,600 U.S. firms had an important presence in the country (Embassy of the United States in Mexico 2008). In 2007, total trade between the United States and Mexico reached U.S. $347 billion, up from just $82 billion in 1993, the last year before the creation of the free trade area (United States Bureau of the Census 2008). More than one million Mexican workers labored, often in sweatshop conditions, in assembly plants known as maquiladoras, whose output was directed toward the U.S. market (Comité Fronterizo de Obrer@s 2007). Mexico exported around one-third of its total production, with 90 percent going to the United States (EarthTrends 2003). Wal-Mart was the largest private employer in each country (Weiner 2003). As economic integration proceeded apace with the implementation of NAFTA, manufacturing employment in Mexico grew only sluggishly, agricultural employment declined precipitously, real wages fell, and income inequality grew substantially (Polaski 2004). At the outset of the twenty-first century nearly 40 percent of Mexicans lived on less than two dollars a day (EarthTrends 2003), and Mexican maquiladora workers only earned $250 to $300 per month (Instituto Nacional de Estadística, Geografía e Informática 2008), a small fraction of what comparably employed workers would earn in the United States. Indeed, contrary to expectations of free-trade advocates, Mexican wages declined significantly relative to those of U.S. workers in NAFTA's aftermath (Polaski 2004).

The global apartheid frame lends itself well to analyzing both contemporary and historical conditions along the border between Mexico and the United States.[14] Ever since this border was imposed by military conquest in the mid-nineteenth century, it has demarcated a low-cost labor pool that can be tapped by U.S. capitalists as needed, whether by stimulating Mexican workers to migrate into U.S. territory, a phenomenon that began in the late nineteenth century and continues to this day, or by relocating manufacturing plants to Mexican territory, something that began in the 1960s and developed into a mass phenomenon by the 1980s. Since the 1920s, this system has depended on the U.S. Border Patrol to carry out the interdiction function at the international boundary and on other law enforcement agencies to police the Mexican migrant workforce in the U.S. interior. Today, U.S. border-control measures serve primarily as a forceful reminder to Mexican and other Latin American migrants of the unfreedom that they can expect once inside U.S. territory, that is, a warning that they are entering an apartheid police state. Rather than actually preventing or deterring entry, today the Border Patrol and its sister agencies within the Department of Homeland Security inflict ever-greater risk, suffering, humiliation, and expense on migrants who have not had their passage properly "documented" by the relevant state agencies.[15]

Although race is not the *official* criterion used by U.S. immigration authorities to decide toward whom to direct their unwanted attentions, it is strongly correlated with the official criteria—national origin, assets, income, educational qualifications, and "suspicious" behaviors—that *are* used.[16] Thus, in operational terms, the Border Patrol dedicates the overwhelming bulk of its personnel and resources to the surveillance of a Latin American "suspect population" in the southwestern U.S. borderlands, from which it identifies and arrests hundreds of thousands of "illegals" annually (Heyman 1998, 159, 166–67). At the same time, the Border Patrol and its sister agency ICE virtually ignore non-Hispanic whites. Indeed, it seems that the Border Patrol's principal function is to police the Mexican population residing in or passing through the U.S. borderlands, so much so that members of all other ethnonational groups fall into a single residual category in agency parlance—"other than Mexicans" or OTMs (Heyman 1995, 268). OTMs accounted for just 8 percent of apprehensions made by the Border Patrol in FY2004 (U.S. Department of Homeland Security 2004).

In addition to apartheid having never been "only" about race, neither has it ever consisted solely of the forcible separation of groups in physical/territorial space. It also operates in deterritorialized social, cultural, political, and economic "spaces" in which races and ethnic groups engage in a variety of relations with one another in relatively close physical proximity. The U.S.-Mexican case is an instructive example in this regard. For migrants, the task of crossing the border neither begins nor ends upon crossing from one side of the international line to the other, since the border continues to surround them even after they step onto U.S. territory (see Spener 2003b, 384). This virtual border surrounding migrants is constituted by ongoing surveillance and the denial by agents of the state of access to the full rights of personhood. The imposition of an apartheid border on Mexican migrants even after they have entered U.S. territory depends on the state stigmatizing them as "illegal" (Bacon 2007; Heyman 1999b). According to De Genova (2002, 427), the border enveloping such migrants consigns them to a "social space of 'illegality'" that accomplishes the "erasure of their legal personhood." Migrants inhabiting this space are subjected to "forced invisibility, exclusion, subjugation, and repression" that systematically inflict suffering on them. De Genova (2002, 492) further argues that the "illegalization" of migrants by the state is not primarily intended to physically exclude them but to incorporate them in U.S. society "under conditions of enforced and protracted vulnerability" that "serve as a disciplinary apprenticeship in the subordination of their labor" (see also Heyman 1998, and Sharma 2006).

This radical "othering" of Mexican migrants in the contemporary period harkens back to the evils of black-white segregation outlined by Martin Luther King Jr. in his "Letter from Birmingham Jail." King denounced this U.S. version of apartheid using the moral terminology developed by the Jewish philosopher Martin Buber. Segregation, argued King, "degrades the human personality" by substituting "an 'I-it' relationship for an 'I-thou' relationship" that "ends up relegating persons to the status of things" (King 1963, 85). Recent psychological research has found that "undocumented immigrants" have become one of the most negatively stereotyped out-groups in the United States, with the negative personal traits attributed to them mainly based on their lack of legal status (Lee and Fiske 2006). According to Massey (2007, 150), this finding "implies that undocumented migrants are not perceived as fully human at the most fundamental neural level of cognition, thus opening a door to the harshest, most exploitive, and cruelest treatment that human beings are capable of inflicting on one another." The radical "othering" and stigmatization of "illegal immigrants" constitutes a form of *cultural violence*, defined by Galtung (1990, 291) as "those aspects of...the symbolic sphere of our existence" that can be used to rationalize, legitimize, or obscure the operation of structural violence in a society. Thus, commonly held beliefs and attitudes about race and nation operate as cultural violence that legitimizes global apartheid as a system of structural violence.

Today global apartheid, as manifested in the deterritorialized border relations between Mexico and the United States, relegates undocumented migrants to the status of a commodified thing—labor power—while denying their essential humanity. This commodity, as noted by De Genova (2002, 438), can be readily disposed of physically through deportation by the state acting in the service of capital.[17] At the economic level, U.S.-Mexico border apartheid works today to facilitate the superexploitation of Mexicans on both sides of the border. The illegalization of Mexican labor owing to the imposition of employer sanctions by the 1986 Immigration Reform and Control Act (IRCA) reduced the wages earned by undocumented Mexican immigrants relative to their documented counterparts (Phillips and Massey 1999). Increased U.S. border enforcement since the implementation of NAFTA has been shown to have significantly depressed wages of workers in Mexico (Robertson 2005), while other research has indicated that increased border enforcement during the same period did nothing to boost the wages of workers in the United States (Hanson, Spilimbergo, and Robertson 2002). Evaluating the results of a variety of studies, Massey (2007, 145–46) concluded that the intensified criminalization and policing of migrants in the United States over the last two decades depressed wages and worsened working conditions for both immigrant *and* native workers. Taken together, these findings suggest that border apartheid imposed by the state is effective in maintaining a low-wage Mexican labor reserve available to capitalists in the United States and Mexico, one that mainly benefits capitalists, not workers in either country. Just as important, it serves as a barrier that prevents Mexican and U.S. workers from associating with one another to defend their common interests as workers vis-à-vis capitalists.[18]

Mexican Migrants and Global Apartheid: *Resistencia hormiga*

Sociologist Néstor Rodríguez (1996) introduced the term *autonomous international migration* into the scholarly lexicon as a way of referring to "the movement of people across nation-state borders outside of state regulations." This type of migration, he argued, was essential to the formation of transnational migrant communities, whose growing size and significance had become the object of considerable scholarly inquiry by the mid-1990s (e.g., Basch, Schiller, and Blanc 1994; Portes 1996). Crucial to Rodríguez's formulation was not just that the state failed to effectively regulate this type of migration but that the individuals and communities that engaged in it did so according to their own interests and agendas, regardless of the position adopted by states. He borrowed the autonomy/autonomous terminology from the work of scholars of class and labor relations, who used it to characterize as "worker self-activity" the spontaneous class struggles of workers in Italy and elsewhere that occurred independent of official unions and political parties. Rodríguez (1996, 24–25) argued that the autonomous self-activity of migrants was analogous to the autonomous self-activity of workers insofar as "autonomous" migrants a) were not organized into overtly political groups; b) challenged "capital's global stratification" through their migration from low-wage to high-wage regions of the world economy; and c) pursued the goal of survival, not the taking of political or economic power.

One of the great analytical strengths of the autonomous migrant/autonomous migration terminology is that it avoids defining migratory activity in ways that reproduce and legitimate state-centric perspectives. It does this by clearly casting migrants as the authors of their own history and as protagonists of wider socio-historical changes taking place in the global capitalist system. As Portes (1996) has observed, the formation of transnational migrant communities challenges one of the presumed defining features of the capitalist world-system, namely that capital is global and labor is relentlessly local in its purview (see also Ross and Trachte 1990). In this regard, Rodríguez argues that the round of border fortification we are currently witnessing in the United States needs to be understood as a reaction to the apparent disregard for state regulations with which migratory communities of Mexicans and other Latin American nationalities have acted, that is, as a reaction to migrants' challenge to the right of states to control their movements and labor-market behavior.[19] Migrant autonomy, then, challenges both the forcible segregation of populations into zones of affluence and zones of poverty that defines global apartheid as well as the monopoly exerted by nation-states over the "legitimate means of movement."

Despite the dramatic increase in U.S. border-enforcement efforts over the last two decades, Mexicans have continued to migrate autonomously north of the border. The circumstances that drive their migration—lack of job opportunities with decent wages, benefits, and working conditions and lack of adequate social welfare programs from the state in the absence of such jobs—have failed to improve or even worsened with the deepening of neoliberal development policies in Mexico that are ratified and to a large extent underwritten by the U.S. government and multilateral institutions based in Washington, DC (Bortz and Aguila 2006; Pozos 2003; Scott, Salas, and Campbell 2006; Salas 2003; Salas and Zepeda 2003). With intensified fortification of the Mexico-U.S. border, migration conditions have become considerably more adverse. We can interpret the simultaneous deepening of the neoliberal model in Mexico and the intensified policing of the border as an intensification of the exercise of power over peasant and working-class Mexicans by the U.S. and Mexican states. The fact that peasants and workers continue to migrate autonomously rather than accept conditions in Mexico represents an intensified *resistance* on their part to the exercise of state power over them.[20]

If autonomous migration represents a type of resistance to the global apartheid system, how might we characterize the specific ways in which it is enacted? The anthropological approach taken by James C. Scott to understanding peasant resistance to their exploitation offers some valuable conceptual tools. Scott (1985) originally developed this approach in an attempt to explain the forms of class struggle engaged in by Malaysian peasants in the mid-to-late twentieth century. He sought to reorient scholars away from instances of overt peasant rebellion and insurrection—which he noted were historically few and far between, and usually quite quickly crushed—and toward the ways in which peasants advanced their class interests through everyday forms of resistance to exploitation by landlords and regulation by the church and state. Scott referred to these everyday forms of resistance as *weapons of the weak* and offered the following initial formulation of what he meant by these terms:

> It seemed…important to understand what we might call *everyday* forms of peasant resistance—the prosaic but constant struggle between the peasantry and those who seek to extract labor, food, taxes, rents, and interest from them. Most of the forms this struggle takes stop well short of collective outright defiance. Here I have in mind the ordinary weapons of relatively powerless groups: foot dragging, dissimulation, false compliance, pilfering, feigned ignorance, slander, arson, sabotage, and so forth. These Brechtian forms of class struggle have certain features in common. They require little or no coordination or planning; they often represent a form of individual self-help; and they typically avoid any direct symbolic confrontation with authority or with elite norms. To understand these commonplace forms of resistance is to understand what much of the peasantry does "between revolts" to defend its interests the best it can. (Scott 1985, 29)

Although in this initial formulation Scott describes such forms of resistance as the anonymous acts of individuals, later in the text he describes how a "venerable popular culture of resistance" supported individual acts and how, despite their lack of formal coordination, such acts were widespread enough and presented themselves in a consistent-enough pattern to be regarded as *class* resistance (Scott 1985, 35).

In a subsequent work that attempts to generalize the description of everyday resistance on the part of Malaysian peasants to a broader set of contexts, Scott (1990, 118) explains that "none of the practices and discourses of resistance can exist without tacit or acknowledged coordination and communication within the subordinate group." For this to occur, he says, "the subordinate group must carve out for itself social spaces insulated from control and surveillance from above." It is within this space of mutualism, he argues, that members of subordinate groups can be socialized into "resistant practices and discourses." Although such resistance is socially organized and culturally and class based, Scott argues that it is not consciously political. Rather, its conscious motivation is *survival*: "We need assume no more than an understandable desire on the part of the peasant household to survive—to ensure its physical safety, to ensure its food supply, to ensure its necessary cash income—to identify the source of its resistance to the claims of press gangs, tax collectors, landlords, and employers (Scott 1985, 295). According to Scott, peasants who engage in these everyday forms of resistance may or may not have a vision of a world in which class relations and the relations between governments and the governed would be transformed to their benefit.[21] They do, however, have a fairly realistic assessment of the small likelihood of their being able to effect such transformations in the immediate term. Everyday forms of resistance, then, represent key elements in the pragmatic survival strategies elaborated by subordinate classes as they wait for structural changes that seem unlikely to occur in the foreseeable future.

The "weapons of the weak" perspective developed by Scott can be fruitfully applied to analyzing international migration by Mexicans as a form of resistance to global apartheid and the state's monopolization of the legitimate means of movement.[22] Analogous to the situation confronting the Malaysian peasants studied by Scott, Mexican migrants confront a structural situation of poverty and deprivation in Mexico and lack of legal access to the U.S. labor market that is beyond their ability to change through concerted collective action in the short term. The form taken by their resistance—withdrawal of their labor from the low-wage market in Mexico and clandestine participation in the U.S. labor market in order to retain a greater share of the surplus generated by their labor—is not consciously political but, rather, a survival strategy pursued at the household level. Although the migration strategies pursued by Mexican households are not centrally organized or coordinated, they are quite widespread in working-class and peasant communities, and are supported by a "venerable popular culture" of autonomous migration that has developed over the course of more than a century (Durand and Massey 2003; Massey, Durand, and Malone 2002). Household migration strategies are elaborated in a social space of mutualism that is impervious to "surveillance from above" and within which individuals are socialized into the "practices and discourse" of migration-resistance. An additional way in which Mexican migration fits the "weapons of the weak" approach is that the practices of migrant resistance are almost uniformly *covert* insofar as they typically involve either evading detection by the authorities when entering the United States or presenting documents to the authorities that make them appear to be complying with the U.S. immigration and employment statutes when in reality they are not (Heyman 1998; van Schendel 2005).

Another aspect of Scott's perspective that is relevant to the present discussion of autonomous Mexican migration to the United States is the way he describes the relationship between subordinate and superordinate groups as one in which members of each group constantly probe the line of defense of the other for a potential weakness: "It is in this no-man's land of feints, small attacks, probings to find weaknesses, and not in the rare frontal assault, that the ordinary battlefield lies" (Scott 1990, 193). This probing is especially important to the subordinate group as it attempts to advance its interests vis-à-vis its more powerful and institutionalized rival. Scott characterizes the everyday resistance of the subordinate group thusly: "Any weakness in surveillance and enforcement is likely to be quickly exploited; any ground left undefended [by the superordinate class] is likely to be ground lost" (Scott 1990, 195). This passage is quite applicable to Mexicans' attempts to enter the United States surreptitiously. Every obstacle placed thus far in their path by U.S. apartheid police at the border has been probed, evaluated, and ultimately evaded or overcome by millions of migrants whose principal "weapons" in their struggle against their involuntary territorial confinement are their collective inventiveness, persistence, and traditions of mutual aid in the face of adversity. We hear this reflected in the comments of a Mexican man I interviewed in San Antonio in the early years of the twenty-first century, who expressed the sentiments of many other migrants I interviewed elsewhere:

Yo sé que la gente nunca se va a rendir. Nunca los va a detener nadie, ni con muro, ni con nada. Para todo hay una solución. Son como las hormigas que entran por cualquier agujero. [I know that the people are never going to give up. Nobody is ever going to stop them, not with a wall or anything. There's a way around everything. They are like the ants that come through any hole].

Salomón, Mexican migrant in San Antonio, Texas.

In Mexican Spanish, the clandestine passage of goods and people across the Mexico-U.S. border is commonly likened to the passage of ants through a crack or hole in a wall, hence the often-used term *contrabando hormiga*, referring to the surreptitious movement of merchandise across the border in small quantities, often hidden in suitcases, under blankets in cars, or in a pedestrian's knapsack.[23] In light of Scott's description of the "line of battle" between the weak and the powerful and Salomón's likening of migrants to ants searching for a "hole" leading into the United States, I use the term *resistencia hormiga* in this book to refer to the specific forms that everyday resistance takes with respect to clandestine border-crossing by autonomous migrants. We might think of resistencia hormiga as the peaceful analog in contemporary migrant struggles against global apartheid to the "war of the flea" tactics used by guerilla fighters in many twentieth-century anti-imperialist struggles around the world.[24]

Migrant Mutuality: The Resources of Resistance

The resources that peasant and working-class migrants draw on to engage in resistencia hormiga are predominantly social and cultural. Sociologists and anthropologists have referred to these resources as "social capital" and "funds of knowledge." French sociologist Pierre Bourdieu (Bourdieu 1977 and 1986) is credited with coining the term *social capital* to refer to the way in which social relationships constitute a resource to individuals and groups that can grant them access to other types of resources possessed by people with whom they have relationships.[25] Bourdieu (1977 and 1986) developed the concept of social capital in conjunction with several other types of capital—economic, cultural, and symbolic—that he linked in a framework he referred to as the "economy of practices." Each type of capital could be accumulated by individuals or groups as a consequence of the social labor they invested in acquiring it and via their exchanges of one form of capital for another.

Already by the beginning of the 1980s, University of Texas researchers studying "undocumented" migration to Austin and San Antonio (Browning and Rodríguez 1985) recognized that clandestine border-crossing and settlement in the United States by Mexicans depended fundamentally on migrants' networks of kin and friends in the receiving country, just as rural to urban migration within Mexico depended on migrants' networks in their urban destinations (Balán, Browning, and Jelín 1973). Autonomous Mexican migrants counted on members of their social networks who were already in Texas to lend them money to cross the border, provide them with an initial place to stay, help them find work, and teach them how to negotiate U.S. institutions. These authors were among the first to use the term *social capital* with regard to Mexican migration to the United States, referring to its accumulation by migrants as "the development of interpersonal bonds that not only facilitate overall social adjustment in a new locale, but also enhance the opportunities for other forms of resource accumulation (Browning and Rodríguez 1985, 287).[26]

Subsequently, many other analysts used the social capital concept to explain various aspects of the phenomenon of international migration, including and especially the case of Mexican migration (e.g., Durand 2001; Kyle 2000; Massey et al. 1987; Massey, Durand, and Malone 2002; Phillips and Massey 2000; Portes 1995; Portes and Sensenbrenner 1993; Singer and Massey 1998). As Durand (1998 and 2001) has documented, various forms of mutual aid among Mexicans that could be labeled "social capital" have played an important role in facilitating migration since at least the beginning of the twentieth century, soon after Mexican laborers first began to migrate north of the border. Not surprisingly, more than one hundred years of migration to the United States led to the accumulation of tremendous stocks of migration-related social capital in Mexico, especially in the "traditional" sending states in western Central Mexico, including Aguascalientes, Colima, Durango, Guanajuato, Jalisco, Michoacán, Nayarít, San Luis Potosí, and Zacatecas (Durand and Massey 2003; Phillips and Massey 2000).

The "funds of knowledge" concept was developed by Chicano anthropologist Carlos Vélez-Ibáñez (1988 and 1996) to refer to the information, skills, and expertise developed within Mexican working-class communities on both sides of the border as ways of coping with the challenges brought about by their precarious economic situation.[27] Members of these communities draw on such knowledge through informal apprenticeship to members of the community that serve as "repositories" for specific funds. With regard to Mexican migrant communities, this means drawing on these communities' accumulated knowledge about all aspects of the migration process, including the strategies and tactics of clandestine border-crossings, the key aspect of resistencia hormiga to global apartheid discussed in this book.[28] The "funds of knowledge" concept succinctly captures Scott's (1990, 118) analytical point that subordinate groups are socialized into "resistant practices and discourses" in a social space of mutualism. Taken together, the social capital and funds of knowledge accumulated in autonomous migrant communities form the resource base that constitutes the "venerable popular culture of resistance" that supports the individual acts of their members.

The interpretive framework used in this book to approach clandestine border-crossing practices in the Northeast Mexico-South Texas boundary region permits us to understand migration in terms of domination and resistance that are deeply rooted in political economy and culture. This framework adds a moral, human rights dimension that is too often absent in the contemporary debate over Mexican migration to the United States by explicitly casting the actions of a pariah group as morally justifiable resistance to oppression. Mexican migrants resist their territorial confinement within a low-wage labor reserve by mobilizing the social and cultural resources at their disposal to cross a heavily policed border into the United States where they can realize a far higher reward for their labor.[29] This resistance strategy is not consciously political, but instead has household survival and reproduction as its goal. Even when the goal of *resistencia hormiga* is achieved—as it has been by millions of autonomous Mexican migrants who have lived and worked in the United States—migrants' labor is policed and stigmatized north of the border in such a way as to guarantee its super-exploitation relative to comparable native labor.[30] The policing and stigmatization of Mexican labor today is no longer legitimized primarily on racial grounds, but rather on the basis of its nationality and illegality. Although resistencia hormiga as expressed in clandestine border-crossing is not by itself capable of overcoming the extraterritorial dimension of apartheid-induced inequalities, it shows itself to be quite effective in reversing a significant portion of inequalities based on the physical territory within which Mexicans toil; in other words, resistencia hormiga permits migrants to partially reconfigure their relation to capital by evading interdiction at apartheid's territorial border. Although, in the immediate term, such resistance poses no threat to global apartheid as a system, over the long term the demographic changes it brings about in both the United States and Mexico have the potential to bring about changes in the political and moral economy of this "peculiar institution," a point to which I will return in the book's conclusion.

Mexican Clandestine Border-Crossing as a Unique Case

Throughout this introduction I have used the Mexico-U.S. border as an example of *global* apartheid and, by extension, the case of Mexican autonomous migration as an example of global resistance to apartheid at national boundaries. Nonetheless, it is important to recognize that this case is unique in at least three ways identified by Durand and Massey (2003), each of which impacts our understanding of resistencia hormiga. First, unlike the situation facing all other autonomous migrants from the Global South and the formerly communist countries of eastern Europe and northern Asia, Mexicans enjoy close geographical proximity to the United States and must negotiate only one international boundary to get there. Moreover, Mexicans are able to freely organize their attempts to penetrate apartheid at their country's northern border from within their own national territory, where they do not face the logistical challenges and dangers faced by other nationalities as they pass through Mexico. The geographical adjacency to the United States and the relative simplicity of crossing a single national border combine to make the costs of autonomous migration considerably lower for Mexicans relative to other nationalities. Second, Mexican autonomous migration to the United States has been occurring continuously from certain regions for over a century. As a consequence, migrant communities in "traditional" sending states like Guanajuato, Zacatecas, San Luis Potosí, Jalisco, and Michoacán have many decades of accumulated experience in making autonomous border-crossings. Third, the sheer scale of Mexican migration to the United States sets it apart from migration from all other nations. Most recent estimates indicate that around 11.5 million Mexican-born persons live in the United States (Batalova 2008), while many thousands of former migrants have returned to Mexico, making it the largest contemporary migration between any two countries in the world (Durand 2000, 29).

While Mexicans in general have important advantages in resisting global apartheid, we must not lose sight of the tremendous heterogeneity to be found within the contemporary Mexican autonomous migration process. In recent years, new regions have emerged in southern and central Mexico (Durand and Massey 2003) that are now sending ever-larger numbers of their residents to the United States. These regions, including the rural areas of states such as Chiapas, Guerrero, Hidalgo, and Veracruz, do not have the long migration history of the traditional regions of departure, nor have they established large populations already living in the United States. In addition, the distance of these states from the northern border is greater, raising the costs of transportation. As a consequence, migrants from the new sending regions are likely to be at a considerable disadvantage in terms of resisting their territorial confinement relative to their counterparts from the country's traditional regions of emigration. Moreover, the exodus from Mexican states like Veracruz was brought about by sudden economic crisis in the latter half of the 1990s that propelled thousands to leave the country in just a few years.

Another important factor to take into account is that U.S.-Mexico border space is quite heterogeneous. Topographical, climatic, vegetation, demographic, social, and cultural characteristics vary considerably from one stretch of the border to another. In this sense, it is important to recognize that migrants' experiences in making clandestine border-crossings in one part of the border region may be quite different from those in another. Today, the largest autonomous flow of Mexicans bound for the United States passes through the 350-mile wide Arizona-Sonora corridor, a lightly populated desert region with sparse vegetation and only a handful of sizeable human settlements. Conditions there differ dramatically in a number of ways from what migrants encounter in the 575-mile-wide Northeast Mexico-South Texas corridor or in the binational metropolis of Tijuana-San Diego. It is for this reason that I endeavor throughout the remainder of this book to highlight the particular geographic, social, cultural, and historic characteristics of the South Texas-Northeast Mexico region that are indispensable to understanding the specific ways in which clandestine border-crossing is practiced there.

CHAPTER 1

The Unfolding of Apartheid in South Texas

Domination, Resistance, and Migration

The Northeast Mexico-South Texas border region has been one of the principal corridors for Mexican migration to the United States since the late nineteenth century. It was the single most important migratory corridor between the two countries until the 1960s, when a variety of factors combined to redirect much of the flow of migrants toward California through the Tijuana-San Diego corridor. In order to understand the dynamics of resistencia hormiga at the beginning of the twenty-first century, we must first examine the particularities of the region's history and its social, economic, and geographical characteristics. A vital part of this history involves the region's status as a major transit corridor for migrants from specific sending regions in Mexico. By focusing on these particularities, I will recount the historical unfolding of the apartheid system in this region as well as describe the cultural underpinnings of autonomous migration through it. I do so in order to emphasize how the contemporary practice of clandestine border-crossing in the region remains strongly influenced by the unique aspects of its history and culture.

The Northeast Mexico-South Texas Migratory Corridor

About 30 percent of autonomous Mexican migrants to the United States at the beginning of the twenty-first century entered by crossing the Northeast Mexico-South Texas border. These migrants encountered a variety of social, cultural, and economic conditions that simultaneously facilitated their transit through the area and made it unattractive as a final destination. Several characteristics of the region lent themselves to facilitating the movement of migrants, including those who did not have permission from the U.S. government to enter the country.

First, the South Texas border was geographically closer to the major population centers of Mexico, as well as the traditional migrant-sending regions, than any other stretch of the border. Moreover, the Northeast Mexico border cities were served by a well-maintained highway system over which traveled a variety of modern and affordable passenger buses and vans. The South Texas border cities were similarly well served by high-speed highway connections to the interior of the state and beyond. At the border, these two highway systems were linked by seventeen international bridges that spanned the Río Bravo/Rio Grande and one ferry that served motor vehicles. The river was also spanned by three international rail bridges (International Boundary and Water Commission 2004; map 1.1). This infrastructure facilitated a tremendous amount of cross-border movement by both people and vehicles: in 2005, 57.7 million passenger vehicles, 20.6 million pedestrians, 4.9 million commercial trucks, and 556,000 railcars crossed the South Texas-Northeast Mexico border.[1]

Migrants arriving at Mexico's border with South Texas at the beginning of the century had five urban areas with over one hundred thousand inhabitants to choose from as places to stage their crossings—Reynosa, Matamoros, Nuevo Laredo, Piedras Negras, and Ciudad Acuña. Several other smaller Tamaulipas towns along the river were also good options, including Ciudad Camargo, Ciudad Miguel Alemán, and Ciudad Gustavo Díaz Ordaz. In addition to offering a material infrastructure to serve migrants in transit, these cities and towns were also home to a large population of internal migrants from some of the same states that also sent large numbers of migrants to the United States.[2] The presence of a large number of border residents from migrant-sending states in the Mexican interior constituted an important element in the social infrastructure of clandestine migration that I discuss in greater detail in subsequent chapters.

Immediately across the river in Texas, migrants found three significant metropolitan areas—Laredo, McAllen-Edinburg-Mission, and Brownsville-Harlingen—and many smaller towns and villages, including Del Rio, Eagle Pass, Zapata, and Roma, that they could use as layovers before continuing their journeys into the U.S. interior. The eight South Texas counties along the Rio Grande—Cameron, Hidalgo, Starr, Zapata, Webb, Maverick, Kinney, and Val Verde—had a combined population in 2000 of 1.3 million inhabitants. Not only were these counties home to a substantial population, but this population was overwhelmingly Mexican: 88 percent of these counties' residents

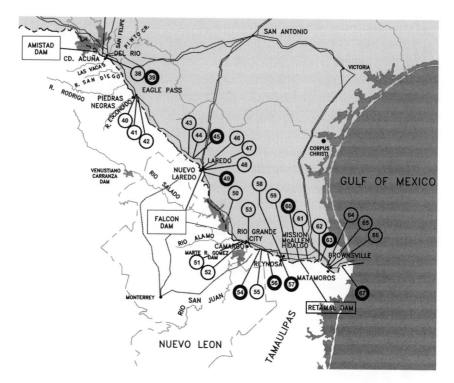

Map 1.1. International Bridges and Border-Crossings, Northeast Mexico-South Texas Border.
Source: International Boundary and Water Commission, United States and Mexico, United States Section. 2004 (May). *International Bridges and Border Crossings: United States Names.* El Paso, Texas. Online at http://www.ibwc.state.gov/Files/Bridge_Border_Crossings_.pdf.

MAP LEGEND

BRIDGE OR CROSSING	MILES ABOVE MOUTH	STATUS
38. Del Rio II (proceeding)	N/A	Proposed
39. Del Rio-Ciudad Acuña (U.S. 277)	561.0	Existing
40. Eagle Pass-Piedras Negras (U.S. 57)	496.3	Existing
41. Eagle Pass-Piedras Negras II	495.8	Existing
42. Eagle Pass-Piedras Negras (railroad)	495.7	Existing
43. Dolores-Colombia Solidarity Bridge	392.5	Existing
44. Laredo-Nuevo Lardo IV (Hwy. 3484)	369.7	Existing
45. Laredo Railroad Bridge	367.8	Proposed
46. Laredo-Nuevo Laredo Railroad Bridge	361.5	Existing
47. Laredo-Nuevo Laredo I (Convent Street)	360.9	Existing
48. Laredo-Nuevo Laredo II (Lincoln-Juárez)	360.6	Existing
49. Laredo International Bridge V	353.0	Proposed
50. Falcon Dam (Hwy. 2098)	274.8	Existing
51. Roma-Ciudad Miguel Alemán (Hwy. 200)	255.0	Existing
52. Roma-Ciudad Miguel Alemán (Suspensión bridge)	255.0	Historical
53. Rio Grande City-Ciudad Camargo	234.8	Existing
54. Los Ebanos-Ciudad Díaz Bridge (on hold)	204.7	Proposed
55. Los Ebanos-Ciudad Díaz Ferry	204.4	Existing
56. Mission International (on hold)	173.2	Proposed

BRIDGE OR CROSSING	MILES ABOVE MOUTH	STATUS
57. Anzalduas International (proceeding)	167.4	Proposed
58. Hidalgo-Reynosa (Spur 115)	159.5	Existing
59. Pharr-Reynosa (U.S. 281)	154.6	Existing
60. Donna-Rio Bravo International (proceeding)	138.6	Proposed
61. Progreso-Nuevo Progreso (Hwy. 1015)	123.4	Existing
62. Los Indios-Lucio Blanco (Free Trade Bridge)	98.5	Existing
63. Westrail railroad bridge (proceeding)	71.7	Proposed
64. B&M railroad/vehicle (Mexico Street)	56.4	Existing
65. Brownsville-Matamoros Gateway (Hwy. 4)	55.7	Existing
66. Los Tomates-Matamoros III	51.3	Existing
67. Port of Brownsville (proceeding)	24.7	Proposed

were Latino and 29 percent were immigrants. The vast majority of people in these counties spoke Spanish at home, ranging from 79 percent in Cameron County, to 92 percent in Webb and Maverick Counties.[3] In addition, many residents of the Texas border cities had friends and family members across the river in Mexico, with whom they maintained ties and were in routine contact. These demographics also formed a significant part of the social infrastructure of clandestine border-crossing into the United States, insofar as it was possible for migrants crossing in urban areas to quickly blend in with the local population, with whom they could communicate in Spanish to obtain things they needed for their journey into the interior. Moreover, the cross-border ties among members of the local population could also serve as the basis for business enterprises whose objective was to assist migrants in their passage through the region. As migrants traveled away from the border itself into the seventeen counties that made up the remainder of the South Texas region,[4] they entered twenty thousand square miles of ranches and farms dotted with small towns. Sixty-two percent of these counties' 592,377 inhabitants in 2000 were Latino, almost all of whom were of Mexican origin, with most speaking Spanish at home.[5] Given the cultural continuities between the border and nonborder counties of South Texas, Arreola's (2002) characterization of the region as a whole as a "Mexican American cultural province" is entirely apt.

Although the characteristics described above made South Texas an attractive transit corridor for many migrants from the Mexican interior, it had other characteristics that made it an unattractive place for them to settle relative to other parts of the United States. Although Texas border cities like Laredo and McAllen had experienced strong population and economic growth following the implementation of NAFTA in 1994, a study by the Texas Comptroller of Public Accounts characterized the economy of the border region as featuring "growth without prosperity" (Sharp 1998). In 2000, the South Texas border counties were among the poorest in the nation, with nearly 35 percent of the population living below the official poverty line, compared to just 12 percent in the United States as a whole. Median household income in the border counties ranged from $16,504 in Starr County to $28,376 in Val Verde County, compared to $41,994 in the entire United States.[6] Unemployment in the border counties similarly was considerably higher than elsewhere in the state and nation.[7] The nonborder counties of South Texas also exhibited much higher poverty rates and much lower median household income than the rest of the state and the nation.

The second principal reason that most clandestine Mexican labor migrants did not choose South Texas as a final destination was the omnipresent vigilance of the U.S. Border Patrol in the region. *Mexicanos* were more likely to come into contact with U.S. immigration authorities on a daily basis here than practically anywhere else in the country. Although the Border Patrol and its sister force ICE (Immigration and Customs Enforcement) did not routinely engage in raids of workplaces and residences in the region, their presence in public places in the community was ubiquitous, and they frequently set up temporary checkpoints on roadways traveled by local mexicanos on their way to work. Similar situations prevailing elsewhere along the U.S. border with Mexico led human rights activists to speak of the *cotidianidad* (everydayness) of the surveillance and repression to which Latinos were subjected by the immigration authorities (Heyman 1998, 166). Such surveillance and repression of the Mexican population by the Anglo authorities had a long history in South Texas and constituted a key element of apartheid policies at the border.[8]

Heritage of Conquest and Resistance in Mexican Texas

In order to properly understand the dynamics of the clandestine passage of Mexican migrants through South Texas in the contemporary period, it is important to interpret today's events in light of the history of Anglo conquest and colonization of the region's territory and people. This history is highly significant to the phenomenon of clandestine border-crossing, insofar as it continues to reverberate in the relations between the region's Mexican-majority population and federal law enforcement authorities, between Mexicans living in Texas and across the river in Tamaulipas and Coahuila, and between Texas Mexicans and Mexican migrants passing through on their way to points in the U.S. interior.

The land that is today known as South Texas has been a predominantly Spanish-speaking cultural region ever since the time of its first European settlement in the eighteenth century. When Texas seceded from Mexico in 1836, the majority of its population was Anglo American, but the majority of residents between San Antonio and the Rio Grande were Spanish-speaking ranchers and small farmers. Although the new republic of Texas claimed territory all the way to the Rio Grande, this claim was never recognized by Mexico (Arreola 2002, 30). After Texas seceded, most *mexicanos* who had lived in San Antonio and points east were driven from their homes into Mexico or the disputed territory south and west of the Nueces River (Montejano 197, 27–30; Paredes 1993, 7). The territory between the Nueces and the Rio Grande remained in dispute after the United States annexed Texas, until the present boundary between the two countries was established by the Treaty of Guadalupe Hidalgo in 1848, which concluded the war between Mexico and the United States (Arreola 2002, 30). These territorial changes are illustrated in map 1.2. In the decades following the U.S. military conquest of South Texas, Mexican ranchers, shepherds, and small farmers were systematically dispossessed of their property by a coterie of newly arrived Anglo elites, whose acquisition and enclosure of Mexican lands was backed by the U.S. Army and the Texas Rangers (Alonzo 1998; Montejano 1987; Rosenbaum 1998). According to Montejano (1987, 113–14), by the end of the second decade of the twentieth century "the Texas Mexican people had generally been reduced…to the status of landless and dependent wage laborers," who "found themselves treated as an inferior race." The arrival of railroads and the discovery of bountiful underground aquifers in South Texas at the beginning of the twentieth century set the stage for the development of year-round commercial farming in the Lower Rio Grande Valley. This set off a real estate boom and an influx of Anglo farm families from the U.S. Midwest and Mexican immigrant laborers from across the border (Montejano 1987). Now fully proletarianized, Mexicans cleared the land of brush and prepared it for cultivation by hand, getting paid less than a dollar a day for this back-breaking labor (McWilliams 1990, 163; Zamora 1993, 33).

Violent Rebellion and Repression

Mexicans in South Texas did not submit passively to their dispossession and subjugation by the new Anglo landowning class. They rose up in arms on multiple occasions in the late nineteenth and early twentieth centuries. In 1859–60, for example, a rebellion against Anglo domination led by a *tejano* (a Texan of Mexican descent) rancher named Juan Nepomuceno Cortina disrupted trade, led to the destruction of many farms and ranches, and forced much of the population of the Lower Rio Grande Valley to flee the region, before being put down by the Texas Rangers and U.S. Army (Montejano 1987, 32–33). With the rapid deterioration of their status and their increasing economic desperation in the early twentieth century, some Mexicans engaged in banditry in the new

Map 1.2. Changing boundaries of Texas in the nineteenth century.
Source: Raat 1996, 72.

Anglo farming areas. The Texas Rangers took on the task of enforcing the new economic and racial order with a "shoot first and ask questions later" policy that left many Mexicans dead (Rosenbaum 1998, 49). In 1915, a small group of South Texas Mexicans attempted to spark an insurrection against Anglo rule in the U.S. Southwest. Though the insurrection detailed in their Plan de San Diego never materialized, the conspirators staged a series of thirty raids from across the border, attacking Anglo properties, including elite properties such as the massive King Ranch, and killing a total of twenty-one Anglo Texans (Coerver and Hall 1984, 106). The response of U.S. authorities in South Texas was to launch what historian Walter Prescott Webb called a "reign of terror" against Mexicans, carried out by the Texas Rangers and fifty thousand U.S. Army troops and members of state militias (Montejano 1987, 122–23). Lynchings and summary executions of Mexicans were widespread, as was the burning of Mexican homes and property. Estimates of Texas Mexicans killed in reprisal for the cross-border raids ranged from several hundred to as many as five thousand (Coerver and Hall 1984, 107; Johnson 2003, 118–20; Paredes 1958, 26; Rosenbaum 1998, 51).

It is not surprising, given the conflictive history of the region, that *tejanos* did not regard Anglo authorities as acting legitimately in their observation or enforcement of the law. Even at the end of the twentieth century, many South Texas Mexicans continued to see the loss of their lands as the consequence of "wholesale Anglo thievery" (Alonzo 1998, 7). Américo Paredes (1958), in his pioneering exploration of the folklore of border Mexicans in the Lower Rio Grande Valley, reported that Mexican residents vilified the Texas Rangers as racist and bloodthirsty, on the one hand, and mocked them as braggarts and cowards, on the other. They gave the name "rangers" a special border Spanish rendition—*rinches*—that came to be applied indiscriminately and pejoratively to all Anglo law enforcement authorities. Paredes argued that Anglo abuses actually promoted Mexicans taking the law into their own hands, adding "to the roll of bandits and raiders many high-spirited individuals who would have otherwise remained peaceful and useful citizens." Those who forcefully resisted the agents of Anglo domination in the region became "the heroes of the Border folk." In addition, the exploits of *contrabandistas* (smugglers) and *mojados* (wetbacks) in the region came to be associated in the popular mind with the bravery of the border-conflict heroes, since "they came into conflict with the same American laws and sometimes with the same individual officers of the law." Moreover, many Texas Rangers involved in suppressing Mexican rebellion in the early years of the twentieth century were later recruited as the first agents of the U.S. Border Patrol, who, in addition to tracking down migrants, did battle with Mexican smugglers of tequila during Prohibition (Paredes 1993, 27).

Although by the early years of the twenty-first century, the majority of Border Patrol agents were Latino,[9] hostility toward them was still prevalent among South Texas Mexicans. As Maril (2004, 74) noted in his ethnographic study of the Border Patrol, "Mexicans and Mexican Americans in the Valley who suffered at the hands of the Border Patrol...did not forget what they had endured. They could not ignore the history. Many Hispanic residents...neither trusted nor respected the Border Patrol and never would." Moreover, their hostility toward the Border Patrol as the symbol of the domination of Mexicans in the region meant not only that they would not help agents carry out their job of policing fellow Mexicans, but that some would also go further and deliberately interfere with agents doing their job (Maril 2004, 180–81).

Transgressing Boundaries as a Way of Life

According to Paredes (1993, 25–26), the situation prevailing along the South Texas-Tamaulipas border in the decades following the establishment of the

Rio Grande/Río Bravo as the international boundary in 1848 was substantially different than it was elsewhere along that two thousand mile-long boundary. The difference, he argued, was that the region along the Lower Rio Grande was already home to settlers on both sides when the river became the border. Thus, "friends and relatives who had been near neighbors—within shouting distance across a few hundred feet of water—were now legally in different countries." Alonzo's (1998, 120) social history of life in South Texas in the eighteenth and nineteenth centuries describes *tejanos'* view of the river as an "imaginary line" that they crossed at will, without regard to the legality of their movements. This made sense insofar as it would be decades before either Mexico or the United States stationed sufficient personnel along the river to enforce customs and immigration regulations. Similarly, Coerver and Hall (1984, 8) reported that "inhabitants of the region viewed the Rio Grande as a connecting force rather than a line of division," given that "physical and legal obstacles to movement across the border were virtually non-existent." Under these circumstances, Paredes (1993) identified "smuggling" and "illegal immigration" as integral elements of the borderlands way of life:

> It goes without saying that [residents] paid little attention to the requirements of the law. When they went visiting, they crossed at the most convenient spot on the river; and, as is ancient custom when one goes visiting loved ones, they took gifts with them: farm products from Mexico to Texas, textiles and other manufactured goods from Texas to Mexico. Legally, of course, this was smuggling, differing from contraband for profit in volume only. *Such a pattern is familiar to anyone who knows the border, for it still operates, not only along the Lower Rio Grande now but all along the boundary line between Mexico and the United States.* [emphasis added]...Unofficial crossings also disregarded immigration laws. Children born on one side of the river would be baptized on the other side, and thus appear on church registers as citizens of the other country. This bothered no one since people on both sides of the river thought of themselves as *mexicanos*.[10] (Paredes 1993, 26)

Smuggling remained a common cultural practice in the South Texas-Northeast Mexico border region throughout the twentieth century and continued as such in the early years of the twenty-first century. In the 1970s and 1980s, for example, merchants in South Texas border towns routinely sold merchandise to Mexican customers who smuggled the goods into Mexico without paying the corresponding tariffs or in outright violation of a ban on imports. In some cases, the merchants themselves smuggled the goods or worked directly with Mexican customs officials who carried the merchandise for them (see, for example, Miller 1981, 48–64). Used clothing, whose importation from the United States was banned by Mexican law (*El Informador* 2008), continued to be sold to Mexican customers by the bale in South Texas towns, who then took it across the river to sell door to door or in flea markets (Hellman 1994). U.S. tourists smuggled alcohol and prescription pharmaceuticals across the Rio Grande bridges on a routine basis. And, of course, the region remained one of the chief drug-smuggling corridors between Mexico and the United States, providing a significant direct or indirect source of income for many of its inhabitants. As had historically been the case, the very law enforcement officials whose job it was to combat this smuggling were frequently found to be engaging in it (Maril 2004, 188–90; Pomfret 2006; Vartabedian, Serrano, and Marosi 2006).

Mexican Migration in South Texas in the Twentieth Century

Not only does the history of South Texas as a region continue to reverberate in the relations among actors in the contemporary border-crossing drama, so does the history of Mexican migration through the region. Moreover, an examination of the history of this migration sheds considerable light on how the apartheid system in place at the border today came into being and evolved over the course of the twentieth century. Specifically, we can see how Mexican migration to the United States has been a story about labor mobilization, control, exploitation, and expulsion, all of which constitute key elements of an apartheid system. In addition, it calls our attention to the ever-intensifying criminalization of Mexican labor over time, a process that reached crisis proportions in the first years of the twenty-first century. By briefly reviewing the history of Mexican migration through South Texas, we can see more clearly how current U.S. border enforcement represents not a break with a more tolerant past but, rather, an attempt to restore order to an apartheid system threatened by growing migrant autonomy.

Although Mexicans had begun to be recruited from across the border to work in Texas cotton fields as early as the years immediately following the end of the Civil War (Foley 1997, 25–26), it was not until the 1880s when rail lines began to connect the border region with the interior of both countries that mass migration of Mexican labor through South Texas to the United States began (Massey, Durand, and Malone 2002; Montejano 1987). Along with El Paso, San Antonio became one of the most important labor recruitment and contracting centers for Mexican migrants in the early twentieth century, and by the 1920s its contracting agencies dominated the market in Mexican labor in the United States (Cardoso 1980, 85). Mexicans in search of work traveled to the city by the thousands in the first three decades of the century, crossing through Eagle Pass, Laredo, and Brownsville and shipping out to work in the cotton fields of central Texas, the sugar beet farms of the upper Midwest, the slaughterhouses in Chicago, the steel mills of Pennsylvania, and to lay rails throughout the country (Clark 1908; Durand and Arias 2004; Foley 1997; McWilliams 1990; Reisler 1976; and Zamora 1993). These workers came in response to active (and often illegal) recruitment drives in Mexico by U.S. farmers and railroad companies.[11] After revolution broke out in Mexico in 1910, the flow of migrants accelerated as many thousands of peasants were freed from their feudal obligations on haciendas and thousands of other peasants and workers were displaced from their homes by violence and economic disruption (McCaa 2003; Reisler 1976, 15).

In 1917, the United States government imposed its first serious restriction on the admission of Mexicans along its southern border. It did so by requiring all foreign nationals entering the United States to pass a literacy test and pay an $8 "head tax" (about $125 in 2008 dollars), something that most Mexican laborers at that time were incapable of doing (Reisler 1976, 24; Scruggs 1960, 320). This marked the beginning of the system of apartheid-style pass laws that have attempted to regulate the movement of Mexicans across the U.S. border ever since. The new policy did not appreciably deter Mexicans from coming, but instead prompted most of them to enter away from legal ports of entry to avoid these requirements (Slayden 1921, 122). Their motivation for avoiding the legal ports of entry increased after 1924, when a $10 visa fee (around $120 in 2008 dollars) was added to the requirements (Corwin 1978, 144). Although no figures are available specifically for South Texas, Cardoso (1980, 94) estimated that of the approximately 160,000 Mexicans who entered the United States each year in the 1920s, 100,000 did so outside the law; while Morales (1981, 88) reported that for every Mexican who entered the United States with proper documents during the 1920s, as many as five entered without them.

In the face of labor shortages during World War I, railroad and agricultural interests obtained waivers of the literacy and head-tax requirements from the U.S. Department of Labor to legally contract Mexican workers (Reisler 1976, 24–29). Eighty thousand Mexicans participated in this first guest-worker program that ran from 1918 to 1921, though many more entered surreptitiously and worked without getting waivers (Reisler 1976, 83; Scruggs 1960, 321–23). Following the war, the U.S. experienced a brief but strong economic depression. As unemployment surged, the federal government led a drive to arrest and deport thousands of Mexican immigrants, complemented by threats of violence against Mexicans from organized groups of white nativists. Twenty-four thousand Mexicans were officially deported by the government, with as many as one hundred thousand others intimidated into returning to Mexico "voluntarily" (Corwin 1978, 141; Reisler 1976, 50–54).

Demand for Mexican labor rebounded as soon as the U.S. economy recovered from its postwar slump. The desire for Mexican workers by U.S. employers was intensified by federal legislation passed in 1921 and 1924 that severely curtailed the arrival of immigrant workers from Europe (Cardoso 1980, 83). One of the results of this was that sugar beet farmers and other employers in the East and Midwest recruited ever-more Mexican laborers, mainly through contracting agencies in San Antonio. As a consequence, by the mid-1920s South Texas had become the principal corridor for Mexican international migration to the United States (Durand and Massey 2003, 104). The creation of the U.S. Border Patrol in 1924 did little to slow the movement of Mexican migrants across the Rio Grande, given that as late as 1928 it had a total of only 747 agents to police both the Mexican and Canadian borders and most of their efforts went into enforcing Prohibition and customs laws rather than arresting unauthorized Mexicans (Cardoso 1980, 84; Corwin 1978, 149).

Strong demand for Mexican workers elsewhere in the United States created problems for Anglo farmers in South Texas, who had come to rely on an abundant and exceptionally low-wage Mexican workforce to plant and harvest their crops. Given that wages and working conditions in South Texas were considerably worse than in other parts of the country, Mexicans were quick to abandon work in the region to pursue better earnings elsewhere. Growers responded by employing a variety of tactics to forcibly keep Mexicans from leaving the region, including holding them on their farms under armed guard and colluding with local law enforcement officials to arrest and fine migrants for vagrancy, then offering the jailed migrants the "opportunity" to work off their fines in the fields. In addition, toward the end of the decade growers succeeded in getting the Texas legislature to pass a law restricting out-of-state employers from recruiting Mexican workers in Texas (Montejano 1987, 203–13).

As had been the case with the economic downturn following the end of World War I, the Great Depression that began in 1929 prompted a wave of deportation drives aimed at Mexicans around the United States. Between half a million and a million Mexican immigrants and their U.S. citizen children were "repatriated" to Mexico, with some formally deported, others intimidated into leaving, and still others deciding on their own to weather the storm back home in Mexico (Acuña 2003, 209; Balderrama and Rodríguez 1995, 120–22;

Hoffman 1974, 126–27). Although there were many Europeans residing in the United States at the time whose immigration status was also doubtful, Mexicans were the only nationality singled out for repatriation during the Great Depression (Durand and Massey 2003, 58). South Texas, especially, was the scene of federal deportation raids and widespread intimidation and hostility toward Mexicans (Balderrama and Rodríguez 1995, 59; McKay 1981 and 2001).

Less than a decade after the mass expulsion of Mexicans at the outset of the 1930s, agricultural labor shortages developed because of the United States' entry into World War II. To meet the demand for farmworkers, the U.S. and Mexican governments negotiated an agreement to implement an agricultural guest-worker program that became known as the Bracero Program. During the twenty-three years the program lasted, over 4.5 million contracts for *braceros* were issued to Mexican men to work in the United States, the vast majority (more than 4.3 million, or over 95%) issued in the eighteen years after the end of the war (Calavita 1992, 218).

The Mexican government insisted on the exclusion of Texas farms from bracero contracting, based on Texas farmers' and law enforcement authorities' historical and contemporary mistreatment of Mexicans (Calavita 1992, 20; Samora 1971, 45). The exclusion of Texas from the program meant that most Mexican nationals laboring there did so as undocumented migrants. The so-called Texas proviso included in the 1952 Immigration and Nationality Act permitted U.S. farmers to employ "illegal" Mexicans without fear of prosecution for "harboring" aliens who were unlawfully in the country (Corwin 1978, 152; Massey, Durand, and Malone 2002, 36). By the late 1940s, South Texas was home to tens of thousands of undocumented Mexicans migrants and served as the transit corridor for tens of thousands of others headed to interior points in the United States. In their 1951 report *The Wetback in the Lower Rio Grande Valley,* Saunders and Leonard estimated that there were at least one hundred thousand unauthorized Mexicans working in the Lower Rio Grande Valley counties of Cameron, Hidalgo, and Willacy (p. 83), reckoning that there were as many "wetbacks" as there were authorized workers. The authors described deplorable wages, living conditions, and working conditions endured by undocumented laborers in the Valley, as well as stereotypes of racial inferiority widely held by Anglos in the region that were used to justify the ill-treatment of these Mexican workers.

Although the Border Patrol apprehended and expelled thousands of migrants from South Texas during this period, including 220,000 from the Rio Grande Valley sector alone between July 1, 1949, and June 30, 1950 (Saunders and Leonard 1951, 56), they were careful not to take unauthorized laborers from growers during harvest time, lest the season's crops be lost (Corwin 1978,

152). In general, Border Patrol agents avoided carrying out raids of farms, instead focusing on picking up migrants along the region's principal roads, thus making their presence felt without disrupting farm production (Saunders and Leonard 1951, 79). In the same way that employers could count on the Border Patrol not to arrest "wets" they wanted to keep working, they could also count on agents to arrest and deport any Mexican who complained about or otherwise resisted exploitation (Saunders and Leonard 1951, 55). Such was the system of apartheid labor control in South Texas at mid-century.

Another effect of the growth of undocumented migration to South Texas and the role played by the Border Patrol in policing it were the hundreds of Mexicans who drowned in the Rio Grande as they attempted to cross it surreptitiously (García 1980, 144; New York Times 1954b, 9; Saunders and Leonard 1951, 38). Although the Border Patrol was insufficiently staffed to prevent unauthorized entry in South Texas, it was still able to apprehend many migrants at strategically located highway and rail checkpoints. This forced migrants to walk the back roads and through the brush to avoid detection, exposing them to the dangers of rattlesnake bites, extreme temperatures, and dehydration. Many migrants died from these causes during the years of the Bracero Program (García 1980, 144–45). Their many travails were memorialized in Luis Spota's 1948 novel, *Murieron a mitad del río* (They Died Halfway across the River).

In the context of the Cold War, the ongoing influx of thousands of Mexican workers across the border alarmed government officials and others who feared that communist "subversives" were infiltrating the United States by hiding among Mexicans (see, for example, American GI Form of Texas 1953, 30–32; Calavita 1992, 49–50; García 1980, 122–23; New York Times 1954a, 23). Concerns about a border out of control were fanned by sensationalist press accounts, such as a *New York Times Sunday Magazine* article titled "Two Every Minute across the Border: Mexican 'Wetbacks' Continue to Invade U.S. in an Unending—and Uncontrolled—Stream" (Hill 1954, 13). In response, in June 1954 the Border Patrol launched a series of immigration raids throughout the Southwest under the name Operation Wetback, resulting in the apprehension and return to Mexico of tens of thousands of undocumented migrants and the "voluntary" return of thousands more who fled across the border in advance of raids on their communities and workplaces (García 1980; Koestler 2002; Massey, Durand, and Malone 2002, 37; Samora 1971, 51–55). In conjunction with the operation, the U.S. Commissioner of Immigration offered South Texas growers a streamlined process for contracting workers and a guarantee that sufficient contracts would be expeditiously offered to meet their needs (García 1980, 208–9). In the following years, migrant apprehensions along the length of the U.S.-Mexico border fell precipitously from their peak of 1.1 million in 1954 to 243,000 in 1955, and then to just 30,000 in 1960 (Samora 1971, 46, table 4). The major reasons for this were the incorporation of formerly excluded areas of Texas into the Bracero Program and the border-wide doubling of visas issued annually for braceros.[12] Between 1955 and 1960, over four hundred thousand braceros were legally admitted every year, with Texas accounting for the bulk of the increase (Galarza 1964, 79; Massey, Durand, and Malone 2002, 37).

The Bracero Program was finally terminated unilaterally by the U.S. government at the end of 1964 in response to pressure from organized labor, as well as religious and civil rights organizations. The next year, the Hart-Celler Act placed, for the first time ever, a numerical limit (120,000) on the number of immigrants who could be admitted from Western Hemisphere countries, including Mexico. Visa applicants without immediate relatives who were citizens or legal permanent residents of the United States were required to have a job offer from a U.S. employer, who, in turn, had to obtain a certification from the U.S. Department of Labor that no U.S. citizen workers were available to do the job and that local wages and working conditions would not be worsened as a consequence. A subsequent law passed in 1976 limited the number of visas issued to Mexicans to just 20,000 a year (Cerrutti and Massey 2004, 18; Cornelius 1978, 18).[13] Mexicans continued to cross the border in large numbers, despite the dramatic decline in legal opportunities to migrate to the United States, building on the experience of millions of men who had worked north of the border and knew where to find the higher-waged jobs that awaited them there.

Whereas in the decade prior to 1965, most Mexican migrants came as legal contract workers, after 1965 a very large proportion came without work or residence documents, spurred by recurring economic problems in Mexico and ongoing demand for their labor in the United States. Not surprisingly, the apprehensions of "deportable aliens" by the U.S. immigration authorities, the vast majority of whom were Mexicans caught by the Border Patrol, rose from 87,000 in 1965 to 345,000 in 1970 to over 1 million in 1978, reaching a peak of 1.8 million in 1986 (United States Department of Homeland Security 2004, tables 35 and 36, and p. 146).[14] Another significant development in the post-bracero period was the dramatic drop in the demand for farm labor due to the mechanization of production and the introduction of chemical pesticides in the fields, so that by 1970 less than half as many farmworkers were employed in Texas as in 1950 (Foley 1997, 207; Montejano 1987, 272–74). As a consequence, South Texas ceased being a principal destination for Mexican migrants, many more of whom sought employment in urban occupations in major cities. At the same time, California replaced Texas as the leading recipient of Mexican migrants, with Tijuana-San Diego consequently replacing Northeast Mexico-South Texas as the leading corridor for Mexicans' clandestine crossings (Durand and Massey 2003, 104). Nevertheless, Texas remained the second-most-important destination for undocumented Mexican migrants, and many also continued to cross through the Northeast Mexico-South Texas region on their way to jobs in Chicago and other destinations in the upper Midwest, in addition to major Texas cities like Houston, Dallas, and Fort Worth.

Operation Rio Grande: Barricading the Border in South Texas

By the 1980s, "illegal immigration" had become a topic of great public concern in the United States (Chávez 2001; Dunn 1996; Nevins 2002). In 1986, after a long and rancorous debate, Congress passed, and President Ronald Reagan signed into law, the Immigration Reform and Control Act. On the one hand, IRCA allowed around 3 million migrants, including 2.3 million Mexican nationals, to legalize their residence in the United States under its "amnesty" provisions (Massey, Durand, and Malone 2002, 90). On the other hand, IRCA contained two major provisions designed to curtail autonomous migration to the United States. First, it repealed the Texas proviso that, since 1952, had allowed U.S. employers to legally hire "undocumented" workers. After IRCA's passage, employers who knowingly hired "illegal aliens" could be fined and face criminal sanctions. The purpose of this provision was to cut demand for "undocumented" workers. Second, IRCA dramatically increased resources available to the Border Patrol to apprehend migrants attempting to enter the United States clandestinely from Mexico. By 1992, the enforcement budget for the INS authorized by Congress grew to $702 million ($1.1 billion in 2008 dollars), up from just $352 million in 1986 ($690 million in 2008 dollars) (Dunn 1996, 180–81). With this added money, the Border Patrol expanded its arsenal of equipment with new helicopters, motion sensors, night-vision scopes, and other remote-surveillance equipment. It also built a new steel fence on a seven-mile stretch of the border between San Diego and Tijuana (Dunn 1996, 68–69 and 183–184). The intensification of U.S. efforts to deter unauthorized entry into its territory did not begin in earnest, however, until September 1993, with the launching of Operation Blockade in the Border Patrol's El Paso sector. Operation Blockade served as a model for other heavily trafficked sections of the border, first in California, then in Arizona, and finally in South Texas. The model represented the culmination of the progressive intensification of the interdiction aspects of apartheid policies at the border that had begun with the application of the head tax and literacy test on entering foreign nationals three-quarters of a century earlier.

Operation Blockade as the New Border Control Model

Operation Blockade radically altered the deployment and duties of agents in El Paso in an attempt by the sector chief of the Border Patrol to prevent unauthorized entry of U.S. territory and, thus, reduce the friction between his agents and the residents of El Paso, around 70 percent of whom were Mexican Americans or Mexican immigrants. This radical redeployment was undertaken suddenly and without prior announcement in the early morning hours of September 19, 1993. Of the 650 agents assigned to the El Paso sector, 400 were deployed "forward" to the banks of the Rio Grande, where agents took up twenty-four-hour, seven-days-a-week sentry duty in their vehicles within sight of one another overlooking the river, in a twenty-mile-long row from one end of the El Paso metropolitan area to the other. The goal of the operation was to create a "wall" of agents in their vehicles to deter migrants from crossing in the urbanized areas of the sector (Bean et al. 1994, 7–8). Operation Blockade, which initially lasted just three weeks, was subsequently made permanent and renamed Operation Hold the Line, in deference to critics who found the implications of the term "blockade" objectionable with regard to the U.S. relationship with Mexico on the eve of the ratification by the U.S. Congress of the North American Free Trade Agreement (Bean et al. 1994, 10).

The blockade appeared to immediately achieve its primary objective of preventing the unauthorized entry of migrants into El Paso city limits from Mexico. The number of apprehensions by Border Patrol agents within the city dropped precipitously, as far fewer migrants attempted to penetrate the imposing line of agents stationed along the river. Although it had not originally been supported by the INS bureaucracy in Washington, the operation was soon judged to be a resounding success, and its essential elements were taken as a model for the Border Patrol to follow to gain control of the other major migratory corridors running north from Mexico into the United States. The Border Patrol attempted to replicate Operation Blockade's presumed successes, beginning with Operation Gatekeeper in the San Diego sector in 1994, then following it with Operation Safeguard in 1995 in Nogales, Arizona, and finally with Operation Rio Grande (ORG) in Brownsville, Texas, in 1997, each of which was subsequently extended from its original locale to cover adjacent stretches of the border (Andreas 2000; Nevins 2002; Spener 2000).

In many ways, however, Operation Blockade's success with regard to stemming the flow of unauthorized migrants was more apparent than real. While it is true that there was a dramatic reduction in unauthorized border crossings in the urban area as a consequence of the operation, much of the reduction owed to the response of Ciudad Juárez residents from the Mexican side of the river who had formerly crossed to work in El Paso on a daily basis. These local residents responded to the operation by reducing the frequency of their crossings, either by working less often in El Paso or by extending their stays in U.S. territory when they did cross, or by using false or borrowed documents to cross on one of the international bridges.[15] Thus, the obstacles created by Operation Blockade led to a much greater reduction in the number of illicit *border crossings* than in the number of unauthorized *border-crossers*. Moreover, to the extent that undocumented migrants prolonged their stays in El Paso after entering in search of work, the blockade actually tended to increase the undocumented migrant population of the city.

Similarly, long-distance migrants from the interior of Mexico who were headed to interior locations in the United States did not desist from doing so as a consequence of Operation Blockade. In the past they might have forded the river in downtown El Paso, but after the blockade they staged an end run around the twenty-mile line of agents on the riverbank. To be sure, this meant they had to walk longer distances over mountains and through harsh desert terrain, perhaps having to hire a now much-more expensive coyote to guide them and exposing themselves to greater risk of accident, injury, and death, but those whose decisions to migrate were made based on factors far removed from changing conditions at the border continued to come. Moreover, because most agents in the sector had been deployed "forward" to the international line itself, migrants who trekked around the blockade were actually substantially less likely to be apprehended after entering the United States than they were before it was launched. In summary, the dramatic drop in apprehensions of migrants made by the Border Patrol in the El Paso sector, from 285,781 in FY1993 to just 79,688 in FY1994,[16] was a result of, not only an actual deterrent effect, but also the new strategies undertaken by migrants as a response and the reduced likelihood that they would be apprehended once they made it into U.S. territory (Bean et al. 1994, 123–24; Spener 2003a).

In subsequent years, it was apparent that as it became more difficult for long-distance migrants to stage their crossings in the Ciudad Juárez-El Paso and Tijuana-San Diego corridors, some shifted their crossings to other stretches of the border where the Operation Blockade model had not yet been implemented. (Figure 1.1 shows the changing patterns of migrant apprehensions along different stretches of the border from FY1993 to FY2005.) Following

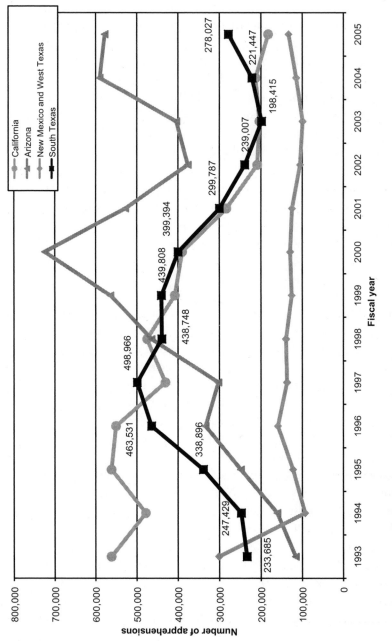

Figure 1.1. Apprehensions of Migrants by U.S. Border Patrol, by Fiscal Year and Southwest Border Region.
Source: Data obtained by author from the U.S. Border Patrol.

the implementation of the new patrol strategies in El Paso and San Diego, the fall in apprehensions in those two sectors was accompanied by a dramatic increase in apprehensions in South Texas, from a little more than two hundred thousand in FY1993 to around half a million in FY1997.[17] After Operation Rio Grande was launched in South Texas near the end of FY1997, apprehensions there fell significantly but skyrocketed in Arizona; whereas in FY1997 there were only about three hundred thousand apprehensions of migrants made by the Border Patrol in Arizona, by FY2000 over seven hundred thousand apprehensions were made in the state. In addition, and more significantly, as shown in subsequent studies, the impacts of Operation Blockade detailed in the Bean report became generalized across the entire length of the border as the main elements of the deterrence strategy were implemented in each of the other major migratory corridors (Andreas 2000; Massey, Durand, and Malone 2002; Nevins 2002; Reyes et al. 2002).

Operation Rio Grande: Implementing the New Border Control Model in South Texas

In the four years following the launching of Operation Blockade in El Paso, annual apprehensions of migrants made by the Border Patrol in South Texas more than doubled. Of greater concern to U.S. authorities was the fact that many hundreds of thousands of migrants eluded capture as they passed through the region. At the end of July 1997, Commissioner Doris Meissner of the INS announced in Brownsville that the Border Patrol in the Rio Grande Valley sector would receive additional funding and one hundred new agents to launch a new initiative, dubbed Operation Rio Grande. She promoted the operation as a way of bringing the remainder of the Texas border "under control" in the face of the new pressures brought about by tighter enforcement to the west. Joe Garza, the chief of the Rio Grande Valley sector, explained to reporters that ORG would begin in the "hot spot" for illegal crossings in the Matamoros-Brownsville urban corridor and would follow the "high profile, high visibility" model used in Operation Blockade. Agents would be stationed every one-eighth mile along the riverbank, the area would be floodlit, and agents would be assisted by motion sensors, night-vision scopes, and low-light television monitoring. Once Brownsville was brought under control, the operation would be extended farther up and down the river (Allen 1997). On August 25, 1997, Meissner returned to Brownsville to officially launch the operation. On this occasion, she declared that the new strategy would be permanent and would be extended upstream in stepwise fashion over the next two to three years until "the entire Texas border" was brought under control. Chief

Garza bragged that the new operation would deter would-be crossers from making the attempt: "Tonight they'll all see the lights....We're gonna take the night away from the smugglers and bandits and thieves in this area. If anyone crosses here, there's a 99-percent chance of them being arrested" (MacCormack 1997, 1A).

Over the next several years, ORG substantially beefed up Border Patrol enforcement capabilities in South Texas, as it moved steadily upstream from Brownsville. The total number of agents assigned to the region grew from 1,627 in FY1997 to 3,445 by FY2003, an increase of 1,818 agents on patrol (see figure 1.2). In the Rio Grande Valley sector, which covered 284 river-miles of the border from the mouth of the Rio Grande upstream to Falcon Dam, ORG's "operational enhancements" included the clearing of brush along roadsides; installation of thirty-nine elevated observation posts with LORIS night-vision scopes and the deployment of nine mobile LORIS scopes mounted on pickup trucks; installation of thirty permanent floodlights along the river and the rotating deployment of 184 portable light units; erection of forty-six remote, 360-degree video surveillance towers near the border; use of twenty-three high-speed patrol boats; and deployment of seven helicopter and three fixed-wing aircraft surveillance units (United States Border Patrol 2003). In the Laredo sector, the Border Patrol, with the assistance of the U.S. Army, built or improved 240 miles of dirt roads on lands adjacent to the international boundary and installed a dozen new helicopter landing pads and other facilities (Schiller 1998). In 1999, the Border Patrol in Laredo began testing the use of "unmanned aerial vehicles" or "drone" aircraft to conduct surveillance by flying over territory adjacent to the border and beaming back video images to agents at stations on the ground (Schiller 1999a). By the end of the decade, portable floodlights were in use and video surveillance towers had also been erected in the Laredo sector, and more were planned for the riverbank upstream toward Eagle Pass.[18]

Operation Rio Grande also incorporated use of the recently developed IDENT system, which involved taking digital photographs and fingerprints from migrants detained by the Border Patrol and entering this biometric information in a centralized database. The data collected could be used to identify suspected drug smugglers as well as "recidivist" unauthorized entrants and coyotes for prosecution. Prior to the introduction of IDENT, individuals who were apprehended by the Border Patrol on more than one occasion would simply give agents a different pseudonym each time they were arrested, making it impossible to know how many times they had been apprehended previously or where. With IDENT, the strategy of using a different name was rendered useless, since "new" fingerprints and photographs were matched with old

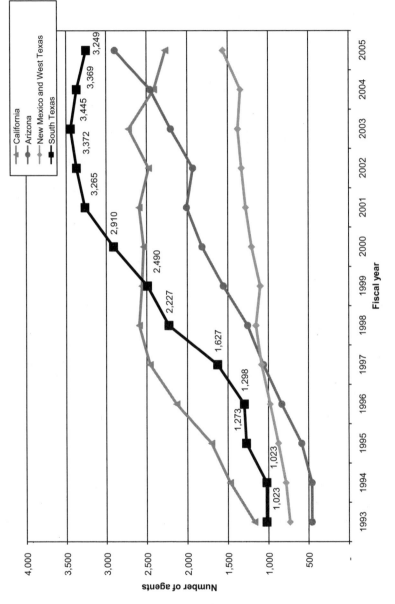

Figure 1.2. Border Patrol Agents Assigned to Different Regions of U.S. Southwest Border, by Fiscal Year.
Source: Data obtained by author from the U.S. Border Patrol.

images contained in the database. By 2002, IDENT had become linked to the FBI's databases, so that agents were quickly able to determine whether a given individual had been previously convicted of or was a suspect in other crimes (Associated Press 2002a). Along the Texas border, the use of IDENT proved to be a powerful U.S. government tool in the intensified criminalization of migration. Whereas in 1997 the INS referred only 2,140 criminal immigration cases along the Texas border to the U.S. Attorneys Office for prosecution, by 2003 the number had more than tripled to 7,411 cases. The bulk of these cases involved charges of misdemeanor illegal entry and felony illegal reentry into the United States (Transactional Records Access Clearinghouse 2005).

As with Operation Blockade, migrant apprehensions in South Texas fell sharply as Operation Rio Grande was implemented. From their peak of nearly half a million in FY1997, South Texas apprehensions fell to just under four hundred thousand in FY2000, and continued to drop through FY2003, when they reached a low of just under two hundred thousand (see figure 1.1). Also, as had happened with Operation Blockade, long-distance migrants continued to pass through the South Texas border region, but in the face of Border Patrol saturation of urban crossing areas, they tended to stage their crossings a few miles upstream or downstream from urban areas and then began their treks around the highway checkpoints. Not surprisingly, given the hazards of the terrain and the increased length of the treks involved, the number of migrants dying en route in Texas jumped markedly, from just 34 deaths registered in FY1997 to 269 in FY2000 (Cornelius 2001, 669).[19] This jump in migrant deaths in Texas post-ORG led researchers from the University of Houston to conclude that it was "unambiguous" that the redirection of migrant flows into more remote sections of South Texas ranchlands was the cause of many deaths from drowning and exposure to the elements (Eschbach, Hagan, and Rodríguez 2003, 13). This rising death toll was a grim consequence of the intensification of apartheid policies in the region at the end of the century.[20]

In addition, the rapid increase in the number of Border Patrol agents in the region brought with it intensified surveillance of many roads away from the river itself and, concomitantly, an increase in the number of interrogations of local drivers and their passengers. This led to widespread complaints by Mexican Americans and Mexican immigrants in South Texas—who were the vast majority of the population—that many of them were being pulled over and having their documents and vehicles inspected by Border Patrol agents for doing nothing more than "driving while Mexican."[21] The Harlingen-based Immigration Law Enforcement Monitoring Project (ILEMP) of the American Friends Service Committee reported in 1998 that documented human rights abuses by immigration authorities in South Texas grew by 38 percent following the launching of ORG. The types of abuses the group complained about included the following:

- psychological or verbal abuse, "such as abusive language, sexual harassment, threats or coercion, aggressive interrogation techniques, and…racial insults";
- physical abuse, such as "hitting and kicking, inappropriate use of firearms, injury during arrest, and reckless treatment during transport";
- sexual assault;
- violation of due process;
- "illegal or inappropriate seizure of people in illegal law enforcement raids, questioning based solely on ethnic appearance, arrest made without cause, unlawful temporary detention, unlawful deportation, and deprivation of food, water, and medical attention";
- illegal searches;
- unlawful seizure or destruction of property; and
- unlawful cooperation with local law enforcement.

According to the report, around 35 percent of the complaints involved U.S. citizens, legal permanent residents of the United States, or people seeking asylum in the United States (Seltzer and Kourous 1998).

By the first years of the new century, the Border Patrol had undertaken a number of measures to address human rights concerns in South Texas in response to complaints from the community and the mounting death toll among migrants attempting to circumvent Operation Rio Grande. In October 2001 the Border Patrol put its BORSTAR (Border Patrol Search, Trauma, and Rescue) teams into the field to search for, rescue, and provide emergency medical care to migrants in distress, though, as Maril (2004, 302) notes, this came four years and hundreds of migrant deaths after the launching of ORG. And, of course, many migrant deaths and injuries continued to occur in spite of the agency's efforts to minimize the dangers brought about by the new enforcement strategy. In Border Patrol detention facilities, signs in Spanish were posted that invited migrants to call a toll-free number to report abuses of their rights. Agents and supervisors were trained in respecting migrants' human rights, and periodic meetings between the Border Patrol and human rights advocates had begun to take place. Conducting fieldwork in 2000 and 2001 for his ethnographic study of the Border Patrol in the Rio Grande Valley sector, Maril (2004, 261–62) found an organizational culture in which overt abuse of migrants or residents by agents would be quickly investigated and prosecuted. Still, in 2004, the Valley Movement for Human Rights, a Harlingen-based successor to ILEMP, received 149 complaints involving the same categories of human rights abuses by government authorities in the Lower Rio Grande Valley as in the 1998 ILEMP report. Of the abuses documented by the group, 65 percent were alleged to have been committed by agents of the Customs and Border Protection (CBP) unit of the Department of Homeland Security, which included the Border Patrol (51%) and U.S. Customs (14%), with the most of the remainder attributed to local law enforcement agencies (Valley Movement for Human Rights 2005, 32–33).

In my own fieldwork, it was evident that many Mexican migrants continued to successfully pass through the South Texas border region in spite of Operation Rio Grande and the great increase of Border Patrol enforcement capability. With the Border Patrol, I visited numerous migrant landings on the banks of the river in the Laredo and Rio Grande Valley sectors where piles of clothing, plastic bags, inner tubes, and beaten paths leading away from the bank into the brush were evidence that a great many people continued to cross the river in or near the border cities. The Border Patrol agents I interviewed knew that ORG had not stopped migrants from entering the United States through South Texas; at best it had reduced the flow somewhat. The migrants I interviewed continued to make most of their entries into the United States along this stretch of the border, since most of them had a city in Texas as their primary destination and because South Texas was the route they knew and where their social support networks continued to operate.

In the 1970s and 1980s, migrant sojourns north of the Texas-Mexico border were often seasonal and could be measured in months. Few of the migrants I interviewed after Operation Rio Grande went back and forth across the border that frequently. Given the increased difficulty and expense associated with the crossing, they typically spent years at a time in the United States. As I discuss in greater detail in subsequent chapters, much of the continued movement across the border and through South Texas was facilitated by coyotes of one type or another, who raised their fees to cover the greater risks and efforts needed to move their customers through the Border Patrol's heightened defenses. The rising costs of making the crossing contributed to migrants staying longer periods in the United States before returning home, as had happened generally along the border (Massey, Durand, and Malone 2002, 128–33; López, Oliphant, and Tejeda 2007, 79; Reyes et al. 2002).

For his 2004 ethnography of Border Patrol operations in the Rio Grande Valley sector, *Patrolling Chaos,* Robert Lee Maril spent two years studying the implementation of Operation Rio Grande in depth with agents in the field. In his judgment, the control-through-deterrence strategy developed in the El Paso sector had not worked in South Texas. It was, he said, "a terrible dud" in terms of reducing clandestine migration through the region (Maril 2004, 164). There were multiple reasons for this. First, the dense vegetation in South Texas, especially along the winding river, made visual surveillance by agents much more difficult than it had been in the open, sparsely vegetated desert around El Paso (Maril 2004, 167). Second, the strategy of agents staying in their vehicles in a single spot near the river meant that agents were unlikely to actually apprehend migrants in their area unless they walked right past their vehicles. Third, once migrants made it past the river, the "frontal deployment" strategy used in ORG meant that fewer agents were left behind the front line to apprehend them. One important indicator of this was that many apprehensions continued to be made at or near the immigration checkpoints on highways leading out of the Valley. Finally, he found that the new equipment and technologies deployed in the operation, including boat patrols on the river itself (235) and electronic motion sensors buried in the ground along its bank (76–77; 202–3), did little to improve agents' chances of apprehending migrants.

Another possibility to consider here is that even as late as 2005, after the huge increase in Border Patrol personnel assigned to South Texas, Operation Rio Grande remained insufficiently staffed to deter unauthorized entry of U.S. territory in the region. In 1999, researchers from the Center for U.S.-Mexico Border and Migration Research of the University of Texas presented a research report to a U.S. House of Representatives committee that estimated the number of Border Patrol agents that would need to be stationed in each sector of the country's border with Mexico in order to permanently sustain the level of control/deterrence that had been achieved by Operation Blockade in the El Paso sector in the fall of 1993. According to their estimate, the South Texas Border Patrol sectors of Rio Grande Valley, Laredo, and Del Rio would together require at least 6,006 agents to replicate the level of control achieved by Operation Blockade permanently (Bean, Capps, and Haynes 1999). In FY2005, the three sectors combined had only slightly more than half that number of agents (see figure 1.2). Of course, even with a doubling of agents in the region, the effects would only be what those from Operation Blockade had been: pushing migrants around the end of the line of agents on the river, raising the costs and dangers of their journey, and instead of deterring them from attempting to enter the United States, encouraging them to stay ever longer before returning home to Mexico. The abject failure of border operations like Blockade and Rio Grande to deter autonomous migration to the United States was reflected in the rapid growth of the "illegal" immigrant population residing in the United States, which grew from a postlegalization low in 1989 of 2.5 million to an estimated 11.1 million by 2005 (Passel 2006, 3).

Mexican Clandestine Border-Crossers in the Northeast Mexico-South Texas Corridor: A Sociodemographic Profile

Who were the migrants crossing this stretch of the border at the outset of the new century in terms of their sex, age, occupation, income, place of origin in Mexico, and intended U.S. destination? In other words, toward whom were U.S. apartheid policies directed, and who were the practitioners of resistencia hormiga? Data collected by the Encuesta sobre Migración en la Frontera Norte de México (EMIF),[22] allow us to answer this question by creating a sociodemographic profile of autonomous migrants.

The overwhelming majority of autonomous migrants were young men of working-class and peasant background with low levels of formal education (table 1.1). According to the EMIF, 95 percent of autonomous migrants arriving at the border with the intention to cross in the 2000–2003 period were men. Sixty percent of these migrants were under the age of thirty, and 90 percent were under the age of forty. Nine out of ten of them had dropped out of school before *preparatoria,* the Mexican equivalent of U.S. high school. Most of the migrants were married and were the heads of their households in Mexico, while a substantial minority were the children of household heads. Although the EMIF would seem to underestimate the presence of women in the flow of clandestine migrants across the border, given that 46 percent of Mexican immigrants living in the United States in 2003 were female,[23] other data confirm that males made the overwhelming majority of clandestine border-crossings during this period. For example, in the first five years of the new century, only about 15 percent of apprehensions made annually by the Border Patrol were of women.[24] The low proportion of women in the EMIF sample and among persons apprehended by the Border Patrol reflect differences in male and female migratory behavior, insofar as women were more likely than men a) to enter the United States legally or to use fake or rented documents to enter and b) to make definitive, one-time-only moves to the United States, often for the purposes of family reunification (Cerrutti and Massey 2001; Donato 1999; Donato and Patterson 2004; Valdez-Suiter, Rosas-López, and Pagaza 2007; Woo Morales 2001, 70–72).[25]

It is also evident that difficult economic circumstances motivated migrants to attempt to enter the United States clandestinely. Over 40 percent had not worked the month prior to their departure. Those who had been employed had typically worked six days a week for 500 pesos, less than fifty dollars at the prevailing exchange rate. Only about a fifth of those who had been employed received any type of fringe benefit (paid vacation, health care, retirement, end-of-year bonus, etc.). Almost all worked in some manual occupation

Table 1.1. Selected characteristics of autonomous migrants crossing the Northeast Mexico-South Texas border at the beginning of the twenty-first century

Migrant characteristic	Percentage, except as noted	Sample
Place of crossing		Migrants arriving at the
Crossing in Northeast Mexico-	30	border from the south,
South Texas corridor in 2002–3		2002–3, $n = 5,111$
Crossing elsewhere along border	70	
Gender of migrants with no crossing		Migrants arriving at the
documents, no work documents		border from the south,
Male	95	2000–3, $n = 3,319$
Female	5	
Gender of migrants with crossing		Migrants returning to
documents, but no work documents*		Mexico voluntarily, 2000–3,
Male	85	$n = 226$
Female	15	
Age		Migrants arriving at the
Under 30 years	60	border from the south,
Under 40 years	90	2000–3 $n = 3,319$
Marital status and household role		Migrants arriving at the
Married	53	border from the south,
Head of household	55	2000–3 $n = 3,319$
Child of household head	40	
Highest level of education attended		Migrants arriving at the
Primaria (elementary) or secundaria	89	border from the south,
(junior high) highest level		2000–3, $n = 3,319$
Preparatoria (high school) highest	9	
level		
University highest level	1	
Employed/not employed before leaving		Migrants arriving at the
Not working during last month	42	border from the south,
before departure		2000–3, $n = 3,213$
Working during last month before	58	
departure		
Last occupation before departure		Migrants arriving at the
Agricultural worker	30	border from the south,
Construction worker	26	2000–3, $n = 1,669$
Factory worker	14	
Personal services worker	12	
Mechanic or related trade	5	
Some other occupation	13	

(continued)

Table 1.1. *(continued)*

Migrant characteristic	Percentage, except as noted	Sample
Days worked, income earned, fringe benefits received at last job in Mexico		Migrants arriving at the border from the south, 2000–3
Median days worked per week, in days	6 days	$n = 1,222$
Median weekly income, in Mexican pesos	500 pesos	$n = 1,222$
Receiving any fringe benefits (vacation, health care, etc.)	21	$n = 1,684$
Mexican region of origin		Migrants arriving at the
Historic region	54	border from the south,
Central region	23	2000–3, $n = 3,319$
Southeast region	12	
Border region	11	
Mexican state of origin		Migrants arriving at the
Guanajuato	22	border from the south,
San Luis Potosí	10	2000–3, $n = 3,319$
Michoacán	7	
Veracruz	7	
Intended U.S. regional or state destination		Migrants arriving at the border from the south,
Texas	58	2000–3, $n = 2,274$
Houston	18	
Dallas–Fort Worth	14	
Austin	7	
San Antonio	6	
Texas border region	3	
Other Texas	10	
California	2	
Arizona	4	
Southeastern states	18	
Midwestern states	13	
Rocky Mountain States	3	
Northeastern states	2	
Northwestern states	<1	
Longest place of residence in United States		Migrants returning voluntarily to Mexico, 2000–3,
Texas	50	$n = 627$
Southeastern state	34	
Midwestern state	8	
Some other state	8	
U.S. occupation		Migrants returning voluntarily to Mexico, 2000–3,
Construction worker	31	$n = 604$
Agricultural worker	29	
Factory worker	19	

(continued)

Table 1.1. *(continued)*

Migrant characteristic	Percentage, except as noted	Sample
U.S. occupation (continued)		
Personal services worker	8	
Mechanic or related trade	5	
Domestic service	4	
Some other occupation	3	
U.S. earnings		Migrants returning volun-
Median weekly earnings, in U.S. dollars	$300	tarily to Mexico, 2000–3, $n = 400$
Median earnings during most recent U.S. sojourn, in U.S. dollars	$14,100	

Source: Consejo Nacional de Población. 2004. *Encuesta sobre Migración en la Frontera Norte de México (EMIF). Mexico City.*
*All other results presented in this table are for migrants who possessed no valid documents allowing them to enter the United States legally.

commensurate with their low level of formal education, with the majority employed in agriculture or construction.

Although migrants crossing this stretch of the border came from all over Mexico, the majority were from states in what Durand and Massey (2003) have referred to as the "historic region" of migration, that is, Aguascalientes, Colima, Durango, Guanajuato, Jalisco, Michoacán, Nayarit, San Luis Potosí, and Zacatecas, which had been sending migrants to the United States in large numbers for over a century. Among these states, Guanajuato and San Luis Potosí figured especially prominently, accounting for nearly one-third of the total. A substantial part of the clandestine migratory flow across this stretch of the border also came from states in central and southern Mexico that had only recently begun to send large numbers of their residents to the United States. Especially prominent among these was Veracruz, where an economic crisis in agriculture since the 1990s propelled ever-growing numbers of farmers and farmworkers to seek their fortunes north of the border (Hernández Navarro 2004; Mestries Benquet 2003). The northern border states of Mexico, mainly Tamaulipas, Nuevo León, and Coahuila, accounted for 11 percent of the clandestine flow.[26]

The majority of clandestine migrants arriving in the Mexican border cities of the northeast were headed to Texas and around half of migrants returning to Mexico across this stretch of the border reported that Texas was where they had lived longest in the United States. A substantial minority of arriving migrants were headed to the U.S. Southeast or Midwest, and a substantial minority of return migrants also reported having lived in those areas the longest before returning home. Texas-bound migrants listed, in rank order, Houston, Dallas-Fort Worth, Austin, and San Antonio as their principal destinations. Not surprisingly, in light of the discussion at the beginning of the chapter, only 3 percent of migrants surveyed reported the Texas border region as their intended destination, while 10 percent listed a variety of other destinations in the state. Migrants returning to Mexico during this period had been employed primarily in construction, agriculture, or as factory workers, especially in poultry-processing plants. Agricultural work was far more common among migrants returning from the Southeastern United States, where 56 percent reported having worked in the fields, compared to just 14 percent who were returning from Texas. Meanwhile, migrants returning to Mexico from Texas were far more likely to have worked in construction, with 41 percent employed in that sector, compared to just 21 percent of migrants returning from the Southeastern states. Median weekly earnings at migrants' last U.S. job were $300, around six times what they could have expected to earn in their home communities, had work been available.

In sum, the autonomous migrants coming across the Northeast Mexico-South Texas border at the beginning of the twenty-first century were largely from working-class and peasant backgrounds. They came mainly from the traditional areas of emigration in Mexico, but also from the northern border region and the new sending regions such as Veracruz. In Mexico, they had worked in a variety of manual occupations, especially in agriculture and construction, where pay was low and employment was intermittent. In the United States, they also found employment as manual workers, at wages considerably higher than they could earn in Mexico, but considerably lower than what most U.S. workers would accept. Consistent with the concept of global apartheid, we see that the state directed its repressive apparatus toward regulating the mobility, conditions of labor, and ability to press political demands of the nonwhite working poor who were born and raised in low-wage homelands. Consistent with the concept of resistencia hormiga, the migrants gained considerably in economic terms from their refusal to accept their territorial confinement within Mexico, but at the same time in the United States they occupied an illegal status that made them vulnerable to superexploitation relative to native and legal immigrant workers.

Autonomous Mexican migrants who crossed the northeast border with the United States at the turn of the century entered a territory with a particular history and specific set of social, cultural, and economic characteristics that strongly influenced the dynamics of migration through it. South Texas was and always had been Mexican Texas. In the contemporary period, the history of conflictive relations between a conquering Anglo American elite and a subjugated Spanish-speaking populace continued to color residents' attitudes toward one another, Mexicans across the river, federal law enforcement authorities, and migrants passing through on their way to destinations in the U.S. interior. More specifically, transgression of the international boundary was a part of everyday life in the region as was hostility toward federal authority for a significant part of the Mexican immigrant and Mexican American population. The history of migration to and through South Texas was one of labor mobilization, coercion, exploitation, and, at times, mass expulsion. The overall trend through the course of the twentieth century is one of ever-more-intensive surveillance and regulation of the mobility of Mexican workers at the border, beginning with the imposition of entry controls in 1917 and culminating in the launching of Operation Rio Grande in 1997. Throughout the history of their migration, Mexicans have actively evaded this surveillance and resisted regulation of their mobility by U.S. authorities, such that state-authorized labor flows from Mexico have always coexisted with substantial autonomous flows. As indicated by earnings data, evading state attempts to interdict them at the border paid significant dividends, even though their earnings were substantially lower than what U.S. citizens and legal immigrants could expect in return for their labor. Most of the autonomous migrants entering South Texas in the early 2000s came from regions in Mexico with a long history of emigration to the United States. Such migrants, relative to those coming from communities in Mexico that only recently began sending their members to work in the United States, had access to considerable accumulated social and cultural resources in their communities that could help them successfully negotiate the ever-more-serious obstacles and hazards that faced them at the border. In the next chapter, I examine in detail the ways in which a group of autonomous migrants from a small settlement in rural San Luis Potosí organized themselves to make the crossing through South Texas.

CHAPTER 2

Clandestine Crossing at the Beginning of the Twenty-first Century

The Long March through the Brush Country

Absent the possibility of supporting themselves and their families at a decent standard of living at home, communities in many parts of Mexico at the end of the twentieth century continued to do what they had been doing for most of the previous hundred years—they took matters into their own hands and sent thousands of their members north to work in the United States. Reacting to this autonomous movement and the political headaches it provoked, the U.S. government dramatically intensified policing of its southern border. As described in the previous chapter, this policing took the form of a series of paramilitary operations, including Operation Rio Grande. Taking place in the context of the creation of the North American Free Trade Area, the launching of such operations by the Border Patrol could be seen as an intensification of the state's attempt to interdict labor at its border while it simultaneously facilitated the transborder movement of commodities and capital. It represented, in other words, an increasingly militarized segmentation of the North America labor market within an ever-more-integrated North American market for goods, services, and investments. Without any realistic political possibility of altering the macro structures of inequality that consigned them to poverty and a precarious existence in Mexico in the short term, Mexican workers and peasants pursued a variety of survival strategies, including figuring out ways to overcome their interdiction by U.S. authorities at the border, using whatever resources and knowledge they could access within their communities. In this

For more detailed border-crossing stories collected by the author from individual informants, see http://www.trinity.edu/clandestinecrossings.

chapter I describe the most common way in which migrants at the beginning of the new century carried out their resistencia hormiga to the intensification of apartheid at the border. I do so through an examination of the prosaic details of border-crossing experiences of a group of men from a single rural community in the arid altiplano region of the state of San Luis Potosí. In this way, I illustrate how the practice of resistencia hormiga was lived by the autonomous migrants who engaged in it.

The basic elements of the clandestine-crossing process through South Texas had changed little since the creation of the Border Patrol in the 1920s, even after increased U.S. government enforcement with Operation Rio Grande. Aspiring migrants had to successfully negotiate the same series of obstacles as before the operation. First, they had to finance their journey from their homes in the Mexican interior to the point along the border where they planned to enter the United States. Second, they had to make a furtive crossing of the Rio Grande away from the legal ports of entry on the international bridges, avoiding immediate detection and apprehension by Border Patrol agents who lay in wait on the opposite bank. Once across the river, they had to hike through the brush to a point beyond the last immigration checkpoint on the highway leading away from the border, an arduous journey that took anywhere from two days to a week. Detection and arrest by the Border Patrol could occur at any moment during these treks. Finally, once they were past the immigration checkpoints, migrants had to either continue walking out of the border region until they reached the outskirts of San Antonio, Corpus Christi (each 150 miles from the border), or another town such as Uvalde (65 miles from the border), Kingsville (110 miles), or Alice (120 miles). Alternatively, they could try to hitch a ride from some local person or arrange for friends or relatives in the Texas interior to come pick them up. In subsequent chapters, I detail how migrants entered into relationships with coyotes in order to help assure their successful negotiation of these obstacles. It is important to recognize, however, that for most migrants the nature of the journey itself remained essentially the same, whether or not they employed coyotes to make it: get to the border, cross the river, walk around the checkpoints, and get a ride to a Texas city in the interior.

The Men from La Carmela*

La Carmela was a small town located in the foothills of the sierra about an hour's drive from the state capital of San Luis Potosí. It was home to several hundred inhabitants. Its residents raised cattle and goats, and cultivated some

---

*The names of the town and the migrants in this section are pseudonyms.

of the surrounding lands with corn, chilies, beans, tomatoes, and onions. These activities were no longer sufficiently remunerative to support the community, however, and some of its members "commuted" to work in construction, manufacturing, and domestic service in the state capital. In addition, some of its residents earned extra cash from the cottage industry of sculpting *molcajetes* (a type of mortar used for making salsa) from volcanic rock. Men from La Carmela long had migrated to the United States to work, mainly in Texas. By the beginning of the new century, some women had also joined the migrant stream. As was the case in the relationship between the town of Aguililla, Michoacán, and Redwood City, California, described by Rouse (1991), La Carmela as a community existed as much in Texas as it did in San Luis Potosí. Many of its migrants had settled more or less permanently in several places in Texas, having legalized their residence in the United States through the amnesty provisions of the 1986 Immigration Reform and Control Act. These immigrants had adult U.S.-citizen children who had spent their childhoods making periodic visits to La Carmela, which was just a day's drive from the largest cities in Texas, and some of these children had married friends of their families who grew up in La Carmela. The presence of a diaspora from La Carmela in Texas facilitated the ongoing out-migration of its residents, who typically received assistance in making the trip and finding a job from friends and relatives across the border. Although since the launching of Operation Rio Grande in 1997 more of them had contracted professional coyotes to make the crossing than in the past, the men of La Carmela whom I interviewed still had a preferred route through Laredo that they followed north to Texas and continued to use without hiring professionals to guide them. The following account of how migrants from La Carmela went about organizing and making their cross-border journeys is based on in-depth interviews I conducted with a dozen migrants in 2004. I refer specifically to the experiences of six men, all of whom knew or were related to one another (see below for short biographical sketches of the men).[1]

BIOGRAPHICAL SKETCHES OF SIX MIGRANTS FROM LA CARMELA, SAN LUIS POTOSÍ

• **Álvaro,** twenty-two, was married and had a three-year-old daughter. He had experienced two sojourns of living and working in Texas, having first gone there in 1999 when he was sixteen. Each had ended when he was picked up by immigration authorities and sent back to Mexico. The second sojourn had lasted four years and had ended a month before I interviewed him. Álvaro met his wife, who was the daughter of a couple from La Carmela and a U.S. citizen by birth, while he was living in Texas.

His daughter had also been born in Texas. Both of them were living in Texas and awaiting his return. Álvaro was born and raised in La Carmela. He had attended school through the end of *secundaria,* the equivalent of a ninth-grade education in the U.S. system. His parents had lived in La Carmela their whole lives and were *campesinos* (peasants).

- **Jorge,** twenty-seven, was one of Álvaro's older brothers. Like Álvaro, he had finished *secundaria* before going to work in the fields and then going to Texas to work in construction. He made his first trip north in 1996 and a second in 1999. He had attempted to cross again a few months before I interviewed him, but he had not made it. Jorge was married with two children, a five-year-old boy and a two-year-old girl, and lived with them in his own house in La Carmela. He now worked in the fields and making *molcajetes.*

- **Lorenzo,** twenty-five, was the older brother of Álvaro and the younger brother of Jorge. He had completed the sixth grade of elementary school before going to work in the fields. He was the first of the three brothers to travel to Texas in search of work when he was just seventeen. He had gone back and forth between Texas and La Carmela several times. He had returned to La Carmela in 1998 and 1999 after he had been picked up by the Border Patrol at construction sites in Texas. When he was picked up by immigration authorities at work on a third occasion in December 2000, a judge sentenced him to 180 days in prison for illegally entering the United States. Lorenzo had a Mexican American fiancé in Texas whose parents, like those of Álvaro's wife, were from La Carmela. His imprisonment and subsequent deportation derailed their plans to marry. In spite of the risk of further imprisonment if he was caught by the Border Patrol, Lorenzo planned to head north again as soon as he could. He didn't see a future for himself in La Carmela working the fields and making *molcajetes.*

- **Efrén,** twenty-three, was born and raised in La Carmela and completed *secundaria* before heading north in search of work. He had found work in construction in Texas 1998 and stayed for three years. While he was there he worked for Mexican construction contractors applying stucco to walls of private residences, earning eight dollars per hour in cash, with no taxes deducted. The money he sent back to La Carmela served to build a house for him and his parents. He had tried to go back to Texas in early 2003 but got picked up by the Border Patrol and returned to La Carmela. Efrén married a few months before our interview. He had no immediate plans to return to Texas to work. Although money was short—he made very little from chiseling *molcajetes* and working in the fields—he and his wife had their own quarters in the house he had built for his parents.

- **Fermín,** thirty-three, was born and raised in La Carmela. He had only completed the third grade and went to work in the fields after that. He also worked in construction in the capital city of San Luis Potosí on occasion. Fermín had been married for fifteen years, and his wife and five children lived in La Carmela. He did not have any immediate relatives living in the United States. To support his wife and children, Fermín had made four sojourns to work in construction in Texas over the last five years. His migratory career started much later than Álvaro and Efren's had begun: he was twenty-eight when he crossed the border for the first time.

- **Pancho,** twenty-six, was married and had two children with whom he lived in La Carmela. He had crossed the border and worked in Texas for nine months in 1998, first in a restaurant and then in construction. He had tried to go back in early 2001 but had been picked up by the Border Patrol near Dilley, Texas, after nearly a week of walking in the brush. Pancho had not tried to cross again and had been working in the fields and making *molcajetes* in La Carmela since then. He wasn't sure if he would go back to Texas in the future.

Getting Ready to Make the Trip

Men from La Carmela usually made the trip north together in small groups of five to ten people. Younger men and first-time migrants traveled with older, more experienced men who had made the trip before and knew the way. Thus, the first challenge facing novice migrants was finding someone experienced with whom they could travel.[2] The second challenge was to save or borrow the funds needed to buy a bus ticket to the border, pay for a night's food and lodging at the border, buy food and water for the long hike through the brush and for other incidental expenses that might be incurred along the way. At a minimum, a successful trip made without hiring a coyote would cost about $100, a significant amount of money for residents of La Carmela, most of whom were only irregularly employed and made very little money when they did have jobs.[3] I met several men in La Carmela and elsewhere who were waiting to make their next trip north as soon as they could get the funds together to leave, something that could take an especially long time for those who did not have friends and relatives in the United States to lend them the money. Once migrants assembled their group and scratched together the money needed to purchase bus tickets for everyone, they would take off for the border. Although the Mexican constitution guaranteed them the right to move about freely within their own country and to leave it, migrants from La Carmela would sometimes have that right abrogated by government agents and other countrymen as they approached the U.S. border.

Extortion and Robbery on the Mexican Side of the River

As they approached the border, the men from La Carmela had to negotiate the hurdle of getting through the customs and immigration checkpoint a couple of dozen kilometers south of Nuevo Laredo on the highway to Monterrey. Pancho described how he and his companions were ordered off the bus in June 1998 by Mexican immigration officials at the checkpoint and shaken down for money. He said the police singled them out because of their rural appearance and mannerisms:

> I believe that it was mainly our country looks, like we were from the country. You look different than the city folks who travel more. We're more innocent looking, since we've hardly traveled anywhere.

The men from La Carmela also had to be on guard against shakedowns from the local police in Nuevo Laredo. Lorenzo told me of a trip he'd made in 1996 in which police in Nuevo Laredo accused him and his friends of being coyotes and threatened to arrest them all. He'd had to pay the police 800 of the 1,000 pesos he was carrying.[4] Other men from the village had faced trouble along the riverbank in Nuevo Laredo, not only from police, but from gang members and thieves. According to Fermín:

> Before you cross the river, here on the Mexican side of the border, when you go down to the river, there are bad people over here. Members of gangs watch you. They beat you up and take your food and your money. The police do, too.

Migrants I interviewed from other towns in San Luis Potosí, Nuevo León, and Guanajuato related similar experiences with, and opinions about, Mexican police officers in the border cities. The priests and nuns who operated shelters for migrants in Reynosa and Nuevo Laredo also related stories about police abuse of members of the population they served. Fortunately, the men made it to Nuevo Laredo without incident most of the time. Once there, they would prepare as best as they could for the bigger hurdles that awaited them at the river and beyond.

Stocking Up on Provisions in Nuevo Laredo

On arrival in Nuevo Laredo, the group of migrants from La Carmela sometimes would check into an inexpensive hotel, but, trying to save money, more often they would not. Instead, they would go to a supermarket to buy supplies for the crossing and the trek around the checkpoints on the Texas side, a trip that usually took several days. The typical rations included cans of beans, tuna, and corn, flour tortillas, and one or two gallon-size jugs of water per person. They might also bring a plastic bag of *pinole,* a sugar-sweetened corn powder that could be eaten dry or as a porridge, and that was lightweight, filling, and rich in calories and carbohydrates. Each member of the group brought his own small *mochila* (knapsack) from home to carry his own food, a minimum of clothing, and perhaps a light blanket and plastic tarp to sleep on. Rain jackets, sleeping bags, tents, and camp stoves were unheard of. Not only were these items not affordable for the typical migrant leaving La Carmela, but they also fell outside his set of cultural experiences. Moreover, the migrants' goal was not comfort but to make as fast and direct a trek through South Texas as possible. Camping equipment of the sort commonly used by U.S. recreationists would not only slow down the migrants in the brush but could dangerously weigh them down as they attempted to cross the river. Depending on where along the river the group intended to make its crossing, or if the river was running high, they might also stop by a *vulcanizadora* (tire-repair shop) to purchase some inflated *cámaras de llanta* (inner tubes) to use to float across the river.

Crossing the Río Bravo del Norte/Rio Grande

The middle of the channel of the Rio Grande marks the international boundary between South Texas and Northeast Mexico. Known as the Río Bravo del Norte by Mexicans—"the rough/wild river of the north"—the river begins its life as a clear snow-fed stream in the Rocky Mountains and flows 1,896 miles to its mouth at Boca Chica in the Gulf of Mexico (Metz 2004). Below the Amistad Dam at Ciudad Acuña, Coahuila-Del Río, Texas, the river is no longer clear or *bravo;* rather it runs a generally slow, muddy, and meandering course to the southeast over the next 575 miles to the Gulf. The width, depth, and flow of the river—all extremely relevant characteristics from the point of view of migrants who must cross it—vary considerably, depending on precipitation, irrigation, and amount of water released from the Amistad and Falcon dams (International Boundary and Water Commission 2006 and 2007). Regardless of this variation, compared to the other major rivers of North America, the river is hardly *grande:* one journalist writing from Brownsville in the second year of the twenty-first century reported that he had visited places "where the river is so narrow you can wade across and not get your trousers wet" (Davis 2001).

Although the Rio Grande/Rio Bravo in the study area was easily forded on foot in many places and was a much diminished river from what it had been historically, it still represented a substantial drowning hazard for migrants seeking to cross it clandestinely. In 1998, for example, a drought year in which river levels were generally quite low, a study conducted by the Center for Immigration Research of the University of Houston documented the drowning deaths of thirty-six migrants along this stretch of the international river boundary (Eschbach, Hagan, and Rodríguez 2001, 46). The number of drowning deaths tracked strongly with measured flows in the river: in their study of border deaths, the University of Houston researchers found that in 1992, a wetter-than-normal year, fifty-two migrants drowned in the river while attempting to cross (Eschbach, Hagan, and Rodríguez 2001, 46, 53). The river had a reputation among migrants, amplified by the U.S. Border Patrol and the Mexican government's migrant protection unit known as Grupo Beta, as being *traicionero* (treacherous) and full of unseen hazards, such as unexpectedly deep holes at low-water crossings and deceptively strong currents and undertows. Certainly much of the fear—and danger—generated by the river had to do with the fact that unlike most middle-class U.S. residents, many Mexican migrants from peasant or working-class backgrounds, especially those from arid regions in states such as San Luis Potosí, Guanajuato, and Nuevo León, were very weak swimmers or did not know how to swim at all.

Arriving at the banks of the Río Bravo at the turn of the twenty-first century, migrants from La Carmela generally looked for a shallow place where they could wade across, holding each other's hands to prevent any member of the group from being swept away. If they couldn't cross in a shallow place and one of the group's members knew how to swim, he would pull the other members across on inner tubes. Several of the men I interviewed in La Carmela had also crossed on one or more occasions with *pateros,* men who ferried people across the river using boats or inflatable rafts. These migrants found it terrifying to cross the river, even when they crossed it in shallow spots, where the water barely came up to their knees. Worse still, they sometimes made their crossings in the dark to avoid detection by the Border Patrol. Their sense of vulnerability was undoubtedly heightened by having to strip naked to make the crossing, stashing their clothes in plastic bags to keep them dry. In the winter months, it was a frigid crossing. On reaching the other bank of the river, they would hide in the dense thickets of *carrizo* (a tall, bamboo-like reed), hurriedly put their clothing back on, and head into the brush above the riverbank as quickly as possible. As discussed with regard to the effectiveness of Operation Rio Grande, it was important for the migrants to move away from the river quickly because the Border Patrol had buried motion sensors near the most frequently used landings, which meant that agents were likely to arrive on the scene shortly after migrants hit the ground. Although they might be captured at any point during their trek, they were most likely to be apprehended close to the river where the terrain was most heavily patrolled.

Trekking through the Brush Past the Immigration Checkpoints

At this point migrants had already run the gauntlet of police bent on extorting them and gang members waiting to rob them on the Mexican side of the river. They had braved the treacherous currents of the Río Bravo. Yet this had been the easy part of the trip. The biggest challenge was still to come: traversing the unforgiving South Texas brush country that lay between the river and the immigration checkpoints on the highways leading away from the border. In South Texas, the greatest difficulty for migrants had never been crossing the border itself. That had always been and still remained relatively easy. The big challenge was to get past the immigration checkpoints to the towns and cities in the U.S. interior where jobs awaited them. Migrants referred to these checkpoints as the *segunda garita* (the second sentry post or guardhouse), with the *primera garita* being the immigration stations located at the official U.S. ports of entry on the international bridges.

The U.S. Border Patrol operated more than a dozen immigration checkpoints along the region's thoroughfares, each located a considerable distance from the international boundary itself (see map 2.1). The checkpoint along Interstate Highway 35 north of Laredo had historically been one of the closest to the border, located just fifteen miles from the city's international bridges downtown.[5] The Falfurrias checkpoint, on U.S. 281 north of McAllen, was located over eighty highway miles from the international bridge that connected Hidalgo, Texas, with Reynosa, Tamaulipas. The Sarita checkpoint, on U.S. 77 north of Harlingen, was located a similar distance from the international bridge connecting Los Indios, Texas, with Indio Blanco, Tamaulipas. The Del Rio sector of the Border Patrol operated several checkpoints on the highways leading away from Del Rio and Eagle Pass. These checkpoints normally consisted of mobile home–style trailers; they were moved closer to or farther from the border on several occasions in the 1990s and early 2000s, but they were always located on stretches of highway between the Rio Grande and U.S. 83. All vehicles traveling away from the border on the highways where checkpoints were located had to exit and pass through them. Drivers and passengers were greeted by Border Patrol agents and could be required to produce valid identification documents that permitted them to be in the United States. Vehicles might be opened and their contents inspected. The purpose of the checkpoints was to prevent "aliens" who had managed to enter U.S. territory from traveling farther into the interior of the country. Shipments of illegal narcotics were also seized at these checkpoints.[6] An article in the June/July 2006 issue of *Customs and Border Protection Today,* published by the Department of Homeland Security, reported that since 1999, the Laredo checkpoint had been responsible for over 28,000 apprehensions of migrants and the seizure of 450,000 pounds of marijuana and 10,000 pounds of cocaine, with a combined value of $680 million (United States Department of Homeland Security 2006).[7]

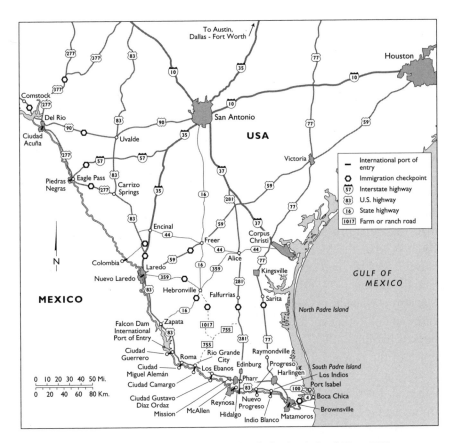

Map 2.1. Routes away from the border and immigration checkpoints in South Texas, 2005.

The land that lies between the Rio Grande and the highway checkpoints forms part of the region known to geographers as the South Texas Plains (Johnson 2001). As the name suggests, the topography of the region is generally flat to rolling. It ranges in elevation from about 1,000 feet above sea level along the southeastern edge of the Edwards Plateau to sea level along the Laguna Madre (McNab and Avers 1994). At the turn of the century, vast tracts of land in this region were dedicated to cattle ranching, while vegetable farming was important in the "winter garden" area around Uvalde and Crystal City, as well as in the Lower Rio Grande Valley in the corridor running from Brownsville to Rio Grande City, where citrus production was also important (Jordan et al. 1984, 155, 178). Cotton was an important crop in the farmlands surrounding Brownsville, Harlingen, McAllen, and Corpus Christi (Jordan et al. 1984, 169). In the southernmost portions of the region, where the

Brownsville-Harlingen and McAllen-Mission-Edinburg metropolitan areas were located, farm and town were interspersed and blended into each other. Although most of the counties along the border itself were home to substantial populations, most of the South Texas counties away from the border were only sparsely populated.[8]

Ecologists describe the South Texas region as a semiarid chaparral or savanna zone whose natural vegetation consists of grasses, mesquite and other thorny bushes, scrub oaks, and prickly pear cactus (Jordan et al. 1984, 33; McNab and Avery 1994). In the nineteenth and twentieth centuries, overgrazing, restriction of natural fires, soil compaction, and drought led to a dramatic increase in brush density in this region (Texas Parks and Wildlife Department 2005). Writing in the 1920s, renowned Texas author J. Frank Dobie declared that "the worst brush in the United States of America that I know anything about is what the Mexicans used to call the *Brasada,* in McMullen, Webb, Duval, Live Oak, and other counties between the Nueces River and the Rio Grande" (Dobie 1929, 201). The brush was so dense and full of thorns that the Mexican cowhands, or *vaqueros,* who worked this country typically wore an entire suit of leather and cloth armor to protect them as they rode through the thickets herding cattle (Dobie 1929, 204). At the end of the twentieth century, much of the ranchland in the South Texas Plains remained a nearly impenetrable "tangle of xerophytic vegetation" with extremely limited visibility (Jordan et al. 1984, 33). Unlike the vaqueros of a century ago, Mexican migrants traversing the brush in the contemporary period did not enjoy the benefits of the protective armor described by Dobie.

Although South Texas is not a desert, rainfall is sparse and erratic, and surface water is in short supply.[9] Because of the lack of surface water, both farming and cattle ranching in the region are dependent on pumping water from aquifers deep beneath the ground.[10] Migrants' treks across the region during the time of this study were made possible in large measure by their knowledge of where *papalotes* (windmills) pumped water from the ground to fill cattle troughs and ponds, which they used to refill their jugs and canteens. In addition to the dense brush and scarce water, migrants had to contend with the region's extreme temperatures. In the summer, high temperatures are frequently over 100° Fahrenheit in the shade, with shade from trees in short supply and little relief in the way of cloud cover (Bomar 1983, tables B-9 and F-6). Not surprisingly, migrants trekking through the brush in the summer usually did most of their walking at night or in the early morning hours, sleeping and resting in what shade they could find during the heat of the day. Winters in South Texas are colder than many think, with average lows in the 30s and 40s Fahrenheit and routine freezes (Bomar 1983, tables B-2 and B-5). Given the extremes of heat and cold that characterize South Texas, combined with the scarcity of surface water, it is understandable why so many migrants have died in this region. The University of Houston study cited earlier with regard to drowning deaths found that thirty-one migrants perished from environmental causes (i.e., heat, cold, and/or dehydration) in 1998 as they trekked through South Texas on foot (Eschbach, Hagan, and Rodríguez 2001, 35).[11] Fortunately, the seasonal pattern of labor migrants' cross-border trips through this region was such that far fewer migrants attempted the crossing during the deadly hot summer months, making the bulk of their crossings during the first few months of each year, when temperatures were far cooler.[12]

Once migrants from La Carmela had crossed the river near Laredo, their goal was to walk to Encinal, Texas, the nearest town beyond the checkpoint on Interstate 35. Encinal is located just off the interstate, about forty driving miles north and east of downtown Laredo. Migrants guided themselves to Encinal by either walking through the brush parallel to the interstate highway or by following a power line mounted on tall posts that ran through unpopulated ranchlands from Laredo right into the town. It was a small settlement, with just a few hundred inhabitants who lived on unpaved streets in mobile homes or small, irregular houses they had constructed themselves. The residential area was surrounded by ranches, and yards transitioned quickly into dense brush. There were a couple of convenience stores and other small businesses in town, mainly along the highway at some distance away from the main residential area. When migrants arrived in Encinal, they would hide in the brush and send one or two of their members into town to use a telephone to place a call to friends in San Antonio, Austin, or Houston and ask them to come pick them up and drive them the rest of the way out of the border region.[13] Unfortunately, Encinal was regarded by the Border Patrol as a hub for drug and "alien" smuggling. As a result, it was regularly patrolled by agents, making it risky for migrants to enter town. Indeed, in 1996 a group of men from La Carmela was captured by the Border Patrol when two of its members went into Encinal to call ahead for their ride. Sometimes Encinal was so heavily patrolled that migrants did not dare enter it. Other times, the rides they expected would fail to materialize. In these cases, groups were forced to continue their march through the brush to the towns of Cotulla or Dilley, located another thirty and forty-five driving miles, respectively, up Interstate 35. Walking on to one of these towns not only involved trekking a longer distance after provisions had been exhausted, but it also meant having to ford the Nueces River, which, after a rain, might be no less of a challenge than crossing the Rio Grande.

Even under the best of circumstances, it was always at least a two-day walk from Laredo to Encinal. Before the Border Patrol stepped up its patrols in the mid-1990s, the men from La Carmela could walk in the right-of-way of the power line from Laredo to Encinal, which was regularly cleared of brush. By 2004, migrants bold enough to walk in the right-of-way were likely to be quickly apprehended by the authorities, who kept the route under heavy surveillance. This did not mean that migrants had abandoned the route, however. Rather, they followed what they called the *postería* (line of posts, as in "fence posts") from a distance, hidden in the brush. This was possible to do, given that the terrain was flat and the power lines were on such tall posts.[14] It meant, however, that walking was considerably slower and more laborious, given the thicket of branches and thorns which migrants had to battle outside the power line right-of-way. It was also more dangerous, since accidents befalling migrants a mile or more from the power lines in the brush were much more likely to have tragic consequences than if they took place in plain view in the right-of-way.[15] Migrants from La Carmela left home for the first time with the knowledge that the passage through the border region, even if it ended well, would be very, very tough. Men from the community told others of finding corpses along the trail and of their own suffering and near-death experiences. Efrén had this to say about what he was thinking when he left for the border on his first trip in 1998, when he was just seventeen:

> EFRÉN: When someone leaves here, well, he's heading off to suffer, to face whatever comes his way. If he has to face death, he just has to face it. He knows that the river is *traicionero*. He doesn't know if he's going to return or not. He just takes off with the blessing of his parents and asking for God's blessing.
>
> SPENER: What had they told you about the crossing before you attempted it?
>
> EFRÉN: That it wasn't too complicated, but that you had to battle to make it.
>
> SPENER: You had to battle. What kinds of things did they tell you? In other words, what did the battle consist of?
>
> EFRÉN: There was the danger of dying on the trail, because there are many dangers, like rattlesnakes, spiders, things like that. And you could even break your leg in the *monte* [brush] and be stranded out there.

One of Efrén's comrades, Álvaro, averred that everything about the trip was dangerous and that as you were leaving on your first trip, "you're thinking about things that one can't even imagine." Álvaro was just sixteen and making his first crossing with some friends in February 1999 when he saw a dead man along this route. The body was still clothed, but badly decomposed, lying on the ground underneath a mesquite, covered with flies. The men noticed a rope with a noose hanging from one of the branches of the mesquite and concluded that the man had hung himself or perhaps been lynched. Álvaro guessed that maybe he had committed suicide after having been left behind on the trail. They left the body where they had found it after covering it up with a bit of dirt—it was already half-buried, he told me. The experience was sobering for everyone in the group:

> We continued on our way, but it wasn't the same after that. All I could think of was that it could have happened to us.... It really scared me and made me sad, too, at the same time, since it could have been me. And that was an experience I'll never forget. And this makes you think about all the people that cross the border, day after day, day after day. People cross, people die along the way. Many make it to their destination and many do not. And these are things that make you sad, but you just have to do them.

In spite of this scare, Álvaro had crossed the border several times since his first trip. Neither he nor his friends and family in La Carmela had been dissuaded from making the crossing by their own experiences or by the public-service announcements on Mexican radio and television that warned migrants about the perils of the journey north:

> I don't think [the public-service announcements] matter at all. In my case, and I think that everyone feels the same in these cases about those announcements they make, they're worthless. Because our situation is really difficult. You know that you're going to be risking your life. But a lot of the time it's poverty that obliges you to go. It forces us to leave our lands, regardless of what we see on television or what they're publishing. A lot of the time it's just irrelevant to you [*sale sobrando para uno*]. I'll tell you again, because of poverty, people are always going to be crossing the border.[16]

In the early twenty-first century, the men of La Carmela typically arrived in Encinal exhausted, with blistered feet, and full of thorns after two nights and three days (or three days and two nights) of walking through the *monte*. Their clothes were often in tatters from catching on the barbs of mesquite, *nopal* (prickly pear), and *maguey* (agave or century plant), which they had trouble avoiding during the daytime and collided painfully into at night, when they walked without flashlights to avoid being seen by the Border Patrol or ranchers on whose land they were trespassing. The men especially feared running into the ranchers, for they had heard that they were armed with rifles and wouldn't think twice about shooting migrants they found trespassing on their land. They might or might not see other groups of migrants in the brush.

If they did, they kept their distance, since drug runners might also transport their merchandise on such routes, and they did not trust the coyotes who were based at the border, worrying that they might rob them of their food, water, and money. The men of La Carmela were never alone in the *monte,* though. They typically encountered cattle, javelinas (wild boars), jackrabbits, deer, and rattlesnakes on the trail. At night, they might be surrounded in the darkness by howling coyotes. They catnapped on the barren ground, under the stars at night or in the sparse shade of a mesquite during the day. They had to be careful to lie down in a place that was free of grass and brush, lest they cuddle up to a rattlesnake.[17] If it rained, they got soaked, leading to painful chafing of their legs from walking with wet pants. If they were crossing in the hot summer months, they would be blasted by an unforgiving sun and would surely run out of water after the first day of walking. They would then be obliged to look for a *papalote,* which pumped water from under the ground into a cattle trough. The water was typically brackish (*salada*), dirty, and often filled with green algae, but they had to drink it, even though it made them nauseous and gave them diarrhea later. If they were crossing in January and a cold front blew through, the temperatures could drop into the 20s or 30s Fahrenheit at night, and the men would be faced with the dilemma of whether or not to build a small fire—which was likely to attract the attention of the Border Patrol—in order to stay warm. This was what the trip was like under the best of circumstances.

Pancho was lucky enough to make the trek in just two days of nonstop walking when he made it for the first time in 1998, at the age of twenty. When he and his friends finally reached Encinal at nine or ten in the evening and began to wait for their ride, he was so exhausted that he collapsed and immediately fell asleep on the ground. When he awoke in pain a little while later, he realized he should have inspected the spot more closely for he had lain on top of a mound of fire ants. Painful as fire ant bites can be, worse things had happened to men from La Carmela as they journeyed north into Texas.

The migrants often lost their bearings while hiking around the checkpoints. The word they used to describe this happening was ironic: as they headed to *el Norte,* it was not uncommon for them to *nortearse* (to get disoriented). Fermín explained how it was surprisingly easy to get lost in the brush, even for migrants who had made the trip several times before and despite the terrain between Laredo and Encinal being generally flat, so that you could usually see landmarks like the *postería* from a great distance:

Well, sometimes we cut a stick so we can knock down the *nopal* because there are times we get all boxed in and can't find a way out! Because of this we can't get out to the road because the *monte* is so thick! It's really dense! And so sometimes you get turned around and head back in the direction you've come from because you've gotten lost.

In the grueling summer months, the heat and lack of water meant that getting lost could easily be fatal. Moreover, at any time of year the physical stresses of the trek—fatigue, hunger, heat or cold, and dehydration—could contribute to migrants losing their way.

Lorenzo made his first trip along the Laredo-Encinal route in April 1996 when he was seventeen. His group included seven other men from La Carmela, including one of his cousins. One of the older men had made the crossing once before and served as the group's guide. He did not know the route well enough, however, and got the group lost in the brush. Instead of taking two or three days, it took four days and four nights of walking to get to Encinal. It was a dreadful trip. It was hot and they ran out of water on the second day, lost deep in the brush, out of sight and sound of any road. Lorenzo's teenage cousin, Ismael, got sick from dehydration and began vomiting a yellow bile. Lorenzo and another companion carried Ismael in search of water, though he begged to be left behind. With no roads or houses nearby, the boy surely would have died. Finally, the group came across a mobile home that had a garden hose they could drink from. The home was unlocked and had a little bit of food in the refrigerator. The group rested there for the afternoon and then headed back into the brush that evening. Still with no food, they used the *resorteras* (slingshots) they had brought to kill a couple of jackrabbits along the trail. They cooked the jackrabbits on a small fire they built in a gully under some trees so they would not be seen by the Border Patrol. They finally got to Encinal at the end of their fourth day, having run out of food and water again by that time. It was this group that was apprehended by the Border Patrol when two of its members went into town to call for a ride.

Some of the other men from La Carmela told me that they, too, had killed rabbits on the trail to eat, but they had dried their meat in the sun and eaten it raw, so as to avoid having to light a fire. Pancho, the man who had fallen asleep on a mound of fire ants, said that he and his fellow travelers had even killed and eaten an armadillo out of desperation once, on a week-long trek to Dilley, Texas, in 2001. They peeled its shell off using a knife and attempted to cook it over a fire, but it had been raining and they couldn't keep the fire going. The armadillo's meat was like a pig's, he said, and they'd had to eat it raw and bloody. Their food had run out after two days. Before catching the armadillo, they had already eaten feed corn left by hunters in deer blinds, raw *nopales* (prickly pear leaves) and sour *tunas* (prickly pear fruit) along the trail. When a rattler struck at the legs of one of the men, they killed it with a rock and then cooked and ate it. Pancho said that when you're out in the *monte*, "you don't think twice about it. You just do what you have to do to survive."

Getting a Ride out of the Border Region

The migratory strategy of people from La Carmela following the Laredo-Encinal route depended on the willingness of people they knew in San Antonio, Austin, Dallas, and Houston to drive to Encinal (or Dilley) in their cars to pick up them up and drive them surreptitiously out of the border region to one of the aforementioned cities.[18] It was a strategy that would not work unless migrants in La Carmela had friends and relatives who lived in Texas and were willing to aid them in this way. Drivers who picked up groups of migrants emerging from the brush in Encinal ran considerable risks by doing so. They might be spotted by the Border Patrol loading people up on the side of the road. Alternatively, they might be pulled over by an agent driving on Interstate 35 who developed a "reasonable suspicion" that their car was transporting undocumented migrants, based on factors such as how low the vehicle was riding to the ground, the speed at which it was traveling, or, more nebulously, the driver's failure to make eye contact with the agent as he passed the car.[19] Many traffic stops of this sort were made by the Border Patrol between Laredo and San Antonio. When unauthorized migrants were found in the vehicle, the driver could be charged with "harboring and transporting illegal aliens," a felony that could result in a significant period of imprisonment and forfeiture of the vehicle he was driving.

In some cases, drivers picked migrants up in Encinal free of charge, based on altruism or noncash forms of reciprocity. In most cases, however, the friends, family members, and acquaintances who picked up people from La Carmela in Encinal charged for the service, with amounts ranging from $400 to $700 per person.[20] Generally, someone in the group made arrangements in advance with a driver before they left La Carmela, telling him approximately when they expected to get to Encinal. One of the problems with the arrangement, obviously, was that it was hard to predict how long it would take to make the trek through the brush. As a consequence, even drivers who had promised to come for a group in Encinal might not be able to do so immediately when the call came, given their other commitments to work and family in San Antonio or another city. In these cases, migrants might be forced to wait in the brush for a day or more or might simply have to try to locate someone else who was willing to come for them. Or, they might just have to keep walking until they could find a ride.

Pursuit and Capture by the U.S. Border Patrol

The men from La Carmela also told me stories of capture and near capture by the Border Patrol on the Laredo-Encinal route, which had been under heavy surveillance since the launching of Operation Rio Grande in 1997. The Border Patrol's light planes and helicopters had swooped over them from the sky and had radioed their location to agents in vehicles on the ground, who then captured them as they emerged from the brush to cross a road a bit farther toward Encinal. Sometimes the migrants were able to hide under bushes and trees and avoid detection from the air, but they worried from then on that they had been spotted. Other times agents had surprised the men on the trail. Then the men would all run in opposite directions, diving into the brush to hide until the agents found them or gave up trying. On the trip where Pancho and his friends ate the raw armadillo, they were spotted by agents as they crossed a dirt track in the brush just before reaching Dilley, after a full week of walking. Agents let loose their dogs to chase the men down and they were captured. Pancho said that at times like that, "you feel like an animal, with them chasing you. That's when I would feel worst. When you're running like that, you don't care that you might fall in a gully in the middle of the night, you just want to get away. It's horrible!" Others said they had been treated relatively well by Border Patrol agents when they had been apprehended, although several said they had friends who complained of agents who spoke to them rudely and had roughed them up when they were arrested.

There were times when migrants from La Carmela were actually glad to see the Border Patrol. If they become too exhausted on the trail, they would walk out to the nearest main road to wait for a Border Patrol vehicle to pass by in order to be picked up and taken back to Laredo to be "voluntarily returned" to Mexico.[21] Ironically, it was not always easy to find the Border Patrol when you really wanted them. Such was Jorge's experience. In March 2004, Jorge made the crossing with eight other men from La Carmela and neighboring settlements. One of Jorge's cousins served as the group's guide. They waded across the river successfully in the middle of the night and started their march through the brush toward Encinal without problem. It began to rain heavily, however, shortly after they crossed the river, and they were buffeted by storms for several days. They were soaked to the bone, it was cold, and the trails they were following turned into seas of mud. It took them five full days to reach Encinal, instead of the usual two or three. When they arrived in town, they were unable to reach by phone the friend who had agreed to pick them up. Two of the men had an aunt in Houston who knew a woman who ran a *camioneta* (van) company that ran people and merchandise back and forth between Texas and Mexico. The aunt gave them the woman's number, and she agreed to pick them up in Encinal at four in the morning the day after they arrived. She would charge them a total of $4,000 for the service, payable on the group's arrival in Houston. They waited for the van in the rain in the *monte* at the outskirts of Encinal, but it never came. Wet, cold, hungry, and exhausted, the group decided to press on to Dilley, another forty-five miles of walking. Jorge wished them luck, but said he was going no farther: "I don't think anyone had ever felt as desperate as I did that time. I had really lost all hope. I just couldn't go on any farther. We were so hungry, and we had no money for food, and the weather was so terrible."

Jorge bid his companions good-bye. They took off into the brush toward Dilley and were eventually successful in reaching San Antonio, their final destination. Jorge walked out onto State Highway 44 and waited in the rain for a Border Patrol vehicle to come by. When none came, he started walking toward the intersection with Interstate 35, a mile or so away. He walked onto the southbound shoulder of the Interstate to look for a Border Patrol vehicle. Still, none appeared. After walking for a mile or two, he began to try to hitch a ride from passing vehicles headed toward Laredo. Finally, a Spanish-speaking Mexican American man stopped and gave him a ride, dropping him off a few blocks from the international bridge. Walking through the downtown Laredo business district, Jorge passed by several uniformed Border Patrol agents on bicycles and another in a vehicle, but much to his surprise, they paid him no attention whatsoever.[22] He walked across the bridge, called home with a phone card he still had, and made arrangements to return to La Carmela by bus.

Other migrants from La Carmela seemed to have much better luck getting the Border Patrol to pick them up. On his last trip to Texas following the Laredo-Encinal route in March 2002, Fermín was apprehended by agents *eight times.* After each apprehension, he was quickly processed in the Border Patrol station and walked back across the bridge to Nuevo Laredo by the U.S. authorities. And just as quickly, he crossed the river again and began marching toward Encinal. After the eighth apprehension in the course of a week or so, the authorities charged Fermín with misdemeanor illegal entry of the United States. He was taken before a judge where he readily admitted his "crime" and was sentenced to three years of probation. The judge warned him that if he got caught returning to the United States before the three years were up, he would be sent to jail for at least six months. Fermín was then either formally deported or "voluntarily returned" to Mexico—he wasn't sure which—and did not plan to return to the United States until the three years had elapsed.[23] He knew that if he were caught again, the Border Patrol would know that he had violated the judge's order and would prosecute him. He knew this because each of the times he was apprehended on his last trip, he was photographed, fingerprinted, and had his data entered into the Border Patrol's IDENT database. That was how they knew that he had kept coming back, even though they warned him not to try again. Fermín claimed that people in La Carmela knew that the Border Patrol in Laredo wouldn't prosecute you until you've been apprehended at least eight times.[24] In other words, their migrants' calculus was that they could keep trying to enter clandestinely many times in a row before they would run the risk of prosecution.

Much to my amazement, Fermín planned to return to Texas following the same route he had always taken. He had five young children and a wife to support, and he could not earn enough income from farming or jobs available around La Carmela to do it. He could not arrange for a good coyote to take him across the border using less arduous methods because he did not have sufficient savings to pay for the trip and did not have any relatives living in the United States who could lend him the $2,000 it would cost. And he did not personally know any other route to follow. In other words, the limits to his social capital and funds of knowledge left him with no alternative but to use the same route from Laredo to Encinal or Dilley that he knew so well. The difference would be that he would walk farther away from the power line, hidden deeper in the brush. Fermín told me that people from La Carmela still managed to make it through this way.

Of course, the farther into the brush Fermín and his friends walked, the rougher the terrain would be, the more likely they would be to get lost or injured, and the farther they would be from potential help. In June 2004, I explored different parts of the route Fermín and his friends followed and wondered how he and the others could make it through there in the blazing summer months. The landscape was a sea of thorns, the heat was unbearable, there was little shade to be found, and the *papalotes* were miles apart. No wonder the early Spanish settlers referred to this country as La Brasada, the land of burning embers (Alonzo 1998, 18; McGraw 2003). Traipsing along the power line right-of-way and then following paths worn through the brush by deer, javelinas, and humans on foot, I found evidence of the migrants who had passed before me—a baseball cap, an empty gallon water jug, a can of tuna, wrappers from a packet of tortillas, a small fire ring, a torn flannel shirt hanging from the branch of a mesquite. In many places off the roads and set back from the power line right-of-way, the brush seemed to swallow you right up. It was easy to see how you could get lost and hard to imagine how you could hike very far without water. The security guard posted at the entrance of a large ranch told me that a migrant woman had died on the property a few weeks earlier, after having been bitten by a poisonous spider and succumbing to the intense heat.

And I wondered what would become of Fermín if he attempted to traverse this route again, "más escondido en el monte" [hidden deeper in the brush], as he had said he'd do. I also realized that he would *have* to be well hidden to escape detection by the authorities, for I seemed to attract Border Patrol vehicles nearly every time I stepped out of my own car to walk around. Yet I knew that some of the men from La Carmela had successfully run this gauntlet since Fermín's last trip, propelled by necessity, undeterred by the suffering and danger.

Turning to Coyotes to Cross the Border

Given the trials and tribulations faced by La Carmela men on their favored Laredo-Encinal route, some veteran and first-time migrants were turning to professional coyotes to make an easier and more secure passage to the interior cities of Texas. Migrants from the village had used coyotes in the past when they could find no one in the community who was available to guide them, but by 2004 even migrants who knew the Laredo-Encinal route well were hiring them. The main attraction, they said, was that with at least some of the coyotes who operated in their area, you didn't have to walk at all. The cost was very high, though, as much as $2,000. As a consequence, whether or not a man from La Carmela hired a coyote depended principally on two factors, which were frequently interrelated. First, not surprisingly, was the ability to pay. Virtually no one in La Carmela could pay for the trip out of personal savings or by selling some of their meager assets. This meant that they had to borrow money from someone they knew to pay the coyote. In most cases, the money came in the form of several micro loans from friends and family members who were already living in the United States and, therefore, earning a dollar income. The men whom I interviewed in La Carmela who did not intend to use a coyote on their next trip north—or who had given up hope of traveling north again at all—told me that one of the main reasons was that they didn't have anyone living in the United States who they could count on to pay the coyote when they arrived, which was the usual arrangement.

The second determinant of coyote use was the urgency the migrant felt to get back to life and work in the United States. Not surprisingly, those who felt the need to return most urgently were men who had spent enough time in the United States to consider it their real home at that point in their lives. These men had wives, children, and regular jobs there, as well as other family members living nearby. Thus, if they had returned to La Carmela for a visit or had been picked up by la migra on a job site and sent back across the border, they needed to return to the United States as quickly and reliably as possible, rather than wait to get a group of local men together and embark on a very uncertain journey. Happily, the men who felt the need to return most urgently, and therefore were most likely to require the services of a coyote, were also those most likely to be able to pay for one, since the friends and family members waiting for them were typically quite willing to front the money to bring them back.

Findings I obtained from the Encuesta sobre Migración en la Frontera Norte de México indicated that the apparently increasing use of coyotes by migrants in La Carmela was typical for all Mexican migrants making clandestine crossings of the Northeast Mexico-South Texas border (see table 2.1). Whereas, before the launching of Operation Rio Grande, only about 21 percent of clandestine migrants reported hiring a coyote to cross this stretch of the border on their last trip to the United States, in the ORG period through 2003, slightly over 50 percent of migrants reported doing so. Another result I obtained from the EMIF data appeared to be consistent with the experiences of the migrants from La Carmela: since the launch of Operation Rio Grande in 1997, autonomous migrants who reported living in the United States were considerably more likely to have hired a coyote to make their last border-crossing than migrants who reported living in Mexico. Sixty-four percent of the U.S. residents had done so, compared to just 46 percent of migrants residing in Mexico. Migrants from "traditional" migrant-sending states in Mexico like San Luis Potosí, the state in which La Carmela was located, were

Table 2.1. Reliance on coyotes by autonomous Mexican migrants, Northeast Mexico-South Texas corridor

Type of migrant	Percentage using coyote	Sample size
All migrants, before Operation Rio Grande (ORG)	21	1,151
All migrants, after ORG	50	982
Migrants residing in United States, after ORG	64	155
Migrants residing in Mexico, after ORG	46	827
Migrants from traditional region of emigration, after ORG	37	513
Migrants from nontraditional region of emigration, after ORG	57	327

Source: Author's calculations using the Encuesta sobre Migración en la Frontera Norte de México (EMIF), *levantamientos* (rounds) 1–3 and 6–8, consisting of a sample of migrants returning voluntarily to Mexico.
Note: "Before Operation Rio Grande" refers to clandestine crossings made in 1997 or earlier. "After ORG" refers to crossings made from 1998 through 2003. Following Durand and Massey (2003), "traditional region of emigration" refers to the Mexican states of Aguascalientes, Colima, Durango, Guanajuato, Jalisco, Michoacán, Nayarit, San Luis Potosí, and Zacatecas.

considerably less likely to hire coyotes in the period since the launch of Operation Rio Grande than were migrants from nontraditional migrant-sending regions, such as the state of Veracruz on the Gulf of Mexico. Only about 37 percent of migrants from traditional sending regions hired coyotes on their last trip across the border, compared to 57 percent of migrants from nontraditional migrant-sending states.[25]

The Old-Timer's Perspective: The More Things Change, the More They Stay the Same

The challenges on the Texas-Mexico border facing migrants from La Carmela, San Luis Potosí, at the beginning of the twenty-first century were the same as those facing migrants from many other parts of Mexico. Their experiences confronting those challenges were quite similar to those of migrants I interviewed from other towns in San Luis Potosí, as well as from other states, including Nuevo León, Guanajuato, and Michoacán, whether they made their treks in the Laredo-Encinal corridor, the Piedras Negras-Uvalde corridor, or through sections of the Lower Rio Grande Valley. More interestingly, perhaps, was the extent to which the strategies pursued and the suffering endured by La Carmela migrants, after the enormous intensification of border enforcement efforts in the region with the launching of Operation Rio Grande in the summer of 1997, appeared to be little different from the experiences of earlier generations of migrants. Part of the reason was that the basic logistics of making the crossing remained the same. The major hurdle facing migrants had never been crossing the international boundary itself and getting *into* South Texas. Rather, the major difficulty had always been getting *out of* South Texas, that is, getting past the immigration checkpoints on the principal thoroughfares located a considerable distance from the Rio Grande, thus escaping the zone where Border Patrol surveillance was most intense.

Although the increase in agents, vehicles, and application of surveillance technologies by U.S. authorities seemed to have made apprehension more likely and extended the distance migrants had to trek through the brush, in South Texas these appeared to be changes in degree rather than changes in kind. The impact of stepped-up border enforcement on migrants' crossing behaviors appeared to have been less radical on this stretch of the border than in other areas, such as the Tijuana-San Diego corridor. In Tijuana-San Diego, the imposition of Operation Gatekeeper turned what had formerly been a quick dash across the border within a binational metropolis into a days-long trek through unpopulated desert and mountains (Alonso Meneses 2001; Andreas 2000;

Cornelius 2001; Nevins 2002). In contrast, migrants in South Texas *already* had to make long treks through the brush well before the launching of Operation Río Grande. As discussed in the previous chapter, the historical record suggests that already by the 1950s the Border Patrol in South Texas was fairly effective in forcing migrants to travel away from the region's major thoroughfares lest they be apprehended by agents who focused their efforts on picking up migrants traveling along the roads headed north. Although the Border Patrol's presence along the roadways was insufficient to slow the movement of Mexicans into and through the region in the 1950s, it does appear to have ensured that many migrants would be exposed to the same types of dangers and suffering as inflicted on today's migrants (García 1980, 144–45; Saunders and Leonard 1951, 79). Today's dangers and sufferings certainly date back to at least the late 1960s, when they were vividly documented by Jorge Bustamante in his crossing of the border near Reynosa with two "wetbacks" as a participant-observation researcher for Julian Samora's (1971) book, *Los Mojados.*

Interviews I conducted with several older migrants from rural Guanajuato, who were in their forties and fifties, confirmed that there was a great deal of continuity in border-crossing conditions since the early 1970s. For example, Aurelio, a fifty-six-year-old farmer living in Rancho San Nicolás (both names are pseudonyms) in a rural section of northern Guanajuato told me of the annual border-crossings he made starting in 1972, when he was just twenty-three, and ending in 1988, when he finally received documents that allowed him to travel back and forth legally between Mexico and the United States. According to Aurelio, he used to cross the Río Bravo between Nuevo Laredo and Piedras Negras and then walk a full week through the brush before taking the bus or getting a ride to San Antonio. In those days, he had many of the same experiences the La Carmela migrants described with regard to the Laredo-Encinal route—nearly drowning in the river; running out of water and having to drink from cattle troughs, then getting sick from it; running out of food and eating raw *nopales* and hunting jackrabbits on the trail; getting stuck by thorns and struck at by rattlesnakes; losing his way in the brush; and having to hide from the Border Patrol's aircraft. Sometimes, when he couldn't get a ride, he would walk all the way to the outskirts of San Antonio, a distance of around 150 miles. The hike from the border would then take up to two full weeks.[26] Aurelio said it had always been dangerous crossing the river and then hiking through the *monte:* "You always were taking your chances of whether you'd die on the way.... And you'd always arrive all blistered, chafed, and hungry, really hungry." One difference between the "old days" and the time period studied for this book was that during the years when he regularly crossed without papers, Aurelio was apprehended only once by the Border Patrol, though he'd nearly been captured on several other occasions. Generally, he didn't see many agents in the brush, just along the highways. In addition, he noted that by the time I interviewed him, some men from around his rancho had been threatened with jail by the Border Patrol after being apprehended several times,[27] as had happened to Fermín, though he didn't know of anyone from his rancho who had actually been incarcerated for illegal entry.

I also spoke with another man from Guanajuato, Fernando, who had crossed the border into South Texas on multiple occasions in the 1970s and 1980s. Like Aurelio, Fernando had legalized his status in the United States under the 1986 U.S. immigration reform. Unlike Aurelio, Fernando had settled permanently in Texas and had recently become a U.S. citizen when I interviewed him in early 2002. Fernando worked as a construction contractor, doing painting and carpentry, and hired other Mexicans to work for him, all from Guanajuato, including some family members. Since legalizing his status in the late 1980s, he had gone back to visit his hometown regularly and had received many new *guanajuatense* migrants in his home and talked with many others in his circle of family, friends, and acquaintances. Fernando argued that in some ways, at least, entering the United States through South Texas had gotten easier than when he used to cross.

> It has changed a lot because it used to be that almost everyone had to walk, and now almost nobody walks. Now, most of the people who walk only walk for one night and then the coyotes pick them up, so these days almost nobody wants to walk. But now they're paying a lot more money than was paid in the past. Back then if you paid $400 or $500 it was a fortune [*un dineral*], and now they're paying $1,500 or $1,900 just to get to San Antonio.... Now the same guides who used to walk and know the route, now they have contacts here. So when they go and bring people with them from [Mexico] they walk them a ways, and then they call ahead and say, "I'm going to arrive at such-and-such a place at such-and-such a time." And then they [the contacts in San Antonio] say, "I'll send the truck at such and such a time," depending on the number of people [the guide] is bringing, and they send the truck to meet them.... They keep coming that way. Twenty-seven people just got here [a few days earlier] in one of those big tractor-trailers...and they charged them $1,100 each when they got here.

Aurelio offered a similar assessment of the current situation, based on the experiences his sons continued to have crossing the border with coyotes. Fernando believed that migrants who could pay for it had the opportunity to travel and be housed more comfortably by coyotes because coyotes by the early

2000s were able to use the higher fees they charged to offer a better quality of service. Of course, we should note here that Fernando's comments were made over a year before nineteen migrants perished while sealed in the unventilated trailer of an eighteen-wheeler in Victoria, Texas, and clearly underestimated the potential dangers migrants were exposing themselves to using this "higher quality" service. Regardless of the risks they faced, with coyotes or without, migrants from his rancho continued to migrate clandestinely to Texas, with no end in sight to the practice:

SPENER: So these people you're telling me about, from your rancho, they keep coming from there?

FERNANDO: Oh, yes, it's routine. This has not stopped at all, it hasn't stopped at all.

SPENER: Do the people arrive without problems most of the time?

FERNANDO: The majority do. Eighty percent get here.

SPENER: And what happens to the rest?

FERNANDO: They go back [to Mexico] and then they cross over here again. Everybody makes it. The ones who don't make it the first time make it after two or three more tries. But in the end they always make it.

In the face of the collapse of their rural subsistence economy and the absence of jobs paying a living wage in Mexican cities, the long march across the border and over the South Texas Plains became one of the principal household survival strategies pursued by members of the community of La Carmela, San Luis Potosí. It was a strategy that required a tremendous amount of effort, stamina, and valor on the part of the men who engaged in it, and one that subjected them to extraordinary risks. The migrants I spoke with were well aware of the dangers they would face before they left home and were also aware that the trip had become more difficult every year since the Border Patrol's imposition of Operation Rio Grande in 1997. They also knew that the government of the United States was ratcheting up its efforts to prevent them from reaching their intended destinations beyond the border, including arresting and imprisoning them. Nonetheless, they continued to pursue this risky strategy because the precarious conditions of life they and their families endured in La Carmela obliged them to do so. The intensification of apartheid at the border, embodied in measures such as Operation Rio Grande, represented a change in degree of the difficulties and dangers facing migrants, but not a change in kind. The nature of the long march across this stretch of the border had not, in fact, changed remarkably in the years following the operation's launch. It was already an arduous journey before the operation. It was worse afterward, but not so much worse as to deter many migrants from undertaking it.

The prosaic details of migrants' experience of making the crossing of this stretch of the border also shed light on an important aspect of their practice of resistencia hormiga. As discussed in the introduction, this type of resistance is experienced by those who practice it as a survival strategy rather than as conscious resistance to any identifiable political or economic system. Migrants I interviewed from La Carmela and elsewhere consciously took matters into their own hands when it came to assuring the well-being of themselves and their families. They did not wait for governments to either come to their assistance or grant them permission to migrate. They were, in this limited sense, conscious of taking autonomous action to resolve their situation. Nevertheless, to the extent that they consciously experienced their autonomous migration as struggle, they experienced it most immediately as a primal struggle to overcome the material hazards and obstacles they encountered en route rather than as a struggle against the paramilitary forces arrayed against them at the border or the apartheid system such forces embodied. At the same time, as outside observers, we can see clearly how their actions constituted resistance to their forcible territorial confinement within Mexico. We can also see the dangers and suffering they endured as an example of the structural violence that the apartheid system imposed on Mexicans at the border. As discussed earlier, autonomous migration as a form of resistance had a long history along this stretch of the U.S.-Mexico border. With heightened militarization of the border at the end of the twentieth century, migrants increasingly entered into relationships with coyotes of one kind or another in order to overcome their territorial exclusion from the United States. In the following chapters, I turn my attention to these relationships between migrants and coyotes as a central feature of the practice of resistencia hormiga.

CHAPTER 3

Coyotaje as a Cultural Practice
Applied to Migration

With intensified surveillance of the South Texas border by U.S. authorities in the 1990s and early 2000s, autonomous Mexican migrants have increasingly turned to coyotes to help them enter the United States to live, work, and reunite with their families. Though the proportion of migrants hiring coyotes today may be higher than in the past, the practice itself is far from new: coyotes have played a significant role in the migratory process since Mexicans first began traveling to the United States to work in large numbers at the end of the nineteenth century. Indeed, the role played by coyotes in the migration process is but a contemporary variant of the roles they have played historically in other institutional arenas of Mexican cultural life, dating back to Spanish colonial times. Moreover, it is no accident that the people playing these roles came to be called *coyotes,* given the attributes displayed by this animal character in Mexican mythology and folklore dating back to before the Spanish conquest. In Mexican society, the services provided by coyotes are referred to as *coyotaje.*[1] In this chapter, I will explain how the practice of *coyotaje* operates in Mexican society, discuss its cultural and historical origins, and explain how it came to be practiced in the border-crossing arena. In doing so, I will argue that the term *coyotaje* better describes the types of paid services provided to migrants to help them enter the United States than do other commonly used terms such as *smuggling* and *trafficking.* Finally, I will describe the three general forms that coyotaje has taken in the migration process on the South Texas-Northeast Mexico border—*bureaucratic evasion, labor brokerage,* and *clandestine crossing*—during different periods in the history of Mexican migration to the United States. In reviewing the history of coyotaje in this migratory corridor, I will discuss how at some points it contributed to the development of apartheid as a form of labor control and at others represented a strategy pursued by migrants to resist such control.

About Coyotes and Coyotaje

The word *coyote* in Spanish and English comes from the Náhuatl word *coyotl,* referring to the small wolflike mammal native to Meso and North America that is classified by biologists today as *Canis latrans* (Larousse Editorial 1998, 408). The coyote plays a colorful role as creator, a trickster, and a clown in the folklore of the indigenous peoples of both Central and North America. Important elements of this mythical characterization carry over into the term's colloquial use in modern Mexican Spanish. A complete analysis of the evolution of the colloquial use of the term *coyote* in Mexico is beyond the scope of this book, but it is clear that the mythical attributes of coyotes have been used by human beings to characterize the behavior of their peers since ancient times. As noted by Meléndez (1982, 295), "the coyote figure of indigenous traditions has been a source of considerable wealth in Mexican folklore, history, and language usage," owing to the "multivalent nature" attributed to him: "The coyote's remote past in Mesoamerican cultures associates him with music and war; in written history, with class and racial terminology; and in folk traditions, with a witty trickster and a sympathetic *pícaro.*"

The Coyote in Mexican Mythology and Folklore

The coyote figure played a significant role in the cosmology of Mesoamerican peoples prior to the arrival of Cortés. At Teotihuacán, centuries prior to the rise of the Aztecs to power, the coyote symbolized military might, and warriors often dressed in coyote costumes to draw upon the creature's predatory power. Coyotes continued to be associated with warrior cults in Central Mexico through the centuries leading up to Aztec rule (Schwartz 1997, 146–49). The Aztec god Huehuecóyotl (Old Coyote, sometimes rendered Ueuecóyotl) appears in several codices in which he is depicted as having a human body and the head of a coyote. Huehuecóyotl was the god of dance, music, and carnality (Miller and Taube 1993, 92), but also of discord and trickery (Anders, Jansen, and Reyes García 1991, 130). According to Olivier (2003, 32), Huehuecóyotl was also known as a seducer of women; indeed, in some interpretations of the codices in which he appears, he has been seen as responsible for the "original sin" of seducing Xochiquetzal (Flower Feather), the Aztec goddess of love, and bringing war into the world as a consequence. In addition, the figure of the coyote was associated with thievery in ancient Mexico, both with regard to the original "theft" of fire by a coyote (Olivier 1999, 117–18) and insofar as the god Tezcatlipoca took the form of a coyote to warn people that they were about to be robbed (Aranda Kilian 2005, 65). For his part, Kelley (1955, 397) argued that Quetzalcóatl, the plumed-serpent god that plays a central role in the mythology of ancient Mexico, had its origins in the earlier myths of the Uto-Aztecan tribes of the southwestern United States and northern Mexico, where the coyote was portrayed as "the 'Elder Brother' of mankind, a Creator, erotic trickster, and culture hero identified with the morning star." Quetzalcóatl, among other things attributed to him in stories from the Postclassic Nahua period, was believed to have participated in the creation of the cosmos along with his brother Tezcatlipoca (Almere Read and González 2000, 223; Kelley 1955, 397). In other words, the coyote figure has played a central role in Mexican cosmology since ancient times.

By the twentieth century, the coyote's attributes of trickery, thievery, and creativity appeared in mestizo as well as indigenous Mexican folklore. Often these tales involved coyotes outwitting farmers to steal their crops or livestock. For example, Dobie (1947, 274–76) collected a tale from a ranch hand in northern Coahuila that described how a coyote had escaped from an angry farmer by playing dead after having gorged himself on the farmer's chickens. The moral of the story, according to Dobie's informant, was that the coyote was "muy astuto, muy diablo" [very astute, very clever]. As Herrera-Sobek points out, this type of depiction of the coyote figure carries over to the colloquial use of the term to refer to border-crossing guides:

> The crafty coyote (smuggler) takes advantage of innocent undocumented pollos [chickens]. In barnyard lore, the coyote is the animal who sneaks in at night and steals the farmer's chickens to eat them. The pollos waiting to be smuggled across the border are thus perceived in this barnyard metaphorization as innocent victims who must fall into the claws of the coyote in order to be guided out of the "chicken coop." The coyote is the figure who can successfully evade the watchful eye of the "farmer" (read I.N.S.) and in the dead of night sneak them into the United States. (1993, 204)

In this formulation we clearly see the coyote's dual characterization as both a guide clever enough to help migrants evade the "watchful eye" of the immigration police and an untrustworthy predator who is just as likely to devour his *pollos*, if given the chance, as deliver them safely to their destination in the United States. The folkloric meanings attached to the coyote figure in indigenous and mestizo folklore in Mexico also appeared in the twentieth-century speech of Texas Mexicans. One common expression heard in Texas was "es más listo que un coyote" [he is smarter/shrewder than a coyote], connoting a person who was intelligent and cunning (Cerda, Cabaza, and Farías 1953, 269–70). As this expression suggests, calling someone a coyote in Spanish on either side of the border was not usually meant as a compliment.

In spite of the coyote's reputation as an astute trickster, it was also common in Mexican folklore for the coyote to have the tables turned on him and be duped by his intended victims. This is the case, for example, in two Zapotec tales from Oaxaca, *Cuento del conejo y el coyote* (Secretaría de Educación Pública 1994, 17–32)[2] and *Coyote va a la fiesta de Chihuitán* (de la Cruz 1983), both involving a rabbit as the coyote's nemesis. In *Cuento del conejo y el coyote,* the coyote is fooled by the clever rabbit on multiple occasions as the former pursues the latter in order to eat him. Variants of the story have also been heard from nonindigenous tellers in northern Mexico and Texas (Aiken 1935; McKellar 1935). In *Coyote va a a la fiesta de Chihuitán* the rabbit steals a bag of treats that the coyote has stolen from revelers at the fiesta. As I discuss below, Mexican migrants have similarly been known to trick their trickster coyotes during their journeys north.

The anthropologist Marvin Harris (1979, 200–201) has argued that coyotes were given the trickster role in indigenous mythology because the real-life animal is indeed an astute trickster, a "wily predator" and "an extremely cunning carnivore" that has to "compensate for being small by being smart." Indigenous people of North America observed this, Harris argued, and their mythological representations of the coyote reflected the animal's attributes.[3] Because of the animal's "cleverness and adaptability," it has been impossible to eradicate, despite the many attempts by ranchers in the western United States to do so (Cahalane 1947, 253, cited in Harris 1979, 201). In the face of myriad efforts to exterminate it, the coyote actually increased its numbers during the twentieth century and extended its range to the cities and suburbs of the eastern United States (Winkler 2002). As I will make clear below, U.S. efforts to eradicate human coyotes in the twentieth century were similarly futile and will likely continue to be for the foreseeable future.

Coyotes and Coyotaje in Mexico Today: Three Colloquial Definitions Relevant to Migration

In contemporary Mexico, the term *coyote* has taken on several broad colloquial meanings apart from its literal definition. Three of these meanings are particularly relevant for analyzing the migration of Mexicans to the United States. The first colloquial definition of coyote refers to a person hired to help his or her client evade bureaucratic regulations of some kind. The second refers to the middleman role in the marketing and distribution of a commodity, especially an agricultural commodity. The third refers to a guide hired by clandestine migrants to cross the border. Each of these colloquial uses of coyote is diffused widely throughout the country. Although only the third colloquial use is typically understood as relating directly to the migration process, the first two uses are not only applicable to Mexican migration to the United States but have also played an important role in facilitating it both historically and in the contemporary period.

Coyotes as Experts at Evading Bureaucratic Regulations

The word *coyote* is most used colloquially in Mexico to refer to a person who is employed by someone else to help him evade or fulfill, by illicit means, some legal-bureaucratic requirement imposed by the government. Thus, *El diccionario breve de mexicanismos* defines a *coyote* as an "intermediario ilegítimo de trámites burocráticos" [an illegitimate intermediary of bureaucratic procedures] (Gómez de Silva 2001). I was reminded of this meaning of *coyote* by a Mexican consular official I interviewed about migrants hiring coyotes to get across the border:

> The word *coyote* in Mexico is the person who facilitates getting something for you without going through all the legal procedures, whether it's getting a car permit or a driver's license. If I want to get a permit for something but I don't fulfill the requirements, I go to a coyote, who is going to ease my way through the bureaucracy. In Mexico, away from the border, the term *coyote* is used mainly for this. *Coyotaje* in Mexico has this meaning of evading these questions of bureaucratic procedures.

Here it is important to note that employing coyotes is part of everyday life in much of Mexico, as it has been elsewhere in Latin America, where burdensome requirements for documentation imposed by sluggish state bureaucracies can result in lengthy delays in gaining access to even the most basic services (de Soto 1989). Thus, although people employing a coyote may not feel that doing so is entirely proper, they are unlikely to think of doing so as immoral or criminal, either, and may, in fact, be quite appreciative of the coyote's ability to help them deal with the onerous procedures imposed on them by what they consider to be a rigid and inefficient government bureaucracy. At the same time, they are likely to view coyotes as slippery and devious characters, quite in accordance with the cultural mythology surrounding the coyote figure, no matter how valuable the services they provide.

The idea of a coyote as someone to help a person evade regulation by or receive some sort of dispensation from the government dates back to Spanish colonial times. Eric Wolf, in his classic work of cultural anthropology *Sons of the Shaking Earth* (1959), noted that coyotaje was an integral element of Mexican society during the colonial period, which he linked to the racial and cultural mixing known as *mestizaje.* According to Wolf (1959, 237), coyotaje became widespread in New Spain where "there was little correspondence between law and reality," and where the law existed primarily to defend "islands of legality and privilege." He characterized coyotaje and its practitioners as follows:

> Royal prescript supported the trade monopoly over goods flowing in and out of the colony; but along the edges of the law moved smugglers, cattle-rustlers, bandits, the buyers and sellers of clandestine produce. To the blind eyes of the law, there arose a multitude of scribes, lawyers, go-betweens, influence peddlers, and undercover agents, the *coyotes* of modern Middle America, a term that once merely designated one of the physical types produced by mixed unions.[4] In such a society, even the transactions of everyday life could smack of illegality; yet such illegality was the stuff of which this social order was made. Illicit transactions demanded their agents; the army of the disinherited, deprived of alternative sources of employment, provided these agents. (Wolf 1959, 237)

From its outset, then, coyotaje had been practiced by the disinherited members of Mexican society as a way of surreptitiously resisting, in quotidian fashion, their exclusion from wealth and power. Wolf went on to ascribe to mestizos precisely those characteristics that in the contemporary period are attributed to coyotes, which also reflect the preconquest characterizations of coyotes in indigenous mythology. According to Wolf (1959, 238), "the ever shifting nature of his social condition forced [the mestizo] to move with guile and speed through the hidden passageways of society, not to commit himself to any one position or to any one spot." Continuing, he noted how "society abdicated to [the mestizos] its informal and unacknowledged business," making them "brokers and carriers of the multiple transactions that cause the blood to flow through the veins of the social organism" such that "their fingers wove the network of social relations and communication through which alone men could bridge the gaps between formal institutions" (Wolf 1959, 243). In other words, the liminal figures of the coyote and the mestizo played a vital role in allowing Mexican society to function in spite of the fissures generated by its institutionalized inequalities of race and class.

Coyotes as Middlemen in Commodity Chains

The term *coyote* is also used colloquially in Mexico to refer to a broker or middleman, especially with regard to agricultural commodities. The idea of a coyote operating as an intermediary or broker is offered by Santamaría (1983, 309) in the *Diccionario de mejicanismos*, which defines a coyote as "an intermediary, generally speaking, in any kind of transaction, operating on a commission, percentage, or share basis" [*intermediario, en general, en toda clase de transacciones, operando por comisión o porcentaje, o participación*]. As is usually the case in business, both north and south of the border, middlemen are not viewed kindly by either producers or consumers, even though they arguably provide a needed market service. Numerous reports in the Mexican press describe the operation of coyote brokers in agricultural commodities, including lumber, beans, corn, fresh vegetables, and shrimp (see, for example, González and Gómez 2007; Olea 1995; Sánchez Venegas 2007; Santos and Flores 2007; Vásquez 2002). In such reports, the term *coyote* is typically employed pejoratively.

Coyotes as Migration Guides and Facilitators

The term *coyote* has been used with regard to Mexican migration to the United States at least since the early years of the twentieth century. Typically, a coyote is thought of as a person who surreptitiously guides undocumented migrants across the border into the United States away from the legal ports of entry where only those individuals whose legal papers are in order are allowed to enter (see, for example De Mente 1996, 72–75). Coyotes do many more things to facilitate migrants' entry into the United States than just act as their guides, as we shall see. In fact, coyotes facilitate the entry into the United States by Mexican migrants in a variety of ways that we have already contemplated in the first two colloquial definitions of coyote as (1) someone who helps his or her client get around a legal-bureaucratic hurdle of some sort, and (2) a broker of a desired good or service. For example, with regard to the first definition, coyotes both today and over most of the last century have provided documents to migrants, both real and counterfeit, that allow them to enter the United States to live and work. Indeed, we might well consider the coyote "guide" to be fulfilling this definition as well, since in the final analysis leading a migrant into the United States by bypassing the legal port of entry is a way of avoiding the legal-bureaucratic requirement of presenting immigration papers to the authorities. With regard to the second colloquial definition, since the late nineteenth century labor contractors working at the border or in the Mexican interior have effectively operated as coyotes by serving as brokers for U.S. employers seeking to hire Mexican workers who have not yet reached the United States interior. As we shall see, coyotes have provided this labor-brokerage service at times legally and at others quite illegally. When such contractors have engaged in legally proscribed activities—whether surreptitiously guiding migrants on foot across the border, providing them with fake documents, or paying off immigration officials to let them pass through the legal ports of entry—they have fulfilled both of the first two colloquial definitions simultaneously.

To summarize, we can think of coyotes' participation in facilitating Mexican migration to the United States as taking three basic forms, both historically and in the contemporary period, that correspond to the three colloquial Mexican uses of the term *coyote* discussed above. The first form consists of *bureaucratic evasion,* that is, helping migrants overcome legal-bureaucratic obstacles imposed by the state that might otherwise prevent their migration. The second form consists of *labor brokerage,* that is, the recruitment, whether legal or illegal, of Mexican workers by U.S. employers through the use of hired intermediaries. The third form involves the provision of *clandestine border-crossing services,* in which migrants hire a coyote to help guide them into the United States away from the legal ports of entry and transport them away from the border toward their final destination in the interior of the country.

Why Coyotes?

At the outset of the book, I gave several reasons why I use the term *coyote* to refer to people who help Mexican migrants enter the United States without an official invitation from that country's government. These included its widespread use in both the United States and Mexico and that, unlike *patero* and *pollero,* its use was not specific to certain stretches of the border, and that it avoided some of the undesirable connotations carried by the terms *smuggler* and *trafficker.* Here I would like to give two additional reasons for using the term *coyote.* First, the types of activities and actors contemplated by the definitions of *coyote* I have reviewed above are considerably more extensive and varied than those that are typically contemplated for the other terms. This is important because both historically and in the contemporary period coyotes facilitate the entry of migrants into the United States in many more ways than just by guiding them across the border. Second, *coyote* is the term that has been in use historically for the longest period of time and has the deepest set of cultural meanings attached to it among Mexicans. Importantly, these meanings often differ from the meanings U.S. immigration and border enforcement authorities attach to the terms they prefer to use, such as *alien smuggler* or *human trafficker.*

According to *El diccionario breve de mexicanismos,* the term *coyotaje* refers to the "ocupación y actividad del coyote" [the occupation and activity of the coyote] (Gómez de Silva 2001). With regard to border-crossing, we might therefore think of coyotaje as the set of strategies and practices engaged in by coyotes to facilitate migrants' unauthorized entry into the United States. Here, though, we must remember that the hiring of a coyote is also a well-defined strategy for border-crossing on the part of migrants, on the one hand, and for obtaining Mexican workers on the part of U.S. employers, on the other. Moreover, we must bear in mind that wherever coyotaje occurs, it involves coyotes, migrants, and U.S. employers engaging in relationships with one another, sometimes fleeting and anonymous, other times more intimate and ongoing, sometimes solidary and collaborative and other times conflictive and exploitative. It is also significant that when coyotaje occurs at the border today, it has typically been undertaken at the behest of either the migrant or the U.S. employer, or both. In other words, the coyote does not typically initiate the transaction by inducing the migration itself. I believe, therefore, that it is most accurate, for analytical purposes, to extend the definition of *coyotaje* to include the act of hiring the coyote and the negotiation of strategies to follow and practices to engage in that goes on *among* coyotes, migrants, their friends and family members, and U.S. employers. In other words, the participants in the elaboration of the strategies and practices of coyotaje include not only the coyotes themselves but also the people who hire them. Thus, I propose the following formal definition of *coyotaje* as it relates to autonomous Mexican migration to the United States today: *Coyotaje is the set of border-crossing strategies and practices elaborated by coyotes at the behest of and in concert with migrants, migrants' friends and family members, and/or migrants' U.S. employers.* Such border-crossing strategies may include services provided by all three of the types of coyotes listed above—bureaucratic evasion, labor-brokerage, and clandestine-crossing. While coyotaje usually implies a cash transaction between the parties to it, in some instances it can involve reciprocal or in-kind exchanges.

Analytically speaking, I believe it is more fruitful to focus attention on coyotaje as it as practiced on the border, rather than on the individual characteristics of *coyotes* as its professional practitioners. There are several reasons for this.

First, as conveyed by the formal definition of *coyotaje* proposed immediately above, surreptitious border-crossing strategies and practices that include the hiring of a coyote involve a variety of actors in addition to coyotes, including migrants, their friends and family members in both the Mexican community of origin and in the U.S. community of destination, as well as U.S. employers and/or their Mexican *mayordomos* (foremen, work-crew leaders). Thus, if we were to focus attention on coyotes rather than on coyotaje, we would err by excluding from the analysis the roles played by other significant actors who engage in what Heyman (1998, 173) has referred to as "conspiracies to avoid the law" with regard to Mexican migration to the United States.

Second, a focus on coyotaje rather than coyotes foregrounds the processual elements of surreptitious border-crossing, permitting us to analyze the evolving dynamics of the relationships among the various actors who engage in this process, rather than the static, cross-sectional characteristics of the individuals identified as coyotes at any given moment. In other words, a focus on coyotaje rather than coyotes helps us make important analytical distinctions between the dynamics of the *process* of surreptitious border-crossing and the individual traits of the *people* who participate in it. More specifically, it allows us to distinguish between the strategies and practices that constitute coyotaje and the various types of actors who may elaborate them. This is important because a variety of different social actors may participate in any given border-crossing strategy, and any given actor may employ more than one strategy, even on the same crossing attempt. This approach to analyzing the process is also consistent with the fact that a "coyote" is frequently not an individual at all but, rather, a loosely knit network in which different individuals play different roles in enacting specific elements of the crossing strategy or strategies.

The third reason for focusing attention on coyotaje rather than on coyotes is related to the tendency, both in colloquial speech and in intellectual discussion, to narrowly conceive of a coyote as the guide who leads migrants across the border on dangerous treks across inhospitable deserts. As I have already mentioned and discuss in much greater detail below, this is only one type of coyote. Nevertheless, it is the only type to have received much attention in the press, which has portrayed this type of coyote in a relentlessly negative light, consistent with U.S. government officials' contention that such coyotes constitute one of the principal menaces to the health and safety of migrants on the border, on the one hand, and to national security, on the other. Focusing analytically on coyotaje rather than on any single type of coyote allows us to expand the scope of inquiry to include a wider variety of strategies and practices that a broader range of social actors have developed to make possible migrants' surreptitious entry into the United States. Taking this approach also steers us away from potentially misleading stereotypes about individuals and toward a more nuanced and realistic view of how clandestine crossing of the border occurs, both now and in the past.

Coyotaje in the History of Mexican Migration across the South Texas–Northeast Mexico Border

All three of the major types of migration-related coyotaje outlined above—bureaucratic evasion, labor brokerage, and clandestine crossing—have been practiced along the South Texas–Northeast Mexico border since mass migration of Mexicans to the United States began in the late nineteenth century. Nonetheless, the relative importance of each type has waxed and waned considerably, depending on changes in U.S. migration laws and the intensity of their enforcement, as well as the ability of migrant social networks to effectively channel Mexican workers into vacant jobs north of the border. The effectiveness of migrant social networks in this regard is, in turn, a function of their maturity, that is, the amount of U.S. labor-market experience accumulated by Mexicans over time, and of their extent, that is, the number of Mexicans working in the United States and their concentration in specific locales and labor-market niches. Broadly speaking, labor-brokerage coyotaje—the recruitment of Mexican workers for U.S. employers by paid intermediaries—played a major role in initiating the northward flow of Mexican workers across the border in the late nineteenth and early twentieth centuries. Once knowledge of the higher wages available in the United States and how to access them was diffused among Mexican workers more generally, U.S. employers could typically count on their Mexican employees to recruit workers for them by word of mouth through their own networks of friends and kin. They could, thus, dispense with hiring a coyote to obtain them.

In looking at the history of mass migration of Mexicans to the United States, I have identified six major periods whose characteristics determined the extent and types of coyotaje that were practiced in order to effect Mexicans' passage across the border. The prevalence of each type of coyotaje relative to the other types within each period and between different periods is summarized in table 3.1. My periodization of the history of Mexican migration to the United States in this chapter is adapted from Durand (1994 and 1998), with some minor modifications to highlight the conditions giving rise to the practice of coyotaje. The historical discussion of Mexican migration I offer here builds on the outline presented in chapter 1, but more specifically focuses on the legal and law enforcement framework affecting the entry of Mexicans, rather than other factors, such as economic conditions in both countries, that also determined the flow of Mexican labor back and forth across the border at different historical moments.

El enganche, 1888–1917

Among the historical developments that created the conditions for the launching of mass labor migration by Mexicans to the United States in the late nineteenth century, three are especially relevant to the discussion of coyotaje during this period: (1) the passage of the Chinese Exclusion Act in 1882; (2) the 1884 completion of rail lines connecting El Paso, Texas, with the interior regions of both Mexico and the United States; and (3) the passage of the

Table 3.1. Prevalence of different types of coyotaje, by historical period of Mexican migration to the United States

Period	U.S. law enforcement framework	Relative prevalence of type of coyotaje		
		Bureaucratic-Evasion	Labor-Brokerage	Clandestine-Crossing
El enganche, 1888–1917	Chinese exclusion; ban on importation of contract labor; Mexicans exempt from head tax, numerical restrictions on entry; no immigration police force on border	Low	High	Low
Mass migration/mass deportation, 1917–42	Ban on importation of contract labor waived temporarily during and immediately after WWI; Mexicans subject to head tax, literacy test, and medical exam, but no numerical restrictions; creation of U.S. Border Patrol; Texas bans labor recruitment from other states; mass deportations after WWI and again at outset of Great Depression	Low	High	Moderate
Bracero Program, 1942–65	Ban on importation of contract labor waived; labor contracting taken over by Mexican and U.S. governments, but too few contracts awarded to meet demand in Mexico; U.S. Border Patrol expanded to ca. 1,000 agents	Moderate	—	Moderate
Undocumented, 1965–86	Binational contract labor program ended; strict numerical restrictions placed on Mexicans; Border Patrol expanded to ca. 3,000 agents	Low	Moderate	High
Legalization, 1986–93	Legalization of undocumented already in country; employers of undocumented subject to sanctions, but with little enforcement; strict numerical limits on entry of Mexicans remain in place; moderate growth in size of Border Patrol	High	Low*	High
Contemporary, 1993–2006	Strict numerical limits on entry of Mexicans; dramatic expansion of Border Patrol to ca. 12,000 agents; criminalization of migration; employers of undocumented subject to sanctions, but with little enforcement	High	Low*	High

*Outside agriculture, poultry-processing, and meat-packing.

Immigration Act of 1885, which banned the importation of contract labor from outside the United States. The bans on the importation of Chinese and other foreign contract labor created significant labor shortages in the southwestern and western regions of the United States (Cardoso 1980, 28). With the new rail connection to the Mexican interior, it became possible for U.S. employers to import Mexican peasants to work on farms, in mines, and laying track north of the border. Although the 1885 contract labor ban applied to Mexicans as well as residents of other nations, U.S. authorities could not systematically enforce the ban along the porous and largely unguarded land border with Mexico as successfully as they could at the seaports where European immigrants disembarked during this period (Cardoso 1980, 28; Clark 1908, 471).[5]

U.S. employers first accessed Mexican laborers in the interior of Mexico by hiring Spanish-speaking labor recruiters, known as *enganchadores* or *enganchistas* (literally, "hookers," from the Spanish noun *gancho*, hook, and verb *enganchar*, to hook), to convince them to accept jobs in the United States and accompany them on the new trains to the border. This system of labor recruitment, known as *el enganche* ("the hooking"), was already practiced extensively within Mexico as a way of mobilizing peasants in central Mexico to work in expanding factories and mines in the northern region of the country. Following completion of the railroad to the border, U.S. employers tapped into the *enganche* system quite effectively. The enganchadores frequently induced rural men to travel with them by getting them drunk and would sometimes collaborate with local authorities to forcibly recruit vagrants and prisoners. The terms of employment offered by the enganchadores were often changed for the worse once workers were "hooked," and workers were commonly treated as chattel and held against their will until they could work off their transportation debts (Durand 1994, 108–10). The thousands of men who traveled north with enganchadores during this period typically did so without signing a formal labor contract; rather, they would not be asked to sign a contract until they reached a contracting office on U.S. soil. In this way the enganchadores tried to give the appearance that they were not violating the foreign contract labor ban (Reisler 1976, 10). At the same time, it is important to note that they were nonetheless violating U.S. legislation adopted in 1891 that "prohibited the importation of alien laborers by the use of advertisements circulated in foreign countries which promised employment" (Cárdenas 1975, 67).

Although during this initial period of Mexican mass migration to the United States enganchadores did not typically supply clandestine border-crossing services, they clearly fulfilled one of the principal definitions of coyotaje as communicated in colloquial Mexican Spanish—serving as a broker or middleman of a commodity. In this case the commodity was not an agricultural product such as corn, beans, or coffee but another Mexican commodity in high demand in the United States—the labor power of Mexican workers. Enganchadores were coyotes in a second sense as well, that of bureaucratic evasion, insofar as they enabled U.S. capitalists to evade the foreign contract labor ban imposed in 1885.[6]

Although historians of Mexican migration to the United States have not typically referred to enganchistas or other types of contractors of Mexican labor as coyotes, Meléndez (1982, 296) notes that a "well-known connotation of coyote used by Mexicans is associated with the exploitive labor contractor, the enganchista."[7] In addition, she identifies the enganchista as an example of one of the coyote's principal traits in Mexican folklore—in-betweenness. Neither worker nor owner, the enganchista serves as the border-crossing bridge between the two classes and nationalities. In this sense, we can interpret the enganchista's role as analogous to the cultural role of illicit go-between that Wolf (1959) associated with the mestizo population of New Spain in the colonial period. In the same vein, Meléndez (1982, 304) also argues that the enganchista's behavior displays another of the coyote's distinctive folkloric traits—duplicity—with regard to farm-labor relations, insofar as he "works both sides, management and labor" and deceives farmworkers who are not protected by a union.

Although El Paso was the first major labor-contracting center to which enganchadores brought Mexican workers, by the beginning of the twentieth century enganchadores had also become a significant presence on the South Texas-Northeast Mexico border. Reisler (1976, 11) reports that during this period labor-contracting agencies in South Texas, for whom enganchadores often worked, advertised their ability to secure Mexicans to work for any type of employer, at low cost, and in any number needed. According to Durand (1994, 112), contractors located across the river from Piedras Negras, Nuevo Laredo, and Matamoros "only had to wait each day for the train arriving with hundreds of workers and proceed to contract them" [translated from Spanish by Spener]. Writing in 1908, Clark (475) reported that San Antonio had become the biggest contracting center for Mexicans intending to work in Texas, with most of them crossing the border at Eagle Pass, Laredo, or Brownsville.

According to James Slayden, a former member of the U.S. House of Representatives from the San Antonio area, during this period South Texas farmers would sometimes bypass labor-contracting agencies altogether and import Mexican workers directly: "Neighbors would combine and send an agent to Northern Mexico and he would bring back the number needed and distribute them among the farmers contributing to the enterprise" (Slayden 1921, 121).

Because this recruitment was a violation of the 1885 ban on importation of contract laborers, some farmers in his area "found themselves in trouble with the federal courts," and enforcement of the ban "caused a serious stringency in the farm labor market" (1921, 122). Fortunately for the farmers, Slayden said, these problems turned out to be temporary: "However, the Mexicans who wanted to come to Texas to pick cotton and earn in six weeks more than they ordinarily earned at home in six months had learned when they would be needed and many came without contracts but with the certainty of employment" (1921, 122).

Slayden's latter observation accords with Durand's (1994, 111) contention that by the end of the first decade of the twentieth century, the role of enganchadores operating in the Mexican interior had become largely superfluous to Mexican emigration. Instead, Mexicans from the interior would travel to the border on their own and continue on to San Antonio to find work through one of the labor-contracting agencies there. The outbreak of the revolution in Mexico in the second decade of the century also contributed mightily to the flow of unrecruited workers and peasants across the border into the United States.

Although active recruitment in Mexico by enganchistas declined early on in the twentieth century, Mexicans quickly learned that continuing to deal with labor contractors at the border and in San Antonio could work to their advantage. By the second decade of the century, Mexican workers had developed the practice of signing on with labor contractors at the border or in San Antonio in order to obtain free rail transport to the U.S. interior. Contracted to work on the railroads, large numbers of workers would "skip" their contracts, oftentimes before even arriving at their contracted destination, in order to pursue better-paying work opportunities in agriculture and industry. Although the railroad companies complained bitterly about this problem, there was little they could do about it, given the prohibitive cost of tracking down and capturing workers who had deserted their contracts (García 1996, 7–9). Thus, as Mexicans gained knowledge about travel to the United States and an ever-wider range of job opportunities awaiting them there, they began to turn the tables on the *coyotes enganchistas* and *coyotes contratistas* (contractor coyotes) who had originally recruited them. Like the rabbit in the Zapotec folk tales, they learned to trick the trickster coyote. In this sense, we can see that from very early in the history of Mexican labor migration, Mexican workers became relatively autonomous agents in their quest for economic improvement rather than a passive and pliable workforce that was easily taken advantage of by unscrupulous labor agents. We can view migrants' behavior in this regard as an early form of resistencia hormiga, using labor-brokerage coyotaje against itself to free themselves from coercive forms of labor control.

Labor-brokerage coyotaje during the period of *el enganche* played a signifi-cant role in the early development of North American apartheid as a mech-anism for mobilizing Mexican labor for exploitation in the United States, differentiating Mexicans from other racial and ethnic groups as a labor force and controlling them through extraeconomic coercion. At the same time, once they became aware of the opportunities for earning substantially higher cash incomes in the United States than they could at home, Mexican workers willingly entered into relationships with labor contractors to obtain transport and initial jobs in *el Norte*. They quickly learned they could often do even better for themselves by skipping their contracts after traveling away from the border and finding other jobs on their own. With the imposition of new restrictions on the entry of Mexicans into the United States in the late 1910s and early 1920s, migrants began to turn, not only to labor-brokerage coyotes, but increasingly to clandestine-crossing coyotes as well.

Mass Migration/Mass Deportation, 1917–42

As discussed in chapter 1, the new requirements imposed on foreign nationals at the border included in the 1917 and 1924 immigration acts (literacy test, medical exam, head tax, and visa fee) combined with the creation of the Bor-der Patrol in 1924, prompted thousands of Mexican migrants to cross the Río Bravo surreptitiously to enter the country. These migrants were often guided and transported by coyotes. By 1918, just a year after the imposition of the head tax and literacy test, the U.S. Commissioner of Immigration reported to the Congress that these requirements had led to a "new and thriving indus-try...having for its object the illegal introduction into the United States of Mexican aliens on a wholesale scale by means of organized efforts" (United States Department of Labor 1918, 319, cited in Reisler 1976, 25). The demand for coyotaje services by Mexican labor migrants increased further after the U.S. economy recovered from its post–World War I slump and the 1924 immigra-tion act severely reduced the flow of labor migrants from Europe.

By the mid-1920s, large-scale coyotaje operations had emerged in the Ciudad Juárez-El Paso area. These were described in considerable detail by the anthropologist Manuel Gamio (1930) in his pioneering study of Mexican migration. I observed most of the same tactics in use along the South Texas-Northeast Mexico border at the end of the twentieth century (see chapter 4). Coyotes in Ciudad Juárez would hang around the plaza, hotels, restaurants, and even the Mexican offices and U.S. consulate where aspiring migrants would have to go to process their visa paperwork. The coyotes' fees ranged from U.S. $5 to $10 ($60 to $120 in 2008 dollars), considerably less than the

$18 fee (around $220 in 2008 dollars) migrants would have to pay to enter the country legally, on top of the additional costs of food and lodging typically caused by delays in getting the necessary paperwork processed in Juárez. The coyotes would drive migrants across low-water crossings in automobiles, carts, or trucks, or, where the river was deeper, row them across in boats or lead them swimming to the far bank (Gamio 1930, 205–6). Gamio noted that coyotes worked both as individuals and in organized gangs, a structure of the coyotaje "industry" that recurred in subsequent periods and continues to the present day (see chapters 4 and 5). They were quite expert in effecting successful crossings and often did so in concert with both U.S. and Mexican authorities: "These people know their ground thoroughly, and the habits of both American and Mexican authorities, and sometimes even have an arrangement with some district official" (Gamio 1930, 206). According to Gamio, the use of false documents to cross was common, as was the use of valid documents by impostors, who often rented them from coyotes. Gamio found that these organized coyotes sometimes worked for "big commercial, industrial, or agricultural enterprises in the border states and even in the interior of the United States, which have need of Mexican labor" (Gamio 1930, 206).

Although no published account describes the situation prevailing for this type of coyotaje in the South Texas-Northeast Mexico region with the same level of detail and as systematically as Gamio did for El Paso del Norte during this period, scattered references in the extant literature give us a sense of the types of clandestine-crossing coyotaje that occurred in this region.

One of the earliest references to clandestine-crossing coyotaje on the Northeast Mexico-South Texas border comes from an oral history collected by Gamio (2002, 185–86). In it, a woman describes how in 1919 she and her husband each paid a coyote $10 ($135 in 2008 dollars) to cross the Río Bravo into the United States from Nuevo Laredo, Tamaulipas, after the coyote told them that U.S. officials would not permit them to enter legally because they did not know how to read. For his part, Congressman Slayden noted that many of the Mexicans crossing into South Texas from Mexico after passage of the 1917 law did so with the assistance of coyotes, who, in some cases, were in cahoots with Mexican government officials:

There is evidence available to American officials that some of the underpaid officers of Mexico have suggested "through a friend" to intending emigrants to the United States that if they must leave their own country, they can avoid the examination, fumigation, and especially the tax of eight dollars, by crossing above or below the established stations and save at least four dollars, the other four being paid to the "friend" of the officer [about $50 in 2008 dollars]. (Slayden 1921, 122)

Furthermore, Slayden presaged the alarm expressed by subsequent commentators in the 1950s that such coyotes could be linked to foreign communists committed to promoting subversion within the United States:

> Two Mexicans were arrested in San Antonio during the week in which this is written, each of whom had on his person a card, printed in Spanish, saying that the man who presented it would put intending emigrants into the United States for half the head tax exacted at the stations. The card also said that the people who undertook to do this service were headquarters for the distribution of Bolshevist literature. This story is from an absolutely reliable source. (Slayden 1921, 122)

By the 1980s, other commentators were sounding the alarm, not about the possibility of Soviet agents crossing the border into South Texas with the aid of coyotes, but of the potential for Central American guerillas and Middle Eastern terrorists to do so. Today, they claim danger from Islamist terrorists aided by coyotes and members of the Mara Salvatrucha gang,[8] relying on similarly dubious "evidence" (see, for example, Castillo 2004; Chapa 2006; Corchado and Trahan 2006; Hastings and Preston 2006; House Committee on Homeland Security 2006).

As was the case in El Paso, aboveboard labor-contracting agencies based in San Antonio and Chicago often relied, sometimes indirectly and other times quite directly, on clandestine-crossing coyotes to obtain their Mexican workers in the 1920s. For example, Chicago labor contractors would frequently act not only through other labor-recruitment agencies in San Antonio to receive Mexican workers, but also through clandestine-crossing coyotes along the Texas-Mexico border, who would put workers on a train to Chicago after sneaking them across the river. Rail transportation costs from San Antonio to Chicago were typically deducted from the workers' paychecks (Cardoso 1980, 85). Meanwhile, the chief immigration inspector in Brownsville reported that in 1924 at least one hundred Mexicans worked in the area "operating illegal ferries and bringing aliens into the U.S." (Reisler 1976, 74n44). According to McWilliams (1948, 164), by the 1920s the "profits in this racket were really enormous and the smugglers and coyotes and labor contractors constituted an intimate and powerful alliance from Calexico to Brownsville."

Competition for Mexican workers among labor contractors grew so intense that the 1920s also saw the appearance of coyotes on U.S. soil, known as "man-snatchers," who would steal Mexican laborers from work sites in the United States in order to sell them to other employers as if they were chattel.[9] The constant threat posed by the man-snatchers led labor contractors to keep workers en route to employers locked up and under armed guard to prevent their theft. In this regard, McWilliams (1948, 165) tells of Mexican workers being marched through the streets of San Antonio in broad daylight, escorted by gunmen. Of all the types of coyotaje that have existed in this migratory corridor, "man-snatching" is one of the clearest indicators of the coercive control over Mexican labor exercised by the emerging apartheid system.

As discussed earlier, by the end of the 1920s, demand for Mexican workers was so great that Texas, which at that time had the largest Mexican population in the country, began to lose substantial numbers of workers to other states. At the behest of the state's growers, the Texas legislature passed the Emigrant Agent Acts of 1929, which effectively barred labor recruiters acting on behalf of employers in other states from operating in Texas. The sugar beet industry in the Midwest and Great Plains states was especially affected by the new law, for it turned the recruitment of *betabeleros* (sugar beet workers), which had formerly been handled by the sugar beet companies themselves, into an "illegal, underground conspiracy" farmed out to Mexican contractors and truckers, that is, to domestic coyotes. Most Mexican sugar beet workers in the 1920s had entered the U.S. illegally (García 1996, 47).[10]

Although clandestine-crossing coyotaje on this stretch of the border diminished considerably after the onset of the Great Depression, labor-brokerage coyotes continued to operate during the Texas cotton harvests throughout the 1930s. At the end of that decade, there were about four hundred thousand migratory cotton workers in Texas alone, two-thirds of whom were Mexican. About 60 percent of cotton picking was contracted through Mexican labor contractors and truckers. These coyotes drove trucks loaded with fifty to sixty workers following the harvest through the "big swing" of Texas. In an incident presaging tragedies in the contemporary period, an accident occurred in McAllen in 1940 that involved one of these trucks, resulting in the injury of forty-four Mexicans and the death of twenty-nine, including eleven children (McWilliams 1948, 159–60). Following U.S. entry into World War II, the U.S. and Mexican governments, by creating a new agricultural guest-worker program, usurped the role played by labor-brokerage coyotes in providing U.S. farms with Mexican workers. The rise of this new, legal labor-brokerage system eliminated the need for U.S. employers to go to private labor-contracting agencies to recruit Mexican workers. Nevertheless, the new government-run system was accompanied by large-scale bureaucratic evasion and clandestine-crossing coyotaje in the South Texas-Northeast Mexico border region.

The Bracero Program, 1942–65

Although nearly five million guest-worker contracts for agricultural labor were issued to Mexicans during the life of the Bracero Program, the supply of contracts offered by the U.S. authorities was always exceeded by the demand for them on the part of Mexican workers. As a consequence, the number of Mexican men entering the United States *sin papeles* (without papers) during this period was equal to or greater than the number entering with legal work contracts. This phenomenon was especially pronounced in South Texas, since there was a strong demand for Mexican labor by growers and most of Texas was excluded from participation in the Bracero Program until 1954 (see chapter 1). Many thousands of Mexican men who were unable to obtain bracero contracts resorted to either bureaucratic-evasion coyotaje or clandestine-crossing coyotaje strategies to find work in Texas.

   Much of the bureaucratic-evasion coyotaje that took place during the bracero period for Texas-bound workers occurred at the recruitment center set up by the Mexican government in Monterrey, Nuevo León, in the early 1950s.[11] A migrant interviewed by one of Durand's research assistants in Santa María del Río, San Luis Potosí, spoke of how a friend of his, who "trafficked" at the Monterrey recruitment center, got him to the front of the line for a contract in the 1950s (Durand 2002, 36). Two former braceros I interviewed told me of the difficulties they encountered in getting contracts in the 1950s and 1960s at the Monterrey contracting center and how they were able to get contracts with the help of coyotes. Don Ignacio, whom I interviewed in Texas in 2004, told me of paying a coyote $20 (about $160 in 2008 dollars) to get his contract at the Monterrey recruitment center in the 1950s:

Don Ignacio: I went to Monterrey to be contracted several times.

Spener: And how did it work in Monterrey?

Don Ignacio: Well, it was real tough. Real, real tough. Because in Mexico there are many people, a lot of people pile up. In Monterrey, there was a tremendous wait to find work.

Spener: So what did you have to do to get a contract, if it was so tough?

Don Ignacio: It's like this. Sometimes you have contacts so you can get through quickly, but you have to pay a certain amount. Back then, this kind of coyote didn't transport you. This kind was just there to get you in on the contracting. And that was what you wanted, to get contracted.

Spener: And these men that helped you get through the red tape, were they called coyotes back then?

Don Ignacio: Well, like I said, that's what they're called because they aren't authorized to do it, but they do it.

Don Reynaldo, whom I interviewed in Nuevo León in 2002, told me that although "legitimate" coyotes operated at the Monterrey center, there were also men hanging around the contracting office, who posed as coyotes but took aspiring braceros' money, never be heard from again. Many migrants who failed in their attempts to get legal bracero contracts subsequently entered the United States as *mojados* (American G.I. Forum of Texas and Texas State Federation of Labor 1953, 5; Calavita 1992, 110).

Given that by 1950 the U.S. Border Patrol had grown to a force of about one thousand agents, with most stationed along the border with Mexico, a large number of Mexican workers crossing the Río Grande during the bracero years did so with the assistance of clandestine-crossing coyotes. During this period, it was common for clandestine entrants to use the services of a *patero*, or boatman, to cross the Río Grande into the United States (Cockcroft 1986, 24; Durand 2002, 47; Saunders and Leonard 1951, 92). Authors of the report *What Price Wetbacks?*, published in 1953 by the American G.I. Forum of Texas and the Texas State Federation of Labor, described the border towns of Del Río and Eagle Pass, Texas, as a "hot spot" for the "smuggling" of "wetbacks," which they described as a "multi-million-dollar business" (1953, 52). In this report, "smugglers" were described as *pachucos*,[12] and lumped into the same category as other undesirables, including "the criminals, the marijuana peddlers, the falsifiers of identity documents,…the prostitutes, and the homosexuals" (1953, 6). Regardless of the validity of this characterization (and the bigotry of those making it), by the early 1950s there appeared to be a large number of coyotes dedicated to helping Mexicans enter the United States clandestinely: in 1953, the Border Patrol reported apprehending 1,545 "alien smugglers" borderwide (United States Immigration and Naturalization Service 1954, 3, cited in Grebler 1965, 34). Here it is important to note that, under the Texas proviso of the immigration act signed into law in 1952, South Texas farmers could not be prosecuted as "alien smugglers" even though they "harbored" hundreds of thousands of undocumented Mexicans who worked their lands (Calavita 1992, 68).

Similar to the case in the 1920s and again today, some alarmed observers linked the threat of subversion by non-Mexicans entering the United States alongside Mexican workers to the operation of "smugglers" on the border. The authors of *What Price Wetbacks?* raised this specter in particularly florid terms:

Along a wide-open border, such as that of the United States and Mexico, anything can happen. While the nation spends millions of dollars each year seeking out subversives within the country, any given number of them could easily slip in to the country to replace those apprehended.

Who is to say how many Communists mingle with the hordes of wet-backs wandering casually into the country across the Rio Grande? If one out of every two wetbacks—or one out of every five—is arrested, does the same ratio hold true for subversive agents and spies? Or won't the ratio of those unapprehended be much greater, considering the intelligence and training of the subversive or the spy?

In July 1953, the District Immigration Office at San Antonio reported that in two and one-half years, 15 aliens who had come in from Mexico had been deported under subversive charges. They were of the following nation-alities: Mexico, England, Germany, the Philippines, Iraq, Palestine, Poland, Russia, and Chile. How many slipped in without being apprehended? How many from communist-dominated Guatemala came over masquerading as Mexicans? (American G.I. Forum of Texas and Texas State Federation of Labor 1953, 30–32)

The report went on to discuss the case of a "smuggling ring" in Brownsville headed by a Costa Rican woman who had been charging "undesirable Euro-pean aliens" as much as $2,000 each (over $16,000 in 2008 dollars) to enter the country. The authors wondered how many of these "aliens" might have been "subversive elements" who were "using the open border to infiltrate the coun-try." As had been the case in the 1920s, the threat of subversion from across the border proved to be no more than hypothetical—if any communist saboteurs ever made it across the river, they never managed to commit any destructive acts on U.S. soil.

With the end of the Bracero Program, Mexicans lost their principal legal path to work in the United States. Labor-brokerage coyotaje waned with the assumption of the labor-brokerage function provided by the Mexican and U.S. governments. Through the Bracero Program, the neighboring states mobilized and exerted considerable direct control over the Mexican workforce and the terms and conditions of its employment. Nonetheless, bureaucratic-evasion coyotaje was commonly practiced to get aspiring braceros into the contracting queue in the official recruitment centers established in Monterrey and else-where. This represented a way Mexican workers resisted state control over the circumstances in which they sold their labor power in the U.S. market. Because there were never as many bracero contracts made available as Mexican men wishing to work, migrants resorted to hiring coyotes of the clandestine-crossing variety in large numbers in order to enter the United States and work outside the legal guest-worker program. In addition, many workers who worked initially as legal braceros deserted their contracts in search of better wages and work-ing conditions as *indocumentados* (Calavita 1992, 77; Durand 1994, 133–34;

Durand 1998, 33–34).[13] This represented another form of resistance by migrants to noneconomic forms of control over their labor. The end of the Bracero Program brought with it an increased reliance on clandestine-crossing coyotaje by Mexicans as a labor-migration strategy in the face of escalation of U.S. border control efforts in the 1970s and 1980s.

The Undocumented Period, 1965–86

The termination of the bracero program at the end of 1964 and the passage of the Immigration and Nationality Act of 1965 (Hart-Celler Act) effectively precluded the vast majority of aspiring Mexican labor migrants from entering the United States to work with a legal immigrant or work visa. Nonetheless, economic necessity and an undiminished demand for their labor north of the border induced hundreds of thousands of Mexicans to enter the United States each year in search of jobs as *indocumentados*. As the number of undocumented migrants grew substantially throughout this period, so did the number of Border Patrol agents assigned to guard the U.S. border with Mexico, from a total of around 1,500 agents in 1965 to 2,500 in 1980 to around 3,700 by 1986 (Nevins 2002, 197). In the absence of legal opportunities to enter the country in search of work and the presence of an ever-larger Border Patrol deployed to police them, larger numbers of migrants turned to coyotes of the clandestine-crossing variety than ever before.

Based on his experiences in the field along the South Texas-Northeast Mexico border in the late 1960s, Samora (1971, 86) reported that migrants who failed to make it across the border on their first two attempts without the services of a coyote would resort to hiring a coyote by their third attempt. Authors of a study of undocumented immigration conducted in San Antonio and Austin reported that by the beginning of the 1980s "the do-it-yourself approach" to border crossing had become "increasingly rare" and that by then "virtually everyone" was making use of a coyote to get into the United States (Browning and Rodríguez 1985, 287–88). As migrants in the region became increasingly reliant on coyotes to cross the border, U.S. law enforcement began to prosecute significant numbers of individuals for helping migrants enter the country *sin papeles*. Thus, in 1974, U.S. authorities prosecuted 173 coyotes in San Antonio and another 558 in Del Rio (Comptroller General of the United States 1976, 21). In that same year, Mexico passed laws that imposed steep criminal penalties on persons convicted of aiding undocumented workers in illegal entry of the United States. By 1975, the U.S. Immigration and Naturalization Service investigators had begun to cooperate with Mexican authorities in Ciudad Acuña, Coahuila, resulting in the prosecution in Mexico of fourteen members of organized "smuggling rings" in that city (Comptroller General of the United States 1976, 26).

The historical record for this period of migration history on the South Texas-Northeast Mexico border indicates that at least some organizations dedicated to clandestine-crossing coyotaje had grown to a considerable size and degree of professionalism. For example, Lewis (1979, 50) described a large-scale coyotaje operation run out of Nuevo Laredo, Tamaulipas, in the 1970s that continued to operate despite its drivers being repeatedly arrested by U.S. immigration authorities. According to the INS investigator she interviewed, this organization had its own auto maintenance yard in Nuevo Laredo, where it parked as many as twenty-five vehicles. It used juveniles as guides and drivers, since they could not be tried as adults in the United States. It did not limit itself to the clandestine transport of Mexicans but also had a network of contacts throughout Latin America. The INS estimated that this organization moved between eight and ten thousand migrants into the United States annually.[14]

Although the amount charged by coyotes in the early 2000s to guide and transport migrants across the Río Bravo into the United States and out of the South Texas border region had increased to as much as $2,500 since the implementation of Operation Rio Grande in the late 1990s, prices had not actually risen as dramatically as might have been expected. In the late 1960s, traveling away from the South Texas-Northeast Mexican border region by a combination of crossing the Río Bravo/Río Grande, walking through the brush, and being picked up in a car or truck to be driven to a city in the Texas interior appears to have cost around $1,100 in 2008 dollars (Samora 1971, 75). The cost for traveling beyond Texas by land to Chicago in the late 1960s could range from as little as $1,200 to as much as $2,300 in 2008 dollars (Samora 1971, 1–2, 109; Portes 1974, 42).[15]

Coyotes also continued to transport migrants out of South Texas by train in the 1970s and 1980s, as they had done since the previous century, although now they helped them hop into freight cars surreptitiously instead of buying them seats on passenger trains. In addition, by this time tractor-trailers had overtaken rail transport as the chief way to ship cargo around the United States, and, not surprisingly, coyotes had begun to avail themselves of this way of transporting their clients once they had entered the United States. This practice appears to have been especially common in the Lower Rio Grande Valley, decades before the tragic deaths of nineteen Mexican and Central American migrants in the back of an eighteen-wheeler in 2003:

> Typically, an INS agent said, "the [smuggler] will approach a legitimate truck driver and offer him 50 dollars each [about $180 in 2008 dollars] to

haul the aliens one hundred miles past the checkpoint. He is careful to select a driver without a criminal record, someone who will be placed on probation and not sentenced to prison if apprehended." The hundreds of produce trucks leaving the Rio Grande Valley daily cannot be searched individually, according to the agent, and "smugglers often build secret compartments in the floors of truck beds where aliens can hide, covered by loads of produce. (Lewis 1979, 50)

Already by the late 1960s, coyotes were loading Mexican migrants into the backs of other types of trucks to transport them surreptitiously from South Texas to Chicago. Samora (1971, 2–3) described how, in September 1968, forty-six Mexican men were driven away from the border, locked in the back of a rented U-Haul truck. After the truck arrived in San Antonio and its compartment was unlocked, thirteen of the men had to be rushed to the hospital. One was dead on arrival and two others died the following day. Also by the mid-1970s, recreational vehicles had begun to be used as conveyances for transporting autonomous Mexican migrants. In 1975, for example, Border Patrol agents near Laredo stopped a pickup truck and two motor homes carrying 124 migrants; one of the suspected coyotes in the case had $18,000 cash on his person ($72,000 in 2008 dollars) (Comptroller General of the United States 1976, 7).

Coyotaje in the region once again generated fears about national security during this period, especially after the Reagan administration sought to link armed conflicts in Central America and the Middle East in the 1980s with potential terrorist attacks on U.S. soil (Associated Press 1986; Dunn 1996; United Press International 1986). Consistent with the politics of the day, in 1985 Silvestre Reyes, chief of the McAllen sector of the Border Patrol (who less than a decade later would become famous for launching Operation Blockade in the El Paso sector), expressed his concern that it was no longer just Mexicans who were coming across the Rio Grande but "aliens" from around the world. Many of these non-Mexicans were brought into the country by coyotes. "What's scary about this new trend," Reyes said, "is that we're no longer dealing only with hungry Mexicans sneaking across to find a job. We don't know who's getting in—terrorists, criminals. They could be anybody, for any purpose. Unless we stop it, we're vulnerable to anything" (quoted in Loh 1985, 10). As was the case in the 1920s and 1950s, the subversive/terrorist threat never materialized.

When Samora and his research assistants were in the field at the end of the 1960s (1971, 76), they were told that coyotes would lend migrants the large sum of money needed to pay for their crossing at usurious interest rates and threaten to harm their families at home in Mexico if the loan was not repaid.

With the growth of the undocumented Mexican population in Texas in the 1970s, it became less and less necessary for new migrants to go into debt with their coyotes. Rather, they would make use of their accumulated social capital to borrow the needed funds from friends and family members already working in the United States (Browning and Rodríguez 1985). Moreover, as it became clear that most new migrants had contacts in the United States who would pay for their passage, COD payment arrangements with coyotes became common, whereby coyotes would transport migrants for little or no upfront payment, with the confidence that they could collect the money from their customers' "respondents" on arrival in the destination city. For example, Ramón Pérez describes, in his personal memoir *Diary of an Undocumented Immigrant* (1991, 22–28), how he made a border crossing at the two Laredos in the early 1980s in which coyotes refused to take migrants across unless they had a name and a phone number for someone who would pay for their trip on arrival. They complained that too many people had not paid them to risk transporting anyone who hadn't made arrangements with a "respondent" in the United States. During this crossing, he also quotes a fellow migrant as commenting that the "good thing about the coyotes is that they can't collect from a dead man, so they have to protect us against all kinds of dangers" (Pérez 1991, 26–27). I discuss the significance of COD arrangements between migrants and their coyotes in the contemporary period in greater detail in chapter 5.

Upon termination of the Bracero Program, U.S. growers reverted to the use of private labor contractors to recruit Mexican farmworkers. As they had been prior to the taking over of the labor brokerage task by the U.S. and Mexican governments, these coyotes *contratistas* were typically growers' Mexican or Mexican American *mayordomos* (foremen). In agriculture, the contractor recruitment system continues to operate to the present day (see, for example, Krissman 2000). It is nonetheless important to note that the proportion of Mexicans migrants employed in U.S. agriculture dropped precipitously in the post-bracero period, as hundreds of thousands found employment in manufacturing, construction, and services north of the border.[16] Posing as an undocumented migrant for research conducted with Samora in the late 1960s, Jorge Bustamante reported coyotes in the plaza in Reynosa offering to place him in jobs in a variety of locations, ranging from just across the river in Texas to Kansas and elsewhere in the Midwest (Samora 1971, 109). Lewis (1979, 72–80) reported that in the 1970s clandestine-crossing coyotes operating along the South Texas-Northeast Mexico border collaborated with both agricultural and nonagricultural employers in the U.S. interior to provide them with workers, whose pay would be then be garnished to cover the costs of their transit across and away from the border. Similarly, the U.S. Comptroller General reported that many coyotes placed migrants in jobs in the United States in the 1970s (Comptroller General of the United States 1976, 8).

Nevertheless, outside of the agricultural sector, itself declining in importance as a source of employment for Mexican migrants, labor-brokerage coyotaje in this and other regions seems to have sharply declined in importance with the growth of urban Mexican immigrant communities north of the border. Writing about this period, Durand (1998, 44–46) observes that in urban areas employers increasingly relied on the social networks of their Mexican employees to recruit new workers, rather than paying a clandestine-labor broker for this service. By this time, as substantiated in the Texas Indocumentados Study (Browning and Rodríguez 1985), sufficient resources had accumulated in Mexican migrant communities to effectively connect arriving migrants with job vacancies. Indeed, although Lewis sensationalized the seamier and more exploitative aspects of the labor-brokerage coyotaje that she observed in the 1970s—the relevant chapter in her book *Slave Trade Today* was titled "Aliens on Order"—she also recognized that coyotes' labor-brokerage activity rapidly made itself obsolete:

> Once a pattern of alien migration is set, knowledge of where jobs are to be found is spread to friends and family members and the employer no longer has to order a shipment of 'wets' from smugglers. Where migration patterns are the most firmly established, the coyote is no longer a trader in human flesh, but an illicit travel agent operating in an underground labor market where the worker is exploited because of his undocumented status.[17] (Lewis 1979, 79–80)

Meanwhile, Rodríguez (2004, 454) described the situation prevailing by the 1980s as one in which "the employer simply turns over the responsibilities of the labor process to the immigrant workforce, whose members organize and operate the work process through internal social networks and hierarchies."[18]

The Legalization Period, 1986–93

As discussed in chapter 1, the Immigration Reform and Control Act signed into law by President Reagan in 1986 contained three main provisions: (1) a legalization or "amnesty" program to allow undocumented migrants living in the United States to legalize their status and eventually become U.S. citizens; (2) a repeal of the Texas proviso of the 1952 immigration law that had allowed U.S. employers to hire undocumented workers without fear of prosecution for "harboring illegal aliens"; and (3) authorization of increased funds for the

Immigration and Naturalization Service to enhance border security. The first two of these provisions had the effect of promoting an increase in bureaucratic-evasion coyotaje among Mexican migrants in Texas, while the third eventually led, by the late 1990s, to a significant increase in migrant reliance on clandestine-crossing coyotaje relative to the previous period.

IRCA promoted bureaucratic-evasion coyotaje by Mexican migrants for two reasons, both related to the types of documentation needed to show to government authorities and employers as a consequence of its "amnesty" and "employer sanctions" provisions. In order to legalize their status in the United States, migrants had to prove to the INS's satisfaction that they had been living continuously in the United States since January 1, 1982 or earlier, or, if they had not lived in the country that long, that they had worked in agriculture in the United States for at least ninety days during the twelve-month period ending on May 1, 1986. Over two million Mexicans applied to legalize their status, 1.2 million in the "general amnesty" program and another million or so as agricultural workers (Cornelius 1990, 236; Woodrow and Passel 1990, 41). In order to demonstrate continuous residence in the United States, applicants had to present documents including pay stubs, rent receipts, bank statements, and affidavits from persons who knew them during the period they had resided illegally in the United States (New York Times 1987, A16). The documentary requirements for migrants applying as agricultural workers were considerably less stringent. The main thing migrants were required to produce often was simply an affidavit from their agricultural employer (Nordheimer 1988, 14). With regard to employment, after the passage of IRCA, Mexican migrants needed to present employers with a set of documents from an approved list that established their identity and that they were authorized to work in the United States. Such documents included Social Security cards, state-issued birth certificates, legal permanent residency cards, naturalization certificates, driver's licenses bearing a photograph, and the like (Immigration Reform and Control Act, text retrieved on August 9, 2005, from U.S. Equal Employment Opportunity Commission website).

Not surprisingly, thousands of Mexicans residing in Texas had a difficult time documenting their continuous residence in the country, given that they had been living clandestinely up until that point and had not created a paper trail of their lives there. Many of the migrants who lacked the required paper trail invented it by hiring coyotes to obtain the needed documentation. Even before the bill was signed into law by President Reagan, the director of investigation for the INS office in Houston told the press he expected a booming market in false documents to affect the application process: "They are cranking out this stuff all over the world. There is going to be a big market for it. A fraudulent passport with an admission stamp on or before Jan. 1, 1982 is going to be worth its weight in gold" (Tutt 1986). Journalists subsequently documented numerous instances of coyotes providing the documentation needed to qualify for legalization under IRCA (Associated Press 1987a and 1987b; Houston Chronicle 1988; Houston Chronicle News Service 1987; Warren and Wiessler 1988).

Coyotaje enabled migrants and employers throughout the United States to evade the prohibition against employment of undocumented workers in the years following the passage of IRCA. The law only required that an employee present and an employer examine "a document or set of documents that reasonably appears on its face to be genuine" (Title I of the Immigration Reform and Control Act, text retrieved on March 2, 2007, from the U.S. Equal Employment Opportunity Commission website). Very soon after the law's implementation, coyotes began to serve the market for the documents needed to establish eligibility for employment, and at very affordable prices. Some of these documents were counterfeit, while others were valid but sold or rented to persons other than the ones to whom they were originally issued (Anderson and Spear 1988, B9; Andreas 2000, 38–39; Kilborn 1992, E2; Stevenson 1990, 1). This phenomenon was observed in South Texas in the immediate aftermath of IRCA's passage, with the *Houston Chronicle* reporting that "flea markets, grocery store lots, even the more secluded corners of Hispanic restaurants, are increasingly the scenes of blatant wheeling and dealing of phony documents at premium prices" (Rodríguez 1987).

While bureaucratic-evasion coyotaje strategies blossomed in the region as a consequence of IRCA, coyotaje of the clandestine-crossing variety continued unabated, despite the legalization of over two million Mexican residents of the United States. Although apprehensions of migrants at the border fell for several years following the passage of IRCA, by the early 1990s they had returned to pre-IRCA levels. The reasons for this were straightforward. First, only migrants who could "prove" they were in the country prior to 1982 or had worked in agriculture in the months leading to IRCA's passage were eligible to legalize their status in the United States, leaving many Mexican migrants already working in the United States unable to travel legally back and forth across the border. And, second, the reasons Mexicans had sought work in the United States prior to IRCA continued unabated after its passage, in spite of the illegalization of their U.S. employment.

The Contemporary Period, 1993–2006

In 1993 the U.S. government initiated a dramatic buildup of force along its southern border with Mexico, beginning with the launching of Operation

Blockade by the Border Patrol in its El Paso sector in September 1993, followed by Operation Gatekeeper in the San Diego sector in 1994, and Operation Safeguard in the Tucson sector in 1995. In South Texas, Operation Rio Grande made clandestine border-crossing considerably more difficult—though far from impossible—and appears to have significantly increased Mexican migrants' reliance on coyotes to enter the United States.

In addition to the Border Patrol's multiple operations, new federal legislation—the Illegal Immigration Reform and Immigrant Responsibility Act (IIRIRA)—affected the practice of coyotaje by Mexicans after it became law in 1996. Overall the act made U.S. law considerably more punitive with respect to autonomous migration and included a number of provisions that were especially relevant to the practice of coyotaje on this stretch of the border. These provisions included the hiring of five thousand additional Border Patrol agents; extending the IDENT database nationwide; developing new border-crossing documents that were harder to alter or counterfeit; increasing the civil and criminal penalties for "alien smuggling," illegal entry of the United States, and passport and visa fraud; granting law enforcement officials authority to engage in electronic surveillance techniques to combat "alien smuggling"; and increasing the number of INS investigators and assistant U.S. attorneys who prosecuted "alien smuggling" cases (Fragomen 1997; United States Congress Public Law 104–208, September 30, 1996; United States Citizenship and Immigration Services n.d.).

IIRIRA affected the practice of coyotaje along this stretch of the border in several ways. By increasing the number of Border Patrol agents in the region, it made clandestine crossing more difficult. By increasing the civil and criminal penalties for "illegal entry" and "illegal re-entry" and expanding the use of the IDENT database, it made avoidance of apprehension by the Border Patrol more important to a large and ever-growing number of migrants, which, other things being equal, encouraged them to hire professional coyotes. By increasing the criminal and civil penalties for "alien smuggling" and dedicating ever more resources to apprehending and prosecuting coyotes, it increased the risks faced by coyotes and induced them to raise their prices considerably. Intensified prosecution of coyotes, in turn, increased coyote turnover, as experienced coyotes left the field after they were arrested and imprisoned or out of fear that they would be. The extent to which IIRIRA resulted in the intensified criminalization of migration in the Texas border region is illustrated by the skyrocketing number of criminal immigration offenses in the region referred to the U.S. Attorney's Office for prosecution. After illegal entry and illegal reentry of the United States, "bringing in and harboring certain aliens" (i.e., "alien smuggling") was the most common charge (Transactional Records Access Clearinghouse 2005).

In the contemporary period, both bureaucratic evasion and clandestine-crossing coyotaje continued to be especially prevalent in the Northeast Mexico-South Texas migratory corridor. Labor-brokerage coyotaje also continued to be practiced, especially in meatpacking and poultry-processing (Bloomberg News 2001; Schlosser 2001, 160–63; United States District Court, Eastern District of Tennessee 2001) as well as in agriculture. Nonetheless, it is important to bear in mind that the proportion of Mexican migrants finding employment in agriculture in the United States has continued to decline in this period. The most recent figures available indicate that in 2000, just 6.5 percent of Mexican-born workers in the United States were employed in agriculture (Grieco and Ray 2004, graph 2). For this reason, as well as the accumulation of considerable social resources among Mexicans north of the border, labor-brokerage coyotaje appears to be much less prevalent than the bureaucratic-evasion and clandestine-crossing types.[19]

In this chapter, I have reviewed the mythological and folkloric origins of the application of the attributes of the coyote to human behavior in Mexico. I have argued that this association of human cleverness, speed, agility, and duplicity with the coyote figure exhibits itself in the practice of coyotaje in various arenas of cultural life among Mexicans, including international migration to the United States. I have explained how the practice of coyotaje as a strategy for bureaucratic evasion dates back to colonial times in Mexico, and how it was connected to the process of racial and cultural mixing known as *mestizaje*. Coyotaje as bureaucratic evasion continued to be practiced after independence from Spain and still plays an important role in Mexico today as a way for people to cope with what they often regard as arbitrary and capricious laws and regulations that complicate their day-to-day survival. In modern Mexico, coyotaje has also taken the form of brokerage of commodities, with middlemen serving as intermediaries facilitating commercial transactions between geographically distanced producers and consumers. A third form that coyotaje has taken is the guide and transport services provided to undocumented migrants in their attempts to cross the border to work in the United States, which I refer to as clandestine-crossing coyotaje. I have argued that the other two forms of coyotaje—what I have termed bureaucratic-evasion and labor-brokerage coyotaje—also have also played an important role in the process of Mexican migration to the United States throughout its history to the present day.

In the early years of mass Mexican labor migration to the United States, labor-brokerage coyotes known as *enganchistas* were employed by U.S. capitalists to induce Mexican men to head north to work. The role played by these early coyotes was clearly exploitative and directly served the interests of U.S. capitalists rather than the workers they recruited. At the same time, these early coyotes were native to the border region and plied their trade with the traditional disrespect for the externally-imposed international boundary that characterized natives of the Rio Grande Valley until well-into the twentieth century, as detailed in Chapter 1. By the second decade of the twentieth century, however, men in the Mexican interior realized the advantages to them of traveling to the United States to work for far higher wages than were available to them in Mexico, regardless of the degree to which U.S. employers exploited them. Moreover, many of these workers learned to "trick the trickster" by using the transport provided them by *enganchistas* and *contratistas* to travel to worksites in the U.S. interior, only to skip their contracts to search for better jobs elsewhere.

When the door on free transit across the border to Mexicans was slammed shut in 1917 and then barricaded further with the creation of the Border Patrol in 1924, hundreds of thousands of Mexicans continued to migrate north, many of them actively resisting their forcible exclusion by hiring *clandestine-crossing* coyotes, who, for their part, often collaborated actively with labor-contracting agencies in San Antonio. The ambiguities of this situation continue to characterize Mexicans' clandestine migration today, as they resist the apartheid division of the world into high-wage and low-wage regions on the basis of race and national sovereignty, on the one hand, but in so doing make themselves available as a vulnerable and exploitable workforce to capitalists in the United States, on the other. The coyote's role here is also ambiguous and consistent with his representation in myth and folklore, stealthily aiding and abetting migrants' evasion of the laws that exclude them from the "island of privilege" to the north, on the one hand, and delivering them up for exploitation by the owners of that island, on the other.

With the negotiation of the Bracero Program in 1942, the U.S. and Mexican governments took over the brokerage function previously carried out by private enterprises, effectively ending the initial period of labor-brokerage coyotaje. Nevertheless, because the demand by workers for contracts always exceeded their supply, Mexicans turned to bureaucratic evasion coyotes in large numbers as a way to get contracts at the processing center in Monterrey, while other thousands employed coyotes of the clandestine-crossing variety to cross the Río Bravo into South Texas without a contract. When the Bracero Program ended in 1965 and the opportunities available to Mexicans to migrate north legally declined precipitously, migrants kept coming as *indocumentados,* with many placed in jobs by labor-brokerage coyotes, who found a renewed demand for their services. Many of these labor brokers doubled as providers of clandestine-crossing services. As migrant networks matured, however, the need for labor-brokerage services declined, and migrants' friends and relatives in the United States increasingly took over this function, although labor-brokerage coyotaje remained important in agriculture and poultry processing. An ever-smaller proportion of Mexican migrants worked in agriculture during this period, however, further reducing the importance of labor-brokerage coyotes to the overall migration process.

After the passage of IRCA in 1986, clandestine-crossing coyotaje in the region continued unabated, but bureaucratic-evasion coyotaje displayed a resurgence, owing to the paperwork requirements for the "amnesty" process and the new documents Mexicans needed to obtain work in the United States. In the early 1990s, Border Patrol strength in South Texas began to increase significantly, and vigilance intensified even more with the launching of Operation Rio Grande in 1997. In addition, the punitive measures incorporated into IIRIRA in 1996 further criminalized both coyotaje and clandestine migration, leading to an exponential growth in federal prosecutions in the region and a further reduction in the possibilities for legal admission to the United States for a large and ever-growing number of Mexicans. Taken together, IRCA, Operation Rio Grande, and IIRIRA combined to make clandestine migration ever more risky and arduous for migrants and coyotes alike, and led the former to depend more intensively on the latter to avoid apprehension on their journeys north.

Today, coyotes play a role in the Mexican migration process on this stretch of the border that still resembles the role that Wolf described for them in Spanish colonial days. Drawn from among the dispossessed, they help fellow Mexicans overcome laws that are divorced from the reality of their lives and that serve mainly to protect "islands of privilege." Now, however, the islands of privilege are to be found in the United States, and it is U.S. laws, divorced from the reality of Mexican lives, that must be overcome. Given the conditions of material deprivation that they face in Mexico and the lack of legal opportunities open to them to migrate to the United States, it is not surprising that so many Mexicans engage in the deeply rooted practice of coyotaje, in one form or another, to pursue their labor and family-reunification agendas. To the extent that coyotaje over the long term promotes social and cultural blending between the United States and Mexico as a consequence of the massive growth of the Mexican population in the United States, it also remains linked to the process of *mestizaje,* as it was in Spanish colonial times, when the groups in question were Spaniard newcomers and Mesoamerican natives. We also see continuity with the past in the ambivalent attitudes that migrants hold toward their coyotes, which are quite consistent with the dual nature of the coyote as a cultural icon in Mexico. It is not surprising, therefore, that relations between migrants and their coyotes remain fraught with deceit and suspicion, despite the mutual need and shared class and culture that bring them together in the border-crossing project. In the next chapters I analyze the forms that coyotaje takes in the contemporary period on this stretch of the border and how migrants and coyotes manage their uneasy relations with one another.

CHAPTER 4

Coyotaje and Migration in the Contemporary Period

In this chapter I review the range of activities and actors that constituted coyotaje on the Texas-Mexico border in the first years of the twenty-first century as documented in my own fieldwork, in federal court records of cases involving the "harboring and/or transporting of aliens," and in published press accounts.[1] All but one of the coyotaje strategies discussed here (*short-distance coyotaje*) had as their goal the undetected movement of migrants across the Río Bravo into U.S. territory, then through the border region of Texas to one of several cities—San Antonio, Houston, Austin, or Dallas-Fort Worth—in the Texas interior. These cities might be the final destinations of the migrants or might merely be stopover points on the way to other towns and cities in the eastern or midwestern United States. Regardless of the Texas destination city, coyotes had to move migrants across, through, or around several significant obstacles. These were the same obstacles that migrants faced when crossing on their own without a coyote, as described in chapter 2. First, they had to get migrants across the river into U.S. territory, either by boat, inner tube, wading, swimming, or by crossing one of the international bridges and passing through a legal port of entry into the United States. Migrants and coyotes referred to this stage of the trip as getting past *la primera garita* (the first sentry post), and it was generally the easiest stage to complete. Because well-paying

Portions of an earlier version of this chapter appeared in Spanish in the book *Pobreza y migración internacional* (Agustín Escobar Latapí, editor), which was published in Mexico in 2008 by the Centro de Investigaciones y Estudios Superiores en Antropología Social.

jobs were scarce there, unemployment was high, and the immediate border zone was saturated with *migra* [immigration police], relatively few migrants chose one of the Texas border cities as their final destination.

The more difficult challenge facing migrants and their coyotes was getting past *la segunda garita,* that is, the Border Patrol's immigration checkpoints located on all the major roads headed away from the border, and out of the migra-saturated border zone that extended up to 150 miles into the interior of Texas. This could be accomplished in a variety of ways, most of which involved considerable hardship and/or expense. Once out of the immediate border region, migrants and coyotes were relatively unlikely to be detected by U.S. immigration authorities because of the inability of the U.S. government to saturate the big cities of the Texas interior with immigration enforcement agents and because of the large proportion of residents of these cities who were Mexicans or Mexican Americans.

The categories of coyotaje discussed below and summarized in table 4.1 were not mutually exclusive. Some individuals or organizations might engage in more than one type. Similarly, migrants attempting to enter the United States might avail themselves of more than one of these strategies on the same trip. Each type of coyotaje can be viewed in terms of start-up requirements for coyotes and relative advantages and disadvantages as a strategy for migrants. I make no attempt here to estimate the prevalence of one type of coyotaje relative to others. To my knowledge, no data exist that would permit one to do so with any degree of reliability. Some types, such as commercial transport, were evidently quite common in this region, given the high level of prosecution by U.S. authorities of individuals engaged in this type of coyotaje. Indeed, this was the *only* type of coyotaje that generally attracted much public attention. How frequently the other types occurred in the region is a matter of speculation, though I did not have to look long to find specific cases of any of them. The strategies I describe in these pages do not constitute any real secrets that migrants use to fool U.S. authorities—the authorities have seen them all many times over many decades. My purpose in undertaking this extensive description is to demystify and desensationalize how clandestine border-crossing actually takes place. I believe that when U.S. and Mexican citizens understand the prosaic details of clandestine border-crossing strategies, and how they have been undertaken by so many otherwise law-abiding people over the course of a century, they will be less easily swayed by state-sponsored accounts that emphasize autonomous migration's supposedly new and powerful links to organized crime, drug trafficking, and international terrorist networks. These exaggerated accounts, I believe, have the effect—and perhaps also the intent—of generating fear among residents on both sides of the border, which

Table 4.1. Summary of types of coyotaje strategies practiced on the South Texas–Northeast Mexico border at the beginning of the twenty-first century

Type	Minimum startup requirements for coyotes	Advantages to migrants	Disadvantages to migrants
Short distance (*El brinco nomás*)	• Access to Mexican riverfront • Rowboat, motorized launch, rubber raft, or inner tubes	• Low cost • Useful for migrants who cannot swim • Bypasses inspection by U.S. authorities on international bridges	• Risk of assault/robbery along the river • Highway checkpoints remain ahead • Leaves migrants in border zone, where Border Patrol surveillance is intense • Service providers may also ferry drugs
Professional migration	• Knowledge of river-crossing points • Knowledge of roads/trails on Texas side • Knowledge of where and how to hop freight trains on Texas side or • Collaborator with car/truck for pickup	• Low or no cost with easy repayment terms • Coyote is a known and trusted member of the migrants' community	• Service may not be immediately available • Risk of assault/robbery along river • River-crossing dangerous for migrants who do not swim • Long trek through brush around checkpoints or risks of traveling in railroad freight car • Apprehension by Border Patrol relatively likely
Document dispatch	• Cash to purchase documents on black market and/or • Scanning and graphics equipment to produce counterfeit documents and/or • Contacts within U.S. consulate and/or immigration bureaucracy	• Fast, safe, and physically easy • Attractive to women and those not fit to cross on foot	• Expensive • Failure likely if document is inspected closely • May be difficult to locate providers of this type of coyotaje • Failure can result in prosecution, imprisonment, and a bar against legal admission into the United States in the future

(continued)

Table 4.1. (continued)

Type	Minimum startup requirements for coyotes	Advantages to migrants	Disadvantages to migrants
Migra-coyotaje	• Contacts inside U.S. consulates and/or • Contacts inside U.S. immigration enforcement bureaucracy	• Fast, physically easy, and safe • High rate of success	• Expensive • May be difficult to locate providers of this type of coyotaje
Gate-crashing	• Motor vehicle • Licensed driver with valid immigration documents	• Fast and physically easy • Less expensive than document rental or migra-coyotaje • Little risk of prosecution under most circumstances	• Life may be endangered if traveling in trunk or cargo compartment of vehicle • Intensified inspection of vehicles and documents at checkpoints, including use of dogs, has increased the odds of apprehension
For-profit charity	• Food and water • Shelter • Telephone • Motor vehicle	• Low cost • Items and/or services offered are urgently needed	• River crossing and trek around checkpoints must be undertaken on one's own, with exposure to dangers • Encounters with providers of charity may be haphazard
Friendship, not coyotaje	• Access to a vehicle	• Low cost • Drivers are known and trusted by migrants	• River-crossing and trek around checkpoints must be undertaken on one's own, with concomitant exposure to dangers • Not always available when needed
Commercial transport	• *Personnel:* Recruiters, safe house operators, guides, drivers • *Equipment:* Telephones, motor vehicles • *Real estate:* Access to river-crossing points, safe houses, and/or hotel rooms	• Readily available when needed • Relatively high success rate • Partial/complete COD arrangements often available	• Expensive • Exposure to dangers inherent in river crossing, treks through brush, transport in overloaded vehicles in poor condition • Coyotes may not be directly known or trusted

can then be used by the authorities to justify ever-larger police and military budgets and infringement of basic civil liberties, all in the name of guarding against a phenomenon that does not in itself constitute a threat to the health and well-being of the public at large.

Short-Distance Coyotaje

Individuals residing on or near the Mexican bank of the Río Bravo/Rio Grande could earn a living by crossing people to the U.S. bank in a boat or using inner tubes. Such individuals, known as *lancheros* (boatmen, from the Mexican word *lancha,* meaning "launch") or pateros, the operators of shallow-draught boats known as *patos* or "ducks," typically dedicated themselves exclusively to the *brinco* ("hop") across the river. They might sell their services to individual migrants or other coyotes who were headed to one of the Texas border towns or farther into the Texas interior. They might also haul narcotics across the river for drug traffickers, though not necessarily at the same time as they were ferrying migrants (see Richardson and Resendiz 2006, 151). Leonardo, a man from Ejido San Francisco (a pseudonym)[2] near Dolores Hidalgo, Guanajuato, told me how migrants from his town relied on pateros in the state of Coahuila to get across the Río Bravo before trekking through the brush on the Texas side to get around the *segunda garita.* He had crossed into Texas with the help of pateros on three occasions, most recently in 2003:

LEONARDO: It's pretty closely watched [on the Texas side], but pateros take us across, lancheros take us across. We don't wade across anymore. It's more modern now. We pay a lanchero.

SPENER: Do they take you across in boats or on inner tubes?

LEONARDO: Boats with oars, and we pay them 300 pesos [about $30].

SPENER: And you haven't had any problems there with the pateros?

LEONARDO: No.

SPENER: Because sometimes they can have a pretty bad reputation.

LEONARDO: Right, there are some bad ones. I know of some who have bad reputations. And my friends have said that a lot of them will take your money and then not take you across. Or you have other problems with them—they're smoking marijuana or they get drunk and can dump you into the river. There are pateros like that.

SPENER: Are some of them also in cahoots with the drug traffickers?

LEONARDO: Yes, there are some who take drugs across, but I've never seen that myself.

Professional Migration

As discussed in chapter 2 with regard to the men from La Carmela, San Luis Potosí, less-experienced migrants from sending communities in the Mexican interior often depended on more-experienced migrants to lead them across the border. Many times, these migrant-guides charged no money for the service they provided, but rather offered it altruistically or in exchange for unspecified favors to be given in return at some future date. Other times, the migrants serving as guides invited fellow townspeople to make the crossing with them for the security that traveling with others provided them. In some cases, the experienced migrant would ask those whom he guided to cover his expenses for the trip (i.e., food, lodging, and bus fare). Under these circumstances, migrants and their guides did not regard their relationship as involving coyotaje at all, since no one thought of the coyote as being "hired" in the normal sense of the word. As Álvaro, one of the La Carmela migrants told me, "They're migrants, too. They bring people *con el fin de venir acompañados* [mainly to be accompanied]. So they don't have to come alone and to have some company. They may charge people something for bringing them, but not much."[3]

Some experienced migrants from sending communities in the Mexican interior worked intermittently for cash as border-crossing guides. When work was scarce or when they needed money, they led small groups of migrants from their own or neighboring towns or *ranchos* across the border into Texas, accompanying the group along the entire route. Modes of transportation once the group crossed the river varied, but typically they included walking long distances through the brush around highway checkpoints or hopping a freight train bound for San Antonio or Houston. The guide might have occasional collaborators at the border (a reliable patero, for example) or, more likely, friends who would pick the group up in a car at a prearranged meeting point beyond the highway immigration checkpoints and drive them to their destination city in Texas. The amount charged by these coyotes varied considerably, but it was less than full-time commercial coyotes would charge. The clients, who were usually part of the coyote's personal social network, did not typically pay the coyote any money until they arrived at their destination, but were asked to cover their own and the coyote's expenses en route. On arrival, the migrants might pay the coyote his fee immediately, with loans from friends and relatives, or over time after they began working. The coyote, for his part, might stay in the group's destination to work for some period of time or might return to the sending community after a brief visit.

A man I interviewed who lived in the McAllen area and hailed from the town of La Cancha (a pseudonym), Nuevo León, called such professional migrants *coyotes rascuaches* ("bad quality" coyotes) because they were cheap and offered their clients a correspondingly "no frills" service that typically involved walking long distances after crossing the border and hopping freight trains to travel farther into the Texas interior. I met one of these *coyotes rascuaches* when I visited La Cancha in 2002. Joaquín was thirty-four and was married with three young children. He lived with his wife and children at his parents' house and worked in the neighboring fields. He had only finished the sixth grade and had gone to work as a farm laborer after quitting school. Joaquín had traveled to work in construction in Houston on several occasions with a friend of his, who was also a coyote and who had taught him the ropes of taking people across the border.

Joaquín told me about his last trip to the United States, made in January 2002. He and his friend had taken six young men from Veracruz state to Houston. The *veracruzanos* had been working harvesting chiles in the fields near La Cancha.[4] Joaquín and his partner made sure that the six men had enough money among them to pay for everyone's transportation to the border, plus food and other incidental expenses along the way. The two coyotes would charge the men their $1,300 fee once they made it to Houston. "That's cheap," Joaquín said. "Other people are charging as much as $2,500....And then, once we're there, they start working and then they pay us maybe $100 a week, whatever they can manage, so they can still send some money home to their families back here, too."

The group took the bus to Piedras Negras on a Tuesday morning. Then from Piedras, they took a cab to a little town called Torrecita (a pseudonym). According to Joaquín, Torrecita was "out in the middle of nowhere" and the Texas side across the river was barely patrolled by la migra. They waded across the river and spent several days hiking past the checkpoints, going two whole days without eating. Finally, they made it to the town of La Pryor, near Uvalde, where they found a store and bought some food to eat. From there, they took a bus to Austin and got there late on a Sunday evening, They spent the night in the apartment of some friends in Austin and took another bus to Houston on Monday. On Tuesday, Joaquin went back to work in construction with the same friends from La Cancha who always had work for him in Houston. He had just returned from this sojourn in Houston the month before I interviewed him. He planned to take another group across in a few months.

It is not clear what proportion of migrants continued to cross the South Texas-Northeast Mexico border using the professional migration coyotaje strategy in the face of beefed-up surveillance, but I did come across examples of this type in my fieldwork. It was surely not the case, however, that only larger-scale commercial-transport operations could successfully penetrate

U.S. defenses after the launch of Operation Rio Grande, since data from the Encuesta sobre Migración en la Frontera Norte (presented in chapter 2 of this book) indicated that slightly under half of migrants who made their last crossing along this stretch of the border since the launch of the operation did not use a coyote at all.

Document Dispatch

Some coyotes specialized in the selling or renting of U.S. border-crossing documents, including passports, resident cards, and plastic-embossed laser visas (the new version of the border-crossing card, also known formerly as the *pasaporte local* or *mica*). These documents were not necessarily, or even usually, forgeries. Rather, coyotes attempted to match, as closely as possible, photographs and written descriptions of a document's true owner with the physical appearance of their customer. The customer, in turn, memorized the name, date of birth, and other relevant information contained in the document in case she was questioned by U.S. immigration officials. The coyotes would pick a time of day when the number of people crossing the international bridge would be at a peak in hopes that immigration inspectors would not examine the document or question the person too thoroughly. The coyote would follow as she crossed the bridge and meet her on the other side if she got through. If the customer required no further help from the coyote, she would return the document with the fee to the coyote immediately after crossing the bridge. If she desired to travel farther into the Texas interior, the coyote would accompany her, either in a car or on a public bus, through the immigration checkpoint on the highway headed away from the border. Once through the checkpoint, the migrant would pay her fee and return the document, which would then be rented again to another customer.

A variation was when the migrant crossed the river away from an official port of entry and used the rented document only to get through the *segunda garita* (highway checkpoint), where documents and migrants were generally inspected less closely than on the international bridges. Although new-generation crossing documents contained biometric and other personal data about their legal bearers, I observed that agents at ports of entry and highway checkpoints in the region only selectively scanned documents to precisely match their embedded data with the characteristics of the actual persons attempting to enter the United States using them (see also Lipton 2005).[5]

Another variant of the document-dispatch strategy that I encountered in my fieldwork involved migrants purchasing Mexican documents that they would need to present to U.S. consular officials to demonstrate they qualified for a nonimmigrant visa that they could use to enter the United States. The advantage of this strategy was that they would receive a valid U.S. visa that had been issued to them, rather than to someone who looked like them (see also Hernández-León 2008, 159).

Roberto, a forty-six-year-old man from a town outside Monterrey, Nuevo León, had made his last border-crossing using the document-dispatch strategy a few months before I interviewed him in the spring of 2001. In preparation for making his crossing, he interviewed five different *coyotillos* (little coyotes) around his *rancho,* asking them what services they provided, how much they charged, and who could recommend them. The fifth person he interviewed was an older woman who had previously transported several of his wife's family members. She came especially highly recommended but was more expensive than the others. He decided to go with her group of coyotes and paid her $800 up front, with another $800 to be paid on arrival in Houston. He traveled by bus to Reynosa, Tamaulipas. From the bus station he was instructed to go to one of the city's many inexpensive hotels and ask for a certain person. He found this person, who gave him a room to share for the night with another migrant whom he did not know. Early in the morning, they were awakened by a knock at the door and were asked if they were heading to Houston. A man entered with a box full of *micas* that he spread out on a bed. Together, they picked out one that looked like him. The man instructed him to memorize the name on the document and other personal data it contained. Then another member of the coyote's team rehearsed with him how he should converse with the U.S. immigration inspector on the bridge, what questions he would likely be asked, and how to answer them appropriately. They then rehearsed the same types of things for going through the highway checkpoint leading north out of the Valley. One of the coyotes who had papers walked across the international bridge with Roberto and nine other migrants and took them to the bus station in Hidalgo, Texas. From there they took the bus to Houston and went to a safe house where they paid the remaining $800 they owed the coyotes. Two migrants were detained by an inspector on the bridge, had their documents confiscated, and were returned to Reynosa. Another two were taken off the bus by a Border Patrol agent at the checkpoint in Falfurrias. Those that were caught would return to the hotel in Reynosa and keep trying until they succeeded in getting across.

Roberto felt no fear crossing the border with someone else's documents. He could keep very cool when he needed to and was able to lie without showing any nervousness. Moreover, he felt fortunate not to have to cross the river and then hike through the brush country as many of his Mexican co-workers in Houston had been obliged to do. Most important, he never felt like he was placed in any danger while making the trip from his *rancho* to Houston. Roberto had never crossed the border with coyotes before. He calculated that the señora he interviewed back home must have had at least twenty accomplices in this operation.

Despite its greater expense, the document-dispatch method of crossing was attractive to migrants who could afford it because of the lack of physical effort it entailed and its relative speed and safety. Aside from the cost, this method's chief disadvantage was that, if caught, the migrant could be charged not only with misdemeanor illegal entry of the United States, but also with felonious impersonation of a U.S. citizen or legal migrant, which, since passage of the Immigration Reform and Immigrant Responsibility Act of 1996, normally resulted in the imposition of a bar against that person's legal admission to the United States in the future. This bar was extremely difficult to overcome in the case of claiming to be a U.S. legal permanent resident and was nearly impossible to get waived in the case of making a fraudulent claim of U.S. citizenship. For this reason, the Mexican government warned potential migrants against attempting to enter the United States using someone else's legal documents (Secretaría de Relaciones Exteriores 2005a). On the other hand, under present immigration law, most Mexican migrants from working-class and peasant backgrounds who had no immediate U.S. citizen relatives had little real chance of ever migrating legally to the United States whether they had previously violated U.S. immigration statutes or not.

Migra-Coyotaje

Ever since entry restrictions were placed on Mexican nationals at the U.S. border in the early twentieth century, some members of the U.S. immigration police have helped Mexicans evade such restrictions in exchange for a fee, whether paid directly by Mexican migrants themselves or by an intermediary coyote. I call this type *migra-coyotaje*. Available indicators suggest it was fairly common, occurred in a variety of places, and took multiple forms, which I outline below.

On the International Bridges

A well-known secret hit the front pages of the newspapers in South Texas and Tamaulipas in May 2001: in return for a payment of $300–$500, several INS inspectors on the international bridge between Matamoros and Brownsville had been waving cars through the port of entry without inspecting passengers' documents (Benavidez 2001; Burnett 2001; Garrido 2001; Méndez Martínez 2001; Negrete Lares 2001). From the Mexican migrant's point of view, you could not find a better patero than these INS inspectors and their accomplices, who drove migrants across the bridge from Matamoros to Brownsville. It was quick, safe, nearly certain to succeed, and still affordable compared to the rates migrants had to pay to make a hazardous river crossing at night.

Many middle- and upper-class Brownsville women had used the *migra-pateros* (the term coined by the press in Matamoros) to bring Mexican women across the border to work in their households as domestic servants. Some were especially proud to be able to bring their *chicas* (girls) across the bridge this way since it was much more humane than having them cross the river and hike through the brush, exposing themselves not only to the geographical hazards of crossing, but also to the danger of assault and rape on the riverbanks.

The Brownsville case did not appear to have been an isolated incident: migrants and their family members whom I interviewed in a town in Nuevo León insisted that there were coyotes near where they lived who also took people to the United States "cruzando por el puente" [crossing over the bridge], that is, who colluded with immigration agents to take their clients into the United States through legal ports of entry. Other instances elsewhere in the region were reported in the press and by other researchers (Associated Press 2004; Richardson and Resendiz 2006, 150).

In the U.S. Consulates in Mexico

Coyotes also operated in the U.S. consulates in Mexico. In January and February 2003, the U.S. consulate in Nuevo Laredo, Tamaulipas, was shut down for several days as the State Department conducted an investigation into whether visas were being sold there (Zarazua 2003a, 2003b, and 2003c). Four consular employees and a fifth collaborator from Nuevo Laredo were subsequently convicted of selling visas to applicants with no questions asked for fees ranging from $800 to $1,500 per visa. The Nuevo Laredo collaborator served as the "broker" who referred applicants to consulate employees and collected the fee, which was then divided among the other four conspirators. In addition, thirty employees of a security firm contracted to the consulate were dismissed. The investigation into this coyotaje scheme was unable to establish how many visas had been sold before the arrests of the conspirators (Zarazua 2003d and 2003e). Visa selling of this kind also took place at the U.S. consulate in Ciudad Juárez, Chihuahua, during this period, leading to the closing of the consulate on several occasions (López 2003a and 2003b). Informants I interviewed in Monterrey,

Nuevo León, in 1999 claimed that they knew coyotes who brokered visas at the consulate there as well.

At the Highway Immigration Checkpoints in South Texas

Border Patrol agents staffing highway immigration checkpoints might also work as coyotes. One migrant I interviewed described how he rode a Greyhound bus out of the Lower Rio Grande Valley with a coyote who sat in the seat behind him. When the bus stopped at the checkpoint and a Border Patrol agent boarded to check passengers' immigration documents, the agent skipped over him and instead asked the coyote behind him for his documents. Apparently, the man guiding him and the Border Patrol agent checking the passengers' documents were collaborators and the agent did not check the documents of passengers indicated to him by his collaborator. Other migrants I interviewed from different parts of northern Mexico insisted that the coyotes operating out of their hometowns always took migrants across the border and around or through the highway checkpoints on a certain night of the week. According to the migrants, the coyotes never seemed to get caught. They believed it was because on the days they crossed a collaborator inside the Border Patrol was assisting them in some way. In February 2006, a Border Patrol agent in the Rio Grande Valley sector was indicted for allowing narcotics and undocumented migrants to pass through the Falfurrias checkpoint in exchange for bribes from coyotes and drug smugglers (Cavazos 2006; El Mañana de Matamoros 2006).

Border Patrol complicity in coyotaje was also alleged in the case of the nineteen migrants who died in the back of a tractor-trailer in Victoria, Texas, in May 2003. The convicted coordinator of the smuggling operation, Karla Chávez, attempted to withdraw her guilty plea before sentencing after a Houston TV producer interviewed a county constable who said he had been informed by a Homeland Security official that Border Patrol agents were waving truckloads of immigrants through the same Sarita checkpoint that the dying migrants had passed through on their way to Houston. This led Ms. Chávez's lawyers to claim that the government was an "un-indicted co-conspirator" in the smuggling case. Her lawyers also based her claim on the testimony of one of the survivors of the tragedy in the back of the truck, who reported that he had been told that the $1,000 he had paid to smugglers before beginning the ill-fated trip was to be used to bribe immigration inspectors at the Sarita checkpoint (Associated Press 2005a). After the constable recanted his statements to the TV producer, and the federal judge presiding in the case heard from several confidential informants brought forward by Chavez's defense attorneys, the judge found no basis for allowing Chávez to withdraw her plea (Blumenthal 2005; Rice 2005). An additional source of information about the claim that agents at the checkpoint had been bought off comes from Univisión reporter Jorge Ramos in his short book about the Victoria tragedy. There, he recounts an initial encounter between the driver of the tractor-trailer rig and the two men who recruited him to haul migrants in his rig. In this encounter, the driver supposedly asked how he would get through the checkpoint and was told by the two men that "the checkpoint was taken care of." When the men talked to the driver about Karla Chávez, they identified her as "the boss lady" and the one who had the contacts that would allow him to pass through the highway immigration checkpoint without problems (Ramos 2005, 23–24). Although Border Patrol involvement in this incident was not proved, the fact that so many Homeland Security officials since 2003 have been charged with colluding with coyotes and drug traffickers borderwide renders the accusation plausible. According to a 2006 *Los Angeles Times* report, "at least 200 public employees have been charged with helping to move narcotics or illegal immigrants across the U.S.-Mexican border since 2004, at least double the illicit activity documented in prior years" (Vartabedian, Serrano, and Marosi 2006; see also Pomfret 2006).

The Off-Duty Lives of Immigration Agents in South Texas

The extant and potential involvement of Border Patrol and other Homeland Security agents in coyotaje in South Texas was quite comprehensible given the ethnic makeup of the region and of the Border Patrol. Nationwide, a little more than half of the agents in 2007 were Hispanic. Although no official figures were published by the Border Patrol for individual sectors, the proportion of agents in South Texas who were Hispanic appeared to be significantly higher. A substantial proportion of Border Patrol agents in South Texas were Mexican Americans who had relatives and long-standing friends who were born in Mexico, and some were themselves Mexican immigrants. In cities like Brownsville and Laredo, many Mexicans and Mexican Americans had family ties immediately across the river and were in touch with relatives there. Anglo agents who dated or married members of Mexican American or Mexican families could similarly develop these sorts of ties. To be clear, I am not suggesting that Mexican American and Mexican immigrant agents were somehow less "loyal" to the United States than Anglo agents, but rather that ethnic ties could serve as a starting point for this type of coyotaje to take place.

Following an implicit "don't ask, don't tell" policy, off-duty Border Patrol agents sometimes attended local social events at the homes of friends and family where undocumented Mexicans were present, either as family members, social acquaintances, or domestic help. Thus, the social milieu in which Border Patrol agents found themselves could be conducive to exploiting the contacts in their personal networks to engage in coyotaje if they were so inclined. Or they might be recruited by family members, friends, or acquaintances. Commenting on the May 2005 sentencing of two Border Patrol agents for allowing drug shipments to pass through the Hebbronville checkpoint in the Laredo sector, a former federal prosecutor who grew up in Brownsville told reporters that federal officials' involvement in coyotaje and drug smuggling was often based on prior relationships: "In so many of these cases, it seems like the law enforcement officer has a prior relationship with the trafficker, or a relationship with someone who introduces them, or they have a girlfriend who introduces them" (Pinkerton 2005).

In early 2001, a field informant named Mike shared an anecdote with me that offered a vivid illustration of the type of off-hours social mixing that could occur in South Texas between immigration police and the people they are tasked with policing:

> In my soccer league here, we have everyone from one Border Patrol agent to coyotes themselves. I know they're coyotes because they're my friends. The Border Patrol agent isn't aware of the situation, and we try to keep it that way. But then I'm sure he knows most of his team is undocumented. It's a different reality down here. It's amazing how close everything is. Especially looking at a Border Patrol or an INS job. For anybody down here with military experience, it's a great job, man. He's sort of guaranteed a Border Patrol position. And all of a sudden…I mean their parents are immigrants, or even some of them are naturalized themselves…they originally came over as immigrants themselves. It creates some interesting dynamics.

Gate-Crashing at the *Segunda Garita*

Even with stepped up scrutiny of vehicles and passengers following the September 11, 2001, terrorist attacks, significant numbers of migrants managed to pass through the immigration checkpoints on the highways leading away from the border, assisted by family members or by professional coyotes. The most common ways for migrants attempting to get through the checkpoints were by hiding in the trunk of a car, under blankets or luggage in the back of a van or station wagon, or sitting among other passengers who were U.S. citizens or legal residents of Mexican origin. José, a migrant from Rancho San Nicolás near Dolores Hidalgo, Guanajuato, used this coyotaje strategy on his last trip to the United States in December 2001. The coyotes were a Mexican American man, his Anglo wife, and their five-year-old son. José was put in touch with these coyotes by some of his family members living in the Dallas area. The coyotes arranged to have a patero take him across the river on an inner tube from Reynosa, Tamaulipas, to Hidalgo, Texas. Once across the river, the patero took him running to the parking lot of a fast food restaurant and into the open door of a minivan. A short while later the Mexican American coyote came out to the van, saw that José had arrived, and then went back into the restaurant for his wife and son.

> He went back in the restaurant and came out with his wife, *la anglosajona* [the Anglo-Saxon woman], and with their little brown son and we took off in the van. When we got to the checkpoint, they tossed their luggage on top of me, like I was just another piece of luggage. When they stopped at the checkpoint, the agent asked how many people they were. The woman was driving and they spoke to her in English. She answered in English that it was just the three of them, her husband, her daughter, and herself. And then he said, "Fine, have a good trip." And once we pulled away from the checkpoint she said, "That's it. We made it."

Sometimes coyotes come up with more ingenious schemes for getting their clients through the highway checkpoints. One migrant I interviewed in a Texas city reported crossing the river with his coyotes who subsequently took him to a motel where he showered, was given a suit and tie to wear, and was then driven through a checkpoint in a late-model luxury sedan, posing with other migrants as businesspeople returning from a meeting on the border. In a case documented in federal court archives in Laredo, a very fat Anglo woman rode on the Greyhound bus at night, fully occupying two seats with her wide girth. Under her seat, face down on the floor, were three Mexican men dressed all in black hoping to remain hidden in the darkness when Border Patrol agents boarded the bus to inspect passengers' documents. Subsequent interrogation of the woman resulted in the apprehension of six more migrants in a Laredo motel room.

Due to the extensive use of drug- and people-sniffing dogs at the checkpoints and the more intense questioning of drivers and passengers, getting through the checkpoints became considerably more difficult after September 11, 2001. We do not know what proportion of those who made the attempt in the post-9/11 period were successful. Nevertheless, it appears that a significant number of people kept trying: more than 45 percent of prosecutions for the "harboring and transporting of illegal aliens" made in 2002 in the federal courthouse in Laredo resulted from arrests made at highway immigration checkpoints.[6]

For-Profit Charity

As described in chapter 1, the majority of people in the small towns and rural ranches of South Texas were of Mexican origin. Migrants had been crossing through this region on foot for decades, whether guided by coyotes, fellow migrants, or on their own. Groups of bedraggled migrants sometimes emerged from the brush after days of walking and knocked on doors of ranch houses or homes at the edge of small towns to seek water, food, shelter, or the use of a telephone. Fellow Mexican residents of these areas might willingly provide this aid, motivated by religious conviction to help the needy, a sense of ethnic loyalty, or memories of their own families' migratory experiences. Certain individuals became known to migrants and coyotes as people who were willing to help them as they passed through the border region. The charity of these individuals, who were often themselves of limited economic means, could evolve over time into an ad-hoc for-profit enterprise. Migrants I interviewed, for example, told of knocking on the doors of rural ranch houses seeking food and water and receiving it. Subsequently, they might ask the resident for a ride farther up the road away from the checkpoints toward San Antonio, Corpus Christi, or Houston. Or the resident might offer a ride. At this point, though, the proposition was no longer strictly charitable, given that the resident was himself economically needy and, moreover, was running a considerable risk of prosecution if he was apprehended by the Border Patrol. Migrants and their "helper" then would negotiate a price to be driven farther into the interior. This fee might be paid by the migrants through loans from friends or relatives in the destination city, out of funds the migrants were carrying with them, or by working for the resident for some period of time.[7]

Don Ignacio

An example of for-profit charity coyotaje, is the case of Don Ignacio, the same elderly Mexican man from rural Coahuila whom I quoted in chapter 3 about his experiences at the bracero contracting center in Monterrey in the 1950s. Don Ignacio eventually settled in San Antonio, where he worked for many years and raised a family. After retiring from his job, he moved out into the country, since he missed the rural life he had enjoyed while growing up in Mexico. Living in an isolated ranch house with his wife, Don Ignacio occasionally had small groups of migrants knock on his door asking for food, water, a place to sleep for the night, or to use a telephone to call friends to ask for a ride, and he willingly helped them out. After all, he had gone through the same hardships several times when he was a young man. During the 1990s, such encounters became more frequent, and eventually he was asked by a coyote from Queré-taro, who had stopped at his house with small groups on several occasions, if he would be willing to drive migrants in his pickup truck on to San Antonio where his partner had a house. Although Don Ignacio was loathe to do this given the risk involved, he had an ailing sister in Mexico whose nursing home care he was paying for and he was in need of cash to help cover these expenses, so he agreed to do it. He was paid $100 per person. Don Ignacio drove on an occasional basis for this coyote for several years, until he was stopped by local police one night in 2000 on the outskirts of San Antonio for driving too slowly with ten migrants hidden under a tarp in the back of his pickup truck. Fortu-nately, the police officer did not discover the migrants and the old man and his wife in the passenger seat were allowed to continue on without being ticketed. After that scare, Don Ignacio told the man from Querétaro that he wouldn't be driving for him anymore. Later, he learned that the man had decided to stop working as a coyote and to stay on permanently to work in construction in Houston. Since then, Ignacio had been approached on several occasions by people asking him to drive migrants to San Antonio, but he had refused. His sister had since died, so he didn't need the cash anymore, and his eyesight was no longer good enough to drive at night. When I asked him how he felt about having collaborated with this coyote for several years, he had this to say:

DON IGNACIO: On the one hand, I felt guilty because I was breaking the law. And my son told me to stop doing it. He said they were going to catch me. So, I don't do it anymore.

SPENER: And how did you feel about it in a moral sense, as opposed to in a legal sense?

DON IGNACIO: Like I was saying, I regard it as a blessing from God, since I had this expense for my sister, and my [retirement] check was so little.

SPENER: It was a blessing because of the money.

DON IGNACIO: Because of the money.

SPENER: But how did you feel in the sense of your relationship with the migrants and with this guide. Did you think you were doing something good? Or was it bad?

DON IGNACIO: I feel good about it, because, look, I had also suffered a lot....I like to be able to help these people because I know what they suf-fer. And they're my *paisanos* [people from the country, region, or town], they're the same as me.

No Need for a Sanctuary Movement for Mexicans in South Texas

An immigrant-rights activist whom I interviewed in the spring of 2001 cor-roborated what migrants told me about receiving help from Mexican immi-grant and Mexican American residents as they passed through South Texas headed toward the U.S. interior. His organization aided undocumented Mexi-cans in the region in a variety of ways. During the 1980s, other religious and human rights activists had participated in the Sanctuary movement, which, on religious grounds, helped Central American refugees enter and remain in the United States despite U.S. immigration authorities' efforts to arrest and deport them (Coutin 1993). These activists had run a shelter for Central Americans near Brownsville, and some had helped spirit refugees away from the heav-ily patrolled border region to places in the U.S. interior where immigration surveillance was less intense (Sedeno 1986). When I asked this man why his organization did not offer the same help to Mexicans in the early 2000s that it had offered to Central Americans in the 1980s, he had this to say:

> For decades you've had poor *mexicano* families over here that were help-ing folks out. Whether they're from Mexico or Central America. I know a number of folks who live along the train lines. You talk about care and aid? People regularly come to their doors asking for food and water, and they set them up. And even connections that they may have to someone who can move them on up the line. I don't know about how much people charge. Al-though I guess I understand how the Sanctuary movement sort of captured everyone's imagination as the new underground railroad, this type of resis-tance has been going on a long time. Ultimately, I think you're really looking at the folks who live in the *colonias* [squatter settlements], who live in the rural areas. They're the ones who have really done the most. And continue to do the most because that's just part of their reality.

Friendship, Not Coyotaje

Members of some Mexican migrant communities who crossed this stretch of the border relied on a hybrid coyotaje strategy to reach their destinations in the U.S. interior. These migrants were familiar with particular places to cross the Río Bravo into Texas, with or without hiring the services of a patero, as well as paths through the Texas brush country that enabled them to skirt immigration checkpoints on the highways leading away from the international boundary. Once they reached a town past the last immigration checkpoint, they called ahead to friends, relatives, or acquaintances to come pick them up in private vehicles and drive them on to their destination in the Texas interior. The migrants did not regard the drivers as coyotes, although they paid them a substantial sum for providing this transportation service, often several hundred dollars per migrant. These drivers did not offer to assist just anyone who requested their service, reserving it instead only for people with whom they were personally acquainted in some way. I label this strategy "friendship, not coyotaje" because migrants I interviewed regarded these drivers as just friends, not coyotes, while nevertheless believing they deserved to be paid for the risks they faced when transporting their *paisanos* in this manner. These risks were substantial. They included arrest, imprisonment, confiscation of their vehicles, lost income to their dependents, and deportation to Mexico with a bar on legal admission in the future. This strategy was described in chapter 2 with regard to the experiences of migrants from La Carmela in the altiplano region of the state of San Luis Potosí. One of these men, Pancho, had the following to say about the "friendship, not coyotaje" strategy:

SPENER: This friend, does he make his living picking up people in Encinal? In other words, are these guys just friends or are they really like a kind of coyote?

PANCHO: They're just friends, nothing more.

SPENER: They are people who are working up there [in Texas]?

PANCHO: Right.

SPENER: Then why does this amigo charge you so much? [$400 per person in this case.]

PANCHO: Because of the car, because in any event they're really taking a big risk, too.

SPENER: Of being accused of being coyotes.

PANCHO: Right. And I think it's all right because of the risks they're taking.

SPENER: And how many of you did he pick up? Did you say it was seven?

PANCHO: Right. No wait, there were nine of us.

SPENER: So that's over $3,000 that he's making.

PANCHO: Right, but I think that's OK, you see, because there were so many of us.

SPENER: So it seemed fair to you.

PANCHO: Yeah, it was fine. It was fine with me, right, because he was risking a lot to come get us.

Migrants I interviewed in northwest Guanajuato state also discussed pursuing this strategy. One of its chief advantages was that it was considerably cheaper than hiring a full-service commercial coyote. A variation on this type of cost-saving crossing strategy was for migrants to travel with a paid "professional" coyote either just across the river or to a point just beyond the highway check-points, where friends or family members would come to pick them up. Other migrants I interviewed reported that on the outskirts of certain South Texas towns, there were places where migrants hiking out of the brush knew they would find men willing to drive them farther into the interior for a fee negoti-ated on the spot. Leonardo, the man from Ejido San Francisco, Guanajuato, quoted above with regard to hiring lancheros, said these men *were* regarded as coyotes by him and his townspeople:

SPENER: But how did you connect with these coyotes if you were here [in Guanajuato]?

LEONARDO: My friends told me the place we needed to go. It's called Hixon [a pseudonym], in that area. We walk to there and that's where we would get us a coyote.

SPENER: So all they did was pick you up in pickup trucks and drive you from there?

LEONARDO: Right.

SPENER: And did you consider them to be coyotes or were they, like, friends?

LEONARDO: No, they were coyotes, they weren't friends.

SPENER: So you didn't know them personally.

LEONARDO: Right....In Hixon, there are people there who will give us rides. You get to the edge of town there and the coyotes approach you and they say, "I'll take you for so much."

Leonardo went on to say that the last time he had crossed in 2003 he had paid one of these coyotes $800 on arriving in Dallas, with no money up front. He told me this was a much cheaper way to travel than hiring a coyote in Guana-juato or at the border. Here we see an example of the ambiguities implicit in the process of coyotaje. Migrants from La Carmela, San Luis Potosí, and Ejido San Francisco, Guanajuato, pursued very similar border-crossing strategies. Migrants from both places crossed the border on their own and then hired drivers to pick them up to transport them to their destinations in the Texas interior, to whom they paid considerable sums on arrival. The migrants from La Carmela did not regard these drivers as coyotes because they were known members of their communities, and hence were amigos, even though they were paid well for their services. Migrants from Ejido San Francisco, on the other hand, considered these drivers to be coyotes, since they did not know them in any other way than paying them for rides away from the border.

Commercial Transport

The coyotes most often targeted for prosecution by the authorities and re-ported about in the press during this period were those organized networks of individuals who dedicated themselves to facilitating the entry of migrants into U.S. territory on an ongoing, for-profit basis. Unlike the document-dispatch strategy discussed above, the main service provided by these coyotes was trans-portation, including ancillary food and lodging, as needed or available. Their modes of operation and organizational forms varied, as did the geographical locations of their centers of coordination.

The most common transportation route/strategy taken by commercial transporters was as follows: A group of migrants was either received or as-sembled in a Mexican border town. The group was then taken some distance up or downstream from the town, outside the area on the U.S. side that was most saturated with Border Patrol agents, vehicles, and remote sensing equip-ment.[8] The river was crossed either by wading, swimming, using inner tubes, or contracting with a lanchero. Once across the river on the Texas side, mi-grants might walk or be driven to a safe house in the closest Texas border town, where they would rest and wait to travel away from the border. In other cases, migrants might immediately begin their journey into the interior, either by walking through the brush led by a guide or by being driven to a point closer to the highway immigration checkpoint they must get around. In either case, at some point before reaching the highway checkpoint, migrants would have to trek through the brush with a guide to bypass the highway immigration check-points. Once around the checkpoint, migrants would be picked up by a car, van, or pickup truck and driven to a city in Texas outside the border region. Once in that city, they would either be delivered to friends or relatives who would pay the coyote's fee or taken to a safe house where they would contact the friends and relatives who had agreed to pay for their trip.

As patrolling of the Texas border region intensified, the average distance and time spent walking by migrants seemed to increase, so that what ten years earlier might have been a two-or-three-hour hike around the checkpoint might last two or three days, or even more, if bad weather were encountered along the way, the guide got lost, or the group had to deviate from its intended route after finding their way blocked by the Border Patrol. Although they var-ied considerably depending on the coyotes contracted, the conditions migrants faced at every step of their journey were likely to be bad. Safe houses were often crowded, dirty, and poorly heated or cooled. Transport vehicles were frequently old, badly maintained, and overloaded. Moreover, migrants might have to pile up one on top of the other in the back of a van or pickup truck and ride that way for several hours to avoid being seen by roving Border Patrol agents on the highway. In the early 2000s, there were several multiple-death accidents involving vehicles transporting migrants through South Texas in this way (Brezosky 2006; Schiller and Bogan 2004). Consistent with the experiences of the men from La Carmela, most migrants agreed, nonetheless, that the worst part of the journey was the physically strenuous trek through the brush, which was full of thorns and snakes, often very hot or very cold, and could involve going hungry and thirsty for hours or even days.

Types of Transportation Used

The increasing rigor of the trek through the brush increased the attractiveness of tractor-trailer rigs as a means of transporting migrants through, rather than around, the highway immigration checkpoints.[9] Migrants who knew of the suffering experienced on the treks through the South Texas brush country might find the prospect of spending three or four hours in a truck much more attractive than walking through the brush for three or four days, even if they had to pay considerably more for this type of service and pay a substantial portion of it up front. Coyotaje organizations that moved migrants in tractor-trailers transported migrants across the river in the same way that organizations that walked them around the checkpoints did. Unlike the "trekking" coyotes, the "trucking" coyotes usually needed to house migrants temporarily in a motel or safe house in the Texas border town before transporting them away from the border. This was because they were usually putting together larger groups of migrants (often twenty-five or more) and because a tractor-trailer would not always be immediately available to transport the group.

The main challenge facing this type of coyote organization was finding a trucker who was willing to use his rig to haul migrants. Truckers might be strangers recruited by the coyotes at truck stops near the border-crossing or they might be friends, family members, or acquaintances who drove a truck for a living, whether it belonged to them or the company they worked for. Although inspection of vehicles and interrogation of drivers at the highway immigration checkpoints intensified considerably after 2001, many tractor-trailer rigs continued to pass through without having their cargos examined. Most, if not all, checkpoints by this time were staffed by agents with dogs trained to alert agents if they smelled the odors of humans, but these dogs did not detect all humans hidden in tractor-trailer rigs. In addition, some coyotes had their clients bathe and change into new clothes before boarding a truck in an effort to reduce odors. In the first years of the new century, gamma ray machines became available to view truck cargo at checkpoints on a rotating basis, but they were not always used, especially at times of heavy traffic when there was no special reason for agents to suspect a trucker of hauling human cargo.

In the aftermath of the tragic deaths of nineteen migrants in a sealed tractor-trailer in 2003, coyotes continued transporting migrants in tractor-trailer rigs, but more commonly in the sleeping compartment of the cab than in the trailer.[10] Fewer migrants (a dozen or fewer at a time) might be transported in this manner, but they seemed no more likely to be detected than if they were in the trailer, and they were considerably less likely to face injury or death. Finally, the apprehensions of migrants and the arrest of the driver at the checkpoint were not likely to put the coyote organization out of business: the driver was often a hireling who might not even know the other coyotes, much less where they could be found.[11] The migrants might not have met more than one or two of the other members of the organization and, moreover, might be expecting to make another attempt with the same organization once they were returned to Mexico, thus giving them an incentive not to cooperate with authorities seeking to dismantle the coyotaje enterprise.

Less commonly, commercial-transport coyotes might move their customers by boat or by private plane. U.S. immigration enforcement authorities told me, and press reports have documented, that coyotes occasionally transported migrants by "shark boat" up the Texas coast along Padre Island, either on the Gulf side or the lee side of the island in the Laguna Madre.[12] Depending on where migrants were taken ashore, they might also have to negotiate crossing the Mansfield Channel in inner tubes,[13] as they walked north on the beach to where coyotes arranged to pick them up in vehicles (Associated Press 1998; Schiller 1996a). In 2006, several men were convicted of transporting migrants from Port Isabel, at the south end of Padre Island, to Corpus Christi aboard a luxury yacht owned by a charter boat company (Houston Chronicle 2006). Commercial-transport operations also occasionally rented private planes to transport migrants from Texas border towns to points in the interior such as Austin, San Antonio, or Houston. One migrant I interviewed in San Luis Potosí state described being taken to Houston in 2002 in an *avioneta* (small propeller plane) after his coyotes failed at several attempts to get through Border Patrol defenses trekking through the brush (cost: $2,200). Immigration enforcement authorities I interviewed also recalled a number of cases in which small planes were used to transport migrants.

And, of course, some coyotes continued to transport their clients by rail, as they had done since early in the twentieth century. At the end of the century, this involved hopping freight trains near the border and placing migrants in rail cars. A Border Patrol agent I interviewed in the late 1990s in the Laredo sector told me about the *talacho* (pickax) cases he had seen. In these cases, migrants were loaded into rail cars by their coyotes, who closed and latched the door behind them in order to avoid detection by the authorities. The migrants, sometimes with one of the coyotes inside with them, would be given a *talacho* to use to poke a hole in the top of the freight car in order to exit the train after it passed the *segunda garita*. Freight car travel was quite hazardous, of course, due both to the risk of falling under the train while hopping on or off it and of suffocating inside a sealed car. The dangers of this mode of transport were made tragically evident in 2002, when the skeletal remains of eleven migrants were found in a locked rail car in Denison, Iowa, several months after they had been loaded into it near Matamoros by their coyotes (Associated Press 2002b; Fountain and Yardley 2002).

Organizational Structure

Organizations engaged in commercial-transport strategies could vary considerably in size and complexity, as well as in the frequency of trips they offered and the number of clients they transported. It was a business with very few barriers to entry, and some operations had fewer than a half-dozen members. Others involved considerably more people, with many people at each stage of the journey—recruiters in Mexico; people who provided lodging in the Mexican border town and who contacted migrants' friends or relatives in the United States to collect part of their fee up front via wire transfer or to receive assurances that all the fee would be paid at the end of the journey; pateros dedicated to the *brinco* (hop) across the river; safe house operators in the South Texas border zone; cooks to bring migrants food while they waited in safe houses; guides to lead migrants through the brush; drivers to pick migrants up when they emerged from the brush after bypassing the checkpoints; and operators of a safe house in a Texas interior city who housed migrants, contacted their friends or relatives, and collected any remaining fees they owed. Here I should note that it did not appear to be the case that all or perhaps even most commercial-transport operations were vertically integrated organizations with a top-down command-and-control structure. Rather, they frequently seemed to consist of a more loosely networked set of independent contractors, each of whom handed off migrants to the next "station" on the way to their final destination.[14] Money might be exchanged between groups of coyotes when migrants were handed off in this manner, leading some immigration officials to talk of "loads" of migrants being "sold" from one group of "traffickers" to another. The networked structure of commercial-transport coyotaje made it exceptionally difficult for law enforcement authorities to disrupt it by arresting members of one or more links along the transport chain (see also Miró 2003, 21).

In this regard, we can take as a case in point the arrest, prosecution, and imprisonment of members of the Contreras family of Raymondville, Texas (Schiller 1999b, 1999c, and 1999d). In January 1997, the Border Patrol staged a raid on the family's store and small motel in which 290 migrants were seized (Schiller 1997). Although their prosecution was portrayed in the press as the breaking up of a major "smuggling ring" in the region, the Contreras family neither commanded nor was commanded by the many different transporters who brought their migrant customers to stay with them before continuing north. Similarly, Karla Chávez, the Honduran woman in Harlingen, Texas, who coordinated the ill-fated tractor-trailer trip that resulted in the horrifying deaths in Victoria, Texas, seemed to have done little more than use her telephone to coordinate the arrangements among her network of contacts who could move migrants north. Based on published accounts of the movements of the migrants and coyotes leading up to the tragedy (Ramos 2005; Zernike and Thompson 2003), it seems that it would be a mistake to characterize the twenty-six-year-old former employee of a Levi-Strauss factory in Harlingen as the "capo" of some sort of mafia of traffickers.

In this same vein, migrants I interviewed described arriving at safe houses in South Texas where the residents were surprised by their arrival because their coyotes (to migrants, the safe house operators were not coyotes per se) had not informed them they would be coming and there were other clients already staying there. They also described crossing the Río Bravo with pateros or lancheros who seemed to be providing services to and being paid by a number of different coyotes, each leading a different group of migrants. Assistant U.S. Attorneys I interviewed in 2001 said that in their experience as prosecutors, "smuggling *organization*" was "probably too grand a term" and that the "smuggling business" consisted of a "whole series of independent contractors." Indeed, the Immigration and Naturalization Service's Operation Night Rider in that same year resulted in the arrest of a number of different "independent contractors" after a sting operation that involved the INS setting up its own "safe house" in Houston that its undercover agents offered for use to a number of different coyotes.

As another example, a Mexican consular official I interviewed in Texas believed that some of the cases in which he had intervened for humanitarian reasons involved migrants in safe houses being extorted for more money because of disputes over intranetwork payments between independent coyotes at different points along the transportation chain:

In most cases it's a problem of the prices they've arranged. One of the parties has an expectation that they were going to be paid a different price than the one they're being offered.... It's always, "You owe me $1,000 because that's the amount we agreed on and you only gave me so much. And now the person here who was going to pay me says he doesn't have the money and that he's already sent it to someone else.

This consular official's account is supported by Jorge Ramos's (2005, 27–41) characterization of the relations among individual coyotes in the Victoria tragedy. Karla Chávez, the coordinator of the trip, referred to the individual coyotes she transacted with as the "owners" of the people she arranged to transport in the fatal tractor-trailer (Ramos 2005, 41).

Álvaro, the man from La Carmela quoted previously, described the chain structure of the commercial-transport coyotes who brought him to Texas in a tractor-trailer rig in 2004. He had contracted the coyote who coordinated the trip in another small settlement near La Carmela:

> ÁLVARO: The organization consists of various people, you know? So you get handed off from one person to another.…It's an association, right? So [the first coyote] says [to the next coyote], "You know what, I want you to take these people across the river for me." These people take us across. They walk us from the hotel on the Mexican side down to the river. Then, they get paid for us. Then the others who are at the river, they collect money for us, too. Then we get taken to a house [on the Texas side], and they get paid for us, too. And so the money gets divvied up [*se va distribuyendo el dinero*].
>
> SPENER: But you don't pay until you arrive [in the destination city in Texas].
>
> ÁLVARO: No, no, no, I don't pay until I get here [the destination city in Texas].
>
> SPENER: They're paying each other off, among themselves.
>
> ÁLVARO: Right, each one's paying the other. So, if I can't manage to pay for some reason, there's no money and they lose that money. That's the risk they're taking.

Álvaro went on to explain that he didn't believe that there was any real top-down command-and-control structure to this operation, which involved multiple collaborators at multiple points along the way, all of whom were Mexican nationals, including the truck driver:

> SPENER: Is it your impression that this man from the *rancho* near yours is really the one who heads up this group? Or are they simply people who collaborate with one another?

ÁLVARO: These are people who just collaborate with one another.

SPENER: So, there's no *jefe* [boss]?

ÁLVARO: No, there's no boss in this business, they're all in it together [*son todos entre todos*]. It's like a group. They all support one another. Do you know what I mean? When you work as a group, you know, we all collaborate equally. That's how he works. He just makes a little more than the others because he's the one who brings them together, who brings [the customers] to them. And that's it.

The assessment of a Mexican human rights activist working in a Tamaulipas border city was similar to Álvaro's. She told me in 2001 that even in that city, coyotes were not organized in a hierarchical manner with a top-down command-and-control structure. Instead, they were organized as a network without any single leader, and included everyone from taxi drivers to hotel owners, all "under the inspection of the law enforcement authorities," who tolerated their activities in return for bribes. She said, "It's like a network of people with relationships among them, not so much a single leader." Finally, an FBI agent I interviewed in 2004, who had investigated both drug-trafficking and coyotaje organizations, contrasted the top-down control exercised by drug cartels with the looser forms of association that characterized networks of coyotes:

AGENT: In the alien-smuggling business, they are kind of independent operators that know they have to associate with one another to continue the trade.

SPENER: So you're not going to find really a kingpin where all the money is flowing towards?

AGENT: Not necessarily. Not on this side of the border. Across the border, there definitely are kingpins that kind of coordinate movement. But that's basically getting the process started, and from that point on they lose some of their control.

Locating Commercial-Transport Coyotaje Enterprises

Some commercial-transport organizations were based in the Mexican border cities. These coyotes were the ones whose recruiters approached aspiring undocumented migrants in bus stations and plazas near the international bridges to offer to cross them into the United States. Such encounters were among the most socially disembedded transactions that occurred along the migrant trail, since neither party to the transaction knew anything about the other. Migrants who arrived at the border and contracted coyotes who were unknown to them or other members of their community truly did not know what they were getting themselves into and were vulnerable to all sorts of abuses, especially if they agreed to pay the coyotes all or part of their fee before undertaking their crossing. Because these coyotes actively recruited migrants in public spaces, they might have to pay off local law enforcement authorities who were in cahoots with other organized crime groups, in order to operate freely. When they successfully transported migrants to their destinations in the U.S. interior without overtly abusing them or subjecting them to too much danger or discomfort, and without being apprehended repeatedly by the Border Patrol, they might also receive clients arriving from the Mexican interior who had been recommended to them by relatives and friends who had crossed with them. Paco, a thirty-four-year-old coyote who transported migrants from Matamoros to Houston with a small group of collaborators in the late 1990s and early 2000s, explained his recruitment practices as follows:

> PACO: You "buy" people in Matamoros. The people that are coming here [to the United States]. Normally a person arrives at the bus station in Matamoros where there are people called *enganchadores* [recruiters]. These are the ones who contact people and ask them if they want to go to Houston. Then they come and offer [the migrants] to us. Back then [1995–96], they were worth $20 a head....And that's how we got started, little by little. On a normal day, we'd bring five or six people across. Then we began to make some money, and after a while we were bringing fifteen people across in a pickup truck. And we charged an average of $600 per person, to take them here [Houston]....By then, most of the people we brought were relatives of people we'd already brought, what we used to call *recomendados* [referrals]. By then we didn't "buy" too many people in Matamoros.
>
> SPENER: In the bus station. You mean you didn't work the bus station anymore.
>
> PACO: No, only occasionally to round out a group. Two or three persons. But the majority we'd get with a phone call: "They're in such and such a hotel, go pick them up."

Paco also described how he had to pay off a local "mafia" that worked in concert with law enforcement authorities in order to be able to recruit from the bus terminal. He did not have to start making these payoffs until he had already been working as a coyote for over two years. Two of the recruiters who had been "selling" him migrants from the bus station were arrested and told the police for whom they were recruiting customers. The local police then arrested him and confiscated two of his vehicles. A police agent later contacted him and said he could resume recruiting from the bus station if he could pay a third party $1,000 per month in protection money. Paco agreed to this and was never bothered by the police again. He quit working as a coyote several years later when the monthly payoff rose to $3,000.

In cases where commercial-transport operations consisted of a chain of independent contractors engaged in different activities at different points along a migratory circuit extending from interior migrant-sending communities in Mexico to interior migrant-receiving communities in the United States, it could be difficult to establish just where such operations were "based."[15] Rather than being based in any one geographic point at the border or elsewhere, these coyote enterprises inhabited a binational corridor or circuit that spanned the border and formed part of the social and material infrastructure that permitted the migrant stream to flow north. Thus, migrants living in the United States might organize the trip of a relative in Mexico by contacting a coyote near where they lived in the United States, who, in turn, was connected to coyotes at the border and perhaps also to coyotes in or near where the relative lived in Mexico.

Conversely, the Mexican relative might initiate the trip by contacting coyotes operating in his area in Mexico. These coyotes might work merely as recruiters for commercial transporters based at the border, delivering migrants to them for a "finder's fee," or they might organize all aspects of the trip themselves, working through their contacts at the border through to the destination city in Texas. Migrants from Guanajuato state whom I interviewed in Texas described journeys in which the coyotes they contacted near their hometowns reserved blocks of seats on buses for as many as thirty or forty people to transport migrants from clustered sending communities in the state to the border.[16] Once at the border, they broke the bigger group into smaller bunches and paid local pateros to take them across the river into Texas. From there, the coyotes who had accompanied them to the border led them walking around the highway checkpoints. Once past the checkpoint, the coyotes called ahead to Houston to collaborators, also *guanajuatenses,* who came to pick the migrants up in several cars. On arrival in Houston, friends or relatives came to pay the fee ($1,000 in 2003) directly to the same coyotes who had originally brought the migrants from Guanajuato.

Coyotaje: A Business with Few Barriers to Entry

In spite of the intensified surveillance of the border by U.S. authorities following the launching of Operation Rio Grande in 1997, it remained relatively easy to engage in successful coyotaje. In terms of cash, capital equipment, and level of technological sophistication, there were few serious barriers to working as a coyote, regardless of the type of coyotaje practiced. The main barrier to any physically fit individual considering coyotaje was psychological and consisted of overcoming his or her fear of arrest and imprisonment. This psychological barrier was analogous to the doubts migrants themselves dealt with as they decided whether the potential payoff from crossing the border was worth the risks they would face en route. Given that the social profiles of clandestine border-crossers and coyotes along this stretch of the border were quite similar— both groups consisted mainly of young, working-class Mexican or Mexican American males with little formal education—and that millions of Mexicans had decided that the risks of migration, including possible death, were worth the payoff, it is not surprising that there were plenty of Mexicans and Mexican Americans, not to mention Anglo truck drivers, who were willing to face the risks of being a coyote.[17] Paco, the Matamoros coyote quoted above, had this to say about the people he recruited to work with him:

> SPENER: How do you recruit these people?
> PACO: They're all from Matamoros.
> SPENER: And are they friends or family members?
> PACO: They're friends. *Amigos de la necesidad* [friends in need]. When you don't have any resources, you don't have work. But you do have the strength to work. You think, "Why not? *¿Por qué no le entro?* [Why don't I give it a shot?]."

Moreover, the immediate payoff was potentially far higher for a coyote than it was for a typical labor migrant. It was also not surprising that U.S. and Mexican law enforcement authorities reported that in the first years of the twenty-first century there were between one hundred and three hundred "human smuggling rings" of the commercial-transport type operating in Mexican territory (Miró 2003, 1). These "rings" took migrants into the United States through at least thirty crossing points along the border. Authorities estimated that there were at least thirty such organizations operating along the Texas-Tamaulipas border alone (Notimex 2003a).[18] We should regard these figures with some skepticism, of course, since we have no access to information about how they were calculated. Furthermore, we should take them as lower-bound estimates, since they only include the organizations that authorities knew about and only those that engaged in the commercial-transport type of coyotaje. Regardless, it is clear that no single group or small set of groups monopolized the practice of coyotaje on this stretch of the border in the late 1990s and the first years of the new century.

Minimum startup requirements for each type of coyotaje can be seen in table 4 above. Providers of *short-distance coyotaje* only needed access to a good spot to cross the Río Bravo and some type of flotation device (rowboat, rubber raft, or inner tube) to ferry migrants across. The practitioners of *professional migration* only needed to be familiar with places to cross the river and routes to follow through the brush around highway checkpoints or, alternatively, where to hop freight trains headed away from the border. Other than that, all they needed to know were townspeople and/or relatives who were interested in crossing with them. *Document dispatchers* needed cash to buy laser visas, green cards, or U.S. passports on the black market or a contact within a U.S. consulate or the U.S. immigration bureaucracy who could provide them. They might not necessarily need a great deal of cash to start, since they might be able to purchase a relatively few documents at the outset and then more with the proceeds of their first "deals" with migrants. The principal requirement for engaging in *migra-coyotaje* was either working within the U.S. immigration enforcement bureaucracy or knowing someone who did.

Much was made of the supposed increase in size and sophistication of organizations dedicated to *commercial-transport coyotaje* in response to intensified U.S. border enforcement in since the mid-1990s. A good example from the press is this passage from a story that appeared in the *Christian Science Monitor* in the summer of 2000:

> They've come a long way from the mom-and-pop scofflaws who would guide immigrants across the Rio Grande for a hundred bucks and the thrill of it. These days, smugglers have infrared scopes, two-way radios, and computer databases to keep track of each immigrant, how much they have paid, and where they are supposed to go. It is this new breed of smuggler—call them "Coyote 2.0"—that has forced the U.S. Immigration and Naturalization Service to make monumental changes in its border strategy....The irony [according to Mike McMahon, an INS official in Houston], is that [the agency's] success in shutting down illegal entry points in major urban areas, such as south Texas, El Paso, and San Diego, has forced smugglers to cooperate with one another, and form sophisticated networks capable of delivering immigrants from multiple countries to virtually any destination in the U.S." (*Christian Science Monitor*, August 30, 2000, 1)

While it is true that such coyotaje networks existed, much of the transformation described in this newspaper account had as much to do with the generally increased availability throughout North America of high-tech equipment at a low price as it did with any relative increase in the sophistication of coyotes per se.

The cell phones and pagers that López Castro (1998) used to demonstrate the relative professionalism and sophistication of commercially profitable coyotes based at the border in his research conducted in the mid-1990s were, by the early 2000s, ubiquitous features of everyday life on both sides of the border. Two-way radios were also readily available in Mexico and the United States to the point where Nextel advertised them on billboards in cities in both countries. Effective night-vision equipment could be purchased for as little as $250 in American Airlines flight magazines (American Airlines 2003, 19) and at similarly low prices online (American Technologies Network Corporation 2007). And what business today, no matter how small and unsophisticated, does *not* use some form of computer database as a management tool?

We might also wish to consider that most, if not all, of the largest "alien smuggling rings" known by the authorities to be operating on this stretch of the border during this period would fit the U.S. federal government's official definition of "small business," both in terms of number of employees and gross receipts, were they operating in a legitimate branch of industry (for this definition see United States Small Business Administration 2004). In addition, the alarm expressed by both the U.S. and Mexican governments regarding the growing size and sophistication of "alien smuggling organizations" was sounded previously in the 1970s (Comptroller General of the United States 1976; Halsell 1978; Lewis 1979). According to the 1976 Comptroller General's report, "professional smuggling of aliens is growing in size and complexity. It is a lucrative criminal activity for many persons, often members of large, organized rings" (Comptroller General of the United States 1976, ii). In fact, the overall level of sophistication of early twenty-first-century coyotes did not appear to be especially greater than that described by Gamio (1930, 205–7) with regard to organized bands of coyotes aiding Mexicans in their unauthorized entry in the 1920s.

Setting aside the question of whether the above-described "sophisticated" coyotes were really all that sophisticated relative to other types of businesses, it was also not the case that the types of high-tech tools and extensive networks described above were necessary to successfully engage in commercial-transport coyotaje in the region at the start of the new century. As a federal public defender emphatically put it to me, "All you need to be a coyote is a van!" In fact, the minimum requirements for commercial-transport coyotaje were simple:

- someone to recruit migrants in Mexico;
- someone at the border who could receive migrants, form a crossing party, and verify via telephone that migrants had respondents in the destination city who would pay for their passage;

- someone who could guide migrants through the brush around the *segunda garita;*
- someone with a car, van, or truck who could pick migrants up as they emerged from the brush and drive them on to San Antonio, Austin, Dallas, or Houston; and
- someone living in the destination city who could house migrants in an apartment, mobile home, or private residence and collect the remaining fees from their respondents.

In other words, a viable commercial-transport enterprise could be undertaken with as few as five people, if a different person took care of each part of the operation, or even fewer if, for example, the driver and the provider of the housing in the destination city were the same person. The vehicle or vehicles used need not be recent models or expensive. Indeed, they need not even be owned by the coyotes, since they could also be rented or stolen.

Although coyotes who recruited migrants openly in bus stations and plazas in Tamaulipas and Coahuila border towns typically had to pay significant bribes to Mexican law enforcement to do so, coyotes who recruited elsewhere or more clandestinely might be able to pass through the border towns without paying a *cuota* (fee, bribe), as Paco had done for a time in Matamoros.[19] Here again it is worth remembering that thousands of migrants passed through the region every year without contracting a coyote at all, demonstrating that the border "mafias" that took a cut from the coyotes who operated openly in cities like Matamoros, Reynosa, Nuevo Laredo, and Piedras Negras did not hold a monopoly over clandestine crossing in the region. Thus, aspiring coyotes did not necessarily need to raise capital in order to pay a "toll" to law enforcement authorities or organized crime on the border in order to begin taking people across the border.

We should also note that even small-scale, "unsophisticated" commercial-transport operations were capable of moving substantial numbers of migrants and generating considerable revenue over time. We can take a "ring" based in Austin, Texas as a case in point. This operation (now defunct) consisted of three Mexican men who met each other working in construction in Austin, as well as two collaborators in Mexico—one at the border and one who traveled as a recruiter among migrant-sending communities in his native state of Zacatecas. One of the other collaborators in Austin was also a *zacatecano.* Nearly every Friday two of the men in Austin each drove a van to the border to pick up ten to twelve migrants and transport them back to Austin. One of these men estimated making about thirty trips in a twelve-month period in 1999 and 2000, charging each migrant $1,300. Assuming that the man's memory was correct in terms of the number of total number trips made, migrants transported, and time period elapsed, this would mean that the group transported at least six hundred migrants and generated revenues in excess of $780,000 in that one-year period. The example of this group helps us better understand the comments of a U.S. federal judge I interviewed who had seen hundreds, if not thousands, of "alien smuggling" defendants in his courtroom over the years. At hearings when he received their guilty pleas, the judge typically asked defendants for an explanation of why they did what they did. One of the most common answers he received was, "Se me hizo fácil" [it just seemed easy to me].

Finally, a federal public defender who represented coyotes in one of the U.S. courthouses in South Texas told me in 2001 that nearly all of the coyotes he had defended over the years had been working-class Mexicans and Mexican Americans who were members of small-scale coyotaje operations of limited scope and income:

> The biggest operations I've seen are still "mom and pop." We're not talking here about "Guido the killer pimp"; we're talking about "Mrs. Cavazos." My clients are mostly low down on the food chain. They're anyone who's desperate for a little money. Some of them are freelancers who may not even know who's really hired them. When one of my clients does get "flipped" and fingers somebody else up the line, it usually turns out to be an aunt or an uncle. Almost everyone I see is just trying to make some money for their family. They aren't getting rich....I've defended working people from here who've devised a trunk that'd hold two or three people. They'll drive these cars across the bridge carrying people and then on through the checkpoints. They know when it's easiest to get through the checkpoints. Some of them have been doing this for years. As long as you don't get too greedy or try too often, you don't get caught. The ones who get caught are just unlucky. Or middle-class couples from here who bring people across in their cars, get them ID, and take them to the Harlingen airport to get on a plane!...I don't go home and worry that I've gotten someone acquitted of transporting that's really guilty. Almost all the people I've represented have not violated any of society's general norms.[20]

Aberrant Forms of Coyotaje in the Region

There are several types of coyotaje-related phenomena that I have deliberately excluded from the formal typology presented above. We might refer to these as *false coyotaje*, *narco-coyotaje*, and *sex-trafficking*. I have excluded these from the typology summarized in table 4.1, first because they did not appear to be especially common relative to the other types included in the table, and second because none of them bore any intrinsic relationship with the other types discussed above.

False Coyotaje

At the bus terminals and in the plazas near the international bridges in the Tamaulipas and Coahuila border towns it was common for migrants to be approached by individuals offering to take them to the United States for a fee. Though most of these individuals were offering real coyotaje services, others were merely posing as coyotes in order to swindle unwitting migrants out of their money or to lead them to an isolated place to assault and rob them. An exemplary story I heard from several informants, including staff of a human rights organization that assisted migrants arriving at Mexico's northern border, was that of the first-time migrants who arrived in Reynosa, Tamaulipas, paid a substantial sum of money to a coyote, were guided across what they thought was the Río Bravo, and were left by the coyote on the far bank, in what they were told was the United States. In reality, the migrants had been led across El Anzaldúas, an irrigation canal that runs through part of Reynosa.[21] A close reading of several Tamaulipas newspapers in the late 1990s indicated that some of the abuses that were attributed to coyotes were committed by people posing as coyotes who never had any intention of transporting their victims to a U.S. destination (see, for example, El Mañana de Nuevo Laredo 1998).

Narco-Coyotaje

The second phenomenon, narco-coyotaje, involves unauthorized migrants entering the United States as part of drug-trafficking operations, whether as the *mulas* (mules), *mochileros* (backpackers), or *morraleros* (feed-bag carriers), who carry drugs across the river and through the brush in bundles or backpacks, or as drivers.[22] The migrants involved in narco-coyotaje might or might not be full-fledged members of drug-trafficking gangs. Those who weren't might simply be carrying drugs in exchange for transport across the border. They might be transported by the drug-runners themselves, or they might have their passage with other types of coyotes paid by the drug-runners in return for carrying small quantities of drugs with them. Although the frequent use in the press of the term *trafficker* to describe coyotes has suggested a strong link between drug trafficking and the transporting of people, most of my informants in the field, including migrants, coyotes, U.S. public defenders, human rights activists, U.S. Attorneys, Border Patrol agents, U.S. federal probation officers, an FBI agent, and a U.S. federal judge, believed that in the late 1990s and early 2000s drug smuggling and "human smuggling" were still generally separate businesses. This was also López Castro's (1998, 972) conclusion in his study of coyotes in the mid-1990s.

Mexican public officials also concurred in this point. For example, in March 1998 a high-ranking official in Mexico's National Migration Institute told reporters that "the contraband in human beings was definitely not related to drug trafficking" (Espinosa 1998). Similarly, in 2005, Juan Bosco Martí Ascencio, the director for North American Affairs of the Secretaría de Relaciones Exteriores insisted that "human smuggling" was unrelated to the phenomenon of drug trafficking along the border (quoted in Gómez Quintero 2005, 1). An official of the Secretaría told me in a phone interview in 2005 that Mexican law enforcement officials had informed him on repeated occasions that their investigations of organized crime had not established a link between coyotaje and drug trafficking. He added that such a relationship would be difficult to establish and that he did not believe that the U.S. authorities had been able to demonstrate such a relationship, either. In 2006, Mexico's Attorney General, Daniel Cabeza de Vaca, told reporters that "we have no evidence that [drug traffickers] are getting involved in migrant smuggling" (quoted in Stevenson 2006). Richardson and Resendiz (2006), in their book about crime and deviance in South Texas, also treated drug trafficking and "alien smuggling" as separate activities, with no discussion of any intrinsic connection between the two.[23]

One informant in the U.S. immigration enforcement bureaucracy told me of cases in which drug traffickers gave up dealing drugs in order to move into the "human-smuggling" business because it had become nearly as profitable for them since the launch of Operation Rio Grande and because the penalties for "alien smuggling" were considerably lower than for drug trafficking. Here it is worth noting that Halsell (1978, 82) reported a Border Patrol agent making the same observation to her a quarter-century earlier. On the other hand, some coyotes and migrants I interviewed discussed exactly the reverse—that men who used to work as coyotes "graduated" to drug trafficking, where there was more money to be made.[24] In addition, it is important to bear in mind that the bulk of narcotics being smuggled across the U.S.-Mexico border at the beginning of the twenty-first century appeared to be brought into the country hidden in commercial trucks and private passenger vehicles through the legal ports of entry rather than ferried across the river and trekked through the brush on the backs of individuals, suggesting that most drug trafficking employed substantially different methods than typical commercial-transport coyotaje operations (Andreas 2000, 75; Maril 2004, 277; United States Drug Enforcement Administration 2001; telephone interview on April 6, 2007, with Garrison Courtney, public affairs officer, U.S. Drug Enforcement Administration headquarters, Washington, DC). Relatedly, Richardson and Resendiz (2006, 174) reported that most drugs moving out of the South Texas border region passed through the highway checkpoints staffed by the Border Patrol "in hidden compartments of commercial vehicles."

Whether or not some coyotes might also be *narcos* or vice versa, drugs and migrants did not typically appear to be transported and housed in the same places at the same time. The FBI agent quoted above gave this explanation about why transportation of migrants and narcotics did not typically mix: "A drug trafficker—because the alien smuggling activity is so high profile, because you can't hide bodies as easily as you can hide drugs—they typically don't commingle those kinds of things because they don't want to take the chance of losing their narcotics" (see also Miró 2003, 21). For their part, Richardson and Resendiz (2006, 118) noted that although many drug-runners were also "illegal aliens" in the United States, this did not mean that the flow of migrant labor had any intrinsic relationship to the flow of illegal narcotics across the border. In my own review of 197 "alien smuggling" incidents prosecuted in the Laredo federal courthouse in the first years of the new century, there was only one case in which the arresting officer's report indicated that drugs (47 pounds of marijuana) had been seized at the time of the arrest.

Although some individual coyotes, especially pateros and lancheros who operated along the banks of the Río Bravo, might transport drugs for other organizations when they were not moving people, it did not appear that drug-moving and people-moving were necessarily carried out by a single organization. Instead, there could be some movement back and forth between organizations by certain individuals. Paco, the Matamoros-based coyote quoted above, told me how one of his associates was arrested and convicted for ferrying marijuana across the river. There were times, he explained, when he didn't have any work for the man. On those occasions, the man would look for work where he could find it, and that would sometimes include hiring himself out to drug smugglers. Paco was insistent that the man's arrest was unrelated to working for him: "They didn't catch him with me. *Fue otro baile*" [it was a different "dance"]. He went on to tell me that none of the coyotes he knew were engaged in drug trafficking. "It's a separate business," he said. "Maybe some of my coyote friends might be doing that, but if they do it's real hush-hush [*lo harán muy calladamente*]." What he had seen, he said, was coyotes "graduating" to drug trafficking, that is, saving up enough money to buy a commercial quantity of marijuana and then using their know-how to get it across the border. The FBI agent I interviewed concurred with this assessment. In his experience, drug trafficking remained easier and more profitable than "alien smuggling." As a consequence, "higher-level drug dealers" thought that working as a coyote "was beneath them." On the other hand, "the guys on the street that are trying to make a buck, they would farm themselves out and their capabilities to drug smugglers as well as alien smugglers."

Another piece of evidence that suggests that drug traffickers and coyotes were not necessarily the same people is that only between 10 and 15 percent of "alien smuggling" defendants in Texas during the first years of the new century had prior drug felony convictions on their criminal records.[25] Moreover, my interviews with U.S. federal probations officers suggested that these convictions were often for simple possession of a controlled substance, not for its sale and distribution.[26] Indeed, some interviews I conducted with migrants included stories of their guides using cocaine and/or marijuana during the crossing, suggesting that possession of drugs for personal use might indeed account for some of the drug convictions on coyotes' criminal records. Given that it appears that the processes of autonomous migration and drug trafficking were neither intrinsically nor typically linked in this region when I was in the field, I exclude the phenomenon of *narco-coyotaje* from my coyotaje classification scheme.

As a postscript to this section, I should mention that a number of reports appeared in the press in 2007 that suggested that the so-called Gulf Cartel of drug traffickers had begun to enter the business of moving people clandestinely across the border as a lucrative "sideline" to its main activity. In April 2007, for example, Mexican authorities in Reynosa arrested five leading members of the Gulf Cartel who purportedly engaged in drug, people, and arms smuggling along that stretch of the border (E. Castillo 2007; M. Castillo 2007). The movement of the Gulf Cartel into coyotaje was supposedly related to the bloody turf war with its principal rival, the Sinaloa cartel headed by "Chapo" Guzmán. The battle between the two cartels for control over the movement of narcotics in Nuevo Laredo had been especially violent and had led to a virtual collapse of civilian police authority in the city. With the breakdown of government control of the city, the armed wing of the Gulf Cartel, a group of army deserters known as the Zetas, were reported to have taken over the extorting of businesses there for "protection money" that was formerly paid as bribes to local and federal police authorities. Commercial-transport coyotaje was supposedly one of the types of local businesses affected by this power-grab by the Zetas (Frontera Norte-Sur 2003). Another news report, citing an FBI intelligence report, indicated that the Zetas had begun collecting $1,500 per week from a group of coyotes known as Los Roqueros to allow them to bring migrants across the river into Rio Grande City and El Cenizo, Texas (Doerge 2006).[27] It is not yet clear whether the Gulf Cartel was itself entering the business of commercial-transport coyotaje or if it was simply charging independent operators for the *derecho de piso* (right to trespass) in areas under its control. While English-language news sources such as the Associated Press (E. Castillo 2007) and *San Antonio Express-News* (M. Castillo 2007) wrote reports suggesting the direct involvement of the cartel in transporting people, the Mexico City newspaper *La Jornada* (Castillo García 2007) indicated that the cartel's arrested leaders were involved only in charging coyotes the *derecho de piso* in Reynosa, formerly paid as bribes to local law enforcement authorities. If the *La Jornada* report is accurate, the impact on commercial-transport coyotaje at the border may be less dramatic than might otherwise be presumed.

Sex Trafficking

In the first years of the new century a number of cases in this migratory corridor came to light involving the forced prostitution of migrant women. Some of these cases involved the smuggling of Mexican women across the Texas border for their subsequent trafficking as sexual slaves, working in brothels in Houston, Austin, and Florida (Martin 2004; Rozemberg 2004; Wilson 1998). Another case involved the smuggling of women from Thailand to Houston, where they were forced to work as prostitutes in "modeling studios" until their $40,000 smuggling fee was paid (Associated Press 2000). Such cases, though deeply disturbing, did not reflect the typical coyotaje strategies described in this chapter. While law enforcement authorities in Texas prosecuted thousands of "alien smuggling" cases in the early 2000s, only a few cases involving forcible servitude, sexual or otherwise, were detected in this region annually. According to U.S. Justice Department officials, only fifty-five defendants were convicted of "human trafficking" *nationwide* in 2003. These convictions involved multiple nationalities entering the United States in a variety of places, with and without documents, not all of which involved sexual servitude (Rozemberg 2004).[28] Thus, for the sake of analytical clarity and also to avoid the sort of sensationalism that too often appears in the press, I exclude sex trafficking from my typology of "normal" coyotaje strategies. In doing so, it is not my intention in any way to diminish the seriousness of sex trafficking as a social problem in the South Texas-Northeast Mexico border region or elsewhere, nor do I pretend that women who cross the border with coyotes run no risk of sexual abuse by their coyotes, other men traveling with them, or law enforcement officials on either side of the border. Rather, my intent is to focus squarely on coyotaje as it relates most integrally to the process of the clandestine crossing of this stretch of the border by Mexican labor migrants.

As I have outlined in this chapter, coyotaje on the South Texas-Northeast Mexico border was a multifarious practice at the beginning of the twenty-first century, taking a wide variety of distinct forms, each of which served to facilitate undocumented migrants' clandestine entry into the United States. The forms that this coyotaje took ranged from simple "water taxis" that ferried migrants across the river to paperwork conspiracies in the U.S. consulates in Mexico to fairly elaborate networks of "full package" transportation service providers that organized migrants' trips from their homes in the Mexican interior to their ultimate destinations in the United States. In all cases, the barriers to entry for aspiring coyotes were minimal and consisted mainly of summoning up sufficient nerve to confront the danger of arrest and incarceration by law enforcement authorities. The resources needed to engage in successful coyotaje were not primarily financial or technical but social: knowing collaborators in the right places who were also willing to confront the risks inherent in engaging in this illegal—but not necessarily immoral—activity. Given the poverty lived by so many mexicanos on both sides of the border, it is not surprising that there was no shortage of people willing to confront the risks coyotaje entailed. These were the *amigos de la necesidad* who Paco depended on, who asked themselves *¿Por qué no le entro?* and decided that the potential rewards outweighed the risks.

By detailing the multiple forms that coyotaje took in this region, the lack of control over clandestine border-crossing exercised by any single organization or small set of organizations, and the decentralized, networked structure of some of even the most sophisticated coyotaje operations, I have offered evidence that calls into question the supposed transformation of the "smuggling industry" into one that was increasingly dominated by "transnational organized crime" cartels so often described by government officials and reported in the press. I critique this official discourse about coyotaje in more depth in subsequent chapters. What I wish to emphasize at this point is simply that coyotaje as I found it being practiced on the South Texas-Northeast Mexico border was a quite heterogeneous phenomenon that could still be undertaken successfully by many small groups of individuals with few tangible resources at their disposal and who pursued a wide variety of coyotaje strategies that presented different sets of advantages and disadvantages to migrants. The problem facing government authorities combating coyotaje was not that the types of coyotaje that occurred on the border were unknown to them but rather that coyotaje was so heterogeneous a phenomenon and occurred on such a large scale that they could not hope to put a stop to it without engaging in a wholesale paramilitary crackdown on the movement and activities of large Mexican populations in migrant-sending regions in Mexico, at the border itself, and in migrant-receiving areas of the United States. In other words, it would not be a matter of the authorities taking action against a small number of large-scale criminal organizations that preyed on migrants but would entail a widespread crackdown on migrants themselves, who had come to depend so heavily on coyotaje as a survival strategy in the face of government attempts to territorially confine them to low-wage regions of the North American Free Trade Area.

My purpose in this chapter has been to detail, in a nuts-and-bolts manner, how coyotaje has been practiced in the contemporary period as a form of resistencia hormiga. In the next chapter, I turn my attention to how migrants and coyotes went about mobilizing social resources to successfully realize clandestine crossings of the South Texas-Northeast Mexico border in the face of increased surveillance by U.S. authorities. These social resources were mobilized and deployed strategically in relations among migrants and their networks of family and friends, among coyotes, and between migrants and coyotes in order to finance clandestine migration and minimize the risks to those who engaged in or facilitated it.

CHAPTER 5

Trust, Distrust, and Power

The Social Embeddedness of Coyote-Assisted Border-Crossings

Although the U.S. government's massive investment in border control in South Texas at the turn of the twenty-first century appeared to have done little to prevent clandestine migration through the region, it certainly raised the risks and costs that Mexican migrants had to bear as they attempted to cross the border. As discussed in earlier chapters, the increased risks included drowning, snakebite, dehydration, and death from exposure to the elements. These were symptomatic of the intensification by the U.S. government of apartheid as a system that inflicted ever-greater levels of structural violence against Mexican peasants and workers. The increased costs took the form of increased time and physical effort to make the passage and the greater amount of money that migrants had to raise to pay the coyotes on whom they had come to depend more heavily. Coyotes' fees rose substantially, from the $500–$1,000 range in the period immediately preceding the launching of Operation Rio Grande in 1997 to the $1,500–$2,500 range in the first five years of the new century. Coyotes charged more in order to cover the increased time and effort they had to invest in getting migrants across the border and into the Texas interior as well as to compensate them for the increased risks of arrest and imprisonment they faced. To migrants, this effectively raised the cost of their practice

Portions of an earlier version of this chapter appeared in Spanish in the book *La migración a Estados Unidos y la frontera noreste de México* (Socorro Arzaluz Solano, editor), which was published in Mexico in 2007 by El Colegio de la Frontera Norte and Miguel Ángel Porrúa.

of resistencia hormiga. In the years following the launch of Operation Rio Grande, two questions regarding Mexican autonomous migration across this stretch of the border became more salient than ever. First, how did migrants and coyotes face the problem of the elevated risks they faced as they worked in concert to organize successful trips across the border? And second, how did they mobilize the increased resources they needed in order to undertake ever-more-costly border-crossings? In this chapter, I address these questions, arguing throughout that the solutions that migrants and coyotes found to problems of risk management and resource mobilization are best seen through a lens that focuses on the social and the symbolic, rather than on the material and economic, dimensions of their behaviors. In doing so, I describe coyotaje as a social process that is embedded in networks of social relations and underwritten with social capital and cultural funds of knowledge.

The Embeddedness of Coyotaje in Social Relations

Coyotaje involving cash transactions is exemplary of informal economic activity, that is, those income-generating activities that take place beyond the pale of state regulation (Castells and Portes 1989). Although the transactions between migrants and coyotes take place outside the legal frameworks created and enforced by governments, they are nonetheless regulated by other important social relationships and cultural norms for behavior. Mark Granovetter (1985) has referred to this extralegal nongovernmental regulation of economic action as "embeddedness," and it is an essential concept for understanding how coyotaje takes place. Embeddedness, he argues, takes two forms. *Relational embeddedness* refers to the personal relations between parties to an economic transaction. *Structural embeddedness* refers to the broader network of social relations in which the parties to a transaction are inserted (Granovetter 1990, 98–99).[1] As a result of either or both forms of embeddedness, migrants and coyotes willingly enter into transactions with one another, each trusting the other, however uneasily, to uphold their end of the bargain, even though neither can directly appeal to the law to enforce the informal agreement between them. Unlike the case of human trafficking, in which one set of parties to the transaction takes physical possession of the other set for the purpose of exploiting their labor or their bodies, or both, relations between the participants in coyotaje are not necessarily governed primarily by *la ley del más fuerte* (the law of the jungle). In the remainder of the chapter, I explore how trust can be generated among the participants in coyotaje and the consequences for the parties involved when that trust is violated.

The term *social capital* was introduced into the scholarly literature by Pierre Bourdieu (1977 and 1986) to refer to the resources that individuals are able to access by virtue of their relations with other members of their communities and personal networks. With regard to clandestine border-crossing and coyotaje, it is important to bear in mind that social capital is not simply possessed and used but is also accumulated and exchanged by communities and individuals on an ongoing basis. Moreover, as Bourdieu made clear, social capital can be exchanged for other types of capital—physical, financial, cultural, and symbolic—that can also be effectively deployed in the realization of clandestine crossings of the border. Bourdieu referred to this dynamic process of accumulation, exchange, and deployment of different forms of capital as the "economy of practices," by which he meant to emphasize that the resources accumulated, exchanged, and deployed to undertake a wide variety of human activities were social and cultural as well as economic. Thus we can talk about the role played by "social capital" in an "economy of coyotaje practices." Other analysts have discussed the types of social conditions that give rise to social capital in migrant communities, a topic to which I now turn.

The Sources of Social Capital for Migration

Portes and Sensenbrenner (1993, 1326) and Portes (1995, 15) have developed a four-category typology of social capital as it relates to the economic action of immigrant groups that can be applied fruitfully to the analysis of coyotaje. According to these authors, social capital is available to members of a given social group based on principled, altruistic reasons as well as instrumental, self-interested ones. They identify two sources of social capital in which the donors' motivations are altruistic. First, *values* inspire the transfer of resources from one member of the group to another, as dictated by general moral imperatives to which the donors of capital have been socialized. On this basis, for example, parents give gifts to their children. Second, social capital operates in groups that are unified by external threats made to their members by a hostile wider society. Under these conditions of *bounded solidarity,* donors altruistically extend resources to other members of their group because of their strong identification with in-group needs and goals. The authors also propose two sources of social capital in which donors' motivations are instrumental. The first is *reciprocity,* in which an individual donates resources to another based on the expectation that the gift or favor will be reciprocated at a later time. The second is *enforceable trust,* in which an individual donates resources to another member of the group based on the expectation that the loan of these resources will be repaid by the recipient because the recipient will "be subjected to the full weight of collective sanctions" from the group if it is not repaid (Portes 1995, 13). Enforceable trust is a stronger basis for the generation of social capital than simple reciprocity, the authors argue, because it refers to a situation of deeper structural embeddedness, involving the potential imposition of sanctions by a wider community, rather than one of mere relational embeddedness, which only involves the surveillance of a limited number of individuals (Portes 1995, 6). As I discuss below, we can identify all four sources of social capital operating among the participants in coyotaje. One of the specific questions I address is the extent to which we can observe the operation of the strongest source of social capital, enforceable trust, in the relations between migrants and coyotes.

Using Social Capital to Cross the Border

Singer and Massey (1998) developed and statistically tested a theoretical model for clandestine border-crossing by Mexicans that "views surreptitious border-crossing as a well-defined social process whereby migrants draw on various sources of human and social capital to overcome barriers erected by U.S. authorities" (Singer and Massey 1998, 562). According to the authors, migrants acquire human capital relevant to the crossing both through direct experience and through their social networks, that is, by exchanging their social capital for human capital. The relevant human capital that migrants obtain by "cashing in" their social capital includes being shown the best routes and techniques to follow in making the crossing, including the best coyotes to hire; how to deal with them to best advantage; and what to expect and what to do if they are apprehended by the U.S. authorities. Returning to the interpretive framework for understanding resistencia hormiga introduced in the opening chapter, we can think of what Singer and Massey call "human capital" here as the equivalent of "funds of knowledge" (Vélez-Ibáñez 1988 and 1996) in regard to border-crossing that migrant communities have accumulated. Consistent with the economy of coyotaje practices I discussed above, the authors found that migrants would exchange social capital for economic capital, which they would, in turn, exchange for migration-specific human capital held by a coyote in order to make their first cross-border trip to the United States. After they learned the routes and rules of border-crossing themselves, they would cross the border with no coyote, in effect substituting their own migration-specific human capital for the social and economic capital they used to make their first trips.

Although Singer and Massey's study was ground-breaking in its approach and its findings, it has several limitations with regard to our understanding of coyotaje on the South Texas-Northeast Mexico border from the late 1990s to the present. First, their data did not contain any variables concerning the specific types of coyotaje contracted or the kinds of relations that existed between migrants and coyotes. Second, most of the clandestine border-crossings recorded in their database occurred in the Alta California-Baja California corridor, where crossing conditions were quite different than conditions on this stretch of the border. And lastly, the authors' database only included crossings made through 1995, before the launch of Operation Rio Grande. For these reasons, in-depth consideration of the role played by social capital as it relates to border-crossing and coyotaje along this stretch of the border remains warranted.[2]

In the remainder of this chapter, I apply the concepts developed by the authors discussed above to an examination of three sets of relationships among actors participating in unauthorized border-crossing: (1) relationships among migrants and their families, friends, and work associates; (2) relationships among coyotes participating in networks to transport migrants across the border; and (3) relationships between migrants and their coyotes. In so doing, I illustrate concretely how embeddedness served to regulate the conduct of both migrants and coyotes and how social capital contributed to the financing of coyotaje. At the same time, I analyze cases in which coyotaje was not sufficiently embedded so as to effectively regulate the conduct of coyotes and where stocks of social capital were insufficient for obtaining the resources migrants needed to cross the border.

Social Capital among Migrants

As previously discussed, migrants depended on friends, family, and fellow townspeople in their social networks for the resources they needed to successfully cross the border and find work and a place to live in the United States. With regard to making an unauthorized border-crossing, migrants typically relied on members of their social networks to do some or all of the following:

- accompany and guide/advise them while making the journey across the border;
- give them information they needed to cross the border successfully, including recommending them to affordable and reliable coyotes;
- lend them money at no interest to finance the crossing, including money to pay the coyotes' fee;
- drive them to their final destination in the United States after the migrants got past the last immigration checkpoint; and
- provide them with food, housing, and assistance finding a job after arrival in the U.S. destination.

Mexican migrants who crossed the Northeast Mexico-South Texas stretch of the border to enter the United States demonstrated this dependence on social network assistance. Data from the Encuesta sobre Migración en la Frontera Norte de México (EMIF) show that of clandestine migrants who had last crossed the border into the United States in the 1998–2003 period, 68 percent had friends or relatives living in the U.S. city where they had worked for the longest period of time. Of those migrants who did have friends or relatives living in the same U.S. city, 57 percent had received a cash loan from social network members, 97 percent had been provided food and/or shelter, and 79 percent had received help finding a job.[3]

We can observe a mix of all four sources of social capital proposed by Portes (1995, 15) in this transfer of resources to migrants by members of their social networks. Friends and family provided these resources altruistically because of general moral imperatives related to family and friendship (*values*) and because of identification with the needs and goals of an in-group that faced considerable external threats on both sides of the border, including economic calamity in Mexico and apprehension and deportation in the United States (*bounded solidarity*). Instrumental motivations also played a role in this transfer of resources to the extent that recipients of these resources could be expected to return the favor in some yet-to-be determined way at some indefinite point in the future (*reciprocity*). Moreover, migrants who did not repay the uncollateralized loans from other members of their communities or who failed to reciprocate when called on to do so could be ostracized or otherwise collectively sanctioned by the family, friendship, or hometown migrant community (*enforceable trust*) in which they were structurally embedded. Such ostracism could come at a very high cost to a migrant, given that both in Mexico and the United States a migrant's chief guarantor of social security in the face of the state's indifference or hostility to her well-being was her ability to call on collective resources that could be accessed only through relationships with other members of her social network.

The case of Álvaro, one of the La Carmela migrants, made it clear just how important social capital could be for migrants in moments of crisis. Four years into his second sojourn working in a Texas city, he was picked up by the Border Patrol one spring day while driving a van to a construction site where he and two of his cousins were working. This was the second time he'd been picked up in Texas and sent back to Mexico. By this time Álvaro had made a life for himself in Texas. He had married the U.S.-citizen daughter of a couple from La Carmela. They had a three-year-old daughter to raise. To make ends meet they depended on the $13 per hour he brought home after taxes working as a "master cement-man." When I interviewed him in La Carmela about a month after he was booted back to Mexico, Álvaro was desperate to return to Texas as soon as he could. His life was no longer in La Carmela, he said, but in Texas where his U.S.-citizen wife and daughter lived. There was no remunerative work available for him or his wife in La Carmela. In addition, she had two older children from a previous relationship who had never been to Mexico and could not even speak Spanish. Moving back to La Carmela as a family was not an option. Álvaro could try to walk the Laredo-Encinal route again, following the power lines, but he had no one to travel with. Moreover, neither he nor his wife wanted him to take that risk again—after all, he had once come across a dead man on that trail (see chapter 2). For this reason, Álvaro decided to cross with a coyote. The coyote he would travel with was a "professional" with a good reputation in La Carmela and neighboring settlements. He would have to pay $2,000 on arrival but would not have to walk at all, since he would be traveling through the highway checkpoint in the sleeping compartment of an eighteen-wheeler (chapter 4 also discusses this trip). Álvaro arranged to borrow the $2,000 from a variety of sources. He explained how he had done this when I interviewed him in Texas shortly after he had successfully made the crossing and had resumed working:

> ÁLVARO: You get the funds together with help from everyone. My boss loaned me $1,100. The other boss, the one that gives work to my boss, loaned me $500. My brothers-in-law, my wife's brothers, too, one $280 and the other $200. We got the money together.
>
> SPENER: Remind, me: Your bosses are Mexicans, too, right?
>
> ÁLVARO: Right.
>
> SPENER: So no Anglo American entered into any of this arrangement?
>
> ÁLVARO: No, no. But my boss is a cousin of mine, but he was born here [in the United States].
>
> SPENER: But he's someone who knows what it's like for a Mexican to have to cross the border.
>
> ÁLVARO: That's right, he does. That's why he does so much to help us out, because his parents are from the same *rancho* as me. He is one of my people. And he knows full well everything you suffer coming across and the shape you're in when you arrive. And that's why he helps us out so much, all of us who come here.

Álvaro said that it wouldn't be too hard to pay everybody back. He was earning $550 per week and would pay each of them off, little by little, without having to pay any interest. He reminded me that his wife was also earning about $225 a week at her job, so they wouldn't have to pay all the debt back solely out of his income.[4]

While social capital inhering in migrants' networks certainly made many more border-crossings possible than would otherwise have been the case, we must also bear in mind its limitations under the conditions prevailing at the border after the launch of Operation Rio Grande. Although a great deal of information relevant to making the crossing traveled by word of mouth through migrant networks, that information was often partial, inaccurate, and, at times, even quite misleading. There were several reasons for this. First, migrants relating their exploits "en el Norte" to friends and kin often accentuated the positive and downplayed the negative aspects of their experiences. In so doing, they understated the dangers and difficulties they faced in making the crossing, especially since, if the overall trip achieved its objectives, those difficulties were faced at the very beginning of an extended period of working and living in the United States, so that by the time the story got told they seemed relatively unimportant.

Second, unauthorized border-crossings were typically furtive and hurried events. Migrants, whether they were being led by friends, kin, or coyotes, often did not know exactly where they were, where they were headed, or why exactly things went well or badly for them. Much of the trip could be made under cover of darkness. Sudden detours might have to be made if the migrants encountered la migra on the trail. Rides that were supposed to show up to pick migrants up by a certain fence line along a certain road might never show up, and the group might have to walk farther through terrain unknown to any of them. Exhaustion and dehydration could dull the senses. Moreover, even experienced migrants might make only a handful of crossings over the course of many years, often with several years passing between each crossing. Thus, migrants' memories of the details of what had often been a fairly bewildering experience could be quite fuzzy.

Third, the infrequency of migrants' border-crossings in the period since the launch of Operation Rio Grande created problems with the adequacy of information obtained from even their most recent trips. Operation Rio Grande began in the summer of 1997 in the Brownsville-Matamoros area and was subsequently extended upstream in stages. As described in chapter 1, the increase in the number of personnel, vehicles, helicopters, video surveillance cameras, dogs, X-ray machines, and motion sensors deployed in the Lower Rio Grande Valley was dramatic. Although it by no means made clandestine border-crossing impossible, Operation Rio Grande injected a new dynamism into border-crossing conditions. Old fording spots that had not been patrolled might now be; trails through the brush that once were free from motion sensors might now be under surveillance. Vehicles and agents that one week were concentrated in one area the following week might be deployed in another.

The drug- and people-sniffing dogs that were not present at a checkpoint last month might be there now. And so on. Thus, the border-crossing strategies that were successful last winter might not work in the spring. These border-crossing strategies included the coyotes employed and their accompanying modes of operation: the coyote who delivered the older brother to Houston the previous year without calamity might have to take the younger brother by a different and considerably more arduous route this year.[5]

One of the key insights of Bourdieu (1977 and 1986) is that social capital is fungible and therefore may be exchanged for other forms of capital—physical, financial, cultural, symbolic, and human. Coleman (1988), on the other hand, reminds us that social capital can be quite sticky, that is, that it may not be fungible in a wide variety of circumstances in the way that money or certain kinds of human capital (e.g., knowledge of mathematics) typically are. Coleman's point is especially relevant to the present discussion of border-crossing dynamics. Particular migrant-sending communities in San Luis Potosí, for example, might have accumulated a great deal of knowledge about certain routes across the border as well as specific strategies for getting past both the *primera* and the *segunda garitas* on their way to the Texas interior, including which coyotes to use. That knowledge—migration-relevant human/cultural capital—was accessed by community members through their interpersonal networks, that is, it was obtained in exchange for social capital. The problem facing such communities was that intensified and more dynamic forms of border enforcement by the U.S. authorities could render old border-crossing practices and the social relationships that underwrote them obsolete. This could include the imprisonment or forced retirement of a community's trusted coyotes.

Great hardships might be faced if a migratory community's existing networks of relationships could not connect its members with the new types of resources required to successfully cross the border with a minimum of pain and suffering. One way around this problem would be for the community to mobilize financial capital among its members and substitute that capital for the "funds of knowledge" (human capital) that the new crossing conditions had devalued. Thus, instead of relying on the community's trusted "professional" migrants to get its members across the border, migrants' friends and kin already in the United States would be called on to finance the hiring of a professional coyote, whether a document dispatcher or commercial transporter, since these types of coyotes would have more knowledge of current crossing conditions and connections to collaborators on both sides of the border.[6] Of course, not all members of the sending community would be able to mobilize these financial resources through their network of friends and kin in the United States and might, as a consequence, face serious barriers to migrating relative to those in the community who could mobilize such resources. For example, Fermín, the man from La Carmela discussed in chapter 2, who had been apprehended by the Border Patrol eight times on his last attempt to get into the United States, planned to continue to cross on his own without hiring a coyote. Why? The answer was simple: despite living in a community that sent many migrants north across the border, he himself could not save enough money at home to pay for a coyote, did not have any property he could sell, and had no close relatives or friends living in the United States who could lend him the money to hire one. Furthermore, he knew no other route to follow other than the power lines from Laredo to Encinal, and neither did any of his friends in La Carmela.

Social Capital among Coyotes

Autonomous Mexican migrants' reliance on relationships of trust and reciprocity to underwrite their movement and settlement was conditioned by the common external threats they faced as they journeyed north. Given that the external threats faced by coyotes, both in the United States and in Mexico, were much more severe than those faced by migrants, it should not surprise us that their activities were similarly embedded in such relationships. Given the risks faced by coyotes if anyone alerted law enforcement authorities to their activities, participants in coyote networks needed to be assured of the trustworthiness of other participants in order to collaborate with them confidently.[7] For this reason, coyote organizations often were based on networks involving kinship, friendship, and/or common geographical origin among working-class Mexicans. Thus, one of the federal public defenders quoted in the previous chapter commented that on those few occasions when his clients identified their fellow coyotes to prosecutors, they often turned out to be an aunt, an uncle, or some other relative. In my review of "alien smuggling" cases prosecuted in the Laredo federal court, I came across several examples of defendants who were related to one another by blood or marriage. In addition, a number of high-profile cases prosecuted in Texas during this period involved family-run operations (see, for example, Rodríguez 2002 on a family of coyotes arrested in Kyle, Texas, and Ramos 2005 on the families involved in the Victoria tragedy).

Capital Accumulation and Exchange in Coyotaje Networks

In the same way that migrant networks facilitated the transfer of migration-relevant funds of knowledge, coyotes were apprenticed into their roles as guides, drivers, and safe house operators by their fellow coyotes. For instance, Paco, the commercial-transport coyote discussed in the last chapter, who carried migrants from Matamoros to Houston, got into the business during a bout of unemployment in the mid-1990s. A high school friend of his from Brownsville hired him as a driver and subsequently made him his partner, teaching him other aspects of the operation, including how and where to bring migrants across the river, the routes to follow leading them through the brush, and the best times to bring a load of migrants across to avoid detection by the Border Patrol. Later, after Paco broke with this partner, he recruited other friends to work for him and taught them how to carry out the tasks necessary to the success of his small, but quite lucrative, coyotaje enterprise. Here I emphasize again that, in spite of all the talk in the press about how coyote organizations became much more complex and sophisticated in the face of intensified surveillance of the border in the 1990s and early 2000s, putting together a viable commercial-transport operation still required little in the way of technical expertise or capital expenditures. Indeed, the most vital form of capital for engaging in successful coyotaje appeared to be *social* capital, in the form of social connectedness to trustworthy collaborators willing to assume the risks of engaging in extralegal conspiracies to move migrants across the border. I had the following conversation with Beto, a coyote operating in the town of La Cancha, Nuevo León, in 2002, five years after the launching of Operation Rio Grande:

SPENER: What's going to happen with this business [i.e., coyotaje] now? They tell me it's a lot more difficult to cross.

BETO: No, it's the same as it's ever been. You cross whenever you want. If you really want to cross.

SPENER: And how do you know this?

BETO: Because I know it's easy to do. It isn't hard.

SPENER: But haven't they put a lot more Border Patrol…

BETO: They're putting out a lot more patrols and more people, true, but no, no, no, it's not difficult. It's easy.

SPENER: So, any person who really wants to makes it.

BETO: Exactly. The one who wants to can do it. If he wants to get there, he gets there.

SPENER: And the person who wants to start his own [coyotaje] business can do it, too?

BETO: Not just anyone. You have to know the routes you have to take.

SPENER: How do you learn this kind of thing? Well, in your case, somebody taught you here in the Valley, right?

Beto: Right. Hooking up with somebody who knows the way, and then you know the routes and you can set up your business. You work out an agreement with two or three people over there [in Texas], with two or three people here [in Mexico], and then you rent cars, vans, Suburbans, whatever you can rent. And then you guide them across. That's all you need to get working.

Reiterating a point made in the previous section with regard to migrants, the social capital underwriting coyote operations need not derive entirely from relationships that predated the coyotaje. Transactions that originally were between partners who were little known to one another, if repeated successfully over time, could become embedded in relations of trust and reciprocity, just as many "normal" work relationships could. That social capital can be accumulated by actors participating in a given social activity over time also helps explain the adaptability of coyotaje networks in the face of changing conditions at the border, since they need not depend solely on the trust inhering in preexisting networks based on kinship and geographical community. New contacts with new types of resources could be recruited from outside the original network, and their reliability could be tested before they were brought fully into it. Thus, for example, the previously unknown friend of a friend of a member of a coyotaje operation might be recruited to drive for the organization. Later, after repeated successful trips, he might become one of its integral members. The trust built up over time in this manner helped compensate for the lack of legally enforceable contracts between partners in the coyotaje. Such trust could facilitate, for example, the COD arrangements that characterized many coyotaje operations in place in the Northeast Mexico-South Texas border region, such that lancheros, guides, and safe house operators might willingly provide services to the coordinators of a cross-border trip without the expectation of immediately receiving full payment for them, knowing that they could count on being paid by the coordinator once she collected fees from the migrants after they had arrived in their destination.[8] The COD system underwritten by social capital in this way had the added benefit of expanding the market for coyotaje services, since it indirectly extended credit to migrants who might not otherwise be able to finance their trips across the border.

Coyotes and Reputation: The Importance of Symbolic Capital

Another useful form of social capital accumulated by coyotes over time is their reputation among migrants as being competent and trustworthy, or at least as being less incompetent and less untrustworthy than other coyotes. Bourdieu

(1977, 179) referred to this form of social capital as *symbolic capital,* which he defined as "the prestige and renown attached to a family and a name." Findings from my fieldwork suggest that accumulated symbolic capital played an important role in the context of a competitive market for coyotaje services. No single coyote or group of coyotes monopolized this market. Therefore, migrants were able to choose from among a variety of coyotes employing different crossing methods and charging different amounts of money. Migrants typically chose their coyotes based on information they obtained by word of mouth in their social networks, that is, based on the differing reputations coyotes had among migrants.[9] Thus, to the extent that they needed to attract customers, coyotes needed to be concerned with their reputations "on the migrant street," since word of failure, imposition of hardships, or malfeasance on their part was likely to travel throughout the region in which they operated. In addition, coyotes with bad reputations, that is, those who were known to endanger, abuse, or extort migrants, also appeared to be the ones most likely to be targeted for prosecution by U.S. law enforcement authorities, especially because they were also the ones most likely to be fingered by their dissatisfied customers. I return to this point in chapter 6.

Three examples from my fieldwork indicate that coyotes themselves were aware of the importance of the reputations they had among migrants. Chepe was a twenty-five-year-old bachelor with a pregnant girlfriend when I interviewed him in a Texas border town in 2001. He had come to the border in the early 1990s from Ciudad Mante, Tamaulipas, to look for work, which he found in a body shop on the Texas side. For the last five years he had worked on and off as a guide for a group of coyotes engaged in commercial transport, leading migrants across the river and through the brush around the highway checkpoint. Chepe was aware that migrants had many coyotes from whom to choose. Migrants arriving from the interior often came to the border accompanied by coyotes from their own towns, and many others continued to cross on their own. Those who arrived at the border alone often came with a recommendation for a specific coyote who had successfully crossed their friends and family members without calamity in the past. He would often see other groups of migrants in the brush being led by other coyotes, and all would greet one another. Aside from knowing the routes to take, Chepe said that the main trick to being a successful coyote was knowing how to treat the migrants (*el chiste es saber tratar a la gente*). In other words, it was important to treat migrants well in order to maintain his group's reputation for decent service. His group relied mainly on migrants who arrived at the border already recommended to them. If word got out that he or his accomplices did a bad job or mistreated their customers, it would affect their business: "Word gets out. If you're good, people will seek you out. If you're bad, they won't."

Similarly, Javier, a nineteen-year-old from Guanajuato whom I interviewed in Texas described how his coyote seemed to be concerned with his reputation because women were traveling with them in the group. When they made their crossing in early 2003, the coyote told the migrants that it was the first trip he was making with women and asked that the men respect them because he didn't want any problems. "And that was the deal," Javier told me. "Everybody acted right." A third example comes from Paco, the Matamoros coyote discussed above and in the previous chapter. He bragged to me about the good reputation he had with migrants: "You get a reputation for acting right. You feed them. You make it easy for them. Often I would extend them credit if they had been recommended to me. I'd take them on credit. They'd pay me two or three weeks later."

Problems with Trust in Coyotaje Networks

Although social capital is the product of social networks, the networked structure of some coyotaje enterprises could itself create problems for the maintenance of trust relations among their members, the taking of responsibility for competent transporting of migrants on the part of all participants in the coyotaje, and the maintenance of the reputation of the organization among migrants. When participants in a coyotaje chain were separated from one another geographically, did not engage in frequent and intense face-to-face interactions with one another, and specialized in activities at only one point along the chain, it could be difficult for participants to be very confident about precisely how their collaborators were behaving when they were not physically with them. Information about malfeasance or incompetence on the part of a participant at one point along the chain might not be communicated to other participants by migrants whose main goal was to get to their destination in the United States and move on with their lives as quickly as possible.[10] For this reason, a coyote used by migrants in the town of Moreno (a pseudonym), located on a high-desert plateau in the state of San Luis Potosí, routinely accompanied them all the way to their destinations in Atlanta, Georgia, so that he could maintain control over all aspects of his operation, especially the collection of fees at the end of the trip.

Problems with trust could be exacerbated when a variety of participants rotated in and out of the chain over time. This might be fine as long as money continued to be collected and distributed effectively among all the participants, but trust could unravel if the organization's reputation among migrants was damaged or its operations were exposed to the authorities. As discussed in chapter 4, coyote operations in the Northeast Mexico-South Texas migration corridor tended to be more loosely structured and lacking in the vertical integration that characterized organized transporters of narcotics. Although drug cartels had a hierarchical command structure enforced by violence in order to maintain control over the highly valuable commodity they trafficked, this was not necessarily the case for coyotaje chains, since they normally had no need to guard the migrants they transported against seizure by rivals.[11] As a consequence of their relative lack of hierarchical structure, there might be no single participant in the coyote enterprise who had the authority to enforce specific norms of behavior on other participants and, thus, protect the organization's reputation among migrants. In other words, a coyote chain might only be as strong as its weakest link. These problems with the maintenance of trust among coyotes tended to be less severe in cases where a smaller number of people were involved and they collaborated more closely in more than just one aspect of the coyotaje.

Truckers, Coyotes, and Social Capital: Analyzing the Victoria Tragedy

As discussed in chapter 4, professional drivers of tractor-trailer rigs were sometimes recruited by members of commercial-transport coyotaje enterprises at truck stops in Texas border cities. The case of these participants in coyotaje operations merits special consideration with regard to the role played by social capital among coyotes, for it appears that they were often recruited anonymously and were strangers to other members of a given commercial transporter enterprise. Although around 90 percent of defendants in federal "alien smuggling" cases prosecuted in Texas were Mexican immigrants or Mexican Americans,[12] many of the professional truck drivers who were prosecuted were Anglos who lived in other parts of the United States.[13] Such drivers, at least at the outset of their participation, were not linked to the coyotes who hired them by relationships of blood, marriage, friendship, or common place of origin in the way that other members of the enterprise often were. These drivers had to be offered a high fee (several thousand dollars) to carry migrants and might require a substantial part of it to be paid in advance. This helps explain why migrants who were being transported in tractor-trailer rigs often had to pay half or more of their fee in advance, while migrants transported by other types of coyotes often paid little or nothing until they arrived in their destination city.

The absence of social capital between Anglo truckers and Mexican coyotes could create serious problems for coyotaje enterprises. With regard to the security of the enterprise, lack of solidary relations with the other coyotes meant that, if apprehended, a trucker might have little compunction about fingering other coyotes he could identify. Because his role was typically limited to allowing his rig to be loaded with migrants by the other coyotes, the trucker did not receive a full apprenticeship into working as a coyote, nor did he develop a truly collaborative working relationship with his fellow conspirators at the level of practical detail. This lack of closure of the coyote circle could have disastrous consequences for both migrants and coyotes, as demonstrated in the case of the deaths of nineteen migrants in Victoria in May 2003.

Criminal investigation of the Victoria case and subsequent testimony in the trial of the trucker, a Jamaican immigrant named Tyrone Williams, established several facts relevant to the present discussion. First, Williams was not involved in the actual loading of his truck and had no idea of how many migrants (more than seventy-five) he was hauling until he stopped and opened the rig in Victoria. He was being paid a flat fee of $7,500, while the coyotes who loaded the truck were being paid per migrant transported; no consultation appeared to have taken place between Williams and the other defendants about how many people could be loaded safely into the trailer or how to load them. It is not clear whether the driver was warned by the other coyotes of the danger, that even with night travel and outdoor temperatures in the low 70s, migrants could overheat and quickly run out of oxygen in his trailer. Another defendant testified, as part of a plea agreement, that he had instructed Williams to set the thermostat on the refrigerator at 55° Fahrenheit. One of the great unanswered questions about the case is why the refrigeration unit in Williams' trailer was never turned on, was turned on too late to prevent migrants' deaths, or failed to operate properly after it was turned on (Lozano 2006; Ramos 2005; Rice 2006a and 2006b).[14] Finally, Williams spoke no Spanish and, as a consequence, did not understand the migrants' cries for help from the back of the trailer, although testimony of a female companion traveling in the cab with him indicated that he did know they were in distress. Prosecutors in the case argued that the migrants' deaths were caused specifically by the *total* disregard for their well-being exhibited by the defendants, especially Williams. This claim is tempered by the fact that most of the migrants on board the trailer had only paid part of their fee to the coyotes at the outset of the trip. Most of the Mexicans were paying half their $1,800 fee as a down payment; the remaining $900 would not be collected by the coyotes until the migrants reached Houston, safe and sound (Ramos 2005, 21, 34). Indeed, the jury in the case did not convict Williams of the charges that could have resulted in the death penalty in his first trial, which ended in a hung jury on the most serious counts. (Hart 2007; Lezon and Rice 2005). As reported by the *Los Angeles Times,* the jury in the second trial convicted Williams of all the "alien smuggling" charges against him, but declined to sentence him to death:

Jurors said after the trial that although Williams should have known that the immigrants crammed inside the trailer were in trouble, he didn't set out to kill them. "At no point in time...was there intent for anyone to die," said the jury foreman, one of three jurors who agreed to speak to reporters if their names were not used. "Our conclusion was that he didn't deserve [death]....As a group, we feel good and at peace with ourselves [and] with our decision." (Hart 2007)

For his part, Jorge Ramos, the news anchor for the U.S. Spanish-language television network Univisión, believed that the U.S. authorities' attempt to convince a jury of the coyotes' intent to kill the migrants who died in the trailer was destined from the outset to fail:

> This was obvious to those who followed the phenomenon of undocumented immigration to the United States. It was very clear that the Victoria case was, simply, an operation that turned out badly, very badly. It is not in the interest of any coyote, no matter how insensitive he is, to have the migrants that he is trying to transport die. As cold as it may sound, coyotes don't get paid for dead migrants. They need them alive. (Ramos 2005, 134, trans. Spener)

Another plausible explanation for the deaths could be the group's reliance on a relatively inexperienced outsider, who was neither well integrated into the rest of the coyotaje enterprise nor socially or culturally connected to the migrants he was hired to transport. As noted in the previous chapter, Williams barely knew who the coyotes were who hired him to drive migrants from the border to Houston. In this regard, it appears that Williams's lack of command of Spanish played a role in the migrants' deaths. At one point, Williams stopped the truck and walked to the back of the trailer after realizing that one of its tail lights had been punched out by the migrants. People inside cried out to him about "el niño," referring to a five-year-old boy who was suffocating and near death, but Williams did not understand them. On returning to the cab, Williams asked his companion, a fellow Jamaican immigrant, what "el niño" meant, and she said she thought it referred to a storm, that is, she mistook it for the periodic atmospheric disturbances in the South Pacific known as "El Niño" (Lezon 2005).

Social Capital between Migrants and Coyotes

Although a significant proportion of transactions between coyotes and migrants in this region took place between strangers in socially disembedded contexts, many others were embedded, to varying degrees, in social relations of trust between the parties. As mentioned above, the most disembedded transactions occurred when migrants arrived at border-town bus stations and were recruited by enganchadores who represented coyotes that the migrants had never heard of before. Migrants who connected with their coyotes in this manner were, in effect, giving themselves over to fate, since they had no way of evaluating the relative honesty and competence of the strangers who would be transporting them into the United States, aside from first impressions of the recruiters who approached them. The migrants I interviewed preferred not to contact coyotes in this way, although some had been obliged to do so at times.[15] There were also other contexts in which social capital operated to facilitate transactions between the parties and, to some extent, at least, to reduce the risks facing each in an inherently risky venture. In discussing these contexts, I use the typology of coyotaje strategies outlined in chapter 4 as well as Portes's (1995, 15) typology of the sources of social capital, introduced above.

In-Group Coyotaje Strategies

The most socially embedded transactions between migrants and coyotes tended to occur in the case of professional-migration coyotaje. As the name of this type suggests, the boundary between coyotes and migrants was little defined in this case, in which all parties to the transaction were from the same migrant-sending community and knew or were related to one another in some way. As a consequence, the forms of social capital operating in these contexts mirrored those operating among migrants themselves. This was clear, for example, in the case of Joaquín, the provider of professional-migration coyotaje services in La Cancha, Nuevo León, described in chapter 4. Joaquín characterized his situation as follows:

> The times that we've gone, we've always just brought people from here with us. I know what you're saying. There are coyotes that take people and then they rob them and abandon them in the *monte*. We've never done that because everyone's from here. And if I do something to them, well they're going right away to my family to protest. And there'll be problems for me! I'm happily going about my business here because I've never had troubles with anybody who I've taken across the border, right? And they've gone back and forth and back and forth again with me.

Gabino, another small-time purveyor of this type of service in La Cancha had the same thing to say, only more succinctly: "We all know each other here and we never have any problems."

Social capital in these cases could derive from values (coyotes helping their own family and friends for altruistic reasons), bounded solidarity (coyotes altruistically helping fellow townspeople as a way of benefiting the community in the face of external threats), reciprocity (coyotes helping fellow townspeople with the instrumental expectation that their favor would be returned at some undefined moment in the future or as repayment of favors previously granted to them by migrants or their kin), and enforceable trust (coyotes knowing that if they failed migrants their standing in the community would fall and migrants knowing that they would face community sanctions if they or their families failed to pay their coyotes). Friendship, not coyotaje was another type of socially embedded crossing strategy in which the operation of social capital between migrants and coyotes closely mirrored the operation of social capital among migrants because the boundary between migrants and coyotes was indistinct. The principal difference between this strategy and professional migration was that the amigos linked to the migrants might not be from the same sending community in Mexico, but instead could be Mexican friends or work colleagues the migrants had come to know in the receiving community in Texas.

Social capital also operated in the for-profit charity coyotaje strategy, even though the parties to the transaction were strangers to one another at its outset. Clearly, when a stranger gave aid to a migrant in need, whether her motivations were purely or only partially altruistic, general moral imperatives (values) influenced her behavior. At the same time, in the South Texas-Northeast Mexico border region where most residents were working-class Mexicans and many were themselves migrants (see chapter 1), bounded solidarity also might contribute to the provision of aid to unauthorized migrants, including harboring and transporting them. This sense of solidarity, in addition to being based on ethnicity and class, was reinforced by the external threat represented by U.S. immigration and other law enforcement authorities in the region, whose efforts at repression were disproportionately directed at working-class and peasant Mexicans. As mentioned in the previous chapter, human rights activists in South Texas were well aware of how Mexican families in the region routinely provided aid to migrants passing through because it was the "right thing to do." On the Mexican side, an agent from Grupo Beta, the migrant protection force that patrolled the banks of the Río Bravo, told me how residents of the Mexican border towns also routinely helped migrants in their attempts to cross the river, in part because a large proportion of these towns' population consisted of migrants from other parts of Mexico and/or who had family members living in the United States. That migrants paid something to those who aided them on their journey north does not negate the role that values and bounded solidarity might play in the granting of assistance, even in the case of "commercial" coyotaje.

Reciprocity in Migrant-Coyote Relations

Reciprocity as an instrumental motivating factor contributing to social capital also played a role in the relations between migrants and their coyotes, even those involving commercial-transport coyotaje strategies. To the extent that coyotes depended on word-of-mouth recommendations from migrants, they might make efforts to treat migrants relatively well in the hopes that satisfied customers would send friends and relatives their way later on. As discussed earlier, Bourdieu (1977 and 1986) might have interpreted this behavior as coyotes investing labor in the accumulation of their symbolic capital, which, in turn, they converted to cash in the economy of coyotaje practices. Reciprocity on the part of coyotes could also have a *defensive* instrumental motivation in the sense that good treatment of migrants early on made it less likely for migrants to denounce them to the authorities later if the migrants were apprehended by the authorities. Chepe, the coyote mentioned above who worked in a body shop, told me that it was in his interest to treat his customers respectfully. In safe houses, for example, it was easy for coyotes to push migrants around and behave toward them in a vulgar and aggressive way. This was a poor idea, however, because if the group were later apprehended by the authorities, resentful migrants could exact retribution by denouncing the coyote who had mistreated them. He himself had been apprehended by the Border Patrol on several occasions, but his customers had never identified him as their coyote.

Orlando was a twenty-five-year-old autonomous migrant from a town outside Monterrey, Nuevo León, who was now living in a Texas city when I interviewed him in 2002. In the late 1990s and first years of the new century, he had worked as a coyote with the organization of a relative of his in Piedras Negras, Coahuila. Orlando concurred with Chepe's assessment:

> ORLANDO: Immigration wants to catch the coyote so that the coyote stops bringing people over. People want to come, but they don't know how. But the coyote can get them across. So if you're immigration and you say "Who's the coyote?" and I say, "Well, this man is the one who's brought me," you're going to arrest him and put him in jail. And that's why the migrant never says who the coyote is. The migrant says, "No, the coyote ran off." And if he [the coyote] has treated the migrant well, he's not going to give him up.
>
> SPENER: So they only point out who the coyote is if he hasn't treated them well?
>
> ORLANDO: Right, more or less.

As Orlando's comments indicate, reciprocal motivations could also influence migrants' behaviors toward their coyotes. When a migrant-sending community routinely relied on a more-or-less dependable set of coyotes to cross the border, its individual members might have good reason to treat their coyotes well, by paying them the agreed on amount in a timely manner, for example, or by referring other migrants to the coyotes. Aside from keeping the relied-on coyotes in business for the community, individual migrants might also derive reciprocal benefits in the future from treating their coyotes well now. These benefits could include a discounted price for their own passage the next time they crossed, more relaxed payment arrangements once they arrived at their destinations, or special attention paid by the coyotes to the comfort and safety of the migrants' relatives as they crossed. For example, Adán, a twenty-four-year-old man I interviewed at a fair following a religious pilgrimage in rural northwest Guanajuato, who had lived and worked in Dallas on two occasions, explained to me how going to a coyote recommended by an established customer could help him reserve a "berth" on the coyote's next trip. This was important in the early months of the year when the most-trusted local coyotes often could not take as many people north with them as wanted to go. The coyote was more likely to take the recommended migrant because he knew the established customer had paid him on time, not caused any problems on the trip, and would not send a troublesome or untrustworthy individual his way. On Adán's last trip north, he had reminded the coyote he'd approached that the coyote had taken his brother north before and the brother, who was still in the United States, would be the one paying for Adán's trip. The coyote brightened on hearing this. He remembered the brother and that he had been a good customer when he had traveled with them. He asked Adán how the brother had been doing and to send the brother his greetings. The coyote was especially pleased that the brother would be the one who would pay for the trip. Similarly, Julián, who lived in Rancho San Nicolás, which was near where I interviewed Adán, explained how coyotes who knew you directly or by reputation were more likely to take you north even if you didn't have all the money lined up ahead of time. Julián's brother, José, who had also traveled to Texas on several occasions, had this to say about the coyotes he had traveled with:

> The coyotes show favoritism to the person who has someone who'll "respond" [i.e., pay the migrant's fee to the coyote] for him up there. It's like with my brothers. He's like, "I know your brothers. I know you because I know your brothers, and they've got the money and I know they're straight." Because sometimes the coyotes have complained that they take people across and when they get there they run off. They just jump out of the van and take off without ever paying anything at all. So, the coyote is worried about who

he's taking just like the one who's going with him worries about him. But in this instance they know us and we know them. So I think there's more trust when they know me and my brothers are "responding" for me. They told me there was no problem.... You know, we're not signing any papers or anything, it's just your word. So my brothers told him, "You know what? You have to deliver him to us safe and sound and we'll guarantee you your money."

The Role of Bounded Solidarity in Shielding Coyotes from Prosecution

It was often difficult for U.S. law enforcement authorities to get migrants to identify their coyotes when a group was apprehended hiking in the brush or discovered in a safe house in a Texas border town waiting to head farther into the U.S. interior. Although Border Patrol agents often assumed that migrants refused to finger their coyotes out of fear of retaliation to themselves or their families, other factors involving social capital might be at work. Reciprocity could play a role, insofar as coyotes had promised to make another attempt at crossing with the migrants if the current attempt failed. Bounded solidarity could also play a role, insofar as migrants viewed law enforcement authorities as an external threat to themselves and their group, which, under these circumstances, included their coyotes. This sense of solidarity in the face of an external threat could outweigh any particular grievances that migrants had with their coyotes, as long as those grievances were not so severe as to negate the trust that migrants had placed in them. Sometimes guides would instruct migrants ahead of time that, if apprehended in the brush, they should tell the Border Patrol either that they had no coyote or that the coyote abandoned them before they were apprehended. Chepe, the Texas border-town coyote discussed above, said that he and his collaborators always instructed migrants to tell immigration agents that there was no coyote among them. And migrants always had followed these instructions, he believed, because they had been treated well and, perhaps more important, because they relied on these coyotes for crossing again if they were caught and sent back to the Mexican side. This was what happened with Joel, a Mexico City man who had recently attempted to cross the border with a coyote near Ciudad Acuña, Coahuila-Del Rio, Texas, when I interviewed him in 2001. He explained how he and his companions had covered for their coyote when they were apprehended several times by the Border Patrol:

> JOEL: We tried to cross three times with the same coyote, but we couldn't make it. We'd cross [the river], and then they'd catch us in the brush.
> SPENER: Did they ask who your guide was?

JOEL: They always asked. We'd say that we'd lost our guide. We wouldn't tell them who he was.

SPENER: In other words, that he'd abandoned you?

JOEL: Right. They'd say, "Who's the guide?" And we'd say, "The guide abandoned us." We kept saying that the coyote had abandoned us so as not to get him in trouble.

The irony here is that when migrants would tell Border Patrol agents that their coyotes had abandoned them (while the coyote pretended to be just another migrant in the group) and the Border Patrol repeated their statements to the press, the social capital, born of the migrants' sense of bounded solidarity with their coyotes, could have the unintended effect of devaluing the general value of all coyotes' symbolic capital, as the distorted accounts of their behavior were broadcast by the media to migrant communities on both sides of the border. That solidarity might exist between migrants and their coyotes should not be surprising, even if they are not directly related by kinship or community of origin, since the majority of both migrants and coyotes were young, working-class men of Mexican origin who were struggling to escape the conditions of poverty imposed by powerful elites and enforced by the various police forces that executed said elites' directives.

In this sense, we can regard coyotaje, whatever specific forms it takes, as a business of, by, and for working-class Mexicans. Data collected by the pretrial services units of the federal courts in Texas about "alien smuggling" defendants in the six years following the launching of Operation Rio Grande confirm this point. Of the 7,426 defendants accused of coyotaje in the 1998–2003 period in the Southern and Western Districts of the U.S. Court in Texas, the vast majority were young men of Mexican ancestry with low incomes and limited education. These defendants were mostly men (84%), under the age of forty (70%), and Hispanic (92%). The majority of them (58%) resided in Texas at the time of their arrest, while one-third lived in Mexico, and another 9 percent lived in other U.S. states. Only 0.1 percent lived in some other country. Many of the defendants were "illegal aliens" (47%), while 15 percent were legal permanent residents of the United States and 37 percent were U.S. citizens. The court data did no not distinguish between naturalized and native-born citizens. Three-quarters of defendants had less than a high school education, and 40 percent were unemployed at the time of their arrest.[16]

Data I reviewed in the records of 197 cases prosecuted in the Laredo federal courthouse in 2000 and 2002 produced a similar overall profile of coyote defendants; it also provided some more detailed information. Like the migrants they were transporting, the coyotes who had been working at the time of their arrest

($n = 141$) had been employed mainly in a variety of manual occupations, including construction trades (28%), truck drivers (28%), mechanics (6%), restaurant jobs (6%), and agriculture (4%). The median monthly income earned by defendants at their last job in the United States was just $1,100 ($n = 135$). Less than one-quarter of defendants owned their own home ($n = 166$). Two-thirds ($n = 208$) had dependent children to support. With regard to nationality, 44.5 percent of Laredo defendants were U.S. citizens (includes both citizens by birth and naturalized citizens), 53.5 percent were Mexican nationals, and only 2 percent were from some other country ($n = 256$). In addition to the fact that the majority of defendants were Mexican nationals, most (63%) lived either in the Mexican interior (23%) or the U.S. interior (40%), not in the border region (37%; $n = 254$), suggesting that many of the coyotes had established links to the migrants they served in their communities of origin or settlement. The overwhelming majority of the incidents for which these defendants were being prosecuted in the Laredo federal court involved the transport of Mexican nationals. Only two incidents did *not* include Mexican customers; only 7 percent involved the movement of non-Mexicans, nearly all of whom were Central Americans, principally Salvadorans, Guatemalans, and Hondurans.[17]

The COD System

In my fieldwork along this stretch of the border in the late 1990s and early 2000s, I discovered that it was still common for migrants to pay little, if any, of their fee to their coyotes until they arrived safely in their destinations in a Texas interior city.[18] I've already noted that such COD arrangements were underwritten by social capital among coyotes, but they could also be seen as being underwritten by social capital between migrants and their coyotes. The functioning of this system depended on migrants' reliance on friends and family members in the United States to "respond" for them on their arrival by meeting with coyotes to pay the fee for their trip or by electronically wiring funds to coyotes if they did not live in the destination city. It also depended on coyotes' trusting that the migrants they transported did, in fact, have "respondents" who would pay for their trip when they arrived and that migrants would not try to abscond before making payment. Indeed, Paco, the Matamoros coyote I interviewed said that the principal advantage of working with *migrantes recomendados* (migrants who came recommended) was that you knew that the money to pay for the trip was really there. Similarly, Julián, one of the migrants I interviewed in Rancho San Nicolás, Guanajuato, reported that it was beneficial for the coyotes he knew in his area to work primarily with migrants who came recommended to them by those they had taken to the United States.

Although migrants were sometimes held by armed guards or locked in "cells" in safe houses until their trip was paid for, in many other cases migrants were neither forcibly detained in the destination city nor did they attempt to abscond without paying (though see below for a discussion of the use of physical coercion by coyotes). Rather, migrants typically had made fairly solid arrangements with respondents to assure that payment would be made on their arrival. If their friends and relatives could not make payment immediately, they would wait in the safe house, sometimes for several days, until the payment could be made. A group of migrants from Las Furias (a pseudonym), a small settlement in rural San Luis Potosí near the border with Zacatecas, told me how they waited willingly until their friends and relatives paid their coyotes. They did not expect to leave until then. Tellingly, when I asked them what the coyotes would do if they tried to leave without paying, one of the men got indignant:

RAMIRO: Well, who knows? I don't know. I've never left without paying.
SPENER: Of course not. I wasn't suggesting that.
ROGELIO: Those of us who go [to the United States], we hardly ever do that. The coyotes themselves know ahead of time that you're not going to try to escape [without paying]. And you know it, too. The country people from here aren't *malosos* [bad, untrustworthy].
SPENER: Do the coyotes and migrants know each other?
ROGELIO: No, not necessarily. But even so, you don't see cases like that where they take somebody across and then he tries to skip out on them. It doesn't happen.

Beto, the coyote from La Cancha, Nuevo León, concurred with these migrants' assessment of the typical situation. He had not had problems with customers not paying him, nor had it been necessary to hold anyone against his or her will:

You're in your apartment, in your house. And you say to them, "They're going to come for you. They're bringing the money and you're going to stay here until they bring the money."...You take care that they don't leave, but you just hang out chatting with them, watching television, eating, or whatever, while they're bathing....And everyone who goes, it's very rare that they don't have the money. Everyone has the money lined up....Their relatives up there get the money together ahead of time. It's not in their interest not to be able to pay, because they may have another family member they want to bring later on.

As these examples illustrate, both migrants and coyotes had agreed to these terms in advance and expected that all parties to the agreement would fulfill their obligations under it. A combination of values, bounded solidarity, reciprocity, and enforceable trust combined to ensure that under most circumstances, all parties to the agreement would abide by its terms.[19] And, as noted in the previous section, the social capital at work in these transactions made more migration possible than would otherwise have taken place, since without it migrants would have had to invest borrowed funds at the outset of the trip with no guarantee of success. Moreover, their reliance on members of their social networks to finance their trips considerably reduced the cost. Relatively few migrants had the $1,500 to $2,500 in Mexico needed to pay coyotes, whether from their own savings or the sale of personal property. Those who had no "respondents" in the United States willing to lend them money on concessionary terms would have to rely on loan sharks or the coyotes themselves to lend them travel money on usurious terms, if they were able to make the trip at all.[20]

The Enforceability of Trust between Migrants and Coyotes

Under the right circumstances and within significant limits (see below), enforceable trust could also be an important instrumental motivation for the generation of social capital between migrants and coyotes. Because coyotaje by definition took place outside the protection of the law, none of the parties to it could rely on the law to enforce agreements. Instead, they had to trust one another to uphold their ends of a deal and, in addition, have some confidence that sanctions would be imposed by the community against those who violated that trust. Enforceable trust between coyotes and migrants was most likely to exist where relations were densely embedded in multiplex networks in their communities of origin and/or destination, corresponding most closely to the coyotaje categories of professional migration, and friendship, not coyotaje in the typology presented in chapter 4. Under these conditions, coyotes' reputations were well known, and word of any malfeasance on their part circulated among members of the community. This could lead to their ostracism in multiple aspects of their lives. According to several of the migrants I interviewed from a *rancho* in Guanajuato near Dolores, Hidalgo, this occurred with a local coyote who had a reputation for sexually abusing women he transported and who had led a crossing in the late 1990s in which a couple of local people drowned in the Río Bravo. After that he was kicked out of his house by his parents, shunned by the rest of the community, and ultimately drank himself to death. In other cases, sanctions might simply be economic: members of the community would stop patronizing the coyote or group of coyotes. In this sense, Beto, one of the coyotes operating from La Cancha, Nuevo León, told me he was always under pressure from his community to behave properly: "You have to act right [*portarte bien*] because it's not in your interest to discredit yourself [*no conviene quemarte*] because people won't go to you anymore. You know what I mean? You discredit yourself. It's that simple." The migrants from Las Furias, San Luis Potosí, concurred:

> ROGELIO: The ones who don't treat you right, you don't go with them the next time.
> ROGELIO'S NIECE: Everyone knows who they are. And so they tell you, "Don't go with those guys, because they're going to treat you badly." So they look for somebody who will treat them a little better.

Migrants who behaved badly on the journey north or once in the United States could also gain reputations such that other community members would be unwilling to lead them, travel with them, or finance their trips. This was the case with Memo, an intermittently employed twenty-three-year-old construction worker I interviewed in Moreno, San Luis Potosí, in early 2003. He wanted to return to the United States to work but could not get anyone on either side of the border to lend him the money to hire a coyote to make the trip. Other people who knew him, both in Moreno and in Texas, told me he had spent all his time in the United States drinking and had come back from his last trip with nothing to show for it. On that trip, he had been unable to pay his $1,200 coyote fee because he had not lined up his "respondents" properly. The coyotes, who were from his hometown, agreed to let him pay them off in installments by sending money to the wife of one of them while they stayed in the United States to work. Although Memo told me he had paid off his debt, it seemed unlikely to me, given what others said about him and the fact that he was unable to get these same coyotes to take him north again.

This type of "deep" social embeddedness of autonomous migration, characterized by some degree of enforceable trust, has been encountered by other scholarly observers of the phenomenon in the contemporary period. Evelyne Sinquin Fueillye (2006), for example, found a similar situation prevailing in the communities she studied, although she did not use the idiom of embeddedness, trust, and social capital to describe it:

> What appears determinative is the existence of family and community networks in regions with a long migratory history, such as Zacatecas, Jalisco, Guanajuato, or Michoacán, that facilitate border-crossing. In such "transnationalized" locales, everyone knows the coyotes, their systems for "taking people across to the other side," their terms, and their prices. Everyone also has a relative in the north who will pay the cost of the trip, if the undocumented migrant arrives safe and sound at the address agreed to beforehand.

Lastly, everyone observes a code of honor if they are arrested by la migra; detainees would rather spend three months in jail and then be deported than denounce their guide in court, since they know that later on they or their family members will require their services once again. With regard to the coyotes, contrary to what is said about them, they generally carry out their business "professionally" so as not to lose their clientele. (Sinquin Fueillye 2006, 93–94, trans. Spener)

Another factor that could help enforce trust between migrants and coyotes was that each party to the coyotaje could avenge malfeasance committed by the other by denouncing or turning the other party over to law enforcement authorities. Coyotes, for example, could threaten migrants with turning them over to la migra if they did not pay their fee on arriving in the safe house.[21] Migrants, for their part, under a variety of circumstances had the opportunity to denounce coyotes to the authorities if they suffered abuse at their hands. As already discussed above, this could happen when a group of migrants was apprehended by the Border Patrol while trekking through the brush or driving on a highway headed away from the border. Agents might harshly interrogate migrants, demanding that they identify their coyote and offering them special dispensations if they were willing to serve as material witnesses in court.[22] If they were unhappy with their coyotes' conduct or sufficiently intimidated by the agents interrogating them, they might very well decide to identify the coyotes. If migrants traveled with a group of coyotes, some or all of whose members lived in their home community, their family members could denounce the coyotes to law enforcement authorities in Mexico if some abuse was committed against them. Migrants and their friends whom I interviewed in La Cancha, for example, said that it was for this reason that they preferred to work through Beto, who was connected to a commercial-transport organization at the border. They believed that these coyotes were under pressure to treat migrants better because they could identify Beto by name and knew where he lived. If the coyotes treated one of their friends or kin badly, the coyotes could be denounced to the authorities, and they believed that the Mexican federal authorities would take action, even if law enforcement agencies at the border had been bought off.[23] Finally, if migrants were held in safe houses against their will, their "respondents," who might be legal U.S. residents or even U.S. citizens, might call the police to gain their friend or relative's release. Indeed, this appeared to have been one of the more common ways in which coyotes were arrested in Texas outside of the immediate border region.

The networked, chain structure of commercial-transport enterprises could place important limits on the enforceability of trust by migrants on their coyotes, for some of the same reasons that were discussed above with regard to social capital among coyotes. To the extent that a commercial coyotaje operation consisted of a series of semiautonomous cells that came together on and off again over time, each of which was dedicated to only one stage of the trip with different individuals rotating in and out of the cells, members of migrant communities tended to know the individual coyotes at only one point along the chain. For example, in La Cancha, Beto had come to work exclusively as a recruiter for other coyotes who were based at the border in Piedras Negras, Coahuila. He had formerly worked as a weekday construction worker and weekend coyote in Austin, Texas, with a different set of collaborators (this group was described in chapter 4 in the section on commercial-transport coyotaje) but was arrested, served a prison sentence, and was deported to Mexico. While in prison, he met a man who worked with the Piedras Negras coyotes, and when he got out of prison, he began to work with this group. No longer able to operate easily in U.S. territory, he was paid $100 for each migrant he recruited for the organization, with $50 paid when he delivered the migrant to his collaborators in Piedras Negras, and the remainder after the migrant arrived in his Texas destination and paid his fee.

Beto vouched for his collaborators and said they were reliable. Indeed, there were townspeople who had successfully crossed into Texas through this coyote network without incident (price in 2002: $1,300 to $1,500 per person, COD, Piedras Negras to Austin or Houston). These satisfied customers had recommended the network to others in the community. Nevertheless, Orlando, the other coyote from Nuevo León quoted earlier in this chapter, cast doubt on the real value of working through a "local representative" of such an extensive, commercial coyotaje network. The problem, Orlando said, was that although migrants knew their local coyote, they did not know his other collaborators at other points along the route. When I asked him about the value of the arrangement of working through the "local representative" of the Piedras Negras organization, he said that there was no guarantee that the "good" coyotes who took a migrant across a few months ago would be the same individuals who took his brother across now. Moreover, the local coyote known by the migrants might have no authority over his collaborators to ensure that they treated "his" migrants well. His migrants might know him fairly well, and, in the event of an assault, an abandonment, an extortion, or worse, might be able to take action against *him*, including denouncing him to the authorities, but that did not necessarily mean that the actual perpetrators of the abuse would face serious consequences. The coyote network would lose a member in that particular small town, but the network might have other recruiters working elsewhere that might bring in sufficient clients to more than cover the loss.[24]

If the migrant or her family members wished to press criminal charges against the coyotes who organized the trip, the existence of the international boundary could make it difficult. If the offense occurred on U.S. soil, going after any of the coyotes who resided in or had fled to Mexico would require a level of cross-border collaboration between U.S. and Mexican law enforcement authorities that only seems to take place in the most serious of cases, like that of the tractor-trailer deaths in Victoria. In addition, the organizers might have an immigrant or nonimmigrant visa that allowed them to flee from prosecution or other forms of retribution against them in Mexico by crossing into the United States and disappearing into the large Mexican migrant population there, where the aggrieved migrants and their families could not easily follow. Orlando, the former coyote from Piedras Negras, believed that it was difficult to bring abusive coyotes to justice for this reason: "It's hard for them to prove because they have to conduct a thorough investigation into who was bringing the people [across the border]. And most of the time they don't do much of an investigation. They just arrest the person who was with the group when they caught them."

Even if trust was not enforceable in this kind of arrangement, people from La Cancha could still benefit from arranging their border-crossings with Beto, rather than with coyotes located elsewhere. One of the most important benefits was that he could serve as a conduit of information to family members in the town about what had happened to migrants en route if they did not get to Austin or Houston within the expected time frame. Beto could call his collaborators to find out where the migrants were, why they had been delayed, and give family members and friends a sense of when they might actually get through. All this could give some comfort to families who otherwise would have had no idea what had happened to their relatives during what they knew to be an arduous and dangerous crossing.

It is not surprising, given the chain structure of commercial-transport coyotaje enterprises, that when law enforcement authorities arrested a coyote at one point along the coyotaje chain, the arrest seldom resulted in the apprehension of coyotes at other points along the chain. As mentioned in the previous chapter, two U.S. Attorneys I interviewed in 2001 characterized the structure of "alien smuggling" as a "cottage industry" consisting of "a whole series of independent contractors." They said they only tended to see "one point along the chain" and that it was "hard to move up the chain and get the leaders of smuggling organizations."[25] Those arrested seldom implicated their collaborators, and prosecutors seldom invested the resources needed to engage in a complicated transborder investigation of a "routine alien-smuggling case" in collaboration with law enforcement authorities in the other nation. Summarizing the challenges they faced, the federal prosecutors said, "We get what we can."

Although migrants and coyotes could build trust with one another over time, the growing average length of stay of migrants in the United States and the concomitant decline in frequency of their border-crossings could work against the accumulation of trust between the transacting parties. The accumulation of social capital over time depends in large measure on the expectation of parties to the transaction that their relationship will be ongoing; otherwise neither has much incentive to invest much effort in developing it. To the extent that the character of Mexican migration continues to change so that individual migrants increasingly make single once-and-for-all permanent moves to the United States, migrant-coyote transactions may also tend to be transformed to one-time-only socially disembedded events involving parties who remain strangers. This effect might be avoided, however, to the extent that the one-time moves of individual migrants are repeatedly followed by moves by other family or community members, such that the relevant unit of analysis becomes the relationship between coyotes and the family or the community as a whole, rather than between coyotes and individual migrants.

Power Relations between Migrants and Coyotes

Although social capital appeared to play a significant role in underwriting various types of coyotaje, power relations between the various actors involved must also be taken into account in order to better understand the limits within which social capital operates. This is especially true for the relations between coyotes and migrants, given the many abuses and tragedies that have befallen migrants over the years as they have been guided north by coyotes. Most press accounts, repeating the perspective offered by law enforcement authorities, have portrayed contemporary coyotes as ruthless thugs who prey on defenseless migrants with whom they have no ongoing relationships. While this may be a quite accurate description of some of the coyotes who engaged in the kinds of abuse that made the news, migrants, coyotes, law enforcement authorities, and attorneys I interviewed provided a more nuanced perspective on the power relations between them. In this regard, we should bear in mind that the tragedies that made the news, appalling as they might be, both in nature and in number, accounted for a relatively small proportion of the total number of coyote-led journeys made by migrants across the border.

Migrant Strengths in Dealing with Coyotes

One of migrants' chief strengths in dealing with coyotes was their numbers. At most points along the coyotaje chain, migrants outnumbered their coyotes significantly. When possible, migrants traveled with several other members of their community to increase their security. If a woman was crossing with coyotes, she would often be accompanied by her husband or a male friend or relative who would pose as her husband in order to protect her from sexual abuse by coyotes and other male migrants.[26] On the trail, if a migrant had trouble keeping up with the group, other migrants could insist that the group slow down and help the ailing member, overruling any suggestion by the guide to leave that member behind. The group of migrants I interviewed in Las Furias, San Luis Potosí, told me about a couple of occasions when they overruled their coyotes who wanted to leave one of their companions on the trail. The coyotes were worried that they would miss their ride if they waited for members of the group who were lagging behind. The migrants were able to prevail on their coyotes to wait for the weaker ones among them, not only because they far outnumbered their guides on the trail, but because they had financial leverage over them. Ramiro had the following to say: "All of us were united. We wouldn't leave our companion behind. All of us or none of us! And, well, the coyote had to wait. He was making a lot of money. And the coyote gives in because he has to bring the whole group." In other words, unless the coyote waited for the lagging members of the group, he would not make *any* money on the trip.[27]

Migrants' ability to impose their will in such cases depended on their standing together in an act of bounded solidarity, something that was more likely when all or most of the people traveling together knew one another. In addition, coyotes whose activities were embedded in the social relations of the migrants' communities might be more likely to consent to the will of the group when they knew that consequences could be imposed on them by other community members. For example, in the town of Moreno, not far from Las Furias, another migrant I interviewed insisted that on several occasions local coyotes who behaved badly on a trip had been beaten up by angry customers and their friends and family members.[28]

A second strength possessed by migrants, already discussed, was that migrants had the opportunity to denounce abuses by their coyotes. As Heyman (1998, 169–70) has noted, members of Mexican migrant networks in the United States have long used the tactic of calling la migra as a way of retaliating against clandestine members of these same networks when disputes arise. Thus, it is not surprising that they would use the immigration authorities as a tool to retaliate against coyotes who had abused or otherwise failed their members.

A third strength of migrants had to do with the COD payment arrangements that were common in this part of the border region. Coyotes who would not collect payment from migrants until they arrived safely in their destination had considerably more incentive to get migrants all the way there, despite difficulties along the way, than coyotes who had been paid all or part of their fee in advance. For example, Chepe, the Texas border-town coyote who originally hailed from Ciudad Mante, Tamaulipas, told me that he would not leave a migrant behind on the trail unless he absolutely had to because he was paid *por cabeza* (per head) and not *por viaje* (per trip). Leaving someone behind meant he personally would lose money.

Both migrants and coyotes I interviewed agreed that withholding payment until the end of the trip was one of the most important things that migrants could do to improve their chances of a relatively safe and successful trip with coyotes. Orlando, the coyote who used to work out of Piedras Negras, was insistent on this point: "When they charge up front in Mexico, they're no good." Paco, the Matamoros coyote quoted earlier, said, "The coyote that starts asking for money in Matamoros is up to no good. If he starts asking for money in Matamoros or Brownsville, it smells bad. It's a bad sign. In my experience it's the sign you should turn around and run from him." With COD arrangements, migrants who didn't make it to their destination, for whatever reason, were a total loss to coyotes.

At the same time, coyotes, especially those engaging in commercial transport who had no previous relationships with migrants or their communities of origin, might prefer to abandon a migrant who was being transported on a COD basis if they thought that they might lose fees from the whole group because of her lagging behind on the trail. Orlando, who used to engage in commercial-transport coyotaje in Piedras Negras, had this to say:

> SPENER: Since the coyote is not going to be paid if the person doesn't make it, leaving someone behind on the trail means losing money, doesn't it? In some sense?
> ORLANDO: Well, not much.
> SPENER: But isn't $1,300 or $1,400 a lot of money?
> ORLANDO: It's not a lot of money to the people who do this for a living. That's because what they want is to take ten people across, at least five people or more. And if they lose one, it's like they didn't lose anything.[29]

In addition, guides might be under real pressure to have the group reach the pick-up point in time. Drivers would be loathe to spend much time waiting along the road for a group to emerge out of the brush out of fear of attracting the Border Patrol's attention. Moreover, drivers in small-scale coyotaje operations might have other job and family responsibilities where they resided in the Texas interior. Thus, if a group did not make it to the prearranged pick-up point in time, the driver might find himself obliged to turn around to get back to his regular job in San Antonio, Dallas, or Houston, leaving the guide and migrants stranded without food, water, or shelter in a heavily patrolled area.

Migrant Vulnerabilities as They Deal with Coyotes

Alongside their strengths, migrants also suffered from serious vulnerabilities in dealing with their coyotes. One of their main vulnerabilities when using commercial-transport strategies was their near-total dependence on coyotes for guidance, shelter, food, water, transportation, and first aid once the trip was underway. If they were not happy with a guide's performance or were not convinced of his competence trekking through the brush, there might be little they could do about it, since they would be, quite literally, lost without him. If migrants wanted to leave a safe house near the border or in the destination city, even if they were not being physically restrained from doing so, they might not know where they were, might not speak English, might not be carrying any U.S. currency with them, and might not immediately know how to use the U.S. phone system to contact anyone they knew who might be able to help them. Given their inexperience, coyotes could attempt to instill fear in migrants stuck in a safe house, lying to them that the neighborhood around it was full of criminals, that la migra was patrolling the area heavily, and the like, in order to ensure their docility. A federal public defender I interviewed in 2001 said although he had not seen any true hostage situations involving the "alien smuggling" defendants he had represented, he had observed some of these examples of "psychological coercion." These types of disadvantages vis-à-vis their coyotes were more likely to be true for first-time migrants than for those who had crossed repeatedly and already had experience living and working in the United States. In this regard, however, we must bear in mind that the majority of migrants returning to Mexico in the first years of this century in this stretch of the border appear to have been returning from their *first* undocumented trip to the United States.[30]

The legal status of undocumented migrants in the United States also limited their ability to seek redress against abusive coyotes once they had crossed the border. This was not because U.S. law enforcement authorities were unwilling to act against abuses by coyotes committed against "illegals." On the contrary, the authorities were typically quite willing to act, although inexperienced migrants might not realize this. The problem for migrants was that, unless they could prove that they had been of victims of trafficking,[31] stepping forth to denounce coyote abuses carried the risk of being deported back to Mexico. So, for example, if a migrant was being held against his will in a safe house in Houston, his relatives, who had agreed to be the "respondents" for his trip but were being extorted by the coyotes for a higher fee than was agreed on, would have to weigh contacting the police to rescue him against the risk of being exposed as residing in the country illegally. Under such circumstances, they might decide to pay the additional money if they were able to come up with it. Relatives might be hesitant to contact the police even if they were legal permanent residents of the United States, out of concern that they could jeopardize their legal status by admitting to financing the coyotaje and/or that even if they could use the police to avoid the extortion, the family member whose trip they were financing would get sent back to Mexico. Migrants who went to the police to press criminal charges against coyotes in Mexican border towns such as Matamoros faced another hurdle: coyotes who actively recruited migrants in these towns typically paid hefty bribes to the police to allow them to operate freely.[32] Thus, migrants seeking redress from the border-town police for abuses by coyotes were not likely to find much satisfaction. Migrants looking for help from law enforcement authorities elsewhere in Mexico might also be given pause by the astonishingly high rates of impunity for crimes committed nationwide: a 2004 study, whose results were distributed to the press by the Mexican presidency, reported that of every 100 crimes known to be committed in Mexico, only 25 were reported to the police, only 4.5 were investigated, only 1.6 went to court, and fewer than 1.1 resulted in the application of a criminal penalty to the defendant (Guerrero 2004).

Coyotes and the Use of Force

The final consideration regarding power dynamics between migrants and their coyotes has to do with the use of force by coyotes to exercise control over the migrants they were transporting. As noted above, coyotes were typically outnumbered by migrants at most points along the border-crossing trip, so generally speaking physical strength was not an adequate way to exert control if migrants became "disobedient." For this reason, and also perhaps for protection against enemies, both known and potential, some coyotes carried and brandished firearms, whether pistols or rifles. Thus, there were reports in the press of migrants in Houston, San Antonio, and Austin being locked in rooms under armed guard in safe houses until their passage (or an additional ransom) was paid by friends and/or relatives (see, for example, Crowe 2004; Minaya 2005). Clearly, under these circumstances, it was the coyotes who wielded the power. Another way of making trust "enforceable" was for coyotes to threaten or carry out violence against migrants and/or their families who failed to pay them or denounced them to the authorities. Some cases of this happening were also documented in the press (see, for example, Harmon 1999 and Grupo Reforma 2004).

Nonetheless, it was not clear that in this part of the border region coyotes were typically armed or that they typically brandished these arms to control migrants up through the end of the first five years of the new century. Only a few of the migrants I interviewed reported that their coyotes carried weapons, and none of the coyotes I interviewed admitted to doing so. Federal public defenders who handled "alien smuggling" cases told me that their clients typically were not armed when they were arrested, while U.S. Attorneys reported that most of the cases they prosecuted had not involved the use of firearms. A federal judge I interviewed corroborated these assessments from opposing attorneys, as did federal probation and pretrial services officers. Border Patrol agents I interviewed in the Lower Rio Grande Valley in Texas also reported that coyotes were seldom armed, whether in the brush, driving on the highway, or in safe houses in the border towns. In 2004 I asked one of these agents, who had worked in his sector's anti-smuggling unit before being promoted to a higher-ranking administrative position, whether he had seen coyotes using in South Texas in the same way as had recently been making the news in Arizona:

AGENT: It's different cultures. Different cultures, you know.
SPENER: So you're saying they're not typically armed here?
AGENT: They're not here. Maybe that's the thing to do in Tucson. Maybe that's the thing to do in Arizona. Why we don't see it here, I don't know.
SPENER: But when you find a safe house or a stash house in this area....
AGENT: You typically don't see weapons on anybody. Go in there, take everybody down, and they're just aliens. And the actual guys that are there at the stash house, you know, somebody's guarding them with nothing. They don't have a gun or anything else.

In my review of a sample of the records of "alien smuggling" cases prosecuted in the federal court in Laredo, Texas (197 smuggling incidents, 261 defendants), *none* of the incident reports written by the arresting Border Patrol agents described the presence or use of firearms by the defendants.[33] Moreover, patterns I observed in the sentencing reports prepared by federal probation officers and the sentences imposed by federal judges in these cases did not indicate the use or possession of firearms by defendants, which would have increased the penalties for the coyotaje in which they were engaged. Thus, although there certainly were some documented cases of coyote use of firearms in the region to control migrants, and it could be true that more coyotes in the region were using weapons than was previously the case, available data do not allow us to conclude that most coyotes were armed most of the time or that they typically brandished these weapons against migrants.

Coyotes I interviewed had two main reasons for not carrying weapons with them while taking migrants into Texas. They were quite explicit in their comments about one of these: it simply was not necessary. Migrants were typically quite cooperative and did what they were instructed to do. They wanted very badly to get to their destinations as quickly as possible and placed their trust in the coyotes to get them there. When they got to their destinations, migrants' respondents were prepared to pay their fees, and typically did so promptly, since they had agreed to the terms in advance. Beto, the coyote from La Cancha, Nuevo León, who used to take migrants to Austin, was surprised when I asked him if he ever carried a weapon: "No! They're real peaceful people. All they want is to get where they're going, get reunited with their family members, and get to work. They aren't looking for trouble." In addition, violent disputes between different groups of coyotes were uncommon on this stretch of the border, and, as a result, coyotes did not feel the need to be armed to defend themselves from other coyotes. They were not so explicit about the second reason for not arming themselves: the penalties for "alien smuggling" increased dramatically if they were armed at the time of their arrest. Several of them did, however, tell me of their awareness of intensified prosecution of coyotes by U.S. authorities with longer sentences. They knew that being arrested with a gun would get them into more trouble. If migrants were generally cooperative with you, you weren't afraid of other coyotes attacking you, and your risk of serving a lengthy jail sentence increased if you were carrying a firearm, why would you carry one? Nonetheless, we must recognize some coyotes operating in this part of the region were "armed and dangerous" and used weapons to threaten and extort migrants. It is conceivable that as the risks to coyotes of prosecution and serving lengthy jail sentences increases, as has been the case in recent years, a growing number will resort to arming themselves and threatening migrants with violence in order to enforce the terms of their "contract" and to protect themselves from prosecution. Thus, government efforts to prosecute coyotes, far from protecting migrants, could actually have the effect of placing them at greater risk. Speaking about the escalation of state border control efforts in Canada and Europe as well as on the U.S.-Mexico border, Sharma (2005, 96–97) notes that the main result of anti-trafficking/anti-smuggling campaigns has been to "make illegalized migrations much more dangerous" and to make "the emergence of modern-day Harriet Tubmans even more unlikely."[34]

Paradoxically, such a development could be most dangerous for migrants who contracted coyotes who had established relations with their community, since these "socially embedded" coyotes would be likely to know how to find migrants' friends and relatives in order to exact retribution against them should anyone denounce them to the authorities. Families and friends of migrants who contracted with their coyotes more or less anonymously at the border presumably would not run the same risk of retribution, since the coyotes would not know who they were. Nonetheless, because (1) no single coyote organization or set of organizations monopolized crossing the border between South Texas and Northeast Mexico; (2) not all coyotes were "armed and dangerous"; and (3) information could travel quickly within migrant networks, coyotes who used threats and violence against their customers were likely to be avoided by migrants who had been warned against them by their *paisanos*.

The U.S. government brought tremendous economic and human resources to bear in its attempt to develop a militarized high-tech institutional infrastructure designed to prevent unauthorized incursions across its border with Mexico by peasant and working-class migrants. In this chapter, I have argued that the resources that migrants availed themselves of to resist their forcible exclusion from U.S. territory were mainly social and cultural, not financial or technological. In other words, the principal strength that migrants brought to the "battle for the border" was their tradition of mutual aid, which helped compensate for the overall resource disadvantages they faced in their confrontation with state institutions. To an increasing extent, migrants invested what resources they were able to mobilize within their networks in order to identify, hire, and pay coyotes to help them travel to the United States surreptitiously. Although press accounts highlight their increased revenues and growing technological sophistication, I have argued here that the resources most needed by coyotes to successfully take migrants across the border were social in nature, consisting mainly of connections to willing collaborators on both sides of the border and to a pool of potential customers in migrant communities. Moreover, it appears that benefits could accrue to both migrants and coyotes when the transactions between them were characterized by relations of trust. On the one hand, it helped each manage the risks they faced in making a dangerous crossing. On the other, it gave coyotes the confidence to invest scarce resources at the outset of the undertaking, knowing that they could reasonably expect payment from migrants in the end, which in effect granted migrants a kind of uncollateralized loan to make the trip.

Nevertheless, we must bear in mind that clandestine border-crossing was an inherently dangerous activity, and that trust relations and the social capital they generated were too often insufficient to guarantee migrants' safe passage. In addition, many migrants found themselves obliged to engage in transactions with coyotes who were strangers to *them*, even if they had been recommended

by friends or relatives. We might regard such transactions as partially embedded, with consequently partial protection to migrants, since the strenuous nature of border-crossings could put even the strongest relationships to the test.
Furthermore, our recognition that migrant-coyote transactions were socially
embedded and that social capital was utilized by both parties to clandestine
border-crossing must not blind us to the power relations that also characterized such transactions. In particular, we must recognize that for migrants, risk
management in undertaking a clandestine crossing of the border consisted
largely of attempting to manage their inherent *vulnerability,* for the undocumented migrant was also the *unprotected* migrant. While coyotes were not responsible for migrants' vulnerable condition—capital and the state bore that
responsibility—coyotes could be in a position to exploit their vulnerability,
and some did, quite pitilessly. At the same time, to the extent that information traveled through migrant networks and no single coyote or small group
of coyotes monopolized clandestine transit at the border, coyotes who developed a reputation for mistreating, abandoning, or failing to deliver migrants
to their intended destinations eventually paid a price for their malfeasance or
incompetence, even if no immediate reprisals were taken against them. In this
chapter, I have shown how such reputations mattered to individual coyotes as
they conducted their business. In the next chapter, I turn to the reputation of
coyotes in general through an examination of the ways in which they are portrayed in the stories that different types of informants tell about the process of
clandestine border-crossing.

CHAPTER 6

Passing Judgment

Coyotes in the Discourse of Clandestine Border-Crossing

In the previous chapters, I have described the process of coyotaje on the Northeast Mexico-South Texas border as a heterogeneous phenomenon, involving a range of participants who engaged in a multiplicity of social relations as they pursued a variety of clandestine border-crossing strategies. In so doing, I have tried to offer a more detailed and nuanced account of how clandestine border-crossing occurred on this stretch of the border than was typically offered by government officials and disseminated in media accounts. To the extent that space has permitted, I have used migrants' and coyotes' own descriptions of their experiences in order to give the reader as much insight as possible into how each type of coyotaje strategy worked on this stretch of the border at the beginning of the twenty-first century, from the point of view of those who engaged in it. In this chapter, I examine the variety of ways in which coyotaje and coyotes were normatively characterized by government officials, the news media, human rights activists, migrants, and coyotes themselves. At times the subjective evaluations offered by these different sets of informants coincided to a considerable extent, while at others they diverged markedly.

Not surprisingly, coyotaje and coyotes were portrayed in a relentlessly negative light by government officials, whose authority and control over territories and populations were called into question by clandestine border-crossings. Coyotes, on the other hand, tended to see themselves in a more positive light, as providing a valuable service to migrants that no one else was willing to provide. Meanwhile, migrants and their communities tended to have more equivocal attitudes toward coyotes and coyotaje, depending in large measure on the personal experiences they or their friends and relatives had had crossing the border with coyotes. Regardless of whose account was more accurate, one thing was clear: the government's view was the one that dominated public understanding and discussion of the phenomenon. There were reasons for this that I will outline below. Before doing that, however, I would like to explain why I believe a consideration of the subjective accounts of coyote-assisted border-crossings is in order.

In collecting border-crossing stories from a variety of informants, I have observed that the term *coyote* is polysemous with regard to the contemporary practice of clandestine border-crossing. The Oxford English Dictionary defines *polysemous* as a word "that has a multiplicity of meanings, or bears many different interpretations." Moreover, as discussed in chapter 3, the term *coyote* is polysemous more generally in Mexican society, especially in mythology and folklore, where it exhibits a rich and complex set of metaphorical connotations. The role played by coyotes in the drama of clandestine border-crossing is often morally ambiguous, permitting contradictory evaluations of their character from the point of view of different groups of participants in or observers of the phenomenon and on their performance at different points in migrants' journeys across the border.[1] Meanwhile, public discussion of clandestine border-crossing has been distorted by the paucity of concrete information about the particulars of the process from the point of view of its participants, a distortion that I have attempted to redress in this book. As a result, what is generally "known" about coyotes and clandestine border-crossing by the nonmigrant public in both Mexico and the United States is almost exclusively the product of their discursive construction in the press, which has generally served more to incite "moral panic" about migration than to soberly inform a number of possible moral evaluations of who coyotes are and what they do.[2]

The Dominant View: The State and the News Media

U.S. government officials had very negative opinions of coyotes, in large measure because coyotes undermined what they regarded to be one of the state's basic prerogatives—the regulation of the movement of people across its frontiers. The success of coyotes in penetrating state borders discredited government claims of effectively protecting national territory against foreign incursions and called into question the competence and efficacy of officials charged with the enforcement of customs and immigration controls. Thus, coyotes represented, not only a challenge to state authority, but also a threat to the image of state bureaucrats concerned with keeping their jobs and advancing their careers. At the same time, government officials could find the threat posed by coyotes to be a useful tool in protecting or even expanding their personnel and budgets. To the extent that coyotes, along with smugglers of weapons and illegal narcotics, could be successfully portrayed as a substantial and growing threat to national security that "outgunned" law enforcement authorities on the border, state bureaucrats could use such portrayals to justify ever-increasing budgets for their agencies. This has been done quite successfully by U.S. law enforcement agencies on the border since the 1980s (Andreas 2000; Dunn 1996; Massey, Durand, and Malone 2002; Nevins 2002).

Nevertheless, government officials' negative opinion of coyotes owed not only to the threat coyotes posed to these officials' authority or to some bureaucratic advantage they gained by exaggerating the threat posed by coyotes. Aside from the migrants who were their victims, law enforcement agents were the main witnesses to whatever abuses coyotes inflicted on migrants or on each other. Even if agents did not encounter evidence of overt abuses of migrants in most cases in which they arrested coyotes, the images of the abuses they did encounter—corpses in a rail car, a woman who had been raped and beaten, barefoot migrants locked in a crowded, filthy room—would be indelibly seared into their memories: *"These are the types of things that coyotes do to people."* At the same time, as discussed in chapter 5, law enforcement agents were more likely to make arrests in cases involving abusive or incompetent coyotes than in cases involving less abusive and more competent ones, introducing a selectivity bias that could distort law enforcement's understanding of who coyotes were and what they were like. Adding to this distortion was the fact that providers of services such as *document dispatch* and *migra-coyotaje*— in which the dangers faced by migrants were typically less serious—might not even be considered to be coyotes by government officials, who restricted their use of the term exclusively to refer to full-time, for-profit guides and transporters of migrants.

No quantitative content analysis of news stories is needed to state unequivocally that negative characterizations of "smugglers" and "traffickers" by government officials dominated media coverage of border issues during this period. There are several reasons why the state's perspective on the phenomenon was disseminated by the media to the near exclusion of perspectives that might be offered by other actors knowledgeable about the practices associated with autonomous migration by Mexicans. These are important to understand, since the only knowledge that most U.S. and Mexican citizens have of the social process of clandestine border-crossing comes from what they see, hear, and read in the media.[3]

One of the chief reasons that the views of government officials predomi-
nated in news coverage of border issues was that their views were taken by the
press as newsworthy by virtue of the positions of bureaucratic authority they
occupied. In addition, the U.S. Department of Homeland Security was the only
institution in South Texas concerned with issues of immigration and border
enforcement that had a well-developed public relations infrastructure. Needless
to say, autonomous migrants and their coyotes had no such PR apparatus to
help get out their side of the story. Rather than seek to influence public opinion
about their activities, they did everything possible to protect their anonymity and clandestinity in an effort to evade capture and prosecution by law enforcement authorities. Thus, while reporters working under deadline on tight
budgets found it easy to obtain interviews and information from the Border
Patrol, they had to work hard to even locate migrants and coyotes who had information relevant to the news events they were covering, much less interview
them in depth. Relatedly, most coyote-assisted border-crossings never made
the news at all unless they involved a death, an accident, or an arrest. In other
words, successful crossings in which coyotes rendered services to migrants
competently and without abusing them were not called to the public's attention. When they arrived at their destinations intact, migrants continued to go
about their business clandestinely, as did their coyotes. They did not contact
the press to inform them of their latest successes in overcoming the U.S. government's border enforcement tactics. Even in those relatively few instances in
which journalists were allocated funds and time to undertake special investigative reports about clandestine border-crossing and coyotaje, the legitimating
force of the law itself could influence reporters' perspectives, especially if some
of the most articulate people they found to interview were law enforcement
officials who emphasized the criminality of "smuggling" as an activity and
their own role in upholding the "rule of law."[4] In some cases, reporters might
defer to law enforcement officials' framing of "smuggling" issues so as not to
jeopardize their access to them as valuable sources of breaking news. In other
cases, reporters might not be able to interview migrants and coyotes who had
been apprehended, because most were returned to Mexico quickly after being
detained.[5] The legal jeopardy faced by those who remained in custody as suspects or material witnesses gave them little incentive to speak with reporters.
In principle, some of this information might come out during a trial, but few
cases involving the laws against entering the United States illegally or helping
someone to do so ever went to trial. The vast majority ended with a guilty plea
by the defendant.[6]

In subsequent sections of this chapter, I review the normative characterizations of coyotes and coyotaje offered by a variety of participants in and

observers of the clandestine border-crossing drama. Rather than analyze these characterizations strictly as a function of the type of actor who made them, I categorize the characterizations themselves and examine the varying ways in which different actors employed them as they talked about their experiences with border-crossing. First, I review a set of negative characterizations in which coyotes played the role of villain in this life-and-death drama. Second, I examine a set of more positive characterizations of coyotes made by migrants and coyotes themselves. With these competing sets of characterizations in mind, I then explore the moral ambiguities concerning the particularly troubling issue of who was responsible for migrants who got left behind on the trail in the unforgiving brush country of South Texas.

Coyote as Villain

Although hundreds of thousands of Mexicans living and working in the United States owed their successful border-crossing to a coyote's assistance, coyotes often played the role of "bad guy" in the stories told about the migration process by a variety of social actors who did not otherwise share similar points of view. When I initiated my fieldwork for this book in the summer of 1998, I asked informants to tell me about the different types of coyotes they were familiar with, thinking they would distinguish, for example, between "border" coyotes and "interior" coyotes or "professional" and "occasional" coyotes, using a typology similar to the one advanced by López Castro (1998) in his research for the *Binational Study of Migration between Mexico and the United States.* When I posed this question to a Mexican human rights activist who worked at the border, she listed the following types without hesitation: *los estafadores, los avaros, los violadores, y los asesinos* (the rip-off artists, the greedy ones, the rapists, and the murderers). In her view, "los escrupulosos ya no trabajan de coyotes" [scrupulous people no longer work as coyotes]. Although this activist's view was one of the more extreme characterizations I heard from nongovernmental sources, I found certain "bad guy" tropes recurring in the accounts offered by a variety of informants, including migrants and coyotes themselves, as well as Border Patrol agents and other government officials. Three villainous tropes were especially prominent. The first was that coyotes are not trustworthy. The second was that coyotes are motivated by greed—they look out only for themselves and show no regard for the health and well-being of the migrants they transport. The third was that coyotes are violent thugs, who cheat, rob, extort, and assault migrants when they can. Of course, these tropes were not always stated particularly coherently in conversations with migrants and other informants. Moreover, each of these tropes frequently appeared in combination with one or more of the others, especially insofar as coyotes' avarice was offered as the reason for their other moral failings.

Never Trust a Coyote

In the folklore of Mexican migration, the figure of the coyote is portrayed much the same as in Mexican mythology and folklore more generally, that is, as a clever, self-interested predator and trickster (see, for example, Herrera-Sobek 1993). It is precisely this deep cultural belief in the untrustworthiness of coyotes that government authorities on both sides of the border sought to build on in their public relations campaigns to discourage migrants from contracting guides to enter the United States. We can see examples of this clearly in pages taken from a comic book (fig. 6.1) published by the Mexican secretariat of foreign relations in 2005 titled *Guía del migrante mexicano* (Mexican Migrant's Guide), and in two posters (fig. 6.2) that the Border Patrol exhibited on the walls of its detention centers where apprehended migrants were processed and held pending deportation.

The Mexican government published the *Guía del migrante mexicano* in an effort to warn its citizens of the dangers and risks of attempting to enter the United States without proper immigration documents. One of the principal dangers to migrants that the guide warned against was placing one's faith in a coyote to cross the border. The *Guía* told migrants not to trust coyotes because they would tell them that the crossing was much easier and less risky than it really was, and that coyotes were responsible for hundreds of migrant deaths.

The message of the two Border Patrol posters, one showing a lone grave in the desert ("He trusted a coyote") and the other a Mexican funeral ("Their brother trusted a coyote") is blunt: coyotes kill migrants. These posters were part of the U.S. Border Patrol's Border Safety Initiative, undertaken in the region after the launching of Operation Rio Grande. This initiative consisted of increased search-and-rescue operations and public service announcements broadcast on Mexican radio and television that warned migrants of the risks of crossing with a paid guide. It was undertaken as a response to markedly increased deaths by drowning, dehydration, and hypothermia in remote areas due to increased patrolling of urbanized stretches of the border (United States Customs and Border Protection 2005).

Some of the migrants I interviewed also warned against trusting coyotes. Rafael, a twenty-five-year-old man from rural Michoacán, lived in a Texas city with his sister and her family. He worked in the landscaping business of his U.S.-citizen brother. At the time of my interview with him in 2003, he had

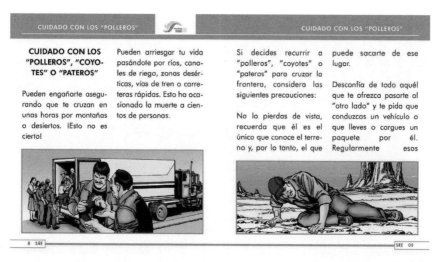

Figure 6.1. Excerpt from *Guía del migrante mexicano* (Mexican migrant's guide), published in 2005 by Mexico's Secretaría de Relaciones Exteriores and distributed at numerous locations throughout the country.

Translation: Be careful with *polleros, coyotes,* or *pateros.* They can fool you, assuring you that they'll take you through mountains or deserts in just a few hours. It's not true! They can put your life at risk, taking you across rivers, irrigation canals, desert zones, railways, or high-speed highways. This has caused the deaths of hundreds of people. If you decide to resort to *polleros, coyotes,* or *pateros* to cross the border, consider the following precautions: Don't let him get out of your sight: remember he is the only one who knows the terrain and, as a consequence, the only one who can lead you out of that place. Don't trust anyone who offers to take you across the border and asks you to drive a vehicle or carry a package for him. These packets often contain drugs or other prohibited substances. If you transport other people, you can be mistakenly thought to be the *pollero* or *coyote,* and you can be accused of the crimes of human smuggling or car theft. Don't put your children in the hands of strangers who offer to cross them into the United States for you.

made three clandestine crossings of the border, with three different sets of coyotes. His first trip in early 1997, when he was just eighteen, had gone very badly. Women were molested, a man was bitten by a rattlesnake and left behind on the trail, and the coyotes had some of the migrants carry knapsacks full of drugs in exchange for free passage. He made it to his destination but was traumatized by the experience. His next two crossings, in 1999 and then again in 2001, both made after Operation Rio Grande was launched, went extremely well. The coyotes behaved professionally and treated their customers considerately. Nevertheless, he believed that migrants should not place much faith in their coyotes, given the dangerous nature of the crossing and their vulnerability to deceit and mistreatment. Although many people in his community had gotten to the United States successfully with coyotes, and the community depended on coyotaje services for its survival, Rafael said there was no coyote

Figure 6.2. These two posters were commonly displayed in the cells in which apprehended migrants were detained in Border Patrol stations in South Texas in the first years of the twenty-first century. *Source:* U.S. Border Patrol.

you could trust. For one thing, he said that the recruiters in Michoacán frequently handed migrants off to other, unknown, coyotes at the border. More important, he believed that migrants were in an inherently vulnerable situation when they crossed the border with coyotes.

> I've been very lucky. I've managed to get here alive. But then I think about what would have happened on my last trip if they'd kicked me or if they'd beaten me up somewhere where I couldn't fight back. I would have been left behind on the trail. That's why you can't trust anyone. No person is trustworthy. Nobody! Making it to the United States is a blessing. You have to be really lucky.

Other migrants I interviewed similarly warned against trusting coyotes. In doing so they employed the next "villainous" trope I will discuss.

The Corrupting Influence of Easy Money

One of the main explanations offered by my informants for why you should never trust a coyote was that coyotes were only interested in one thing—money—and that all other considerations were secondary in their pursuit of that objective. This explanation often took a very specific form: coyotes are in the business of "crossing" migrants today because it is *dinero fácil* (easy money), dishonestly taken from hard-working people who deserve better treatment. A mechanic from Tamaulipas who had lived and worked in the heavily Mexican Pasadena and Magnolia sections of Houston since 1970 had heard numerous stories about coyotes over the years. Although he recognized that many of his family members, friends, and co-workers could not have made it to the United States without the services of a coyote, he remained quite antagonistic toward them: "They pay the coyotes for protection. Some people consider them to be heroes, but for me they're criminals. They're people who are just looking for easy money."

Another migrant employing this trope was Fernanda, a seventeen-year-old woman from a rural settlement in southern Tamaulipas, who in early 2001 had been taken surreptitiously into a Texas border town at her employer's behest to work as a maid. She and her brother had actually been served quite well by their coyotes. Using a migra-coyotaje strategy, Fernanda had been driven across one of the international bridges in the backseat of a car and waved through by a complicit immigration inspector. A year earlier, her brother had made it safely to Dallas, with his professional-migration coyotes making heroic efforts to get him there. He had not had to pay them any money up front. It had taken them two attempts to get him to Dallas, each time crossing the Río Bravo on an inner tube and then trekking three days through the brush to get around the immigration checkpoints. It had cost $2,000, a lot of money, but her brother had been able to pay off the loans from friends and relatives within a couple of months after finding work. The two coyotes that took Fernanda's brother to Dallas were based in her rural village and enjoyed a fairly good reputation in the community for reliability. Both of them lived well, by local standards, but were not rich. Each had become a coyote by building on his own migratory experiences. One of the two had papers and could travel back and forth between Tamaulipas and Dallas by car. Not only did this man arrange residents' crossings into Texas, but he also performed the vital service of carrying migrants' remittances back to the community from Dallas, in the form of both cash and merchandise. Nevertheless, Fernanda was resentful about how much they had charged her brother and used the "easy money" trope to express how she thought the coyotes were gouging their customers:

> The coyotes shouldn't charge so much. They're greedy. They're taking advantage of the situation of the people who want to come [to the United States]. They should charge us less. A few years ago it only cost $500, and now they charge us $2,000. It's greed. They want easy money.

Stories told by other informants went beyond resentment about coyotes' greediness. In these stories, coyotes' obsession with easy money blinded them to the risks that they inflicted on their customers. For example, Vicente, a construction worker living in Texas, who was originally from the town of Moreno, San Luis Potosí, told me of a bad experience he had with a coyote from his town who had failed to deliver a brother whose crossing he had agreed to sponsor. The brother and a friend had been abandoned in the *monte* by the coyote when the friend's feet became so blistered he could not continue walking. Had his brother not stayed back with the friend and carried him out to a road, Vicente said, the friend would have died. Vicente believed that even coyotes who were recommended to you by friends and relatives could not be trusted in the *monte:*

> It doesn't matter how well-recommended they are.... Ask anyone, and they'll tell you that there's no one you can trust in the *monte.* Not even your cousin who's a coyote. Because the coyote only thinks about money. He doesn't care about the people he's taking.

Here Vicente's comments echo those of Border Patrol agents who denounced coyotes for their lack of concern with migrants' safety and well-being. One of these agents insisted to me that all that coyotes cared about was maximizing their profits:

> And as far as the alien-smuggling activities, I don't think it'll ever stop because it's a big enterprise. It's an industry where it's very profitable for a smuggler. And they're not going to stop it. As long as they can make a buck, regardless of saving somebody's life, they're going to do it. Because they're only interested in one thing—and that's the big dollar bill.... We're catching groups, you know, of 99 in the back of tractor-trailers, that we just caught a few weeks ago. You multiply 99 times 3,000! The average fee was $3,200.[7] That's a lot of money to make in a day's work.

An agent in the investigative branch of the INS whom I interviewed in 2001 insisted that the larger sums of money that were by then at play in the "smuggling business" had transformed it into one that was dominated by criminal gangs that had no ongoing relations with or concern for the migrants they transported:

> Smugglers used to have many faces—friends, family, church people, in addition to criminals. Today the smuggler is more likely to be a professional

criminal than a family member....Mexicans are just another piece of merchandise for the smugglers now. This is a business driven by greed.[8]

Law enforcement authorities such as these immigration agents were routinely quoted in news stories about incidents in which migrants had been mistreated, injured, or killed on their coyote-led journeys across this stretch of the border. In these reports, officials often took the opportunity to denounce coyotes' disregard for the well-being of migrants they transported, using the "greed ⇒ disregard for human life" trope to explain the tragedies that had befallen migrants in the region. For example, in June 1996, a year before the launching of Operation Rio Grande, the *San Antonio Express-News* ran a story about migrant deaths from heat and dehydration in Kenedy County in South Texas. The head of the Rio Grande Valley sector of the Border Patrol was quoted as saying that "smugglers" were taking advantage of the weak and people who were desperate for jobs: "They're bringing families to Houston. What's really callous is when somebody gets sick, they're abandoned." In the same story, the reporter quoted a Border Patrol agent named Roy Chávez, who said that the potential for tragedy would get worse as the summer grew hotter and "smugglers" looked for any way to make a buck: "They've been in the business too long, they don't care. They don't have a heart" (Schiller 1996b). The Border Patrol spokesperson for the Del Río sector made similar comments about a tragic incident that occurred near Eagle Pass, Texas, in March 2005, in which a toddler was swept away by the current and drowned as a group of migrants guided by coyotes crossed the Rio Grande: "They [the coyotes] abandoned them at the point where the child was lost because at that point they were screaming for help. These are the dangers of crossing in unknown areas and trusting people who are just out to make money. [The coyotes] have very little regard for human life, and this is just a terrible tragedy" (quoted in Associated Press 2005b).

Sometimes law enforcement agents' comments to the press about coyotes appeared to be almost reflexive, as they fell back on the "greed ⇒ disregard for human life" trope automatically, even if it didn't neatly fit the facts of the case in question. For example, in the early morning hours of January 26, 2006, a pickup truck loaded with migrants was broadsided by a tractor-trailer on U.S. 281 north of the Falfurrias checkpoint as it drove onto the highway from a county road, killing six of its passengers and injuring seven others, some severely. According to an officer of the Texas Department of Public Safety, the driver of the pickup "didn't have any idea what was in store for him" as he turned onto the highway. Although the stop sign that was supposed to have been posted on the county road at the intersection with the major highway was missing—it had been knocked down by another vehicle a day or two earlier—the Border Patrol's spokesperson for the Rio Grande Valley sector blamed the coyotes for the accident: "It's just another example of how smugglers have total disregard for human life. They only care about money" (both men quoted in Zarazua 2006). The driver, a twenty-five-year-old man from a small town in the state of Tabasco, was also seriously injured in the accident. After being released from the hospital and appearing in federal court, where he was charged with "alien smuggling," he hanged himself with a sheet on his first night in jail (Doerge and Vásquez 2006).

Occasionally, however, law enforcement authorities themselves acknowledged another possible product of coyotes' greed for easy money. This occurred in the summer of 2001 when Alvin Santleben, head of the Immigration and Naturalization Service's Anti-Smuggling Unit in Eagle Pass, Texas, was interviewed by a National Public Radio reporter. In the interview, Santleben discussed the difficulties in attacking "smuggling organizations." Although he made clear his low opinion of coyotes, he had the following to say about the incentives that influenced their behavior:

> [The coyote] wants to take care of his people. He wants to be recommended for another load. If a coyote loses his load, he's not very well thought of. If he has a death occur in his operation, the organization is exposed. And if it disrupts the organization, people don't make money. And it's all about the dollar bill. (quoted in Burnett 2001)

Here we find a rather startling reversal of the "greed $\Rightarrow$ disregard for human life" trope. Instead of coyotes being so blinded by greed that they show no concern for the health and well-being of migrants, this INS agent argued that, to a certain extent at least, their greed pushed them to make sure that disasters did not befall migrants in their care.

Data from another part of South Texas lent some limited support to the notion that coyotes most of the time did not entirely disregard the health and well-being of their customers or recklessly endanger them. In my analysis of the records of "alien smuggling" incidents prosecuted in the federal courthouse in Laredo, Texas (see Data Sources and Research Methods), I found the majority of cases—58 percent—showed no evidence of significant endangerment of migrants recorded by the arresting officer, while 39 percent showed evidence of some significant endangerment of migrants, mostly involving the overloading of vehicles in which they were being transported. Only six incidents (3% of cases) exhibited what could be termed severe endangerment of migrants. In one of these cases, 117 overheated and dehydrated migrants were being transported in the back of a tractor-trailer, stacked on one another on top of a load of grapefruit. Four cases involved the Border Patrol engaging in high-speed chases of vehicles being driven by coyotes. One of the cases that took place near Encinal, Texas, involved a coyote who, driving at high speed, flipped a pickup truck in which he was transporting 11 migrants. One of the migrants who was hidden under a piece of plywood in the bed of the truck died at the scene, while several others were seriously injured.

Dangerous *Delincuentes*

If the characterizations above portrayed coyotes as being blinded by greed, others depicted them in an even more negative light, as dangerous thugs who mistreated migrants for their own gratification. In the sexual realm, there were stories of rape and abuse of women. This is not surprising, given that women migrants crossing the border often found themselves in socially unregulated situations, in geographically isolated areas, surrounded by young men and unable to seek help from police authorities. Mariana, one of the women I interviewed in Texas, had crossed the border through the two Laredos in 1989 with some coyotes her husband had contracted for her in Nuevo Laredo. Like many women, it was the first and only time she would make the trip. She came from her hometown in Guanajuato with her brother-in-law in order to reunite with her husband in Texas. They made two attempts to cross the border, with two different sets of coyotes. The first ended in apprehension after a trek of three days through the *monte*. The second was successful. On both trips, the coyotes behaved badly, harassing the other women traveling with them. Mariana was not herself harassed by the coyotes, but on the first trip two other young women who were traveling alone were harassed constantly by their guides, especially by one who had been drinking. On the second trip, the group's guides were snorting cocaine. One of them groped a young woman who was accompanied by her brother. When her brother objected, the coyote lifted his shirt to show that he had a pistol under his belt and told him to shut up or be left behind on the trail—with a bullet in him. As Mariana said, "It's really dangerous for a woman. There are a lot of rapes. And it's especially difficult for women traveling alone." Men I interviewed were also quick to recognize the special dangers women faced when crossing the border. Gerardo, a twenty-six-year-old painter and sometime coyote who grew up in Torreón, Coahuila, related the following:

> Everyone has a story they can tell you. People have told me about awful things. About women who were raped in front of the whole group. These

coyotes raped the women right there in front of everyone. And they beat them up and threatened them.[9]

It is also worth noting that some women's migration is motivated by the desire to escape abusive sexual relationships with men in their communities in Mexico. This was the case of a young woman from Coahuila who had fled across the border with her young son in order to escape a battering husband. Her mother arranged for them to cross with the same coyotes who had safely brought her to the United States several years earlier. Although these coyotes were men, there were also *coyotas* [women coyotes] operating in some places who specialized in helping women cross the border.

Another way that coyotes were portrayed negatively was as "border bandits," who, rather than deliver migrants to their destinations as promised, assaulted and robbed them, either directly or by leading them into ambushes set by other assailants on the banks of the Río Bravo. An agent of Grupo Beta, the special Mexican police force dedicated to migrant protection, told me of the quotidian nature of this phenomenon along the river near Matamoros:

In some way, these people [the coyotes], it's in their interest to just cross people and not commit any crimes against them. Logic tells us this. So that their family members will keep calling them so they'll take the nephew across today and the granddaughter across tomorrow. Common sense, logic, indicates this to you. Nevertheless, there are more criminal criminals [*hay delincuentes más delincuentes*] because, aside from charging the person to take them across, they take him or her to unpopulated areas, risky places, where it just happens that the assailant only assaults the migrants but always leaves the trafficker alone. Because obviously they're in cahoots. These are the cases where we always intervene. In this case the person is not just providing the migrant with a service, by crossing him safely, but instead is attacking him.[10]

In the years following the launching of Operation Rio Grande, the U.S. Border Patrol defended itself against criticism by human rights organizations, which claimed that its new control strategies had placed migrants in greater danger, by emphasizing the degree to which more intensive patrolling of the border protected migrants from the depredations of criminals, including coyotes. This message was promoted especially vigorously by a Border Patrol public affairs agent I interviewed in 2001, who said that "migrants have been the main beneficiaries of this operation because we have more agents on the line." He argued that this meant the Border Patrol was more likely to intervene when migrants were being placed in danger by their coyotes. As an example, he related a case in which several women and children had been literally shoved into the river by their coyotes on a cold January night to force them to make the crossing. Border Patrol agents on the Texas side observed the migrants in distress using infrared telescopes and fished them out of the frigid waters to prevent their drowning. Moreover, he said, the agents had been able to radio authorities on the Mexican side who subsequently arrested the coyotes.

The staff of human rights organizations operating on the Mexican side of the border did not necessarily share this agent's view of the benefit of calling on Mexican law enforcement agents to protect migrants from abuse by their coyotes. When I interviewed an activist with one of these organizations on the border in Tamaulipas, she had this to say:

> A lot of times the migrant is most afraid of the local police that hang out on the banks of the river, supposedly making sure that migrants don't drown there. We've had cases where they are assaulted by those same police. The migrants! By the municipal police! And the police detain them, and they're robbed of all their things. If you ask a migrant who he's more afraid of, the police or the patero, he'll tell you the police.

Data I analyzed from the U.S. federal courts in Texas suggest that this human rights activist may have had a point regarding how fearsome migrants regarded coyotes as being. Less than 10 percent of "alien smuggling" defendants in 2003 had ever been convicted of a violent felony prior to their arrest (see table A in Data Sources and Research Methods).[11] In addition, in my review of the records of 197 "alien smuggling" incidents prosecuted in the U.S. courthouse in Laredo, Texas, I found no records indicating the possession or use of firearms or other weapons by defendants, the taking of hostages to ensure payment of fees, or any overt acts of violence committed against defendants (see Data Sources and Research Methods). This did not mean, of course, that such incidents never occurred, only that they were not so common as to inevitably appear in at least one case in a representative sample consisting of nearly two hundred cases prosecuted in the first years of the new century.

Seeing Coyotes in a More Positive Light

My preliminary research on the topic of clandestine border-crossing in the late 1990s relied heavily on interviews with government officials, especially law enforcement agents. Not surprisingly, I heard virtually nothing positive about coyotes. Once I began talking to other types of informants, I began to hear stories about clandestine border-crossing that portrayed coyotes in less villainous ways. An interview I had with a Mexican immigrant in a South Texas border town who was a naturalized U.S. citizen provided an early illustration of this difference in tone. This informant offered to put me in touch, through an intermediary, with some coyotes across the river in Tamaulipas. Although I eagerly accepted the offer, I expressed some initial apprehension about how safe it would be for a *bolillo* (Anglo, "white bread") college professor like me to go visit coyotes on the other side. The informant assured me that I didn't need to worry, that it wouldn't be dangerous. It wasn't, the informant said, as if I were going to meet with operatives of the Gulf Cartel:

> Unfortunately, we don't see what we're doing as criminal. Because nobody is armed. Nobody is going to kill you. Nobody's going to do anything to you. That doesn't happen with [coyotes]. Where there is a problem is along the river on the Mexican side, where you've got the drunks and the drug addicts. But that's another story—another chapter for your book. They know that the people arriving at the border have money with them…so they're waiting there to rob them. But I repeat, we don't see this as criminal. Now, if you wanted to do a study about drugs, in that case I wouldn't get involved. I'm not anything or anyone to them, and they wouldn't think twice about killing me. But no, not with this.

Although the negative characterizations of the behavior and character of coyotes dominated the public discourse about migration on both sides of the border, this interview fragment serves as an initial example of the counternarratives among migrants and others that cast coyotes in a more positive, or at least a less negative, light. Because they were not backed by the government officials who enforced the laws that made coyotaje criminal and were not promoted in the mainstream media, these counternarratives were not widely heard and ran contrary to the "common sense" that the public had come to hold about coyotes. As discussed above, neither coyotes nor their satisfied customers enjoyed a legal standing in either the United States or Mexico that would permit them to publicly challenge the negative light in which they were usually cast. Hence, coyotes had a serious public relations problem that was unlikely to go away in the foreseeable future, regardless of whether the conduct of a "typical" coyote reflected the bad reputation of the group as a whole. Whatever arguments migrants and coyotes might make in their own defense would have to be looked for in what Scott (1990) referred to as the "hidden transcript" of their surreptitious resistance.

In this section I review some of the counterhegemonic narratives I un-covered in my fieldwork on both sides of the border. These have already been implied or alluded to in previous chapters, insofar as I have demonstrated that there was more than one kind of coyotaje practiced in the region; that some types were embedded in social relations of trust within migrant communities and between migrants and coyotes; that migrants had a variety of coyotes to choose from and relied on the reputations that coyotes had in their communi-ties to decide with whom to cross; that coyotes had some good self-interested reasons for treating their customers as well as they could; and that the control that coyotes exercised over migrants on their journeys was not necessarily ab-solute. In these narratives the following types of normative characterizations stood out:

- Coyotes are providers of a valuable service that migrants strongly desire and appreciate.
- Coyotes are expert migrants who best know how to make the crossing successfully.
- Coyotes are normal people, not that different from the migrants they serve.
- Most coyotes are bad, but not the ones we have used. You have to know which ones to choose.

Although none of these interrelated characterizations cast coyotes in a heroic role in the border drama (even when its author was a coyote himself), neither were they consistent with the portrayal of coyotes as preying mercilessly on innocent migrants. I consider each of these characterizations, in turn.

"El coyote es una ayuda"

Contrary to coyotes' depiction in much of the public debate about migration as dangerous criminals motivated by greed, some migrants I interviewed in several places in Mexico told me that they valued their coyotes highly as pro-viders of a vital service that made it possible for them to cross the border more safely. For example; several young men I interviewed in working-class neigh-borhoods in the Monterrey, Nuevo León, metropolitan area spoke of how they traveled with professional-migration coyotes who knew how to evade or bribe their way past Mexican police on their way to good crossing points on the Río Bravo and who knew the best places and safest ways to ride freight trains away from the border once they were in Texas. Although these men were young and gave the appearance of being tough and street-smart, they emphasized that they preferred crossing the border with a trusted coyote or coyotes because it made them feel safer. A good coyote could show you the ropes and help you avoid mishaps of all kinds along the way.

In a very different context, José, a married man and father of two young daughters from Rancho San Nicolás, Guanajuato, quoted previously, had similar things to say about the coyotes with whom people from his area traveled to the United States. Generally, he said, people in his community regarded their local coyotes positively because of the value of the service they provided:

> José: Normally around here they're considered to be good people because they help you get to the United States and they're seen as helpful to everyone. They see it as a benefit that some poor people will be able to get out of poverty by going to the United States. And if there's someone who's going to help you do it, you look at it positively. That's why you don't think of saying that [the coyote] is a bad guy, or something like that, even though he's charging you money. Because when you get there you know that with any luck you're going to make more money than you're paying him.
>
> Spener: So people around here think of coyotes as being good people?
>
> José: Right, they're people who want to help you. They can help you…it is a big help, because I think that anyone who doesn't know the border runs a lot of risks. He doesn't know the river, he doesn't know the people, he doesn't know the places, the routes. So a person who can guide you like that, I think he's helping you a lot.

In the same vein, Álvaro, the migrant from La Carmela, San Luis Potosí, who hired a coyote from his area to return to Texas and reunite with his wife and daughter after being deported, was extremely grateful to the man for getting him quickly and safely back across the border. This coyote had solved the acute economic and emotional crisis that his unplanned deportation had brought his family. Álvaro knew just how hard it would have been to get back to his family and his job had the coyote not been willing to take him. Shortly after making it back "home" to Texas early in the summer, he sang the man's praises:

> He knew how to get people across. He has never failed. He treats people very well. I have no complaints about him. They only call him "coyote" because he takes people across, but I don't think of him as a coyote, I think of him as *una ayuda* [literally, "a help," i.e., a facilitator] more than anything. He's helping us.

Moreover, Álvaro thought that the $2,000 he had paid to the coyote to be spirited through the highway checkpoint in a tractor-trailer rig had definitely been worth it:

SPENER: So, at this time do you think that these $2,000 were a good investment, or could you just as well have walked yourself?

ÁLVARO: I think it was the right thing to do because I really didn't want to walk. It's a lot of walking, it's all in the brush, and you never know. All in all, I'd say it was the right decision. This way I come a little better protected than if I were walking. It's still safer than walking. Yes, I would say it was a good investment I made. It was a lot of money, but I'd say it was worth it.

SPENER: So, if you were back in your *rancho* again sometime and people came to ask you, "Hey, I'm thinking about going. How should I do it?" What would your advice be?

ÁLVARO: My opinion, my advice that I would give them would be that they should look for someone to take them across. My opinion is that they should get someone to take them, like this man that took me. Because it's very dangerous in the *monte,* especially at this time of year....So doing it this way, you pay a bit more, but it's more secure. You don't walk at all.[12]

"El coyote es el que conoce el camino mejor que uno"

Another characterization of coyotes that emerged in interviews I conducted with a variety of informants on both sides of the border corresponded to the type of coyotaje that I have designated as professional migration. When I asked Simón, a young migrant I met in Monterrey in the summer of 1999, how he would characterize the coyotes with whom he had crossed, he said simply that "el coyote es él que conoce el camino mejor que uno" [the coyote is the one who knows the way better than you do]. In other words, for him, coyotes were simply experienced migrants who learned to capitalize on their knowledge to guide their *camaradas* (companions) across the border. According to Simón, some of the coyotes he knew had become honored community members. They could also be good *compadres* to have, he said, since they tended to have a bit more money than most people and could help you out when you needed it. Simón made clear to me that this characterization of coyotes applied only to the coyotes from around where he lived. According to him, as many other migrants I interviewed in the Mexican interior had told me, it was best to avoid coyotes at the border, for you could not trust them. I will return to this point below.

"Gente normal, gente decente"

Although, as discussed above, migrants might remain distrustful and maintain a low opinion of coyotes even when they had benefited from their services, some other migrants I interviewed had come to evaluate their coyotes more positively. One of the ways that migrants who held their coyotes in higher esteem expressed it was by characterizing coyotes as being "normal" people, more or less like them. In some cases this was because the coyotes in question lived in or near the same communities as migrants themselves, which allowed migrants to observe that the coyotes came from the same background and lived in similar circumstances as they did. For example, Paulino, the fifty-four-year-old brother of Leonardo, the migrant from the small village of Ejido San Francisco in Guanajuato, had the following to say about the coyotes who took people from his area across the Río Bravo into Texas: "They're people like us, only they drive better cars and have nicer houses." Since Paulino and his wife and unmarried children lived in a small cement-block dwelling he had built himself that was located on a dirt track and he drove a battered old pickup purchased on one of his sojourns in the United States, I wondered if he meant by this that the coyotes were getting rich by exploiting their neighbors. When I asked him to clarify what he meant, Paulino said that no, the coyotes he knew were not getting rich, since the money they charged got divided up among a number of collaborators in the "chain of coyotes" that took people north.

Arnulfo was a thirty-four-year-old autonomous migrant living with his common-law wife when I interviewed him in a Texas city in 2004. He hailed from a small town in the Sierra Madre Oriental in the state of San Luis Potosí. He had crossed the border several times in the 1980s and 1990s with coyotes from his town who worked as part of a commercial-transport coyotaje network that spanned the border. These men had learned the route through South Texas to Houston as migrants and later began to work as guides. They specialized in bringing people from Arnulfo's town and the surrounding area. Although he had not crossed with them recently, Arnulfo knew other people who had. According to Arnulfo, these guides were well respected in his town and continued to take people across the border:

They're good people. I never heard anyone complain about them. On the contrary, people always told you not to say who they were, not out of fear that they'd come get you, but rather because they understood that they had families, too. In other words, they were always very sincere and they never lied—I know that for a fact....People understood that they were doing it for everyone's benefit, since, in the end, the majority of people migrate for that reason, to look for a brighter future here. To work here and make a little more money here that you can't there.

Roberto, a forty-six-year-old migrant from the state of Nuevo León who sojourned as a metalworker in Houston, had held a very negative view of coyotes before he successfully entered the United States in early 2001 using a document-dispatch strategy. (See discussion of the logistics of his experience in chapter 4.) In our interview, Roberto told me that prior to making that crossing he imagined coyotes as being a bunch of tough-looking, dishonest hoodlums (*unos mal encarados, de aspecto feo, engañosos, básicamente delincuentes*). Here, though, he had been treated very well. All the members of the organization that he dealt with were courteous and professional. He characterized these coyotes as honorable and trustworthy people who seemed to be concerned about maintaining their good reputation. They were *gente decente* (decent people) in his eyes, "people you could talk with normally, like you and I are talking here right now."

"Most coyotes are bad, but ours are good"

Most of the migrants I interviewed in Texas and Mexico in the late 1990s and early 2000s were conscious of the bad reputation that coyotes had overall. Like migrants elsewhere in Mexico, they were aware of the many reports of coyotes' mistreatment of their clients and of migrant deaths that had occurred as they crossed the border with coyotes, whether they had learned of these tragedies from friends and kin or by watching television (Fuentes et al. 2007). At the same time, many also distinguished between different types of coyotes, especially between coyotes who operated in migrants' hometowns and were well-known by local residents and "unknown" coyotes that people sometimes contracted at the border, with the former being preferable to the latter (see also López Castro 1998). Some migrants expressed this distinction in a very specific way, such that they acknowledged that while most coyotes were bad, their own coyotes had actually been pretty good. We can see this in excerpts from several of my interviews with migrants. For example, Javier, the *guanajatense* quoted in chapter 5 about his first border-crossing in early 2003, had this to say about the local coyote who brought him to Texas:

SPENER: What is your opinion of the coyotes who brought you across?
JAVIER: The coyote who brought me across was a good guy. He kept his word to us. He oriented us and helped us any way he could. Because I've heard from my brothers and other people that a lot of the time they tell you one

thing and then do another. There are coyotes out there that take advantage of people. They take their money but then don't come through.

SPENER: Have you seen him since?

JAVIER: No, I haven't. But if I had to cross again, I'd do it with him. And I'd recommend him to others, honestly. We didn't have to walk a lot. It was safe. He acted right.

In other interviews, when migrants had described generally good conduct on the part of coyotes with whom they had traveled, I would ask them their opinions about the very negative way in which coyotes were portrayed in the press and how it related to their own experiences. Paulino, the migrant from Ejido San Francisco in Guanajuato, had heard a lot of bad things about coyotes elsewhere, but said the coyotes that people in his community had used to travel to the United States had never treated anyone badly. "You're better off going with coyotes from here," he told me. "Who knows about the ones in other places? I've heard bad things about [the coyotes in other places] too, but not around here....Women have even traveled with us and nothing bad has happened. They're respectful."

Don Aurelio, the fifty-six-year-old patriarch of a family of migrants in Rancho San Nicolás, Guanajuato, quoted in chapter 2, believed, like others I interviewed, that the coyotes you had to worry about were the ones you found at the border. Aurelio had crossed the border clandestinely many times in the 1970s and 1980s, and his sons were still traveling to Texas regularly with the assistance of coyotes when I interviewed him in 2005. He had this to say:

AURELIO: The deal is that the ones people are afraid of are the coyotes you hook up with at the border. You don't even know them. With them, there's always the danger that you've got money with you and then they ask you for money: "You know what, you're going to pay me X amount here." Then it's like he's just a bandit. He'll take your money and run off, and you're never going to find him. But the ones from here, they don't do those sorts of things. They really do take you.

SPENER: Other people I've spoken with around here have told me that in other parts of Mexico the coyotes are violent, like the drug traffickers. What about the coyotes around here?

AURELIO: No, not the ones that leave from here, not them. They're people like the rest of us.

SPENER: So you all haven't heard of any problems of that nature?

AURELIO: No, I have heard talk about some coyotes that behave badly, but no.

SPENER: Behave badly—what do you mean?

AURELIO: Well, that they rob people and they kill people.

SPENER: But are those the ones from around here?

AURELIO: No, they're not the ones we know; they're others.[13]

Ambiguities: The Debate about Coyotes Abandoning Migrants

One of the most severe accusations made against coyotes was that they did not hesitate to abandon migrants to their fate if they could not keep up on the arduous trek through the unforgiving brush of South Texas. In the brutally hot summer months, leaving someone behind on the trail could effectively be a death sentence. In the previous chapter I raised the issue about what responsibility fellow migrants had for leaving companions behind on the trail and reviewed an instance in which a group of migrants from Las Furias, San Luis Potosí, had refused to allow their coyote to abandon one of their comrades. I also pointed out that coyotes engaging in commercial-transport strategies, who guided migrants through the brush, faced ambiguous economic incentives. On the one hand, since they typically got paid per migrant, it was in their interest not to lose anyone on the trail. On the other hand, if a migrant couldn't keep up and caused the whole group to turn back and get captured by the Border Patrol or miss its ride out of the border region, it might make economic sense for a guide to "sacrifice" one migrant in order to get paid for the others. Presumably, the morally correct decision for all involved would be to place the survival of any one member of the "crossing party" ahead of the desire of the rest to evade detection by the authorities and make it to their ultimate destination. I was surprised to find that several of the migrants I interviewed did not necessarily agree with this moral logic. In this section I review some of the complexities involved in the question of who was responsible for the deaths of migrants as they trekked through the harsh landscape of South Texas. My purpose is not to exonerate coyotes from failing to act humanely toward migrants but to examine the extreme pressures brought to bear on migrants and coyotes alike by increasingly draconian U.S. immigration and border enforcement policies.

When asked about coyotes abandoning migrants in the brush, Chepe, the Texas border-town coyote, told me, "The Border Patrol says that to take the blame off themselves and because they don't want people to keep coming across." He explained further that as a guide he would not abandon a migrant who couldn't keep up with the group unless it was absolutely necessary and that, even then, he would point him to a nearby highway where he could turn himself in to la migra. This was a reasonable thing to do, he argued, because unlike in the Arizona desert, in the South Texas *monte*, migrants were never very far from the nearest highway, and regional highways were heavily traveled by Border Patrol and other police vehicles (but see migrant testimonies in chapter 2 for exceptions to this characterization). In addition, he said, when migrants did get "abandoned" by their guides it was often because they got lost when they failed to follow a guide's directions, or they got separated from their guides when a group was being pursued by Border Patrol agents and everyone scattered into the brush to avoid apprehension. Thus, he said, coyotes often were blamed for mishaps that were not precisely their fault.

Paco, a coyote quoted in previous chapters, admitted that he would sometimes tell customers *mentiras piadosas* (little white lies) about how long they would have to walk through the brush when they crossed the border with him. If, in reality, they would have to walk nine or ten hours, he might try to encourage a potential customer to hire him by telling him that they would only have to walk four or five hours. Migrants I interviewed in Guanajuato told me that they always *assumed* that they would have to walk farther than coyotes said they would. This, of course, raises the issue about what happened if, during the trek through the brush, a migrant didn't have the strength to go on. Paco admitted that this had happened on occasion as he or one of his collaborators was guiding migrants around the *segunda garita* on the Texas side. According to Paco, they had left migrants behind on the trail from time to time, but never to die:

> Thanks to God, we never had anyone die on us en route. That would be because of our way of working. But what you say about a lot of people being left behind in the brush, yes, it's true, but normally what the guide would do is leave them on ranches so that the Border Patrol would pick them up. But he wouldn't *want* to leave them behind—it was because they wouldn't want to continue, they would tire out. You know what I mean? And yes, I would say that during [the seven years I worked as a coyote], just to give a figure, forty or fifty gave up…out of tiredness.…I'd say that a good percentage, around 50 percent of these people, would return to [the Mexican side] and would want to come across with us again. From experience, I know that they got back safely.

Orlando, the Piedras Negras–based coyote quoted in the previous chapter, said that he believed that sometimes when a migrant died in the brush it was just that his or her body simply could not stand the strain of the trek, especially during the hot months. Although he believed that few coyotes would stay back with a migrant who couldn't keep up with the group out of fear of being thrown in jail by the authorities, he also thought that sometimes the problem was that migrants didn't realize they were physically in trouble until it was too late. He believed that some migrants died in the brush in South Texas because they waited too long before seeking help at the nearest house or along the nearest road, which were often not that far away. They made this mistake because of their understandable desire to avoid contact with the Border Patrol until they absolutely could go no further or perceived their lives to be in imminent danger.

I spoke with several migrants about people from their communities who had died while crossing the border with coyotes. Julián, one of the migrants from Rancho San Nicolás quoted previously, had just returned from his last sojourn in Dallas for Christmas and had made several clandestine crossings of the border over the previous decade. Word had been going around his and other neighboring settlements that a young man had died on the trail crossing with the same coyotes he had used on his last crossing and that he planned to use again to return to Dallas the next time he crossed the border. In our interview, Julián reacted to this tragic incident. "It was the coyotes that I crossed with the last time I went, so I didn't believe it," he told me. "I didn't believe that they would have left him behind." He had asked around about the incident and had heard that the man had gotten sick on the trail and had asked to be left behind. The guide and the group's other members tried to help the man along. Finally, one of the man's friends offered to stay back with the man so the rest of the group could go on. When the rest of the group was picked up by their driver, they stopped to call the Border Patrol and have them search for their two companions. By the time the Border Patrol found them, the young man had died. Julián did not think the coyotes were at fault: "I don't think it was their fault. It's just a question of whether your body will take it or not....The coyote would lose a bit more credibility in my eyes if he hadn't tried to help the people who stayed behind." Julián also told me that he and other migrants he knew were all aware that coyotes usually told you that the hike through the brush will really be shorter than it is. Perhaps the most telling thing about Julián's reaction to the man's death was that he was still thinking about crossing the border again with those same coyotes.

I heard another ambiguous story about abandonment on the trail from Arnulfo, the *potosino* quoted previously. A friend of his from his hometown had begun working as a coyote after first gaining experience as a migrant. On one trip, he had left his own uncle on the trail to die:

ARNULFO: Well, there are stories like ours where people didn't suffer too much and there are other stories where people suffered tremendously. For example, about four or five years ago, a friend of mine from home began working as a coyote. Work was scarce, so he began to take people across. And once he brought a family member with him, another one of my friends. It was his uncle. And he died on him on the trail. He had to leave him there in the *monte*. He was an older guy [*era un señor*].

SPENER: Was it the coyote's fault, or was it simply so difficult that...

ARNULFO: No! It's that it was his family member. I don't think it was his fault. He was bringing him along as a family member. He says he left him behind because he just couldn't go on any farther. The man himself [i.e., the dying uncle] told him he should just leave him there, he couldn't go on.

Here it is worth asking whether such abandonments were precisely the fault of the coyotes, or if such deaths could be better understood as casualties of the structural violence embodied in the way in which the U.S. authorities had militarized the interdiction of migrants at the border in the contemporary period.[14]

The Normalization of Suffering

In order to better understand why migrants sometimes pardon what outsiders might regard as unpardonable abuses committed by their coyotes, we should also consider the way in which global apartheid as a form of structural violence contributes to the worldview and attitudes that migrants hold about life generally and about autonomous migration strategies in particular. In this regard, Bourdieu's (1977, 72) concept of *habitus* proves useful, where habitus refers to the worldview, tastes, and dispositions to which people have been socialized. Migrants' habitus conditions their border-crossing practices in terms of the risks they are willing to assume and the types of behaviors that they are willing to tolerate from coyotes. Several generations of migratory experience in Mexico have led to the accumulation, not only of considerable stocks of migration-related social and human capital, but also of a set of expectations about border-crossing into which aspiring migrants are socialized. This socialization takes place, not only at the face-to-face level among members of the same social network, but also through popular culture and the media, where a variety of forms (e.g., *corridos [ballads]*, films, *telenovelas [soap operas]*, public service announcements on television and radio) warn of the dangers of the crossing and of placing one's faith in a coyote.

Other aspects of migration habitus are attributable to migrants' day-to-day experiences of general living conditions as members of the Mexican working class or peasantry. One of the main aspects of these general living conditions is *precariousness,* as manifested in inadequate and unreliable income, diet, health care, water supply, sanitation, transportation, and security, as a consequence of the prevailing international political economy and the state's neglect of its most basic obligations to its citizens (Bayón 2006). Thus, migrants learn to expect and then bear bad conditions as a matter of course in their lives, including as they make heroic efforts to improve their condition by heading north. It is in this socialized context that migrants transact business with coyotes. They have been warned that crossing the border is dangerous, that conditions will be harsh, that Border Patrol vigilance is intense, that they may have to make several attempts before reaching their destination, and that some people die on the way. In this sense, the generalized situation of structural violence that constitutes their lived experiences can prepare migrants to "pardon" all but the most egregious abuses committed against them by their coyotes.

Another important aspect of male migrants' habitus is their socialization to specific gender norms of masculinity involving strength, toughness, and the ability to withstand pain and discomfort without complaint. This is significant given that the large majority of clandestine border-crossings in this period were made by young men (see chapter 1). Paco, the Matamoros coyote, told me how he preferred *hombres de rancho* (men from rustic, rural areas) as clients:

> The best ones at making the crossing are the *rancheros,* guys from *el rancho,* because they're good for walking. They're real strong; you don't have any trouble with them. Sometimes they even do it wearing boots, cowboy boots. Or they'll hike through the *monte* wearing *huaraches* [leather sandals]. The guys from Michoacán come wearing huaraches. And they don't complain about *anything.*

For adolescent males in many migrant-sending *ranchos* of rural Mexico, the journey to *el Norte* constituted a veritable rite of passage, a way of proving one's manhood by enduring the suffering and overcoming the challenges encountered en route. In hearing men tell their stories of making the crossing, I thought of how in the United States many working-class youths "became men" by joining the armed services. As I listened to migrants' stories, I thought of how older men in the U.S. would regale younger men with their stories about the trials and tribulations they had experienced in "the service." In fact, the stories male migrants told about their journeys across an increasingly militarized border were, in many ways, war stories of a certain kind.

The socialization of men to specific types of hypermasculine heterosexuality also needs to be taken into account with regard to the special vulnerabilities suffered by women border-crossers. Such women face serious risk of sexual violence being committed against them by coyotes, law enforcement officials, and other migrants, though it is only coyotes who are routinely represented as sexual predators in the popular imagination. In this regard, it is important to consider that sexual abuse of women is no more intrinsic to the male coyote role than it is to the male Border Patrol agent or male migrant role.[15] We would do well to recognize that coyotes, migrants, or Border Patrol agents who sexually abuse women do so not as coyotes, Border Patrol agents, or migrants per se, but rather as *men,* whose attitudes and behaviors have been forged in a wider culture of violence toward women. This culture of violence toward women envelops and permeates, not only the relations among actors engaged in clandestine border-crossing, but also relations among actors in many other fields of social activity on both sides of the border.

In my interviews with migrants and other informants besides government officials and law enforcement agents, I found a variety of contradictory opinions expressed about the conduct and character of coyotes. Rather than attempting to determine which characterizations of coyotes were "true" and which were "false" or which opinions reflected the majority view, in this chapter I have tried to explore the range of opinions expressed and the complexities and ambiguities inherent in each type of characterization I encountered. Not surprisingly, given the polysemous quality of the term *coyote* and the morally ambiguous character ascribed to the coyote in Mexican mythology and folklore, many informants had ambivalent feelings about coyotes, even in cases where their own coyotes had served them fairly well. Especially interesting in this regard were the informants who told me that although they knew that most coyotes were unreliable, untrustworthy, and dangerous their own coyotes were relatively safe, reliable, and trustworthy.

In addition, I believe that my review of the issue of migrants being abandoned on the trail by their coyotes indicates that migrants themselves recognized that the situations that arose in making clandestine border-crossings could be morally complex. Thus, it was difficult to pass definitive judgment on the conduct of the individuals making them. One of the reasons for this is that the actions of individuals were considered within the broader context of the structural violence engendered by the system of global apartheid. Not only were the types of actions people could take constrained by the dire circumstances in which they found themselves, but the types of moral judgments they might pass were also influenced by the generalized conditions of structural and cultural violence in which they lived. In other words, as Bourdieu's concept of habitus permits us to see, migrants' reactions to the situations they encountered as they crossed the border were themselves conditioned by the precariousness and deprivation they had endured their entire lives in communities in which the danger of border-crossing was only one risk of many that they faced on an ongoing basis.

Regardless of the moral character of individual coyotes, and the personal opinions migrants might have about coyotes in general or their coyotes in particular, coyotaje constitutes one of Mexican migrants' principal and most effective strategies of resistance to their territorial confinement within a specific low-wage region of the world economy. It remains to be seen if in the future coyotaje will continue to enable migrants to evade interdiction at an ever-more-militarized U.S. border. Similarly, we do not know if law enforcement and labor-market conditions inside the United States will continue to permit migrants to earn high enough wages to keep themselves and their families afloat. Future conditions will depend largely on the resolution of political questions that migrants' resistencia hormiga does not attempt to address. Meanwhile, at the border, migrants and their coyotes are likely to remain locked in an everyday struggle to evade capture by paramilitary forces of the U.S. government.

Ending Apartheid at the Border

In these pages I have employed a framework for interpreting the dynamics of international migration and the border-crossing practices of Mexican migrants that offers a set of alternatives to the conceptual categories and terminology that characterize the mainstream discourse about these intertwined phenomena. Using the concepts of *global apartheid, autonomous international migration, everyday resistance,* and *coyotaje* I have tried to tell a different story about international migration and border-crossing than the usual one that focuses on the illegality and undesirability of the process and the people who are involved in it. The story I have told about border-crossing at the dawn of the new century is one in which working-class and peasant Mexicans refused to submit to a state-imposed situation of structural violence and developed survival strategies drawing on the social and cultural resources they had at their disposal. They deployed these resources effectively in a set of border-crossing practices I have termed *resistencia hormiga,* which permitted them to overcome their territorial confinement to a low-wage region of the world economy in contravention of the will of the U.S. government. In this conclusion, I would like to speak to three systemic questions that the analysis presented in the foregoing pages has not addressed. The first has to do with whether we should interpret the role played by coyotes in the border-crossing drama as assisting migrants in their resistance to apartheid or in contributing to its enactment against migrants. The second involves the accelerating intensification of apartheid policies at the border in recent years as a state response to migrant autonomy. And the third concerns the extent to which resistencia hormiga might ultimately play a role in the dismantling of apartheid on the North American continent.

In speaking about what they call "human smuggling," some analysts have suggested that there exists a perversely symbiotic relationship between the Border Patrol and coyotes insofar as escalation of border control by the state expands the market and increases revenues for coyotes (see, for example, Andreas 2000, 21–26, and Spagat 2006). This raises the question of how to interpret the role played by coyotes in the structure of global apartheid. Clearly, intensified border enforcement induces more migrants to contract the services of coyotes than might otherwise be the case. In addition, some coyotes make mutually beneficial arrangements with agents of the U.S. immigration enforcement bureaucracy to allow them to bring their customers across the border. One could argue, on this basis, that to the extent that migrants are increasingly obliged to contract the ever-more-expensive services of coyotes and, as a consequence, profit from state escalation of border enforcement, the interests of coyotes and the state are somehow allied against migrant interests, that is, coyotes also form an integral part of the repressive structure of global apartheid. I believe that my review of migrant-coyote relations in this book suggests that such a conclusion is misplaced, insofar as (1) the U.S. government expends considerable resources to arrest and incarcerate coyotes; (2) coyotes do not monopolize clandestine border-crossing in the Northeast Mexico-South Texas corridor; and (3) the services provided by coyotes are typically quite useful to migrants. Stepped-up persecution of coyotes by the authorities increases turnover among coyotes as they are captured or abandon the activity in fear that eventually they will be captured and imprisoned. Thus, though the revenue stream flowing into coyotaje as an activity may grow apace with increased border enforcement, that revenue may not flow to a fixed group of individual coyotes or coyotaje organizations in the same measure. We might better characterize the growing amounts of money involved as the growing cost of resistance to apartheid borne by migrants and their communities rather than as a boom in profits to coyotes.

Instead of concluding that coyotes participate in the enactment of global apartheid, and thus in the enactment of structural violence against migrants, I believe it is more accurate to view the relationship between migrants and their coyotes as a strategic alliance in the social field of border-crossing, one of the principal fields in which migrant resistance to global apartheid takes place.[1] This alliance is an uneasy and frequently conflictive one that is entered into for practical reasons rather than moral, affective, or political ones. Nevertheless, it is fostered by shared class and cultural characteristics between migrants and coyotes and their confrontation with a common enemy that persecutes them both in nearly equal measure. As such, intensified persecution of coyotes represents a frontal assault on one of migrants' principal strategies of resistance to apartheid enforced at the Mexico-U.S. border.[2] Over the course of many decades millions of Mexican migrants have successfully relied on coyotaje as a way to increase their share of the economic surplus they produce, by selling their labor power north rather than south of the border. Hundreds of thousands of Mexicans continue to utilize this strategy successfully on an annual basis, albeit with ever-increasing risk and suffering. Although coyotes bear responsibility for any direct and gratuitous abuse they inflict on migrants, the greater portion of the risks and suffering endured by migrants as they cross the border owes to the structural violence manifested in the way their movements are policed in the name of U.S. national sovereignty.[3]

In the years since the deaths of the migrants being transported in the back of a tractor-trailer in Victoria, Texas, we have witnessed an intensification of apartheid-style immigration policies implemented both at the border and in the interior of the United States. Unable to reach an accord to better manage migration between their two nations, the U.S. and Mexican governments worked together instead to dismantle "alien smuggling" and "human trafficking" organizations. Under the name Operation Streamline, the Border Patrol and the U.S. Attorneys Office in the Del Rio, Texas, area began a policy of "zero tolerance" of "illegal entry," meaning all migrants captured by the Border Patrol would be prosecuted and sentenced to jail before being formally deported to their country of origin. This included Mexican nationals, who previously had been routinely "voluntarily returned" to Mexico immediately following apprehension (Contreras 2006). This operation was subsequently extended to the Laredo and Rio Grande Valley sectors of the Border Patrol. The themes of a border "out of control" and under "assault" by organized bands of "criminal aliens" came to dominate news about migration. Civilian vigilantes calling themselves "Minutemen" began to conduct their own surveillance of the border. Immigration reform efforts in the U.S. Congress foundered, while calls to build walls along much of the border were heeded, the National Guard was called out to assist the Border Patrol in arresting migrants, ICE agents carried out punitive raids on immigrant workplaces around the country, and Anglo-majority towns and cities located far from the border passed ordinances intended to discourage autonomous migrants from settling within their limits.

Many of these actions were taken in the name of national security, but credible research indicated that the threat of terrorists entering the United States from Mexico was vastly overstated, especially relative to the U.S.-Canadian border, which continued to receive relatively little attention from the authorities (see Leiken and Brooke 2006). Moreover, decisions to take these actions took place in a climate of "moral panic" and seemed to be intended more to give the appearance of protecting "the homeland" than actually doing so (see Rothe and Muzzatti 2004 and Sharma 2006). This wave of cultural violence served variously to justify, mystify, and distract public attention from the underlying structural violence that at once motivated autonomous migration and endangered those who engaged in it. Not surprisingly, thousands more migrants and coyotes were jailed and hundreds more died as they attempted to traverse the border.

Clearly, the practice of resistencia hormiga will not by itself lead to a dismantling of the apartheid system that characterizes the present operation of the Mexico-U.S. border. Insofar as it provides capitalists in U.S. territory with a ready source of exploitable, low-cost labor, and provokes xenophobic reactions on the part of many Anglo U.S. citizens, its practice may actually deepen apartheid on the continent in the short term. Nevertheless, to the extent that such resistance creates a new set of material conditions in Mexico and the United States and intensifies existing contradictions in the system between political rights and economic necessities, the practice of resistencia hormiga by autonomous migrants may ultimately contribute to the apartheid system's demise. Although migrants do not have structural social change in mind when they cross the border as a household-survival strategy, their actions do have the potential to contribute to such change over the long term. Scott (1985, 36) recognized this in his original writings on peasants' everyday resistance in Malaysia, arguing that "thousands upon thousands of individual acts of insubordination and evasion" accumulate to form new political and economic structures that he likened to a "barrier reef" upon which the "ship of state" can run aground.[4]

One of the main unintended consequences of intensified policing by the United States of its southern border with Mexico has been to encourage an ever-larger number of Mexicans to settle more or less permanently inside its territory (Castañeda 2007). Permanent settlers, regardless of their legal status, begin to develop a new set of aspirations for themselves and their kin in the place of settlement. Their increasing economic, social, and cultural integration into the United States in the absence of their political integration creates contradictions that are not easily resolved by a system that has historically been predicated on their being mere birds of passage, whose labor could be exploited as needed but who seldom asserted collective demands for recognition of their rights. Moreover, many of these autonomous migrants now have U.S.-citizen children who are approaching the age of majority and could begin voting in significant numbers. This new voting bloc, should it become mobilized around issues of human rights and inequalities based on class and race, could well tip the balance of political power in the two largest U.S. states, California and Texas, both of which currently have nonwhite majorities in their populations but white majorities in their electorates. If such mobilization were to occur, the first immigrant generation's *resistencia hormiga* could well become the second generation's *plena participación en la vida cívica*—full participation in civic life.

The massive immigrant-rights demonstrations in many U.S. cities in the spring of 2006 indicate that the cumulative actions of millions of individual Mexican migrants taking matters into their own hands in the face of global apartheid have the potential, under the right conditions, to give rise to organized political action. Taken together, these peaceful marches and assemblies constituted the single largest set of demonstrations for human rights and social justice in the history of the United States. Not surprisingly, politicians of both major political parties in the country have come to actively court Latino voters. The majority of these voters are Mexicans who, if not immigrants themselves, are the children or grandchildren of immigrants.

Although the politics of immigration reform in the U.S. Congress are complicated, the dismantling of the current apartheid system operating at the border need not be. Several straightforward policy measures could be taken that would greatly reduce the need for migrants to engage in resistencia hormiga with the assistance of coyotes in contravention of U.S. laws. The growing size and strength of working-class Latino immigrants and their descendants as a voting bloc could itself contribute to creating the political conditions in the United States that would make implementation of these measures possible. Although undoing apartheid in all its dimensions at the global level looms as an impossibly utopian project, I believe that the more limited measures suggested here could be quite feasibly implemented in North America in the coming decades, if sufficient popular pressure can be brought to bear on the governments involved. Moreover, to the extent that such measures demonstrated the ability of states to permit free movement across national frontiers with expanded political and social rights for migrants, they could serve as an example to other parts of the world where apartheid policies are enforced at international boundaries. These measures include the legalization of autonomous migrants already residing in the United States, an increase in the number of immigrant visas available to Mexicans wishing to live and work in the United States, and investments in Mexico to improve the conditions of life and work in migrant-exporting regions of the country. Let me briefly review each of these measures.

First, the millions of migrants already living and working in the United States would have to be offered some reasonably expedient way of legalizing their status in the country. While it would be understandable to refuse to grant legal status to migrants who have committed serious criminal acts in the United States—research shows that these are relatively small in number—the thousands of migrants whose only "criminal" offenses have been for immigration violations such as reentry after deportation would also need to be allowed to establish legal residence.[5] Those who insisted that it would be unjust to reward lawbreakers by granting them "amnesty" would need to be reminded that laws themselves may be unjust, grievously flawed, or both. Given the history of Mexican migration to the United States and the conflictive history of U.S.-Mexico border relations, the laws presently in place can reasonably be placed in this category.

Second, the United States would need to make far more immigrant visas available to citizens of Mexico than it presently does. Taking special steps to address the Mexican case would go a long way toward diminishing the violence that apartheid inflicts on migrants living in or attempting to enter the United States, given that Mexicans account for around 90 percent of all "deportable aliens" who are apprehended by U.S. federal authorities each year.[6] This would imply recognition by the United States of its unique relationship with Mexico, a neighboring country of more than 111 million people with which it has deep economic, social, and cultural ties and shares more than a century-long tradition of mass migration that has contributed mightily to its own development as a nation. Given the nature of this relationship, it is paradoxical that the United States treats Mexico the same as any other country in terms of the number of immigrant visas its citizens are eligible to receive on an annual basis. It is ironic that in the name of equal treatment of people from all lands, U.S. policy has produced a situation of such profound structural violence at its border with Mexico. As discussed in the introduction to this book, the frequently heard proposal to expand the number of temporary guest-worker visas to Mexicans does not constitute an equivalent alternative to issuing immigrant visas in terms of human rights. Guest-worker visas, insofar as they retain the principle of worker "disposability" that is one of the apartheid system's essential features, are no substitute for expanding the number of immigrant visas available to Mexicans, visas that offer a path to full-fledged citizenship and that do not make human beings' presence in the country contingent on pleasing their employers.[7]

Finally, the governments of the United States and Mexico would need to make considerable investments in developing the economic and social infrastructure of the regions of Mexico that send large numbers of migrants to work north of the border. This could be accomplished in a variety of ways, but a model might be found in the social and regional development funds dedicated to building up the economic and social infrastructure of poorer regions in Italy, Spain, Portugal, and Greece within the European community (Anderson and Cavenagh 2004; European Communities 2007; Geyer 2000; Ireland 1995). Investments made with these funds helped ease the process of European integration by reducing the pressures for cross-border labor migration from poorer to wealthier countries on the continent. Ultimately, it permitted European labor-market integration and the free movement of persons among countries within the European Union without provoking serious economic and social dislocations. With a comparable commitment on the part of the U.S. and Mexican governments, over the medium to long term it ought to be possible to achieve the same result in North America. Such an achievement could be celebrated by tearing down the walls along the border that the U.S. government is so avidly constructing at the time of this writing. From that point forward, the international boundary could cease to be a border of exclusion that the oppressed had to risk their lives to cross. It could become instead a border of inclusion, permitting the unfettered mingling, interaction, and cooperation of neighboring peoples, whose differences it recognized, but whose divisions it no longer enforced.

Data Sources and Research Methods

The principal sources of data for this qualitative study of the clandestine border-crossing experiences of Mexican migrants are field observations and in-depth interviews I conducted intermittently from the summer of 1998 through January 2006. These interviews and observations took place in the Texas cities of Austin, Brownsville, Harlingen, Houston, Laredo, McAllen, San Antonio, and in or near several other small towns in South Texas, and in the Mexican cities of Dolores Hidalgo, Matamoros, Monterrey, Nuevo Laredo, and Reynosa, as well as in several rural communities in the states of Nuevo León, San Luis Potosí, and Guanajuato. In total, I conducted open-ended interviews with 156 clandestine-crossing participants, including 137 migrants and 19 people who had worked as coyotes in some way, that is, they had been paid to help migrants get across the border.[1] I contacted most of the migrants and coyotes interviewed using a snowball method, working outward from initial contacts made with Mexican migrants or members of their families in Austin and San Antonio. The Mexican interior communities I visited were chosen because they were the hometowns of migrants interviewed in Texas who were willing to put me in touch with their friends and relatives still living there.[2] I used my interviews with migrants to construct outlines of their life histories and a detailed account of each of their clandestine trips across the border, including not only the crossing itself but also of their work and living situations in the United States. Interviews with coyotes also included collecting life-history information, but instead of focusing on accounts of each cross-border trip informants had made, I explored how they had come to get involved in coyotaje and what their experiences in providing border-crossing services had been and, if they no longer provided such services, when and why they had stopped.

In addition to direct participants, I conducted key interviews with other informants who had specialized knowledge about varying aspects of the phenomenon of clandestine border-crossing. These included law enforcement officers in the Border Patrol, ICE, the U.S. Drug Enforcement Administration, the FBI, and local police forces in Texas; prosecutors in the U.S. Attorneys' offices, federal public defenders, and private immigration attorneys; personnel of the U.S. District Courts for Southern and Western Texas, including federal judges and magistrates, as well as the staff of the Pretrial Services and Probations divisions; human rights activists on both sides of the border; Catholic priests and nuns on both sides of the border who worked with migrants and their families; agents of Grupo Beta, the Mexican government's migrant protection force; and Mexican consular officials in Texas and U.S. consular officials in Mexico. Interviews with these informants focused on the specific knowledge gained from their particular vantage point of one or more aspects of the clandestine border-crossing phenomenon.

In the course of conducting this research, I made field observations of border-crossing and border-enforcement conditions on numerous occasions. These included several tours of the installations occupied, areas patrolled, and detention facilities and checkpoints operated by the U.S. Border Patrol in its Rio Grande Valley and Laredo sectors, as well as a tour of the region along the Mexican side of the river between Matamoros and Reynosa patrolled by Grupo Beta. I also made visits on my own to areas on the Texas side of the river to examine spots where migrants staged their crossings and observe conditions along routes through the South Texas brush country that they told me they followed on their journeys away from the border. (See chapter 2 for an account of my observation of one such route.) In addition, I visited migrant shelters run by the Catholic church in Nuevo Laredo and Reynosa and explored ways of making "cold" contact with coyotes in Matamoros, Reynosa, and Monterrey. In the course of conducting these field observations I had opportunities to converse more casually with many of the types of informants listed above.

In order to protect them from prosecution by law enforcement authorities and/or from deportation from the United States, I promised migrants and coyotes I interviewed not to include information in my writing that might reveal their identities. In order to encourage other types of informants to frankly express their views on clandestine border-crossing without worrying about how they might be judged by others, including their superiors in bureaucratic agencies, I made them the same promise. Thus, unless noted otherwise, all names of informants given in the text are pseudonyms. The names I have given to several smaller migrant-sending communities in Mexico are also pseudonyms, so as not to draw unwanted scrutiny by the authorities of those communities' migratory practices. I have also omitted or altered some details of informants' testimonies to protect their anonymity and that of their networks of kin, friends, and acquaintances, but have done so in such a way as to not change the substance of their testimonies.

Given the paranoid tenor of the times, I should note here that I am not aware of any specific ongoing conspiracies to violate U.S. or Mexican laws, given that I collected information on border-crossing retrospectively. In addition, I would like to point out that the strategies and tactics of clandestine border-crossing are already well known to the authorities. They are, in effect, an "open secret" along this stretch of the border. The problem is not that authorities are unfamiliar with how migrants go about crossing the border, but rather that so many thousands do so annually with the support of many other thousands in the region that the authorities have been unable to put a stop to the practice. Finally, I should note that in the course of my investigation I did not find any instances of border-crossings engaged in by anyone with any potential connection to international terrorism. Thus, readers need not be concerned that my protection of informants' anonymity has in any way compromised the national security of either Mexico or the United States.

In conducting my study of Mexicans' clandestine border-crossing practices, I made use of three other data sources to supplement my field observations and interviews. One of these was the Encuesta sobre Migración en la Frontera Norte de México, or EMIF, an annual survey of migrants carried out in Mexico's northern border cities as a joint project of Mexico's Consejo Nacional de Población, the Secretaría de Trabajo y de Previsión Social, and the Colegio de la Frontera Norte.[3] A second source was data on defendants prosecuted for the offense of "alien smuggling" that were collected by the Pretrial Services offices of the U.S. District Courts for Southern and Western Texas. The third source was a database on the characteristics of "alien smuggling" defendants and the incidents for which they were prosecuted in the Laredo federal courthouse that I constructed from a sample of case files archived in the Office of the Clerk of the Court.

Data from the Encuesta sobre Migración en la Frontera Norte De México

The Encuesta sobre Migración en la Frontera Norte de México is a survey of migrants in transit through Mexico's northern border municipalities that has been conducted annually since 1993 as a collaboration among three public institutions in Mexico: the Consejo Nacional de Población, the Secretaría de Trabajo y Previsión Social, and the Colegio de la Frontera Norte. The EMIF measures four different types of migratory flows and the characteristics of the migrants found in each type: (1) migrants arriving in the northern border cities from the Mexican interior with the intention of remaining in those cities to live and work; (2) migrants passing through the northern border cities with the intention of crossing the border to live and work in the United States; (3) migrants passing through the northern border cities on their way to points in the Mexican interior after having returned voluntarily from a period of living and working in the United States; and (4) migrants who were apprehended by the U.S. immigration authorities and returned involuntarily to a northern border city. Survey-takers interview migrants at bus terminals, airports, customs checkpoints, and as they enter/exit Mexico at one of the official international border-crossings. EMIF statisticians then use a complex formula to weight each observation in order to tabulate valid results from the survey. (For more information on the EMIF weighting procedures, see Encuesta sobre Migración en la Frontera Norte de México on the website of the Consejo Nacional de Población, http://www.conapo.gob.mx/mig_int/3.htm.)

An important limitation to the EMIF is that it does not capture international migration by residents of the Mexican border cities themselves. This is relevant to this book insofar as there exists a substantial back-and-forth flow of migrants between Texas and Mexico's northeastern border cities.

Using the EMIF, I constructed three databases to establish a sociodemographic profile of autonomous Mexican migrants who had crossed or intended to cross the stretch of the U.S.-Mexico border that ran from Ciudad Acuña, Coahuila–Del Rio, Texas, to Matamoros, Tamaulipas–Brownsville, Texas. All three databases consisted solely of migrants who told interviewers that they did not possess valid documents allowing them to legally enter the United States. The first database consisted of migrants who had returned voluntarily to Mexico from the United States, having made their last crossing into the United States prior to the launching of Operation Rio Grande in July 1997. I constructed this database by selecting cases from the first three rounds of the EMIF, conducted between March 1993 and July 1997. The second database consisted of migrants arriving in one of the northeast border municipalities with the intention to cross into the United States to live and work. I constructed this database by selecting cases from the sixth, seventh, and eighth rounds of the EMIF, conducted between April 2000 and July 2003. The third database consisted of migrants who had returned voluntarily to Mexico from the United States, having made their last crossing into the United States after the launch of Operation Rio Grande in July 1997. I also constructed this database by selecting cases from the sixth, seventh, and eighth rounds of the EMIF. I constructed each of these databases by merging three rounds of the EMIF in order to increase the sample size of each so as to improve reliability of the results. In consultation with one of the designers of the survey, Rodolfo Corona of the Colegio de la Frontera Norte, I deleted a small number of observations from the databases with outlier weights that distorted some of the initial results I obtained.

As noted in chapter 2, the EMIF data show generally lower rates of coyote-usage by migrants than other surveys. Data from the Mexican Migration Project, which is compiled from surveys of households in migrant-sending communities in Mexico, indicate that from 1978 through 1994 between 70 and 80 percent of migrants had hired a coyote to cross the border on their first clandestine border-crossing (Cerrutti and Massey 2004, 29). Similarly, López Castro (1998, 965) reported that surveys conducted by the Colegio de Michoacán found that by the early 1980s a majority of migrants departing from communities in the "traditional" areas of emigration in Western Central Mexico were using coyotes to enter the United States, and that this had continued through the mid-1990s when he conducted research on coyotaje as part of the Binational Study of Mexican Migration to the United States. Research by the Center for Comparative Immigration Studies at the University of California, San Diego, found that more than three-quarters of clandestine migrants surveyed in two small towns in Jalisco and Zacatecas had used a coyote on their last border-crossings, for all crossings made in the 1967 to 1992 period, which rose to nearly 90 percent for crossings made in the 1993 to 2004 period (Fuentes et al. 2007, 65). Although it did not report statistical findings, the Texas Indocumentado Study reported that by the early 1980s "virtually everyone" was using a coyote to enter the country (Browning and Rodríguez 1985, 287–88).

Escobar Latapí (1999, 15–16) has suggested that one of the main reasons for the discrepancies between the figures regarding coyote usage generated by the EMIF and other surveys is that the way that the EMIF is conducted makes it more likely to interview migrants who had weak migratory networks and few resources available for undertaking their migration than surveys that were conducted in households in migrant-sending communities. This suggestion presumes, correctly in my opinion, that migrants with stronger networks and more resources available were more likely to hire a coyote to cross the border than migrants with weaker networks and fewer resources. One reason for this bias is that the EMIF does not collect data from relatively "privileged" undocumented Mexican migrants who voluntarily return home on flights from the United States to cities in the Mexican interior, as had four well-dressed brothers I met on a plane from Houston to Guadalajara in 2005. They had spent several years living and working in New Rochelle, New York, before heading home to see the new house their mother had built with money they had sent home to her in Cotija, Michoacán. All had used coyotes on their last border-crossing, presumably because they knew how to contact reliable ones and could afford to pay them. The EMIF may also underrepresent migrants returning from the United States in private cars, pickup trucks, and vans, who we also might suspect were relatively privileged within the universe of autonomous Mexican migrants. Finally, migrants in transit through border cities might be understandably reluctant to tell interviewers about their behavior with regard to sensitive topics such as the hiring of an illegal border-crossing service, while migrants interviewed in their homes in Mexico might feel less threatened by such questions and more likely to answer them honestly. Despite these caveats, the EMIF remains a rich and unique source of data on the flow of migrants back and forth across the Northeast Mexico-South Texas border, both in terms of the large size of its sample and its measures of migrants' characteristics and behaviors.

Data on "Alien Smuggling" Defendants from the U.S. Pretrial Services Offices of the U.S. District Courts for Southern and Western Texas

When arrested, coyotes may be prosecuted in U.S. federal courts for the felony specified in Title 8, §1324 of the U.S. Code, "bringing in and harboring certain aliens." The courts' Pretrial Services offices collect and record detailed sociodemographic and criminal background data on all defendants passing through each federal courthouse. For the purposes of this book, I was able to obtain annual tabulations of these data for §1324 defendants prosecuted in the Southern and Western districts of the U.S. District Courts for the calendar years 1993 to 2003. The Southern District of Texas includes the federal courthouses located in Brownsville, McAllen, Laredo, Corpus Christi, Victoria, Houston, and Galveston. The Western District of Texas includes the courthouses in El Paso, Midland, Pecos, Waco, Del Rio, Austin, and San Antonio. The vast majority of §1324 cases prosecuted in Texas in this period were prosecuted in these courthouses, with a far smaller number prosecuted in the Eastern and Northern districts of the state.

The raw data used to generate table A were collected by the staff of the Pretrial Services offices in each courthouse listed above through a combination of interviews with defendants and computer checks of relevant federal, state, and local databases to establish defendants' criminal histories. Data collected by Pretrial Services offices are used to guide magistrates and judges in setting bail and other conditions of pretrial release, and are also made available to the U.S. Attorneys Office and defendants' attorneys. Because of the responsibility of the Pretrial Services Office to protect the privacy of defendants, it does not make individual defendants' records available to researchers, only certain types of aggregate data. For this reason, it is impossible to cross-tabulate their data to compare, for example, the levels of education of U.S.-citizen defendants with those of "illegal alien" defendants. Another important facet to take into account regarding the data summarized in table A is that Pretrial Services offices staff did not generally collect information about the criminal histories of defendants in Mexico or other countries, limiting their investigation to data available from U.S. law enforcement agencies. Similarly, Pretrial Services offices do not record any convictions for crimes a defendant committed as a juvenile.

The upward trend in felony convictions on §1324 defendants' criminal records since the launching of Operation Rio Grande in 1997 (see table A) merits some discussion here. Compared to 1996, the last pre-Operation year, the proportion of defendants in 2003 with prior felony convictions of any kind rose by more than twelve percentage points, the proportion with drug-felony convictions rose by over ten percentage points, and the proportion with violent-felony convictions rose by nearly three percentage points. This upward trend in all three categories provides some support to the argument that coyotaje became an increasingly criminal enterprise as border enforcement in the region intensified after 1997. Nonetheless, several other facts must be borne in mind in interpreting this trend.

1. Even with the increased proportions of defendants with prior felony convictions, in 2003 nearly three-quarters of defendants had no felony convictions of any type on their record, nearly 85 percent had no drug-felony convictions, and almost 90 percent had no violent-felony convictions, suggesting that even at the end of the period in question, the large majority of defendants had no proven history of serious criminal activity prior to their arrest.

2. Simple possession for personal use of certain drugs, such as cocaine, is treated as a felony offense in many U.S. states. Thus, the rise in felony drug convictions does not necessarily indicate takeover of coyotaje by drug cartels.

3. The common immigration offenses, §1324 ("bringing in and harboring certain aliens" and §1326 ("re-entry of removed aliens"), are treated as felonies. Thus, increased federal prosecution of immigration offenses

may be contributing to the rise in prior felony convictions in defendants' criminal histories. In addition, the Pretrial Services Office records §1324 convictions as "violent" felonies if they involved any type of endangerment of migrants, such as migrants being transported in a car trunk, lying on top of one another in the back of a van or pickup truck, or traveling in the cargo compartment of a tractor-trailer, even if migrants assented voluntarily to these conditions and no one was injured.

4. During the same period, the proportion of U.S.-citizen defendants rose from 23 percent to 48 percent of the total, while the proportion of "illegal alien" and legal permanent-resident defendants fell from 72 percent to 52 percent. Since Pretrial Services offices do not collect data on defendants' criminal convictions outside the United States, the increase in felony convictions among §1324 defendants may to some extent be an artifact of the increased proportion of defendants who were U.S. citizens and, thus, exposed to the risk of felony prosecution in the United States for a longer period than their noncitizen counterparts. For example, a U.S. citizen cocaine user would be more likely to show a felony drug conviction on his record than a comparable noncitizen cocaine user who had lived most of his life in Mexico.

One final point to bear in mind in interpreting the Pretrial Services offices data is that many crimes, whether committed in the United States or in another country, result neither in the arrest nor in the conviction of the perpetrators. Thus, the lack of felony convictions on a defendant's record does not prove that she or he was not involved in serious criminal activity prior to her or his arrest for a §1324 offense. On the other hand, because the United States criminal justice system operates on the premise of "innocent until proven guilty," giving due consideration to Pretrial Services offices data on the criminal history of defendants seems warranted.

Incident and Defendant Data from the Files of "Alien Smuggling" Cases Prosecuted in the U.S. Courthouse in Laredo, Texas

From 2000 through 2003, about four hundred cases involving violations of Title 8 §1324 of the U.S. Code, "bringing in and harboring certain aliens," were prosecuted each year in the federal courthouse in Laredo, Texas. I obtained permission from the Clerk of the Court to examine case files archived on-site in the courthouse and use them to create an electronic database to analyze for this book. I constructed this database during a series of visits to the Laredo courthouse in spring 2004, entering information contained in hard-copy files

Table A. Selected characteristics of defendants facing alien-smuggling charges in U.S. Federal Courts, Southern and Western Districts of Texas, 1993–2003

	1993	1994	1995	1996	1997	1998	1999	2000	2001	2002	2003
Number of defendants											
Southern District	137	227	386	473	585	519	657	698	726	971	1,072
Western District	82	53	157	312	340	535	547	540	358	430	373
Western and Southern Districts combined	219	280	543	785	925	1,054	1,204	1,238	1,084	1,401	1,445
Gender (%)											
Female	9.1	12.1	11.2	11.7	11.2	13.2	15.8	15.3	15.9	17.9	18.9
Male	90.9	87.9	88.8	88.3	88.8	86.8	84.2	84.7	84.1	82.1	81.1
Age of defendants (%)											
18–30 years	2.3	8.5	9.4	15.7	22.6	24.2	27.3	34.0	36.4	41.3	42.8
31–40 years	45.0	48.8	45.3	46.9	44.4	39.0	39.7	35.1	33.9	33.2	31.4
Over 40 years	52.7	42.7	45.3	37.5	33.0	36.8	33.1	30.9	29.6	25.4	25.7
Marital status											
Single, separated, divorced, or widowed	—	51.8	44.6	41.8	41.6	39.6	40.3	42.6	40.2	41.2	44.0
Married or cohabiting	—	48.2	55.4	58.2	58.4	60.4	59.7	57.4	59.8	58.8	56.0
Highest level of education completed (%)											
Less than high school	—	84.8	88.7	84.9	83.7	84.9	78.8	79.3	77.2	73.1	68.5
High school diploma or equivalent	—	12.3	10.7	13.4	15.0	14.4	20.2	19.4	21.5	25.8	29.8
Bachelor's degree or higher	—	2.9	0.6	1.7	1.2	0.7	1.1	1.3	1.4	1.2	1.7
Employed at time of arrest (%)											
Employed	61.4	58.3	54.7	54.6	61.5	60.3	57.4	63.4	61.5	62.1	56.8
Unemployed	38.6	41.7	45.3	45.4	38.5	39.7	42.6	36.6	38.5	37.9	43.2

(continued)

Table A. (*continued*)

	1993	1994	1995	1996	1997	1998	1999	2000	2001	2002	2003
Race/ethnicity of defendants (%)											
Hispanic	96.4	94.6	97.6	96.1	95.1	94.3	94.0	93.5	90.2	91.2	88.9
Non-Hispanic white	3.2	4.6	1.8	2.7	4.0	4.6	3.8	4.7	6.4	5.6	7.0
Non-Hispanic black	0.5	0.4	0.2	0.3	0.3	0.9	1.1	1.2	2.6	2.3	3.5
Asian	0.0	0.4	0.4	0.8	0.1	0.2	1.0	0.6	0.5	0.6	0.1
Immigration status of defendants (%)											
Illegal alien	45.0	47.9	58.0	55.0	56.0	57.4	50.9	52.1	45.9	41.0	39.5
Legal permanent resident	39.1	33.9	26.3	21.8	22.1	17.7	17.6	16.6	15.6	13.3	12.0
U.S. Citizen	15.0	16.1	14.5	22.5	21.5	24.1	31.1	31.1	38.0	44.5	47.9
Unknown immigration status	0.9	2.1	1.1	0.6	0.4	0.8	0.3	0.2	0.5	1.1	0.6
State of residence (%)											
Texas	52.8	51.9	46.0	48.5	48.3	47.6	57.8	55.7	59.8	62.1	62.3
Mexico	37.9	39.0	48.1	44.9	45.9	45.0	34.3	35.5	29.6	28.5	26.8
Other U.S.	9.3	9.1	6.0	6.6	5.9	7.3	7.8	8.7	10.5	9.5	10.8
Other country	0.0	0.0	0.0	0.0	0.0	0.1	0.1	0.1	0.1	0.0	0.1
Prior felony convictions (%)											
Felony convictions, any type	14.2	16.4	11.6	15.7	18.1	18.6	20.8	24.2	27.0	26.5	28.1
Drug felony convictions	3.7	5.0	5.0	5.7	7.0	11.4	10.3	10.9	12.6	12.9	15.8
Violent felony convictions	5.9	5.0	6.1	6.6	7.8	6.6	8.6	8.2	10.6	10.9	9.3

Source: Author's calculations using data from electronic records maintained by the Pretrial Services Offices of the U.S. Federal Courts, Southern and Western Districts of Texas.

into an Excel spreadsheet on my personal laptop. Because a great deal of information was contained in each hard-copy case file, largely in narrative form, it was not possible to enter data from all cases archived in the Clerk's Office. Instead, I reviewed a sample of closed cases (i.e., cases in which a verdict had been rendered or the case had been dismissed) from the first six months of 2000 and the first six months of 2002.

These two years were chosen for a combination of practical and analytical reasons. Practically speaking, most of the closed files from cases tried prior to 2000 had been transported to a warehouse in Dallas for permanent storage before I had the opportunity to examine them. In addition, many cases brought in 2003 were still open in 2004 when I went to Laredo to examine case files. Analytically speaking, I thought that comparing the last year before the 2001 terrorist attacks on New York and Washington with the first year following them might provide some insight into whether tightened security following the attacks led to observable changes in the patterns of coyotaje practices in the Laredo corridor. Most of the results I present in this book, however, aggregate data from both years taken together.

The Laredo courthouse was chosen as the data collection site because of the many §1324 defendants prosecuted there and because of its geographical proximity to my home in San Antonio. Prior to reviewing Laredo cases, I undertook an examination of §1324 cases prosecuted in the San Antonio federal courthouse, but far fewer defendants were tried there (an average of just 37 cases per year, 2000–2003), limiting the usefulness of statistical analysis of cases from that jurisdiction. Ultimately, I assembled a database in SPSS format consisting of variables constructed from data contained in the files of 197 cases prosecuted in Laredo involving 261 defendants.

The Laredo case files were a rich data source. They included information on defendants' sociodemographic characteristics, including age, sex, race/ethnicity, marital status, number of dependent children, immigration status in the United States, occupation, income, home ownership or monthly rent paid, cash assets, and place of residence. Thus, the case file data on Laredo defendants replicated some of the information on defendants contained in the Pretrial Services offices data, but they also supplemented those data with greater detail. Moreover, because case files were an open public record, I was able to create individual-person files that permitted cross-tabulations not possible with the Pretrial Services offices data.

The Laredo case files also contained a great deal of information about the coyotaje incident resulting in the arrest of the accused defendants. Most of this information was contained in the arresting officer's narrative report establishing the specific criminal acts with which the defendant was charged.

I coded information from these narrative reports into variables documenting the number of migrants being housed/guided/transported and their nationalities, the intended destinations of the trip, the amount being charged and where and when it was to be paid, the location where the arrest was made, the types of vehicles being used to transport the migrants, and what types of specific dangers or abuses migrants had been exposed to on their journey. In this regard, it is important to bear in mind that the arresting officer could only report the facts of the case that he or she was able to ascertain at the time of arrest. Since most arrests during these years in the Laredo sector occurred when migrants were being transported in motor vehicles, the officer making the arrest usually only observed the conditions during transport, unless migrants gave her a detailed account of the conditions they faced during other parts of their journeys. Information from the incident report in each case file was also sometimes repeated or extended in the plea agreement reached between defendants and the U.S. Attorneys Office, which typically contained a description of the factual basis for the defendant's guilty plea. In addition, the case files documented the ultimate disposition of the case, including whether it was dismissed, went to trial, or defendants pleaded guilty to charges, as well as the terms of the sentence imposed on defendants who were found guilty.

Compiling the database from the Laredo §1324 cases was extremely labor intensive and tedious. Given the constraints I faced as an individual researcher, I was able to examine only a small sample of the cases prosecuted in just one courthouse. I believe, however, that the analyses of these data suggest that it would be fruitful in the future for researchers to undertake more thoroughgoing examination and analysis of the data contained in federal court records of §1324 cases around the country to better understand the characteristics and backgrounds of individuals who have been arrested, accused, tried, and punished for being coyotes.

A final consideration in interpreting the findings presented in these pages is how the way in which I conducted my research affected the types of migrants I interviewed. Because I used a snowball method for contacting migrant informants, working outward from contacts I had in Austin and San Antonio, most of the migrants I interviewed came from Mexican states that sent large numbers of people to live and work in these and other Texas cities such as Dallas and Houston. Thus, the bulk of migrants I interviewed were from the states of Guanajuato, Nuevo León, and San Luis Potosí, whether I interviewed them in Texas or in their communities of origin. These communities have a long tradition of sending migrants to the United States, unlike communities in other Mexican states where large-scale emigration began only recently. Also, because I began contacting migrants in *cities* in Texas, very few of the people I interviewed had any experience working in agriculture in the United States. This is important insofar as the dynamics of migration to work in agriculture differ considerably from those of migration to work in urban areas. An additional issue for readers to consider is that the analysis contained in these pages focuses primarily on the migration process from the male point of view. One evident reason for this is that the vast majority of clandestine crossings into South Texas during his period were made by men (see chapter 1). Another is that as a male outsider in the communities in which I conducted interviews, I did not have the same access to female informants as I did with men, and when I did interview women, they may have been less willing to discuss all aspects of their experience with me as openly as their male counterparts were. Given the special dangers and vulnerabilities faced by women migrants, this is an important limitation to the findings of my research.

The qualitative nature of my fieldwork means the findings I report in this book cannot be generalized in any statistically representative sense. Moreover, my findings must be understood as deriving from the experiences only of those Mexican migrants from non-indigenous mestizo communities with a long migratory tradition, who staged their clandestine border-crossings in the Northeast Mexico-South Texas corridor, and who worked in urban occupations in the United States. Because the intensification of U.S. border enforcement has continued in the years since I completed my fieldwork, and because migration flows are dynamic, the findings I report here should be taken to reflect the situation prevailing on this stretch of the border through the end of 2005.

Notes

Terminology

1. The highly denigrating term *wetback* is seldom used in public any longer by any but the most unabashedly racist of English speakers, though its use prior to the 1960s was endemic. Its Spanish equivalent, *mojado,* is still sometimes used colloquially among Mexicans, including migrants themselves, where it does not necessarily carry the same racist connotations.

Introduction

1. This gap in the literature has recently begun to be addressed. See Hernández-León 2008 and Arzaluz 2007.

2. The California Rural Legal Assistance Foundation publishes online data on migrant deaths along the U.S.-Mexico border as part of its project opposing the U.S. Border Patrol's Operation Gatekeeper, launched in the San Diego sector in 1994. It reports these data by U.S. government fiscal year, which runs from October 1 to September 30, and Border Patrol sector. In the Laredo sector, the bodies of forty-seven migrants were recovered in FY2000, twenty-eight in FY2001, and fifteen in FY2002. Data from http://www.stopgatekeeper.org/English/deaths.htm (accessed June 11, 2007).

3. Allegations were subsequently made that the network of coyotes that organized the transportation of these migrants had made arrangements with Border Patrol accomplices at the Sarita, Texas, checkpoint to let this rig through without inspection. The allegations were never proven.

4. Information about this tragic incident was obtained from news coverage from the *Houston Chronicle,* the *New York Times,* the *Los Angeles Times,* and the Associated Press, as well as from Jorge Ramos's (2005), *Morir en el intento: La peor tragedia de inmigrantes en la historia de los Estados Unidos.*

5. This figure is for the U.S. government's FY2004 (October 1, 2003, to September 30, 2004). It was reported in the June 2006 issue of *Migration Information Source* in an article

titled "The U.S.-Mexico Border." http://www.migrationinformation.org/USfocus/display.
cfm?ID=407 (accessed June 12, 2007).

6. The man's name and the name of his hometown are pseudonyms.

7. This figure comes from the Banco de México. See http://www.banxico.org.mx/
documents/%7BA5443598-2DF0-815D-4077-A416D3429AA9%7D.pdf.

8. The source of the estimate of six hundred thousand is Mexico's Consejo Nacional
de Población (n.d.). My own calculations, using data from the Encuesta sobre Migración en
la Frontera Norte de México (EMIF), show that 30 percent of Mexican migrants arriving
at the border with the United States in 2002 and 2003 intended to make their crossings on
this stretch of the border ($n = 5, 111$). For more information on findings derived from the
EMIF, see Data Sources and Research Methods at the end of this book. During the same
period, the United States authorities made 26 percent of the total of 930,000 apprehensions
of migrants on the entire border with Mexico in the Rio Grande Valley, Laredo, and Del Rio
sectors of the Border Patrol that make up the South Texas region.

9. Although in principle Mexicans who have legal-resident or U.S.-citizen relatives living north of the border have a much better chance of obtaining an immigrant visa, they face
extraordinarily long waits to get them. Thus, for example, spouses and minor children of
legal permanent residents from Mexico can expect to wait at least seven years from the time
of application to be admitted legally to the United States; Mexican siblings of naturalized
U.S. citizens can expect to wait at least twelve years (Anderson and Miller 2006, 10, table 4).

10. The U.S. government does run two small "guest worker" programs for manual occupations in agriculture and industry in which around ninety thousand Mexican nationals
participated in 2005, but these programs only offered contracts to work for less than one
year and were rife with abuse of the workers who participated in them. See Bauer and Reynolds 2007.

11. One must always use the term *race* guardedly in social-scientific analysis. Although
race is typically used to refer to a group of people who are perceived by others as shar-
ing some common phenotypical characteristics, racial categorization rests on social rather
than biological bases. Moreover, the racial categorization of groups of people always has
an important political dimension, such that the racial group to which a person is assigned
determines that person's life chances relative to others who have been assigned to a different
group. Of particular interest to the present discussion are the ways in which racial-group
membership determines the role played by members of that group in capitalism's division
of labor, whether this division of labor operates locally, nationally, or globally. For additional discussion of these issues, see Bonilla-Silva 1996; Marable 1991, 188–90; Montejano
1987, 4–5; and Wolf 1982, 379–81.

12. Nevins (2003) himself, however, has argued on human rights grounds *against* accepting border control as a legitimate exercise of state authority. Sharma (2006) makes
similar arguments. Citing a 1914 legal study, Torpey (1998, 250) notes that no consensus
existed in Europe on the eve of World War I about whether or not nation-states had an
unequivocal right to bar foreigners from entering their territory. In the same vein, Wong
(2005, 90) notes that state border controls in Europe and elsewhere did not become widespread until after World War II.

13. While I was conducting field research for this study, non-Hispanic whites arriving
in the United States at one of the ports of entry in South Texas were frequently allowed
to enter without presenting any official identification documents, while nonwhites would
routinely be required to present documents for inspection. Individual immigration inspectors could use their own discretion in asking to see documents. As part of the State Department's Western Hemisphere Travel Initiative, by June 2009 *all* persons entering the United

States through any legal port of entry will have to present a passport or equivalent nationality document to immigration inspectors (Schiller 2006).

14. I am not the first to analyze aspects of the functioning of this border as an example of global apartheid. See Nevins 2002, 185–86, and Nevins 2006. For an earlier work comparing the controls placed on the movement and work of Mexican workers with those placed on black workers in South Africa under the apartheid regime, see Burawoy 1976.

15. Heyman (1998, 165–66) and De Genova (2002, 437) make similar arguments.

16. See Hing (2004, 139–44) for a review of U.S. Supreme Court decisions that permitted the detention in the border region of Mexicans suspected of entering the United States illegally. These decisions carved out a specific set of exceptions to the Fourth Amendment's prohibition against unreasonable search and seizure.

17. Although the creation of new guest-worker programs and the expansion of existing ones might result in a somewhat more humane situation than the current reality of mass illegalization of workers within U.S. borders, such programs retain the basic principle of the disposability of workers that denies their full humanity. See Bacon 2007; Massey 2007; and Bauer and Reynolds 2007.

18. See Sharma (2006) for a discussion of the racial dimension of this "divide and conquer" strategy.

19. For a broader discussion of the interplay of state and nonstate actors in the dialectical process of border formation, see Spener and Staudt 1998.

20. In his analysis of contemporary migratory flows to the United States from Mexico and Central America, Bacon (2007) characterizes migrants as *displaced people,* obliged to leave their homelands as a consequence of the neoliberal economic policies generated by the so-called Washington consensus. While such an understanding of people's reasons for migrating would seem to contradict my characterization of migration as resistance, the contradiction is more apparent than real insofar as autonomous international migration is only one course of action among others that the displaced might pursue. Other options could include internal migration to another region or city, engaging in informal economic activity, looking for work in the burgeoning maquiladora sector, or simply staying put and accepting extreme poverty as a condition of life, none of which involve resisting regulation by state authorities or capital in the way that autonomous migration does.

21. In this way, Scott's vision of resistance is similar to Touraine's (1990) characterization of participants in social movements as not typically seeking system change but rather the redress of particular grievances, and Thompson's (1964) account of the prosaic goals of worker struggles in England.

22. I am not the first scholar to see the utility of Scott's concept in analyzing Mexican migration. Anthropologist Rachel Adler has also described some of the "weapons of the weak" used by the Yucatecan migrants she has studied as they pursue what she refers to as their migratory *agendas* (Adler 2000, 173; Adler 2004, 57–59).

23. For an example of the use of this term in a scholarly article, see Emmerich 2003.

24. For a detailed treatment of "war of the flea" guerrilla tactics, see Taber 2002. Heyman (1999a, 287) has also used the analogy to guerilla warfare with respect to the strategies pursued by Mexican migrants at the border.

25. Sociologist James Coleman (1988) subsequently played a key role in promoting the concept in the English-language literature.

26. The authors soon abandoned their use of the term "capital" to refer to such social resources because of criticism they received from a fellow scholar at a conference in which they initially presented their work. Their critic regarded the term "capital" as too homogenizing and generic (Browning and Rodríguez 1985, 289n11). This is, of course, ironic, given

the prominence that the social capital concept has come to occupy in the field of migration studies and other fields of sociological and anthropological inquiry.

27. *Funds of knowledge* has been used less frequently than *social capital* as a conceptual tool for analyzing international migration. For a study of Mexican migration that employs both concepts, see Hernández-León and Zúñiga 2002.

28. Singer and Massey (1998) referred to these funds of knowledge as *migration-specific human capital.* Bourdieu (1986) would have regarded such knowledge as *cultural capital* within his economy of practices framework. I prefer the *funds of knowledge* term because of the way it highlights the way in which this knowledge is collectively accumulated by communities and distributed in a mutualistic manner among members.

29. Of course, not all Mexican nationals who migrate autonomously to the United States do so in order obtain employment at higher wages. Other considerations, especially the desire to reunite with family members, also enter into people's migratory decisions. Nevertheless, Mexican migration to the United States is still best understood as labor migration, since family reunification migration occurs subsequent to the initial migration of one or more workers.

30. Campbell and Heyman (2007) have pointed to some difficulties in applying Scott's concept of *everyday resistance* to the phenomenon of autonomous migration as I do throughout this book. One issue they raise is the extent to which it is appropriate to classify migratory behaviors as resistance if the migrants are not conscious of the ways in which their behaviors challenge existing power relations. With regard to the specific phenomenon of clandestine border-crossing, I believe readers will find ample justification in these pages for designating it as conscious resistance on the part of Mexicans to their forcible exclusion from U.S. territory. Indeed, Campbell and Heyman (2007, 23–24) recognize that this aspect of the broader migration phenomenon does, in fact, involve "intentional defiance of the laws and police forces of the United States." Of equal concern to the authors is the extent to which migrants' defiance of U.S. laws and their enforcement ironically results in their self-delivery to U.S. employers under conditions of extreme exploitation. The complexity of this situation leads Campbell and Heyman (2007, 24) to argue that we should not categorize autonomous migration dichotomously "as either dominated or defiant." In this regard it is important to bear in mind that the focus of this book is the more circumscribed phenomenon of clandestine border-crossing, rather than the broader phenomenon of autonomous migration in all its aspects. Whether what I call *resistencia hormiga* is applicable to other aspects of migrants' life and work in the United States is a question worthy of further research and debate.

1. The Unfolding of Apartheid in South Texas

1. My calculations using data obtained from the Texas Center for Border Economic Enterprise and Development (2006) at Texas A&M International University in Laredo, Texas. Figures include both northbound and southbound crossings.

2. For example, in 2000 nearly 36 percent of Reynosa, Tamaulipas, residents had been born in another Mexican state. The top four states of origin of Reynosa's migrant population were, in rank order, Veracruz, Nuevo León, San Luis Potosí, and Coahuila, which all sent thousands of labor migrants across the border into Texas each year. The other major cities of Nuevo Laredo and Matamoros exhibited a comparable population composition. My calculations using data contained in the table titled "Población total con estimación por lugar de nacimiento según entidad, municipio y localidad," from the 2000 Censo General de Población y Vivienda, Instituto Nacional de Estadística, Geografía e Informática, http://www.inegi.gob.mx/lib/olap/general_ver3/MDXQueryDatos.asp (accessed June 7, 2006).

3. Data from United States Bureau of the Census, *State and County Quick Facts,* http://quickfacts.census.gov/qfd/states/48000.html (accessed May 24, 2006) and http://quickfacts.census.gov/qfd/states/00000.html (accessed June 1, 2006).

4. These counties were roughly bounded by U.S. 90 to the north, Interstate 37 to the east-northeast, and the Gulf of Mexico to the east. They include Uvalde, Medina, Zavala, Frio, Atascosa, Dimmit, La Salle, McMullen, Live Oak, Duvall, Jim Wells, Nueces, Kleberg, Jim Hogg, Brooks, Kenedy, and Willacy. Although the city of San Antonio is typically thought of as the regional "capital" of South Texas, I exclude Bexar County from my operational definition of this migratory corridor since it constituted a destination rather than a place of transit for many of the migrants I interviewed.

5. Data from United States Bureau of the Census, *State and County Quick Facts.* website (accessed May 24, 2006 and June 1, 2006).

6. Ibid.

7. In January 2005, for example, in Cameron County (Brownsville-Harlingen metro area), unemployment was 8.8 percent; in neighboring Hidalgo County (McAllen-Mission-Edinburg metro area) it was 9.3 percent. Meanwhile, in Texas as a whole it was just 5.9 percent (Texas Workforce Commission 2006).

8. In South Texas, non-Hispanic whites are typically referred to as Anglos, regardless of whether or not they are descendants of people from the British Isles.

9. As of February 2007, 52.5 percent of Border Patrol agents nationwide were Hispanic (unpublished data supplied to me on June 13, 2007, by the Customs and Border Protection unit of the U.S. Department of Homeland Security). Although figures were not available on the national origins of Hispanics employed as Border Patrol agents, in South Texas the large majority appeared to be of Mexican origin.

10. For more on the prevalence and cultural legitimacy of smuggling in the region in the late nineteenth and early twentieth centuries, see Montejano (1987), Mora Torres (2001), and Paredes (1993).

11. For more on the question of the legality of this recruitment, see chapter 3.

12. By the early 1950s, the Mexican government had largely dropped its opposition to its citizens working as braceros in Texas. This change in attitude came when it was apparent that tens of thousands of Mexicans were working in South Texas agriculture without papers (Scruggs 1963, 263).

13. Even before the enactment of the new law, most working-class Mexicans had few opportunities to migrate legally to the United States outside of the Bracero Program, given the costs of applying and the requirement of proof that the applicant would not become a public charge. See Newman 1965, 13–16.

14. The tremendous increase in the number of apprehensions owed not only to the number of Mexicans attempting to enter the United States clandestinely, but also reflected dramatic growth in the number of agents patrolling the border: from 1,566 agents in 1970, the Border Patrol grew to 2,484 agents by 1980 and then to 3,693 agents by 1986, nearly two-and-a-half times the number of agents than just sixteen years earlier (Nevins 2002, 197).

15. This would include, for example, using a valid border-crossing card to enter the United States to work, an activity not contemplated by the terms of this special nonimmigrant visa.

16. These figures are from the *Statistical Yearbook of the Immigration and Naturalization Service* (United States Immigration and Naturalization Service 1993, 1994).

17. It is also worth mentioning, however, that between FY1993 and FY1997, the number of Border Patrol agents assigned to South Texas rose by around 60 percent, from 1,023 agents in 1993 to 1,627 by 1997 (see figure 1.2). Other things being equal, we can assume

that some portion of the increase in South Texas apprehensions was the result of the increased human resources being dedicated to migrant interdiction in the region. In figures 1.1 and 1.2, "South Texas" refers to the Rio Grande Valley, Laredo, and Del Rio sectors of the U.S. Border Patrol.

18. My field observations and meetings with Border Patrol agents in the Laredo sector.

19. Data presented by Cornelius aggregated deaths for the whole Texas border, not just South Texas. Most of the deaths described by Cornelius occurred in the South Texas region that is the focus of this book.

20. In FY2005, migrant deaths on the Texas border totaled 140 (Latin American Working Group n.d.). While this figure was only about half the deaths registered in 2000, it was still more than three times higher than it had been immediately before the operation, even though only about half the number of migrants were apprehended in 2005 as had been in the year before the operation's launch.

21. In one especially notorious case, a federal judge and his aides were pulled over by an agent who had a "reasonable suspicion" that they were drug or alien smugglers (Yardley 2000). In response to human rights complaints, the government of the small town of El Cenizo, Texas, on the Rio Grande a few miles downstream from Laredo, in 1999 ordered its employees not to cooperate with U.S. immigration authorities in order to send the message to the town's residents that their local government was on their side in the conflict with the Border Patrol (author interviews with El Cenizo officials, November 1999; see also Kolker 1999).

22. The EMIF was an annual survey of migrants in transit conducted in the Mexican border cities by the Consejo Nacional de Población, the Secretaría del Trabajo y Previsión Social, and the Colegio de la Frontera Norte. See Data Sources and Research Methods for additional information about this survey.

23. This figure was obtained from a table titled "Población nacida en México residente en Estados Unidos por características demográficas, 1994–2003," Consejo Nacional de Población, http://www.conapo.gob.mx/mig_int/series/030203.xls (accessed June 6, 2007).

24. My calculation using data supplied by the U.S. Border Patrol. This calculation is for the entire U.S.-Mexico border, not just the South Texas-Northeast Mexico stretch and includes other nationalities as well as Mexicans. Nonetheless, it should be noted that Mexicans are the vast majority of persons apprehended by the Border Patrol each year. Findings from the Mexican Migration Project indicated a growing proportion of women among first-time autonomous migrants in the post-IRCA, such that by the mid-1990s as many as one-third were women (Cerrutti and Massey 2001, 187; Massey, Durand, and Malone 2002, 134). This research did not indicate, however, the methods such women used to cross the border.

25. This may be reflected in the other finding reported in table 1.1, which indicates that 15 percent of migrants who had entered the United States with legal crossing documents but had worked without legal work permits were women.

26. Here it is important to note that the EMIF underrepresents the movement of border-state migrants because it does not adequately capture the migration of residents of border cities in its sample (Consejo Nacional de Población 2004). This underrepresentation is significant insofar as San Antonio and other Texas cities were home to a substantial number of Mexican migrants from the northeastern border states of Coahuila, Nuevo León, and Tamaulipas.

2. Clandestine Crossing at the Beginning of the Twenty-first Century

1. Although I interviewed two women migrants from La Carmela, neither had traveled to the United States by undertaking clandestine border-crossings of the type described in

this chapter. Rather, they had entered the United States with legal crossing documents. As discussed in greater detail in chapter 1, clandestine crossing of this stretch of the border in the ways described here remained a largely male experience at the beginning of the twenty-first century.

2. In this practice, migrants from La Carmela seemed to be fairly typical: analysis of data from the Encuesta sobre Migración en la Frontera Norte de México showed that in the 2000–2003 period, 76 percent of Mexican migrants arriving on the Northeast Mexico-South Texas border with the intention of making a clandestine crossing were accompanied by other migrants ($n = 4,426$). The typical migrant came in a group of 5.2 migrants, and 30 percent of migrants arrived at the border in the company of one or more relatives ($n = 3,319$).

3. In this, the men from La Carmela were also fairly typical. Data from the EMIF indicated that the mean amount spent by migrants on their journey to the border was 901 pesos in the 2000–2003 period, somewhere between U.S. $80 and $90 at the prevailing exchange rates ($n = 3,301$).

4. For a published firsthand description of how police in Nuevo Laredo used to extort money from migrants in the 1980s, see Conover (1987, 12–15).

5. In part because the Laredo metropolitan area had grown so much by the early 2000s, nearly swallowing the old checkpoint that used to be located a considerable distance outside town, in April 2006 the Border Patrol closed it and opened a new, bigger checkpoint at mile marker 29 (Castillo 2006).

6. The operation of such checkpoints by immigration authorities was sanctioned by a 1976 Supreme Court decision that "articulated a major exception to the Fourth Amendment's protection against [unreasonable] search and seizure to accommodate the Border Patrol" in its efforts to control undocumented migration from Mexico to the United States (Hing 2004, 140–43).

7. The system of highway checkpoints had been used by the Border Patrol in this region since shortly after its inception in 1924, though in the past they often consisted of little more than a vehicle parked along the road, given the light traffic in the region. Borderwide, the number of checkpoints was expanded and many were made permanent in the 1980s and 1990s. By the late 1990s, the checkpoints shown on map 2.1 were typically open full-time. Nevertheless, even as late as 2005 it was possible to drive around checkpoints located on the main highways by following paved secondary roads or unpaved roads through private ranchland. These lightly traveled secondary roads were very heavily patrolled by Border Patrol vehicles, however, meaning that drivers of suspiciously loaded vehicles were likely to be pulled over (telephone interviews with press officer Carlton Jones, U.S. Border Patrol Del Rio sector, press officer Sara Pocorroba, Laredo sector of the Border Patrol, and Brenda Tisdale, curator of the National Border Patrol Museum and Memorial Library Foundation on June 17, 2005, and July 21, 2005).

8. For example, in 2000, La Salle County, just north of Laredo, had just 3.9 persons per square mile, Brooks County, north of the McAllen metro area, had 8.5 persons per square mile, and Kenedy County, north of Harlingen, was home to just 0.3 persons per square mile (United States Bureau of the Census 2006).

9. Mean annual precipitation in the region ranges from 25 inches in Brownsville to 17 inches in Del Rio (Bomar 1983, table C-2, 221–22).

10. Development of commercial agriculture in South Texas was made possible by the 1898 discovery by rancher Robert Kleberg of "an underground lake three times the size of Connecticut" (Montejano 1987, 106). Near the border itself, water is also pumped from the river and reservoirs for irrigation purposes.

11. In their report, the authors do not disaggregate environmental causes of death. Given that 1998 was an exceptionally hot year and there are relatively few life-threateningly cold days each winter in South Texas, we can assume that most of these deaths were heat related.

12. This pattern could be seen in monthly apprehension statistics supplied by the Border Patrol. For example, in FY2004, apprehensions of migrants by agents in the Del Rio sector peaked in March at 7,983. By July, the hottest month of the year, apprehensions in the sector had fallen to 4,232, only a little more than half the number apprehended in March. Unpublished data supplied by the U.S. Border Patrol.

13. Cell phones worked well in this area, and some migrants from La Carmela owned them. The problem was that unless they had been living in the United States quite recently, they were unlikely to own a phone that would work on the Texas side of the border.

14. Migrants I interviewed from other parts of Mexico that traversed the South Texas border region reported using radio towers, windmills, and highway lampposts to guide them. Some also reported using compasses to forge a route through the brush. Unfortunately, if one member of a group of migrants that was apprehended in the brush by the Border Patrol was holding a compass, agents were likely to accuse him of being the group's coyote.

15. Although some of the land in the Laredo-Encinal corridor had been developed and cleared of brush, migrants were always concerned with staying out of sight and therefore usually confined themselves to the *monte* even when a clearer path was available for them to follow.

16. Álvaro's attitude is consistent with recent studies conducted elsewhere in Mexico. Researchers who surveyed migrants in sending communities in Zacatecas and Jalisco, for example, found that the large majority of intending migrants were well aware of the dangers that faced them at the border but that such awareness did not deter them from attempting to cross the border clandestinely. Just as important, the same researchers found that the vast majority of the migrants they interviewed were able to successfully penetrate the defenses of the U.S. authorities at the border (Fuentes et al. 2007, 54–62).

17. Migrants' fear of sleeping with snakes has, on occasion, had tragic consequences. In October 1998, six men were killed by a Union Pacific locomotive while sleeping on railroad tracks near the town of Norias in Kenedy County. The migrants, whose bodies were so badly crushed that they could not be identified, apparently had believed the myth that by sleeping between the rails they would be safe from rattlesnakes. Railroad officials told reporters that the myth is not true and that rattlesnakes are routinely run over by trains as they slither across the rails (Winingham 1998).

18. By the late 1990s, taking a bus out of the region was not a good option for a couple of reasons. First, it would require migrants to enter public spaces where they could be easily identified by the Border Patrol by their dirty clothing and bedraggled appearance. Second, the Border Patrol monitored bus stations and bus stops in the region and would approach passengers and require them to produce identity documents.

19. These were some of the criteria given by Border Patrol agents in their statements submitted as evidence in the U.S. Federal Court in Laredo as reasons for stopping vehicles on the road to inspect them for the presence of undocumented immigrants. A 1976 Supreme Court decision allowed the Border Patrol to stop vehicles in the border region if agents "were aware of specific articulable facts, together with rational inferences, reasonably warranting suspicion that the vehicles contain aliens who may be illegally in the country" (Hing 2004, 139–40).

20. Interestingly, the migrants did not regard their drivers as "coyotes," although they required payment, but rather simply as friends who deserved to be compensated financially for the risks they were assuming, a phenomenon I analyze more thoroughly in chapter 4.

21. "Voluntary return" is the bureaucratic euphemism for the procedure that allows Mexican nationals to return to their country without spending a long period in jail awaiting

a formal deportation hearing. The vast majority of the million or so apprehensions made on the U.S. border with Mexico every year during the period studied resulted in the apprehended individuals' "voluntary return" to Mexico. Of course, the people who "voluntarily returned" described what had happened to them as "they deported me." This bureaucratic procedure has been practiced routinely on the border since at least the 1920s (Corwin 1978, 148).

22. As noted previously, Border Patrol agents must be able to articulate a reasonable suspicion of illegal behavior in order to interrogate and detain a person on U.S. soil. In Laredo, Texas, where 95 percent of the population is Mexican or Mexican American, simply appearing to be a working-class Mexican is not enough to arouse "reasonable suspicion" on the part of a Border Patrol agent.

23. Mexican migrants who have been charged with criminal illegal entry find the whole process quite confusing. "Improper Entry by an Alien" is a criminal violation of federal law (Title 8, Chapter 12, Subchapter 2, Part VIII, §1325 of the U.S. Code) and is prosecuted in a U.S. district court. Formal deportation proceedings, on the other hand, take place before a judge in a U.S. immigration court. Migrants are unlikely to perceive a meaningful difference between the proceedings, however, and often believe that the federal judges sentencing them to probation for the criminal violation have also ordered their deportation, even though they may have, in fact, been "voluntarily returned" to Mexico. The difference between formal deportation and voluntary return is significant insofar as illegal reentry following formal deportation carries a significantly more serious penalty than illegal reentry following voluntary return to Mexico, although either can result in the imposition of a jail sentence. Fermín was mistaken in his belief that nothing would happen to him if he were apprehended by the U.S. authorities again after his three years of probation had elapsed. Although it is true that he would be subject to more serious sanctions if he violated the terms of his probation by returning to the United States before the three years elapsed, he could still be prosecuted for felonious illegal entry of the United States, which could result in a federal prison term of a year or more. I thank Lee Terán of the Center for Legal and Social Justice of St. Mary's University School of Law for clarifying these issues for me.

24. In reality, the Border Patrol did not set any fixed "permissible" number of apprehensions given to a migrant before he would be prosecuted for misdemeanor illegal entry. The decision whether or not to prosecute a given migrant depended on the discretion of the Border Patrol agents making the arrest and the U.S. Attorneys Office and involved consideration of a variety of factors, not the least of which was the personnel resources they had available to deal with their caseloads at any given time.

25. Other surveys of Mexican migrants showed higher rates of coyote usage than the EMIF, both before and after the buildup of border enforcement in the 1990s. For a discussion of this discrepancy between the EMIF and other surveys, see Data Sources and Research Methods.

26. See Davis (1990, 172–75) and López Castro (1998, 972) for similar accounts of migrants' experiences as they passed through this region in the 1970s and 1980s.

27. The term *rancho,* as used here in Mexican Spanish, does not translate as *ranch* in American English. Rather, it refers to a small, impoverished rural settlement. A *ranchero/a* is the inhabitant of a *rancho.*

3. Coyotaje as a Cultural Practice Applied to Migration

1. Mexican Spanish includes other more or less synonymous variants of this term, including *coyoteada, coyotería,* and *coyoteo* (Santamaría 1983, 309). I use *coyotaje* because it is the one that I have encountered most often in interviews and news reports.

2. Versions of this story also exist in most Mayan dialects of southern Mesoamerica, where it is one of the most widely told folktales (Peñalosa 1992, 46).

3. Harris made this argument to rebut the structuralist explanation of Claude Lévi-Strauss as to why the coyote was assigned the trickster role in indigenous mythology in North America. See Lévi-Strauss (1963, 224–25).

4. Meléndez (1982, 298–99) also discusses the use of this term to refer to mixed-race children in colonial and subsequent periods of Mexican history. Gamio (1930, 233) notes that in the 1920s "half-Mexicans and half-Americans" were called "coyotes" in Texas and New Mexico. Lamadrid (1995, 18) notes that even today in New Mexico "the term is still used to designate those persons who are half Hispanic and half Other, either Anglo American or Native American."

5. In 1900 the United States had only four immigration inspectors along the border, one each in Nogales, Arizona; El Paso, Texas; Laredo, Texas; and Piedras Negras, Coahuila; moreover, these inspectors did not begin to inspect Mexican entrants until 1906, focusing their attention instead on other nationalities, especially the Chinese (U.S. Citizenship and Immigration Services 2004).

6. At the same time, to the extent that the enganchistas violated local laws in Mexico against foreign labor recruitment, they also enabled U.S. capitalists to evade Mexican government regulation. Mexican landowners in states like Guanajuato and Jalisco were often hostile to the recruitment efforts of enganchadores, fearing the loss of a captive rural workforce. They therefore banded together to get local laws passed to prohibit workers from leaving for the United States with enganchadores (Peck 2000, 100). In 1917, article 123 of the postrevolutionary constitution definitively made contract labor recruitment by enganchistas illegal under Mexican *national* law (Galarza 1964, 46).

7. Dobie (1948, 198), in an article titled "The Coyote's Name in Human Speech," also noted that "a smuggler-over of aliens is called a *coyote enganchista.*"

8. This gang was started by young Salvadoran men in Los Angeles in the 1980s. By the early twenty-first century, many of its members had been deported to El Salvador and it had become a transnational gang operating all along the migrant corridor between El Salvador and the United States, involved in drug and arms trafficking, among other criminal activities. See López, Connell, and Kraul 2005.

9. The "man-snatchers" were the forerunners of today's *bajadores* in Arizona and California who kidnap migrants from coyotes bringing them in from Mexico and hold them for ransom from relatives expecting to pay the coyotes. See González 2003.

10. See McWilliams (1948, 167–68) for a vivid description of the inhumane conditions found in the transport of sugar beet workers spirited out of Texas by contractor-coyotes in violation of the state's Emigrant Agent Acts.

11. This type of coyotaje at other recruitment centers in Mexico is also well documented in the literature. See, for example, Calavita 1992 and Galarza 1964, as well as Eugene Nelson's 1972 novel, *Bracero.*

12. *Pachucos* were Mexican and Mexican American members of a working-class youth subculture in the U.S. Southwest that emerged in the 1940s and 1950s. *Pachucos* were denigrated by the wider society as gangsters and delinquents, even though many were not engaged in criminal activity. Here the use of the term to refer to "smugglers" was clearly intended to be derogatory. For a more complete description of *pachucos,* see De León 2001 and Ramírez 2005.

13. Although the historical record seems to be mute in this regard, it is likely that some of those deserters escaped with the assistance of coyotes who spirited them away from the farms where they worked.

14. Writing about the border as a whole during this period, Portes (1974, 43) noted that there had been an "unprecedented increase" in the "efficiency and scope" of "smuggling operations," to the point where "illegal Mexican entry into the United States" had become "an organized profit operation."

15. For reasons that are not clear, given that the mechanics of border crossing changed little during this period and Border Patrol force was growing, coyote land-travel charges away from the Texas-Mexico border appear to have fallen a bit in real terms by the beginning of the 1980s, with several reports in the literature of prices in the $850–$1,100 range in 2008 dollars (Browning and Rodríguez 1985, 287–88; Conover 1987, 16; Pérez 1991, 15–21; Rodríguez and Núñez 1986, 152–53). See Orrenius (1999) for an analysis of borderwide reductions in coyote prices during this period.

16. Data collected by the Mexican Migration Project of Princeton University and the Universidad de Guadalajara indicate that in the first years following the termination of the bracero program around 45 percent of migrants on their first trip to the United States worked in agriculture; by 1975, the figure had dropped to about 35 percent, and in 1985 it fell to barely 25 percent (Durand, Massey, and Malone 2002, 61, fig. 4.6). By 1990, the U.S. Census indicated that only 13 percent of settled Mexican immigrants worked in agriculture (Bustamante et al. 1998, 150).

17. More systematic findings reported by Genicot and Senesky (2004, 14 and table 3), who analyzed data collected for the Mexican Migration Project, support Lewis's journalistic observation: less than 2 percent of labor migrants who hired a coyote to enter the United States for the first time relied on their coyote to find a job. The vast majority (75%) relied on relatives (35%), friends (34%), or community members (6%) for help finding a job in the United States, while 22 percent found a job on their own.

18. Of course, the mutual aid provided by migrant social networks at times can be difficult to distinguish from labor-brokerage coyotaje. This can occur, for instance, in situations where migrants recruit people from their hometowns to accompany them on their next labor sojourn in the United State and work alongside them on the job (Moctuzuma 2000). Employees providing such informal labor recruitment for their employers may be rewarded by their employers in a variety of ways. Such arrangements can be even more ambiguous in instances in which the employer also hails from same town in Mexico, as is sometimes the case with construction subcontractors.

19. Consistent with this interpretation, Gaytán et al. (2007, 43) found that 78 percent of migrants they interviewed in January 2005 in two small towns, one in Zacatecas and the other in Jalisco, had obtained their most recent job in the United States with the help of a friend or a family member.

4. Coyotaje and Migration in the Contemporary Period

1. In constructing the typology that appears in these pages, I have built on, extended, and refined earlier work done by two Mexican scholars, Gustavo López Castro (1998) of the Colegio de Michoacán and Miguel Moctezuma (2000) of the Universidad Autónoma de Zacatecas. Because I have reviewed each of these authors' typologies elsewhere (Spener 2008b) and because their work is not specific to the Northeast Mexico-South Texas corridor, I do not explicitly review them again here.

2. An *ejido* is a plot of land owned and worked collectively by peasants. Ejidos were created as part of the land reforms that followed the Mexican Revolution.

3. In his research on Ecuadoran migration to the United States, Kyle (2000, 95) also encountered migrants who offered this type of coyotaje service to get into the United States. He referred to them as "in-group migration merchants."

4. The fields in this part of Nuevo León were worked by many migrant agricultural laborers from southern Mexico, especially the states of Veracruz and Guerrereo.

5. In principle, laser visas and other new federal identity documents should be more tamper resistant and forgery proof than earlier generations of documents, such as the border-crossing card, even if their biometric features are not fully taken advantage of by scanning them through electronic readers attached to centralized databases. In practice, however, U.S. immigration officials told me that with current widespread availability of scanning/computer technologies, high-quality forgeries of new documents, including the laser visa, typically appeared within a week of issuance.

6. Based on my analysis of a sample consisting of 110 case files archived by the Clerk of the Court in the Laredo federal courthouse. Of a sample of 84 case files of smuggling incidents prosecuted in Laredo in 2000, only 19 percent involved arrests made at highway immigration checkpoints. This difference presumably reflects the intensified inspection of persons and vehicles passing through the checkpoints after the 2001 terrorist attacks on Washington and New York.

7. This type of coyotaje in the South Texas-Northeast Mexico region was mentioned in an oral history collected by López Castro (1998, 972–73) attached to his report on coyotes for the Binational Commission on Mexican Migration to the United States, but he did not make reference to it in his typology of coyotes.

8. Nevertheless, my own field observations and Maril's (2004) study of the Border Patrol in South Texas indicate that many migrants continued to enter U.S. territory in urban areas despite the concentration of agents, vehicles, and surveillance equipment deployed in Operation Rio Grande.

9. As discussed in chapter 3, we should nonetheless note that tractor-trailers have been used to move migrants through this region for at least the last thirty years.

10. In his book on the Victoria incident, journalist Jorge Ramos (2005, 16) reports that some of the migrants had been told they would be transported in the sleeping compartment of the rig that made the fatal trip, rather than in the trailer. This was subsequently corroborated in a *Los Angeles Times* article that reported how the husband of a Honduran woman had paid extra for her to be transported in the truck's cab, only to have her obliged to board the trailer at the last minute with the other dozens of migrants making the trip (King 2007).

11. In the Victoria incident, Ramos (2005, 127) reports that when she was interrogated by law enforcement authorities in Texas after her arrest, Karla Chávez, the coordinator of the operation, did not recognize a photo of the driver of the rig in which the nineteen migrants had perished. Although the driver, a Jamaican immigrant named Tyrone Williams, remembered having seen Chávez on one occasion, he told investigators that he had never learned her name (Ramos 2005, 24).

12. Shark boats are twenty-five-foot open-hull boats that can travel at speeds of up to fifty miles per hour. In Mexico, these boats are used to fish for sharks with nets (Schiller 1996a).

13. Padre Island is a 110-mile-long barrier island along the Texas Gulf Coast. Most of it is undeveloped and protected as a National Seashore. The body of water separating the island from the mainland is the Laguna Madre, which is only about two miles wide. The Laguna Madre is part of the Gulf Intracoastal Waterway used by commercial and recreational boaters. The Mansfield Channel, which bisects the island and connects the Gulf with the Laguna Madre, was dug by the U.S. Army Corps of Engineers in 1962 (Texas State Historical Association 2005).

14. My observation in this regard was corroborated by Miró (2003, 21) in his report on organized crime in Mexico produced for the Federal Research Division of the Library

of Congress: "Unlike other international criminal organizations, some of which smuggle illegal aliens as an adjunct to other criminal activities, alien smuggling groups typically are less hierarchical and more characterized by loose networks of associates to facilitate the movement of illegal migrants across regions and continents." Note that this author is referring not only to Mexican organizations transporting Mexicans across the border, but also to organizations transporting non-Mexican migrants through Mexico to the United States from other countries, a journey that involves considerably more logistical coordination than is the case for Mexican nationals.

15. This ambiguous geography reminds us of Rouse's (1991) description of the emergence of Mexican transnational communities that "are spread across a variety of sites" that he referred to as a "transnational migrant circuit."

16. Some Guanajuato-based coyotes would even rent entire buses to transport their clients to the border, recruiting customers not only from Guanajuato but also from parts of the Bajío, a lowland region in Central Mexico that includes parts of the states of Guanajuato, Michoacán, and Querétaro (Prieto Pérez 2005).

17. The social origins of coyotes in the contemporary period appeared to be similar to those of the coyotes of Spanish colonial times, that Wolf described as being recruited from "the army of the disinherited" who were "deprived of alternative sources of employment" (Wolf 1959, 237). For a statistical profile of the sociodemographic characteristics of today's coyotes, see chapter 5 and Data Sources and Research Methods.

18. In 1998, the head of the intelligence unit of the Laredo sector of the U.S. Border Patrol told reporters that his unit had identified twenty-five "human smuggling" [*tráfico de humanos*] organizations in the Nuevo Laredo-Laredo corridor alone. At the same time, Mexican authorities had identified the five main leaders of the *bandas* (gangs) in Nuevo Laredo itself dedicated to moving migrants across the border (Figueroa 1998), suggesting there were *at least* five significant commercial organizations operating in that city alone.

19. Richardson and Resendiz (2006, 152) also interviewed a coyote who said that it was possible for coyotes in the Mexican border cities to avoid being detected by the police if they were cautious.

20. In this regard, it should be noted that in my review of the official records of 197 "alien smuggling" cases prosecuted in the federal courthouse in Laredo, Texas, in the first years of the new century, 90 percent of the 261 defendants prosecuted in these cases were determined by the court to be indigent and were assigned a federal public defender. In other words, it was not true that public defenders defended only the "low-level" participants in coyotaje operations who got arrested by the authorities. Rather, they defended nearly *all* the participants who were prosecuted. Although the authorities and reporters sometimes argue that only the low-level "mules" get caught, while the "kingpins" never do, it is not the case that all, or perhaps even most, coyotaje is under the leadership of a "kingpin" at all.

21. It appears that swindlers posing as coyotes in Reynosa had been engaging in this ruse for a very long time: Zazueta and Zazueta (1980, 75) commented on it in their 1977 study of Mexican migrants returned by the Border Patrol. It is also possible that the story is apocryphal, taking on the characteristics of an urban legend.

22. See Maril (2004) for a description of the methods used by drug traffickers to bring narcotics across the river in South Texas.

23. In reviewing the operation of "northern border smuggling gangs," Miró (2003) found that only one, the Los Texas gang in Nuevo Laredo, *may* have been engaged in both drug smuggling and "alien smuggling." A Border Patrol agent from the Laredo anti-smuggling unit whom I interviewed in 1998 told me that Los Texas had "graduated" to narcotics smuggling from moving only migrants in the 1980s, but that the authorities had

largely dismantled the gang and jailed its leaders by the early 1990s. A Laredo criminal defense attorney I interviewed shared the assessment of this agent.

24. Miró (2003, 12) gave an example in this regard. Citing Mexican press accounts, he reported that the Colima-based Amezcaua-Contreras drug-trafficking organization began in 1988 as "an alien smuggling ring."

25. Based on my analysis of data on alien-smuggling defendants prosecuted in the courthouses of the Southern and Western Districts of the U.S. Federal Court. These data were provided by the Pretrial Services division of the U.S. Federal Court in San Antonio, Texas. See Data Sources and Research Methods for more information.

26. In Texas, as in many other U.S. states, simple possession of most narcotics other than marijuana is prosecuted as a felony rather than as a misdemeanor. For an example of such a felony cocaine prosecution, see Contreras 2007.

27. It should be noted that such FBI intelligence reports present "raw" intelligence gleaned from unproven sources, which sometimes turns out not to be true.

28. Although there have been documented instances in which migrants have been lured into involuntary servitude by their coyotes, the prevalence of actual trafficking of Mexican migrants along the U.S.-Mexican border overall appears to be fairly limited relative to the number of migrants using coyotes to enter the United States. Indeed, a recent Government Accountability Office report found that very few cases of trafficking in the United States had actually been documented by law enforcement authorities since 2001 (United States Government Accountability Office 2006). Moreover, the report found that government estimates of the total number of people trafficked in the United States were unreliable and might well turn out to be grossly inflated. Wong (2005, 80) has also noted that published statistics about the prevalence of human trafficking worldwide are "highly dubious." As noted in chapter 1, the large majority of Mexican migrants who crossed this stretch of the border clandestinely at the turn of the century were men, who were considerably less likely to be sexually trafficked than women and girls were.

5. Trust, Distrust, and Power

1. This sociological approach to understanding economic activity in modern societies is conceptually similar to anthropologists' understanding of exchange systems among preindustrial peoples. See, for example, Sahlins 1972.

2. Several economists have also examined the phenomenon of coyotaje using data from the Mexican Migration Project, with results generally similar to—and with the same limitations as—those obtained by Singer and Massey (Gathmann 2004; Genicot and Senesky 2004; and Orrenius 1999).

3. My calculations using the EMIF, rounds 6–8, migrants returning voluntarily from the United States, $n = 607$. This subsample only includes clandestine migrants who worked on their last trip to the United States.

4. It is evident that the situation facing most Mexican migrants like Álvaro was dramatically different than that facing migrants from other countries. We can take as an example the case of the Ecuadoran migrants described by Kyle (2000) and Kyle and Siracusa (2005). Ecuadoran autonomous migrants traveling to the United States typically paid their coyotes (known in Ecuador as *tramitadores*) $15,000 to $20,000 (Kyle and Siracusa 2005, 160) with funds raised from local loan sharks known as *chulqueros,* who charged up to 20 percent in monthly interest and held migrants' families' homes, land, and other assets as collateral (Kyle and Siracusa 2005, 168–69).

5. Writing about Mexico's northwest border (Alta California-Baja California and Arizona-Sonora), anthropologist Guillermo Alonso Meneses (2001 and 2004) has argued

that new Border Patrol enforcement strategies there have effectively devalued migrants' accumulated stocks of migration-relevant social and human capital, rendering migrants considerably more vulnerable to a dangerous and rigorous journey across desert and mountains, on the one hand, and to abuses from their coyotes, on the other.

6. Durand (2001, 259) has also discussed this type of conversion of migrants' social capital into economic capital with regard to the costs of crossing the border.

7. Contemplating other cases in other contexts, Portes (1994) has commented on the heightened importance of trust in informal enterprises that, by virtue of the illicit nature of their activities, depend on secrecy for their success.

8. Nevertheless, delayed payment of participants in intermediate links did not characterize all commercial-transport coyotaje chains. See comments from Álvaro and the Mexican consular official quoted in chapter 4.

9. Recent findings by researchers with the Center for Comparative Immigration Studies at the University of California, San Diego confirm this point: in communities in Zacatecas and Jalisco surveyed in 2005, on their last trip to the United States 64 percent of migrants contacted their coyote through recommendations made to them through family or friends who lived in the United States, in their hometown, or elsewhere in Mexico (Fuentes et al. 2007, 64). Even in a "new" sending community in Yucatán, whose members had only recently begun to migrate to the United States in significant numbers, 57 percent found their coyote in this way (Kimball, Acosta, and Dames 2007, 102).

10. The other possibility, of course, is that coyotes might be more concerned about their collaborators' malfeasance and incompetence, insofar as it affected them directly, and less concerned about how their collaborators treated migrants, as long as it did not immediately affect the enterprise's viability.

11. In Arizona, seizure of migrants by rival coyotes or organized gangs of extortionists known as *bajadores* has become a serious problem in recent years (González 2003). Although there have been a few incidents of this sort reported in the Houston area (Crowe and Moran 2007; Rice 2004) this phenomenon does not yet seem to be widespread in Texas. In April 2007, a shootout took place during rush hour on one of Houston's major highways that appeared to involve an attempt to kidnap a group of migrants being transported by coyotes in the back of a pickup truck. One man was killed and several were injured. In response to a reporter's query, Scott Hatfield, an official from Immigration and Customs Enforcement, commented that such incidents remained relatively rare in Houston: "It's uncommon. We don't see that in Houston like we do in other cities in the United States" (Carroll and Glenn 2007).

12. Based on my analysis of data collected by the Pretrial Services Agency of the U.S. Courts in the Southern and Western Districts of Texas, 1993–2003. See Data Sources and Research Methods for more information on this data source.

13. For example, in a sample of 261 defendants in "alien smuggling" cases prosecuted in the Laredo federal courthouse in 2000 and 2002, 89 percent had a Spanish surname. Fifteen of the eighteen Anglos in the sample for whom an occupation could be determined were professional truck drivers. This finding is based on my analysis of a sample of 197 alien-smuggling case files maintained by the clerk of the federal court in Laredo. See Data Sources and Research Methods.

14. Ramos (2005, 12) in his book on the Victoria case reports that one of the coyotes involved offered to get one of the migrants a sweater before he boarded the trailer because he said it would be cold. The Mexican news agency Notimex (2003b) reported that other migrants had been warned to wear warm clothing because the trailer would be refrigerated.

15. Other recent research suggests that a large majority of migrants try to avoid contracting coyotes anonymously at the border (see Fuentes et al. 2007, 64; and Kimball, Acosta, and Dames 2007, 102).

16. For more information on the how these findings were generated see Data Sources and Research Methods.

17. For more information on how these findings were generated, see Data Sources and Research Methods.

18. The qualitative, ethnographic nature of the data generated by my fieldwork does not permit me to make any definitive statistical statements about the relative prevalence of COD arrangements in this migratory corridor. It was the arrangement I heard about most often from both migrants and coyotes. My examination of a random sample of case files of "alien smuggling" incidents prosecuted in the Laredo federal courthouse sheds some additional light on this issue. Of the case files I examined 51 out of 197 contained enough information to specify the payment arrangements between coyotes and their customers. In 38 of these cases (slightly less than 75%) migrants were to pay coyotes on their arrival in their destination, usually San Antonio, Houston, or Dallas-Fort Worth. In another 9 cases (slightly less than 18%), migrants paid some portion of their fee at the outset of their trip, with the remainder to be paid on arrival. In only 4 cases (just under 8%) had migrants paid their full fee to coyotes in advance. Although the sample here is small, the results accord with the qualitative observations I made in the field. See Data Sources and Research Methods for more information about this source.

19. One of the public defenders I interviewed in South Texas said that extortion and kidnapping charges brought against coyotes were often without real merit. Rather, he insisted, prosecutors usually brought them for public relations purposes and/or to pressure defendants into pleading guilty to lesser charges. The COD arrangements typically made for paying coyotes easily lent themselves to extortion charges, such that migrants could be characterized as being held against their will until their friends and relatives paid a "ransom" for their release.

20. These forms of usurious lending have been documented in some of the new Mexican migrant-sending states such as Veracruz. See, for example Mestries Benquet (2003) and Urrea (2004).

21. This threat may not be as far-fetched as it sounds. Migrants often speak little or no English and travel with little cash. They may be staying in safe houses in a city where they have no friends or relatives and where they don't know their way around. In these circumstances, "turning over" the migrant to la migra may mean nothing more than leaving him along the side of the road in an area patrolled by U.S. immigration authorities. Moreover, to first-time migrants the threat may *seem* real enough, even if coyotes have little intention of following through with it.

22. The U.S. Court in San Antonio, for example, had a special program for material witnesses in "alien smuggling" cases that granted them legal status to live and work in the United States for as long as their case was pending and even provided assistance in finding employment.

23. Using just this strategy, the wife and mother of two of the victims of the Victoria disaster confronted Mexico's foreign minister, Luis Ernesto Derbez, at a news conference he was holding. She presented Derbez with the name and the phone number of the coyote her husband had worked through to make the trip and was subsequently offered police protection for her and her family (Millán 2003; Saldierna 2003).

24. One of the victims in the May 2003 Victoria case had been convinced to go on the trip by his brother-in-law, who worked as a recruiter for the coyote network in Linares, Nuevo León. The family and siblings of the recruiter refused to denounce him to the Mexican police, presumably because of his marriage to the sister of the victim (Villaséez 2003).

25. The account by these federal prosecutors was supported by data I reviewed from a sample of 197 "alien smuggling" cases prosecuted in the Laredo federal court in 2000 and 2002. Eighty-four percent of the defendants in these cases ($n = 230$) were arrested for being the driver of a migrant-laden vehicle stopped on the road by the Border Patrol. Only 6 percent of the cases I reviewed were prosecuted as the result of surveillance or investigations conducted by the "anti-smuggling unit" of the federal immigration authorities that brought cases in the Laredo courthouse.

26. López Castro (1998) noted that some commercial coyotes had women working for them to guide and care for female migrants as a way of preventing their sexual harassment by coyotes or other migrants. Migrants I have interviewed have also described crossings where women were lodged in different quarters than male migrants.

27. Another example of migrants exerting control over their coyotes on the trail comes from a newspaper report from the Arizona desert. Seventy-seven Mexican and Central American migrants overpowered their guide, who had gotten lost while leading them and attempted to abandon them, took his cell phone and called 911 to be rescued (Mural 2005).

28. Retaliation against coyotes might also occur in U.S. territory. A coyote named Rubén Rangel was strangled to death in Houston after demanding payment from members of a migrant family he had brought into the country (Houston Chronicle 1999).

29. Guides at the beginning of the twenty-first century in this region were being paid between $100 and $200 per migrant. A coyote guiding fifteen migrants through the brush could, therefore, stand to lose between $1,500 and $3,000 if the whole group were captured due to the inability to keep up of one member, whose loss, aside from the moral costs, would only cost the guide $100 or $200. For the organization as a whole, the difference might be between collecting $21,000 or nothing, assuming a total fee charged per migrant of $1,500. Of course, the migrants from Las Furias used this same logic to ensure that their coyotes waited for their companions who could not keep up the pace: none of them would go ahead with the coyotes without the lagging companions. If the coyote "lost" one member of his "load," he would lose them all.

30. Data from the Encuesta sobre Migración en la Frontera Norte indicate that 72 percent of coyote-users who crossed this stretch of the border in the 1998–2003 period were making their first trip to work to the United States: my calculation using the EMIF, rounds 6–8, migrants returning voluntarily from the United States, $n = 413$. See Data Sources and Research Methods for a more detailed description of the EMIF and my analysis of the data it contains.

31. Under the terms of the Victims of Trafficking and Violence Protection Act of 2000, migrants who can demonstrate that they have been "trafficked" as opposed to merely "smuggled" can apply for a special "T" visa that allows them to stay in the United States for up to three years and then apply for permanent residency (Thomas 2006). In order to qualify for such a visa, migrants have to demonstrate that they were "induced by force, fraud, or coercion" to perform commercial sex acts or subjected to "involuntary servitude, debt bondage, or slavery." Victims of Trafficking and Violence Protection Act of 2000, http://www.state.gov/documents/organization/10492.pdf (accessed May 27, 2007).

32. This is not to say that coyotes were not arrested and prosecuted in the Tamaulipas border cities—they were (see, for example, Bandín 1998; Cárdenas García 1998; García 1998; and Terán González 1998). Nevertheless, according to Mexican human rights activists I interviewed in a Tamaulipas border city, the only coyotes who were prosecuted in the Tamaulipas border cities were the ones who had not kept up with their *cuota*.

33. One case file did mention, however, that a defendant involved in harboring/transporting migrants from Brazil and the Republic of Georgia was subsequently rearrested in a similar case where a semi-automatic weapon was recovered at the scene.

34. Harriet Tubman was the African American woman who is revered for having helped Southern slaves escape to freedom in the North as a leader of what was known as the Underground Railroad. It is worth noting, nonetheless, that prior to the abolition of slavery, paid guides as well as altruistic activists like Tubman helped slaves escape to the north (see Cabrera 2006).

6. Passing Judgment

1. This discussion of the polysemy of the term *coyote* follows Vila's (1998) poststructuralist analysis of the struggle over the meaning of the term *Chicano* among residents of El Paso, Texas, in the 1990s.

2. *Moral panic* is defined by the *On-line Dictionary of the Social Sciences* as "a panic or overreaction to forms of deviance or wrong doing believed to be threats to the moral order. Moral panics are usually fanned by the media and led by community leaders or groups intent on changing laws or practices" (Drislane and Parkinson 2006). For a review of the characteristics of moral panics see Rothe and Muzzatti 2004.

3. Several of the points I make in this section echo similar arguments Klinenberg (2002) made about press coverage of a heat wave that took place in Chicago in 1995, in which over seven hundred people died. See also Gans (2003) regarding the relationship between reporters and government officials.

4. Nevins (2005) has written cogently about the legitimating power of the law with regard to generating U.S. public support for more stringent border enforcement measures. Here I suggest that reporters are no less likely to have been socialized into the default position that the law represents what is right and just than other U.S. residents and that their reporting reflects and reinforces that worldview.

5. This has always routinely happened with Mexican migrants, who typically are "voluntarily returned" to Mexico within a few hours of their detention by the Border Patrol. Now, with the launching of the binational Oasis Program, Mexican nationals who are purportedly engaging in "alien smuggling" and are captured by U.S. authorities on U.S. soil can be turned over to Mexican authorities for prosecution in Mexico. The reason for doing this is that prosecutors of "smuggling" defendants in Mexico do not have to produce "material witnesses" to their "crimes," as is the case in U.S. federal courts. This aspect of the program may remind readers of the practice of "extraordinary rendition" of terrorist suspects by the United States to third countries where legal protections of defendants are less stringent than in the United States. See Cano 2006; El Diario de Juárez 2007; Secretaría de Relaciones Exteriores 2005b.

6. The records I examined of 197 "alien smuggling" cases prosecuted in the federal courthouse in Laredo, Texas, showed that 92 percent of the 260 defendants involved pleaded guilty before going to trial, while 8 percent had charges against them dismissed. *None* of the defendants in the cases whose records I examined went to trial.

7. This amount was far greater than Mexican migrants typically paid at the time. The agent may have been exaggerating to make his point, or there may have been many Central Americans being transported in the truck, who typically paid a much higher fee than Mexicans did.

8. At the same time, it should be noted that the investigations units of the old INS, like today's ICE investigations units, focused their efforts on combating large-scale organizations and/or organizations that were known to abuse or endanger migrants. As an ICE official told me in a later interview, limited resources meant that investigations didn't typically target "your run of-the-mill, mom and pop organizations moving Mexican aliens."

9. The danger of sexual abuse of women by their coyotes was already well-known by the 1980s when Chicana feminist writer Gloria Anzaldúa commented on it in her 1987 literary classic *Borderlands/La Frontera: The New Mestiza* (34–35). Although tales of women's sexual abuse by coyotes are common, occasionally one hears of sexual abuse of male migrants as well. Immigration authorities were able to break up a Houston-based coyotaje organization in 2001 in part because several male migrants denounced the operator of its safe house in San Antonio for allegedly forcing them to perform oral sex on him at gunpoint (Burnett 2001; Hegstrom 2001).

10. In the early 2000s, the Mexican consulate in Brownsville distributed a pamphlet warning migrants about coyotes who conspired with armed bandits along the river to lead their clients into ambushes where they would be assaulted and robbed. Coyotes, the pamphlet warned, were not "white doves."

11. In this regard it is worth noting that the courts classified an "alien smuggling" conviction as a "violent" felony if it involved any type of endangerment of migrants, such as transporting them in an unsafe way hidden under a tarp in the bed of a pickup truck. Nearly three-quarters of defendants in 2003 had no felony convictions at all on their records at the time they were arrested. Some of those who did had been convicted of felony immigration violations, such as reentry after deportation.

12. Other recent research evidence lends a modicum of support to Álvaro's assessment. A 2006 survey conducted in migrant-sending communities in the Yucatán by a team from the University of California, San Diego, found that 92 percent of respondents reported that their coyotes had fulfilled the terms of their agreement with them on their last border-crossing. Unpublished data from the Mexican Migration Field Research and Training Program, Center for Comparative Immigration Studies, University of California, San Diego, 2006 survey in Yucatán. Personal communication from Wayne Cornelius August 11, 2006.

13. The distinctions my informants made between "community" coyotes and "stranger" coyotes operating for profit at the border have been made elsewhere in Mexico as well. See, for example, López 2006.

14. University of North Carolina sociologist Jacqueline Hagan (2008, 67–81) found that few of the autonomous migrants she interviewed for her book about the religious aspect of cross-border journeys were abused or endangered overtly by their coyotes. She found that the main abuse inflicted on migrants by their coyotes took the form of hunger, thirst, and exposure to the elements as they trekked across arid badlands on the U.S. side of the border.

15. Indeed, Hagan (2008, 78) documented cases in which women's coyotes protected them from rape by other migrants on their cross-border journeys.

Conclusion

1. My use of the term *social field* follows Bourdieu and Wacquant (1992).

2. Crépau (2003, 181) makes essentially the same argument with regard to the prosecution of "smugglers" and "traffickers" of migrants in other parts of the world and at other moments in history. He correctly observes that "smugglers save lives" insofar as they permit refugees to escape situations of danger and abuse far greater than any temporary suffering inflicted on them by their smugglers or traffickers. See also Sharma (2005) and Wong (2005), who make similar arguments.

3. For a more extensive discussion of these issues using Galtung's distinctions between personal, structural, and cultural violence, see Spener 2008a. For a related discussion of how current U.S. border-enforcement policies constitute a form of social Darwinism practiced against migrants, see Feldman and Durand 2008.

4. Similarly, Urry (2000) has suggested that the iterative actions repeated by many thousands of people who are linked together in far-flung webs of social relations can cumulatively change the dynamics of the social system in which they are immersed, quite independent of their individual intentions.

5. Research by Rumbaut and Ewing (2007) indicates that Latino immigrants are actually less likely than native citizens to commit crimes in the United States.

6. My calculation using data contained in table 34 of the *2007 Yearbook of Immigration Statistics* (U.S. Department of Homeland Security 2008, 92).

7. It would make sense to make similar adjustments to the number of immigrant visas available to citizens of the Central American countries as well. The great majority (around 70%) of all non-Mexican migrants apprehended by U.S. authorities each year are Central Americans who have passed through Mexico on their way to the United States (my calculations using data contained in table 34 of the U.S. Department of Homeland Security's *2007 Yearbook of Immigration Statistics*). Moreover, like Mexico, the economies of all of these countries except Belize and Panama are highly integrated with the U.S. economy via a comprehensive free-trade agreement.

Data Sources and Research Methods

1. A handful of immediate family members of migrants who spoke about their families' migratory experiences are also included in the total of 137 migrants.

2. Data collected by the Mexican government suggested that the communities I visited in Mexico were reasonably representative of the sources of Mexican migration to the major cities of Texas. The Mexican consulates in San Antonio, Houston, and Dallas issued identity documents known as *matrículas consulares* to their nationals residing in and around these cities, most of whom were not in the United States legally. In both Houston and San Antonio, the three leading states of origin of Mexicans who received *matrículas* were Guanajuato, Nuevo León, and San Luis Potosí. In Dallas, they were Guanajuato, San Luis Potosí, and Zacatecas, in rank order. San Antonio data are found in Schiller 2003. Data for Dallas and Houston were provided by the consulates there.

3. In addition to analyzing data from the EMIF, I also conducted a secondary analysis of data from the Mexican Migration Project, a joint effort of researchers at Princeton University and the Universidad de Guadalajara. Because the MMP data generally corroborated the findings I obtained from the EMIF, I do not report results of that analysis in this book.

References

Acuña, Rodolfo. 2003. *Occupied America: A History of Chicanos.* 5th ed. New York: Pearson/Longman.

Adler, Rachel. 2000. "Human Agency in International Migration: The Maintenance of Transnational Social Fields by Yucatecan Migrants in a Southwestern City." *Mexican Studies/Estudios Mexicanos* 16 (1): 165–87.

———. 2004. *Yucatecans in Dallas, Texas: Breaching the Border, Bridging the Distance.* Boston: Allyn and Bacon.

Aiken, Riley. 1935. "A Pack Load of Mexican Tales." In *Puro mexicano,* ed. J. Frank Dobie, 1–87. Austin: Texas Folk-Lore Society.

Alexander, Titus. 1996. *Unraveling Global Apartheid: An Overview of World Politics.* Cambridge, UK: Polity Press.

Allen, Elizabeth. 1997. "100 INS Agents Headed to S. Texas." *San Antonio Express-News,* July 27, 29A.

Almere Read, Kay, and Jason J. González. 2000. *Handbook of Mesoamerican Mythology.* Santa Barbara, CA: ABC-CLIO.

Alonso Meneses, Guillermo. 2001. "Riesgos y vulnerabilidad en la migración clandestina." *Ciudades* 52 (October–December): 18–25.

———. 2004. "Los peligros del desierto en la migración clandestina por California y Arizona." Paper presented at Tercer Coloquio Internacional sobre Antropología del Desierto: Paisaje, naturaleza y sociedad, sponsored by the Instituto de Investigaciones Antropológicas, Universidad Nacional Autónoma de México and El Colegio de la Frontera Norte, June 2–4, in Tijuana, BJ.

Alonzo, Armando C. 1998. *Tejano Legacy: Rancheros and Settlers in South Texas, 1734–1900.* Albuquerque: University of New Mexico Press.

American Airlines. 2003. *Sky Mall.* Summer. Phoenix, Arizona.

American G.I. Forum of Texas and Texas State Federation of Labor (AFL). 1953. *What Price Wetbacks?* Austin, Texas. Repr. 1976. In *Mexican Migration to the United States.* New York: Arno Press.

American Technologies Network Corporation. 2007. "Night Vision." South San Francisco, CA. http://www.atncorp.com/NightVision (accessed April 1, 2007).

Anders, Ferdinand, Maarten Jansen, and Luis Reyes García. 1991. *El libro del Ciuacoatl: Homenaje para el año del Fuego Nuevo: Libro explicativo del llamado Códice Borbónico.* Mexico City: Fondo de Cultura Económica.

Anderson, Jack, and Joseph Spear. 1988. "Fake Birth Certificates: Hubs of Deceit." *Washington Post,* April 5, B9.

Anderson, Sarah, and John Cavenagh. 2004. "Lessons of European Integration for the Americas." Washington, DC: Institute for Policy Studies. http://aei.pitt.edu/1436/ (accessed January 5, 2009).

Anderson, Stuart, and David Miller. 2006. *Legal Immigrants: Waiting Forever: An Analysis of the Green Card Backlogs and Processing Delays Affecting Families, Skilled Professionals, and U.S. Employers.* Arlington, VA: National Foundation for American Policy.

Andreas, Peter. 2000. *Border Games: Policing the U.S.-Mexico Divide.* Ithaca: Cornell University Press.

Anzaldúa, Gloria. 2007 [1987]. *Borderlands/La Frontera: The New Mestiza,* 3rd ed. San Francisco, CA: Aunt Lute Books.

Aranda Kilian, Lucía. 2005. "El simbolismo del coyote, el zorrillo y el colibrí en el mundo náhuatl y supervivencia en una comunidad huasteca." *Revista de Antropología* 3 (3): 63–73. http://sisbib.unmsm.edu.pe/bib virtualdata/publicaciones/revis-antrop/ n3_2005/a02.pdf (accessed February 23, 2007).

Arreola, Daniel. 2002. *Tejano South Texas: A Mexican American Cultural Province.* Austin: University of Texas Press.

Arzaluz Solano, Socorro, ed. 2007. *La migración a Estados Unidos y la frontera noreste de México.* Mexico City: Miguel Ángel Porrúa.

Associated Press. 1986. "Terrorists Train in Mexico, West Texas Lawman Alleges." *Houston Chronicle,* July 20, Section 1, 31.

——. 1987a. "INS Charges Two in Alleged Sale of False Alien Documents." *Houston Chronicle,* November 11, Section 1, 14.

——. 1987b. "INS Discloses the Breakup of Ring Selling Fake Papers to Illegal Aliens." *Houston Chronicle,* September 11, Section 1, 21.

——. 1998. "Undocumented Immigrants Left on Padre." *San Antonio Express-News,* April 11, 6B.

——. 2000. "Second Man Pleads Guilty to Smuggling Thai Women to U.S. for Prostitution." *San Antonio Express-News,* July 17, online edition.

——. 2002a. "Border Patrol in McAllen Gets High-tech Safety Net." *Houston Chronicle,* July 21, A43.

——. 2002b. "Mexico Family Mourns Rail Car Deaths." *New York Times,* October 18, online edition.

——. 2004. "Agent Accused of Letting Illegal Immigrants into U.S." *San Antonio Express-News,* December 10, online edition.

——. 2005a. "Bribery Details Sought in Smuggling Deaths Case." *San Antonio Express-News,* January 28, online edition.

——. 2005b. "Toddler Swept Away during Rio Grande Crossing." *Houston Chronicle,* March 2, online edition.

Bacon, David. 2007. "The Political Economy of International Migration." *New Labor Forum* 16 (3): 56–69.

Balán, Jorge, Harley Browning, and Elizabeth Jelín. 1973. *Men in a Developing Society: Geographic and Social Mobility in Monterrey, Mexico.* Austin: University of Texas Press.

Balderrama, Francisco E., and Raymond Rodríguez. 1995. *Decade of Betrayal: Mexican Repatriation in the 1930s.* Albuquerque: University of New Mexico Press.

Banco de México. 2007. "Las remesas familiares en México: Inversión de los recursos de migrantes: Resultados de las alternativas vigentes." PowerPoint presentation, http://www.banxico.org.mx/documents/%7BA5443598-2DF0-815D-4077-A416D3429AA9%7D.pdf (accessed January 2, 2009).

Bandín, E. 1998. "'Patero pirata,' detenido." *El Mañana de Reynosa,* May 2. Photocopy from news-clip file, Centro de Estudios Fronterizos y Promoción de los Derechos Humanos in Reynosa, Tamaulipas.

Basch, Linda G., Nina Glick Schiller, and Cristina Szantzon Blanc. 1994. *Nations Unbound: Transnational Projects, Postcolonial Predicaments, and Deterritorialized Nation-States.* Amsterdam: Overseas Publishers Association.

Batalova, Jeanne. 2008. "Mexican Immigrants in the United States." *Migration Information Source.* April, online newsletter. Washington, DC: Migration Policy Institute. http://www.migration information.org/USfocus/display.cfm?ID=679 (accessed June 28, 2008).

Bauer, Mary, and Sarah Reynolds. 2007. *Close to Slavery: Guestworker Programs in the United States.* Montgomery, AL: Southern Poverty Law Center. http://www.splcenter.org/pdf/static/SPLCguestworker.pdf (accessed April 1, 2008).

Bayón, María Cristina. 2006. "Precariedad social en México y Argentina: Tendencias, expresiones y trayectorias nacionales." *Revista de la CEPAL* 88:133–52.

Bean, Frank D., Roland Chanove, Robert G. Cushing, Rodolfo de la Garza, Gary P. Freeman, Charles W. Haynes, and David Spener. 1994. *Illegal Mexican Migration and the United States/Mexico Border: The Effects of Operation Hold the Line on El Paso/Juárez.* Washington, DC: U.S. Commission on Immigration Reform.

Benavidez, Rachel. 2001. "Smuggling Case Goes to Grand Jury." *Brownsville Herald,* May 25, A1.

Bloomberg News. 2001. "Indictment Says Tyson Used Illegals: Chicken Giant Accused in Smuggling Conspiracy." *Houston Chronicle,* December 20, Business section, 1.

Blumenthal, Ralph. 2005. "Twist in Smuggling Case over Complicity in Deaths." *New York Times,* January 21, online edition.

Bomar, George W. 1983. *Texas Weather.* Austin: University of Texas Press.

Bonilla-Silva, Eduardo. 1996. "Rethinking Racism: Toward a Structural Interpretation." *American Sociological Review* 62:465–80.

Booker, Salih, and William Minter. 2001. "Global Apartheid." *The Nation* 273 (2): 11–17.

Bortz, Jeffrey, and Marcos Águila. 2006. "Earning a Living: A History of Real Wage Studies in Twentieth-Century Mexico." *Latin American Research Review* 41 (2): 112–38.

Bourdieu, Pierre. 1977. *Outline of a Theory of Practice.* Cambridge, UK: Cambridge University Press.

———. 1986. "The Forms of Capital." In *Handbook of Theory and Research for the Sociology of Education,* ed.John G. Richardson, 241–58. Westport, CT: Greenwood Press.

Bourdieu, Pierre, and Loic Wacquant. 1992. "The Purpose of Reflexive Sociology (Chicago Workshop)." In *An Invitation to Reflexive Sociology,* ed. Pierre Bourdieu and Loic Wacquant, 61–215. Chicago: University of Chicago Press.

Brezosky, Lynn. 2006. "Investigation Ongoing in Deadly Crash near Border." Associated Press, January 27, online newswire. http://www.mysanantonio.com/news/apwire/texas/storyindex.html (accessed January 27, 2006).

Browning, Harley L., and Néstor Rodríguez. 1985. "The Migration of Mexican Indocumentados as a Settlement Process: Implications for Work." In *Hispanics in the U.S. Economy,* ed. George J. Borjas and Marta Tienda, 277–97. Orlando, FL: Academic Press.

Brubaker, Rogers. 1994. "Are Immigration Control Efforts Really Failing?" In *Controlling Immigration: A Global Perspective*, ed. Wayne Cornelius, Philip L. Martin, and James F. Hollifield, 227–31. Stanford: Stanford University Press.

Burawoy, Michael. 1976. "The Functions and Reproduction of Migrant Labor: Comparative Material from Southern Africa and the United States." *American Journal of Sociology* 81 (5): 1050–87.

Burnett, John. 2001. "Immigrant Smugglers." *Morning Edition.* National Public Radio. June 22. http://www.npr.org/templates/story/story.php?storyId=1124760 (accessed June 6, 2005).

Bustamante, Jorge, Guillermina Jasso, J. Edward Taylor, and Paz Trigueros Legarreta. 1998. "Characteristics of Migrants: Mexicans in the United States." In *Binational Study: Migration between Mexico and the United States*, ed. Mexican Ministry of Foreign Affairs and the U.S. Commission on Immigration Reform, 91–162. Washington, DC: U.S. Commission on Immigration Reform.

Cabrera, Luis. 2006. "Minutemen, Samaritans, and Moral Parallels on the New Underground Railroad." Paper presented at the Annual Meeting of the American Political Science Association, September 1, Philadelphia, Pennsylvania.

Cahalane, Victor H. 1947. *Mammals of North America.* New York: MacMillan.

Calavita, Kitty. 1992. *Inside the State: The Bracero Program, Immigration, and the INS.* New York: Routledge.

Campbell, Howard, and Josiah Heyman. 2007. "Slantwise: Beyond Domination and Resistance on the Border." *Journal of Contemporary Ethnography* 36 (1): 3–30.

Cano, Luis Carlos. 2006. "Activan plan para combatir tráfico de personas en Juárez." *El Universal*, July 11, online edition.

Cárdenas García, Joel. 1998. "Capturan a cuatro 'pateros.'" *El Mañana de Reynosa*, March 4. Photocopy from news-clip file, Centro de Estudios Fronterizos y Promoción de los Derechos Humanos in Reynosa, Tamaulipas.

Cárdenas, Gilberto. 1975. "United States Immigration Policy toward Mexico: An Historical Perspective." *Chicano Law Review* 2:66–91.

Cardoso, Lawrence A. 1980. *Mexican Emigration to the United States, 1897–1931.* Tucson: University of Arizona Press.

Carroll, Susan, and Mike Glenn. 2007. "Southwest Freeway Ambush Ends in Death." *Houston Chronicle*, April 18, online edition.

Castañeda, Jorge. 2007. *Ex-Mex: From Migrants to Immigrants.* New York: The New Press.

Castells, Manuel, and Alejandro Portes. 1989. "World Underneath: The Origins, Dynamics, and Effects of the Informal Economy." In *The Informal Economy: Studies in Advance and Less-Developed Countries*, 1–40. Baltimore: Johns Hopkins University Press.

Castillo García, Gustavo. 2007. "Captura PGR a *El Barbas* y otros cuatro presuntos narcotraficantes." *La Jornada*, April 18, online edition.

Castillo, E. Eduardo. 2007. "5 Members of the Gulf Cartel Arrested in Reynosa." Associated Press, April 17, online newswire.

Castillo, Mariano. 2004. "Al Qaida Rumors in Valley Confuse." *San Antonio Express-News*, September 27, online edition.

———. 2006. "Checkpoint to Speed Traffic on I-35." *San Antonio Express-News*, April 15, 5B.

———. 2007. "Officials Trumpet Drug Arrests in Wake of Reynosa Raid." *San Antonio Express-News*, April 18, online edition.

Cavazos, Mary Ann. 2006. "Border Agent Accused of Assisting Smugglers." *Corpus Christi Caller-Times*, July 1, online edition.

Cerda, Gilberto, Berta Cabaza, and Julieta Farias. 1953. *Vocabulario español de Texas.* Austin: University of Texas Press.

Cerrutti, Marcela, and Douglas S. Massey. 2001. "On the Auspices of Female Migration from Mexico to the United States." *Demography* 38 (2): 187–200.

——. 2004. "Trends in Mexican Migration to the United States, 1965–1995." In *Crossing the Border: Research from the Mexican Migration Project*, ed. Jorge Durand and Douglas S. Massey, 17–44. New York: Russell Sage Foundation.

Chapa, Sergio. 2006. "Infiltration from the South Feared: Terrorist Smuggling Denied by Admitted Drug Runner." *Brownsville Herald,* January 15, online edition.

Chávez, Leo R. 2001. *Covering Immigration: Popular Images and the Politics of the Nation.* Berkeley: University of California Press.

Christian Science Monitor. 2000. "U.S. Tries Spy Tactics to Stop Human Smugglers." *Christian Science Monitor,* August 30, 1.

Clark, Victor S. 1908. "Mexican Labor in the United States." *Bulletin of the Bureau of Labor* 78:466–522.

Cockcroft, James D. 1986. *Outlaws in the Promised Land: Mexican Immigrant Workers and America's Future.* New York: Grove Press.

Coerver, Don M., and Linda B. Hall. 1984. *Texas and the Mexican Revolution: A Study in State and National Border Policy, 1910–1920.* San Antonio, TX: Trinity University Press.

Coleman, James S. 1988. "Social Capital in the Creation of Human Capital." *American Journal of Sociology* 94:S95–S121.

Comité Fronterizo de Obrer@s. 2007. "Algunos datos de la industria maquiladora de exportación." Piedras Negras, Coahuila. http://www.cfomaquiladoras.org/numeralia. es.html (accessed March 30, 2008).

Comptroller General of the United States. 1976. *Report to the Congress by the Comptroller General of the United States: Smugglers, Illicit Documents, and Schemes are Undermining U.S. Controls over Immigration: Departments of Justice and State.* Washington, DC: Comptroller General of the United States.

Conover, Ted. 1987. *Coyotes: A Journey through the Secret World of America's Illegal Aliens.* New York: Random House.

Consejo Nacional de Población. 2004. *Encuesta sobre Migración en la Frontera Norte de México (EMIF).* Mexico City. http://conapo.gob.mx/migracion_int/principal.html (accessed January 24, 2004).

——. n.d. "Flujo de migrantes temporales que se dirigen a Estados Unidos por período de levantamiento de la EMIF, 1993–2003." Mexico City. http://www.conapo.gob.mx/ mig_int/series/g13.ppt#512,1,Slide 1 (accessed January 4, 2007).

Contreras, Guillermo. 2006. "Immigrants Flooding Del Rio Courts." *San Antonio Express-News,* 1A.

——. 2007. "Nearly 3-year Immigration Nightmare Appears Over." *San Antonio Express-News,* January 22, online edition.

Corchado, Alfredo, and Jason Trahan. 2006. "FBI Bulletin Outlines Possible Terrorist Plot at Texas Border." *Dallas Morning News,* July 16, online edition.

Cornelius, Wayne A. 1978. "Mexican Migration to the United States: Causes, Consequences, and U.S. Responses." Working paper. Cambridge, MA: Migration and Development Study Group of the Center for International Studies of the Massachusetts Institute of Technology.

——. 1990. "Impacts of the 1986 Immigration Law on Emigration from Rural Mexican Sending Communities." In *Undocumented Migration to the United States: IRCA and the Experience of the 1980s,* ed. Frank D. Bean, Barry Edmonston, and Jeffrey S. Passel, 227–49. Washington, DC: Urban Institute Press.

———. 2001. "Death at the Border: Efficacy and Unintended Consequences of U.S. Immigration Control Policy." *Population and Development Review* 27 (4): 661–85.

Corwin, Arthur F. 1978. "A Story of Ad Hoc Exceptions: American Immigration Policy toward Mexico." In *Immigrants—and Immigrants: Perspectives on Mexican Labor Migration to the United States,* ed. Arthur F. Corwin, 136–75. Westport, CT: Greenwood Press.

Coutin, Susan Bibler. 1993. *The Culture of Protest: Religious Activism and the U.S. Sanctuary Movement.* Boulder, CO: Westview Press.

Crépau, François. 2003. "The Fight against Migrant Smuggling: Migration Containment over Refugee Protection." In *The Refugee Convention at Fifty: A View from Forced Migration Studies,* ed. Joanne van Selm et al., 173–86. Oxford, UK: Lexington Books.

Crowe, Robert. 2004. "Immigrants Found in Squalor." *Houston Chronicle,* October 28, online edition.

Crowe, Robert, and Kevin Moran. 2007. "Freeway Gun Battle Ends in Death." *Houston Chronicle,* April 18, online edition.

Davis, Rod. 2001. "A Río Runs Through It: Part 1." *San Antonio Express-News,* June 3, 1L.

Davis, Marilyn. 1990. *Mexican Voices, American Dreams: An Oral History of Mexican Immigration to the United States.* New York: Henry Holt.

De Genova, Nicholas P. 2002. "Migrant 'Illegality' and Deportability in Everyday Life." *Annual Review of Anthropology* 31:419–47.

de la Cruz, Víctor. 1983. *Coyote va a la fiesta de Chihuitán.* Juchitán, Oaxaca: H. Ayuntamiento de Juchitán, Oaxaca.

De León, Arnoldo. 2001. "Pachuco." *Handbook of Texas Online.* Austin: Texas State Historical Society. http://www.tsha.utexas.edu/handbook/online/articles/PP/pqp1.html (accessed September 2, 2005).

De Mente, Boye Lafayette. 1996. *NTC's Dictionary of Mexican Cultural Code Words.* Chicago: NTC Publishing Group.

de Soto, Hernando. 1989. *The Other Path: The Invisible Revolution in the Third World.* New York: Harper and Row.

Dobie, J. Frank. 1929. *A Vaquero of the Brush Country.* Dallas: Southwest Press.

———. 1947. *Tongues of the Monte.* Boston: Little, Brown, and Company.

———. 1948. "The Coyote's Name in Human Speech." *The New Mexico Quarterly Review* 18 (2): 195–99.

Doerge, Olivia. 2006. "El FBI vincula a Segura con el crimen organizado." *Rumbo-Valle,* March 10, online edition.

Doerge, Olivia, and Arianna Vásquez. 2006. "Ilegal hallado muerto en cárcel." *Rumbo,* February 9, online edition.

Donato, Katharine M. 1999. "A Dynamic View of Mexican Migration to the United States." *Gender Issues* (Winter 1999): 53–75.

Donato, Katharine M., and Evelyn Patterson. 2004. "Women and Men on the Move: Undocumented Border Crossing." In *Crossing the Border: Research from the Mexican Migration Project,* ed. Jorge Durand and Douglas S. Masssey, 111–30. New York: Russell Sage Foundation.

Drislane, Robert, and Gary Parkinson. 2006. *Online Dictionary of the Social Sciences.* Athabasca, Alberta: Athabasca University. http://bitbucket.icaap.org/dict.pl (accessed June 30, 2008).

Dunn, Timothy J. 1996. *The Militarization of the U.S.-Mexico Border, 1978–1992: Low-Intensity Conflict Doctrine Comes Home.* Austin: CMAS Books.

Durand, Jorge. 1994. *Más allá de la línea: Patrones migratorios entre México y Estados Unidos.* Mexico City: Consejo Nacional para la Cultura y las Artes.

——. 1998. *Política, modelos y patrón migratorios: El trabajo y los trabajadores mexicanos en Estados Unidos.* San Luis Potosí: El Colegio de San Luis.

——. 2000. "Tres premisas para entender y explicar la migración México-Estados Unidos." *Relaciones: Revista de El Colegio de Michoacán* 21 (83): 17–36.

——. 2001. "Origen es destino: Redes sociales, desarrollo histórico y escenarios contemporáneos." In *Migración México-Estados Unidos: Opciones de política,* ed. Rodolfo Tuirán, 248–61. Mexico, DF: Consejo Nacional de Población, Secretaría de Gobernación y Secretaría de Relaciones Exteriores.

——. 2002. *Rostros y rastros: Entrevistas a trabajadores migrantes en Estados Unidos.* San Luis Potosí: El Colegio de San Luis.

Durand, Jorge, and Patricia Arias. 2004. *La vida en el Norte: Historia e iconografía de la migración México–Estados Unidos.* Guadalajara, JA: Universidad de Guadalajara.

Durand, Jorge, and Douglas S. Massey. 2003. *Clandestinos: Migración México–Estados Unidos.* Mexico City: Universidad de Zacatecas and Miguel Ángel Porrúa.

EarthTrends. 2003. "Economic Indicators—Mexico." Washington, DC: World Resources Institute. http://earthtrends.wri.org/pdf_library/country_profiles/eco_cou_484.pdf (accessed March 30, 2008).

El Diario de Juárez. 2007. "Acuerdan México y EU extender el programa Oasis a Coahuila," June 8, online edition.

El Informador. 2008. "Afirma Cámara del Vestido que seis por ciento del contrabando es ropa usada." *El Informador,* May 7. http://www.informador.com.mx/jalisco/2008/10533/1/afirma-camara-del-vestido-que-seis-por-ciento-del-contrabando-es-ropa-usada.htm (accessed June 3, 2008).

El Mañana de Matamoros. 2006. "Vinculan a un agente con narcos y polleros." *El Mañana de Matamoros,* February 7, online edition.

El Mañana de Nuevo Laredo. 1998. "Rescatan a quince ilegales." *El Mañana de Nuevo Laredo,* March 31.

El Sol de Irapuato. 2005. "Reportan a policía finca de posible pollero con ilegales." *El Sol de Irapuato,* April 28, online edition.

Embassy of the United States in Mexico. 2008. "U.S.-Mexico at a Glance: Trade at a Glance." Mexico City: United States Department of State. http://www.usembassy-mexico.gov/eng/eataglance_trade.html (accessed March 30, 2008).

Emmerich, Gustavo Ernesto. 2003. "México–Estados Unidos: Frontera eficiente, pero no abierta." *Frontera Norte* 15 (29): 7–34.

Eschbach, Karl, Jacqueline Hagan, and Néstor Rodríguez. 2001. "Causes and Trends in Migrant Deaths on the U.S.-Mexico Border, 1985–1998." Working Paper Series No. 1–4. Houston: University of Houston, Center for Immigration Research.

——. 2003. "Deaths during Undocumented Migration: Trends and Policy Implications in the New Era of Homeland Security." Paper presented at the 26th Annual National Legal Conference on Immigration and Refugee Policy in Washington, DC. http://www.uh.edu/cir/Deaths_during_migration.pdf (accessed July 19, 2006).

Escobar Latapí, Agustín. 1999. "Utilidad, potencial y limitaciones de la Encuesta sobre Migración en la Frontera Norte de México (EMIF), desde la perspectiva de un antropólogo interesado en la migración." *Migración internacional: Boletín editado por el Consejo Nacional de Población* 3 (9): 14–16. Special edition "Comentarios a la Encuesta sobre Migración en la Frontera Norte de México."

Espinosa, Raúl. 1998. "Guerra a los 'pateros'." *El Mañana de Matamoros,* March 6.

European Communities. 2007. *European Social Fund: 50 Years Investing in People.* Brussels. http://ec.europa.eu/employment_ social/esf/docs/50th_anniversary_book_en.pdf (accessed January 4, 2009).

Feldman, Andreas, and Jorge Durand. 2008. "Mortandad en la frontera." *Migración y desarrollo* 10:11–36. English-language version, http://www.migracionydesarrollo.org/.

Figueroa, Carlos. 1998. "60 mdd ganaron en 1997 *polleros* que operan entre Tamaulipas y Texas." *La Jornada,* February 10. Photocopy from news-clip file, Centro de Estudios Fronterizos y Promoción de los Derechos Humanos in Reynosa, Tamaulipas.

Foley, Neil. 1997. *The White Scourge: Mexicans, Blacks, and Poor Whites in Texas Cotton Culture.* Berkeley: University of California Press.

Fountain, John W., and Jim Yardley. 2002. "Skeletons Tell Tale of Gamble by Immigrants." *New York Times,* October 16, online edition.

Fragomen, Austin T. Jr. 1997. "The Illegal Immigration Reform and Immigrant Responsibility Act of 1996: An Overview." *International Migration Review* 31 (2): 438–60.

Frontera Norte-Sur. 2003. "Los Zetas: Armed Branch of Gulf Cartel Extorts Nuevo Laredo Businesses and Underworld." *Frontera Norte-Sur,* June 16, online synopsis of news reports published about the U.S.-Mexico border, Center for Latin American and Border Studies of New Mexico State University.

Fuentes, Jezmin, Henry L'Esperance, Raúl Pérez, and Caitlin White. 2007. "Impacts of U.S. Immigration Policies on Migration Behavior." In *Impacts of Border Enforcement on Mexican Migration: The View from Sending Communities,* ed. Wayne A. Cornelius and Jessa M. Lewis, 53–73. San Diego, CA: Center for Comparative Immigration Studies, University of California, San Diego.

Galarza, Ernesto. 1964. *Merchants of Labor: The Mexican Bracero Story: An Account of the Managed Migration of Mexican Farm Workers in California, 1942–1960.* Charlotte, NC: McNally and Loftin.

Galtung, Johan. 1969. "Violence, Peace, and Peace Research." *Journal of Peace Research* 6 (3): 167–91.

——. 1990. "Cultural Violence." *Journal of Peace Research* 27 (3): 291–305.

Gamio, Manuel. 1930. *Mexican Immigration to the United States: A Study of Human Migration and Adjustment.* Chicago: University of Chicago Press.

——. 2002. *El inmigrante mexicano: La historia de su vida: Entrevistas completas, 1926–1927,* ed. Devra Weber, Roberto Melvilla, and Juan Vicente Palerm. Mexico City: Board of Regents of the University of California and Miguel Ángel Porrúa.

Gans, Herbert J. 2003. *Democracy and the News.* New York: Oxford University Press.

García, Juan R. 1996. *Mexicans in the Midwest, 1900–1932.* Tucson: University of Arizona Press.

García, Juan Ramón. 1980. *Operation Wetback: The Mass Deportation of Mexican Undocumented Workers in 1954.* Westport, CT: Greenwood Press.

García, Onésimo. 1998. "Pateros fueron capturados por agentes policiacos." *El Bravo,* March 25.

Garrido, Ernie J. 2001. "INS Inspectors' Arraignments Set." *Brownsville Herald,* June 13, A3.

Gathmann, Christina. 2004. "The Effects of Enforcement on Illegal Markets: Evidence from Migrant Smuggling along the Southwestern Border." Discussion Paper No. 1004, January. Bonn, Germany: Institute for the Study of Labor.

Gaytán, Seidy, Evelyn Lucío, Fawad Shaiq, and Anjanette Urdanivia. 2007. "The Contemporary Migration Process." In *Impacts of Border Enforcement on Mexican Migration: The View from Sending Communities,* ed. Wayne A. Cornelius and Jessa M.

Lewis, 33–51. San Diego: Center for Comparative Immigration Studies at the University of California, San Diego.

Genicot, Garance, and Sarah Senesky. 2004. "Determinants of Migration and 'Coyote' Use among Undocumented Mexican Migrants to the U.S." Paper presented at the 9th Annual Meeting of the Society of Labor Economists, April 30, San Antonio, Texas.

Geyer, Robert R. 2000. *Exploring European Social Policy.* Cambridge, UK: Polity Press.

Gómez de Silva, Guido. 2001. *El diccionario breve de mexicanismos.* Mexico City: Academia Mexicana de la Lengua and Fondo de Cultura Económica. http://www.academia.org. mx/dbm/DICAZ/c.htm (accessed June 21, 2005).

Gómez Quintero, Natalia. 2005. "SRE: Crece violencia fronteriza por 'polleros.'" *El Universal,* August 30, 1.

González, Daniel. 2003. "Gangs Are Menacing 'Coyotes,' Immigrants." *Arizona Republic,* August 17, online edition.

González, Rocío, and Laura Gómez. 2007. "*Coyotes*, ganones con hortalizas de los productores de Tláhuac." *La Jornada,* February 7, online edition.

Granovetter, Mark. 1985. "Economic Action and Social Structure: The Problem of Embeddedness." *American Journal of Sociology* 91 (3): 481–510.

———. 1990. "The Old and the New Economic Sociology: A History and Agenda." In *Beyond the Marketplace: Rethinking Economy and Society,* ed. R. Friedland and A. F. Robertson, 89–112. New York: Aldine de Gruyter.

Grebler, Leo. 1965. *Mexican Immigration to the United States: The Record and Its Implications: Mexican American Study Project,* Advance Report 2. Los Angeles: Division of Research, Graduate School of Business Administration, University of California, Los Angeles.

Grieco, Elizabeth. 2003. *The Foreign Born from Mexico in the United States.* Washington, DC: Migration Policy Institute.

Grieco, Elizabeth, and Brian Ray. 2004. "Mexican Immigrants in the U.S. Labor Force." *Migration Information Source* (March). http://www.migrationinformation.org/ USfocus/print.cfm?ID=206 (accessed March 12, 2007).

Grupo Reforma. 2004. "Retan a Migración polleros de Coahuila." *El Norte,* April 4, online edition.

Guerrero, Héctor. 2004. "Alcanza impunidad 98.4% en delitos: Presidencia." *Noticiero Televisa,* July 15. http://www.esmas.com/noticierostelevisa/mexico/377994.html (accessed February 11, 2005).

Hagan, Jacqueline. 2008. *Migration Miracle: Faith, Hope, and Meaning on the Undocumented Journey.* Cambridge: Harvard University Press.

Halsell, Grace. 1978. *The Illegals.* Briarcliff Manor, NY: Stein and Day.

Hanson, Gordon, Antonio Spilimbergo, and Raymond Robertson. 2002. "Does Border Enforcement Protect U.S. Workers from Illegal Immigration?" *Review of Economics and Statistics* 84 (1): 73–92.

Harmon, Dave. 1999. "Don't Ask, Don't Tell: Austin's Red Hot Economy Relies Heavily on Illegal Immigrants." *Austin-American Statesman,* December 5, online edition.

Harris, Marvin. 1979. *Cultural Materialism: The Struggle for a Science of Culture.* New York: Random House.

Hart, Lianne. 2007. "Driver Gets Life in Prison in Deadly Human Smuggling Case." *Los Angeles Times,* January 19, online edition.

Hastings, Karen, and Julia Preston. 2006. "Threat of Terrorist Crossings Is Stressed at Border Hearing." *New York Times,* July 8, online edition.

Hegstrom, Edward. 2001. "Local INS Sting Yields 21 Arrests for Smuggling." *Houston Chronicle,* May 15, online edition.

Hellman, Judith Adler. 1994. *Mexican Lives.* New York: The New Press.

Hernández-León, Rubén. 2008. *Metropolitan Migrants: The Migration of Urban Mexicans to the United States.* Berkeley: University of California Press.

Hernández-León, Rubén, and Víctor Zúñiga. 2002. "Mexican Immigrant Communities in the South and Social Capital: The Case of Dalton, Georgia." Working Paper No. 64. La Jolla: Center for Comparative Immigration Studies, University of California, San Diego.

Hernández Navarro, Luis. 2004. "To Die a Little: Migration and Coffee in Mexico and Central America." *Counterpunch,* December 15. http://www.counterpunch.org/navarro12152004.html (accessed June 5, 2008).

Herrera-Sobek, María. 1993. *Northward Bound: The Mexican Immigrant Experience in Ballad and Song.* Bloomington: Indiana University Press.

Heyman, Josiah McC. 1995. "Putting Power in the Anthropology of Bureaucracy: The Immigration and Naturalization Service at the Mexico–United States Border." *Current Anthropology* 36 (2): 261–87.

———. 1998. "State Effects on Labor Exploitation: The INS and Undocumented Immigrants at the Mexico–United States Border." *Critique of Anthropology* 18 (2): 157–80.

———. 1999a. "State Escalation of Force: A Vietnam/U.S.-Mexico Border Analogy." In *States and Illegal Practices,* ed. Josiah McC. Heyman, 285–314. Oxford, UK: Berg.

———. 1999b. "Why Interdiction? Immigration Control at the United States–Mexican Border." *Regional Studies* 33 (7): 619–30.

Hill, Gladwin. 1954. "Two Every Minute across the Border: Mexican 'Wetbacks' Continue to Invade U.S. in an Unending—and Uncontrolled—Stream." *New York Times Sunday Magazine,* January 31, 13+.

Hing, Bill Ong. 2004. *Defining America through Immigration Policy.* Philadelphia: Temple University Press.

Hoffman, Abraham. 1974. *Unwanted Mexican Americans in the Great Depression: Repatriation Pressures, 1929–1939.* Tucson: University of Arizona Press.

House Committee on Homeland Security. 2006. *A Line in the Sand: Confronting the Threat on the Southwest Border.* Prepared by the Majority Staff of the House Committee on Homeland Security, Investigations Subcommittee, Michael T. McCaul, Chairman. Washington, DC.

Houston Chronicle. 1987. "INS Agents Reviewing Files of Food Chain in San Antonio," October 24, Section 1, 16.

———. 1988. "9 Arrested for Allegedly Selling Fake Paperwork to Illegal Aliens," December 9, A34.

———. 1999. "Strangulation Investigated," October 9, 3 Star edition, Section A, 36.

———. 2006. "Men Sentenced for Smuggling Immigrants aboard Yachts," December 9, online edition.

Instituto Nacional de Estadística, Geografía e Informática. 2008. "Banco de Información Económica: Industria Maquiladora de Exportación: Indicadores Mensuales." Aguascalientes, AG. http://dgcnesyp.inegi.gob.mx/cgi-win/bdieintsi.exe/NIVJ15000200 0300050005#ARBOL?c=1414 (accessed March 30, 2008).

International Boundary and Water Commission. 2004. International Bridges and Border Crossings: United States Names. El Paso, Texas. http://www.ibwc.state.gov/Bridge_Border_Crossings_.pdf (accessed May 24, 2006).

———. 2006. Rio Grande Flow Conditions. http://www.ibwc.state.gov/wad/flowdata.htm (accessed June 9, 2006).

———. 2007. Rio Grande: Stage and Discharge Charts. http://www.ibwc.state.gov/Water_ Data/rtdata.htm (accessed June 8, 2007).

Ireland, Patrick R. 1995. "Migration, Free Movement, and Immigrant Integration in the EU: A Bifurcated Policy Response." In *European Social Policy: Between Fragmentation and Integration,* ed. Stephan Leibfried and Paul Pierson, 231–66. Washington, DC: Brookings Institution.

Johnson, Benjamin Heber. 2003. *Revolution in Texas: How a Forgotten Rebellion and Its Bloody Suppression Turned Mexicans into Americans.* New Haven: Yale University Press.

Johnson, E. H. 2001. "South Texas Plains." In *Handbook of Texas Online,* ed. General Libraries of the University of Texas, Austin, and the Texas State Historical Association. Austin: Texas State Historical Association. http://www.tsha.utexas.edu/handbook/ online/articles/SS/ryslr.html (accessed June 12, 2006).

Jordan, Terry G., with John L. Bean Jr. and William M. Holmes. 1984. *Texas: A Geography.* Boulder, CO: Westview Press.

Kelley, David H. 1955. "Quetzalcoatl and His Coyote Origins." *El México antiguo: Revista internacional de arqueología* 8: 397–416.

Kilborn, Peter T. 1992. "Counterfeiters Prosper: Law Fails to Protect and Curb Migrants." *New York Times,* October 25, E2.

Kimball, Ann, Yesenia Acosta, and Rebecca Dames. 2007. "Impacts of U.S. Immigration Policies on Migration Behavior." In *Mayan Journeys: The New Migration from Yucatán to the United States,* ed. Wayne Cornelius, David Fitzgerald, and Pedro Lewin Fischer, 91–113. La Jolla: Center for Comparative Immigration Studies, University of California, San Diego.

King, Martin Luther Jr. 1963. *Why We Can't Wait.* New York: Harper and Row.

King, Peter H. 2007. "Immigrants' Journey Took a Deadly Turn." *Los Angeles Times,* March 18, online edition.

Klinenberg, Eric. 2002. *Heat Wave: A Social Autopsy of Disaster in Chicago.* Chicago: University of Chicago Press.

Koestler, Fred. 2002. "Operation Wetback." *Handbook of Texas Online.* Austin: Texas State Historical Association. http://www.tshaonline.org/handbook/online/articles/OO/pqo1. html (accessed June 4, 2008).

Kohler, Gernot. 1978. "Global Apartheid." World Order Models Project, Working Paper No. 7. New York: Institute for World Order.

———. 1995. "The Three Meanings of Global Apartheid: Empirical, Normative, and Existential." *Alternatives* 20: 403–13.

Kolker, Claudia. 1999. "Town Speaks the Language of Its People." *Los Angeles Times,* August 13, online edition.

Krissman, Fred. 2000. "Immigrant Labor Recruitment: U.S. Agribusiness and Undocumented Migration from Mexico." In *Immigration for a New Century: Multidisciplinary Perspectives,* ed. Nancy Foner, Rubén Rumbaut, and Steven J. Gold, 277–300. New York: Russell Sage Foundation.

Kyle, David. 2000. *Transnational Peasants: Migrations, Networks, and Ethnicity in Andean Ecuador.* Baltimore: Johns Hopkins University Press.

Kyle, David, and Christina A. Siracusa. 2005. "Seeing the State Like a Migrant: Why So Many Non-criminals Break Immigration Laws." In *Illicit Flows and Criminal Things: States, Borders, and the Other Side of Globalization,* ed. Willem van Schendel and Itty Abraham, 153–76. Bloomington: Indiana University Press.

Laczko, Frank. 2002. "Human Trafficking: The Need for Better Data." *Migration Information Source*. November, online newsletter. Washington, DC: Migration Policy Institute. http://www.migrationinformation.org/Feature/display.cfm?id=66 (accessed June 15, 2005).

Lamadrid, Enrique R. 1995. "The Rogue's Progress: Journeys of the Pícaro from Oral Tradition to Contemporary Chicano Literature of New Mexico." *MELUS* 20 (2): 15–34.

Larousse Editorial. 1998. *Gran diccionario usual de la lengua española*. Barcelona, Spain.

Latin American Working Group. n.d. "Immigrant Deaths, Fiscal Year 2005." Washington, DC. http://www.lawg.org/countries/mexico/deaths_2005.htm#top (accessed July 2, 2008).

Lee, Tiane L., and Susan T. Fiske. 2006. "Not an Out-group, Not Yet an In-Group: Immigrants in the Stereotype Content Model." *International Journal of Intercultural Relations* 30 (6): 751–68.

Leiken, Robert S., and Steven Brooke. 2006. "A Quantitative Analysis of Terrorism and Immigration: An Initial Exploration." *Terrorism and Political Violence* 18:503–21.

Lévi-Strauss, Claude. 1963. *Structural Anthropology*. New York: Basic Books.

Lewis, Sasha Gregory. 1979. *Slave Trade Today: American Exploitation of Illegal Aliens*. Boston: Beacon Press.

Lezon, Dale. 2005. "Rider Tells a Stark Story of Fatal Trip: Witness Says Williams Ignored Immigrants' Cries from inside Trailer." *Houston Chronicle*, March 17, online edition.

Lezon, Dale, and Harvey Rice. 2005. "Trucker Spared Death—for Now: Jury Finds Him Guilty of Lesser Counts; a Mistrial Is Declared on the 20 Tougher Ones." *Houston Chronicle*, March 23, online edition.

Liñan, Francisco. 2003. "Cae presunta líder de banda de polleros." *Reforma*, June 16, online edition.

Lipton, Eric. 2005. "Hurdles for High-Tech Efforts to Track Who Crosses Borders." *New York Times*, August 10, online edition.

Loh, Jules. 1985. "Aliens Smuggled over Border Come from All Parts of World." *Houston Chronicle*, December 1, Section 3, 10.

López, Henry, Rob Oliphant, and Edith Tejeda. 2007. "U.S. Settlement Behavior and Labor Market Participation." In *Impacts of Border Enforcement on Mexican Migration: The View from the Sending Communities*, ed. Wayne A. Cornelius and Jessa Lewis, 75–96. La Jolla, CA: Center for Comparative Immigration Studies, University of California, San Diego.

López, Robert J., Rich Connell, and Chris Kraul. 2005. "Gang Uses Deportation to Its Advantage to Flourish in U.S." *Los Angeles Times*, October 30, online edition.

López, Sonny. 2003a. "Consulate Halts Issuing of Visas." *Dallas Morning News*, June 19, online edition.

———. 2003b. "Consulate in Juárez Reopens after Visa Woes." *Dallas Morning News*, June 20, online edition.

López, Viridiana. 2006. "Aumentan los polleros sus tarifas." *Cambio Michoacán*, July 21, online edition.

López Castro, Gustavo. 1998. "Coyotes and Alien Smuggling." In *Binational Study: Migration Between Mexico and the United States*, vol. 3, *Research Reports and Background Materials*, 965–74. Mexico City and Washington, DC: Mexican Ministry of Foreign Relations and U.S. Commission on Immigration Reform.

Lozano, Juan. 2006. "Truck Driver in Immigrant Deaths 'Vile, Heartless.'" Associated Press, November 27, online edition.

MacCormack, John. 1997. "Patrols Beefed Up on Texas Border." *San Antonio Express-News*, August 26, 1A.

Marable, Manning. 1991. *Race, Reform, and Rebellion: The Second Reconstruction in Black America, 1945–1990.* Jackson: University Press of Mississippi.

Maril, Robert Lee. 2004. *Patrolling Chaos: The U.S. Border Patrol in Deep South Texas.* Lubbock: Texas Tech University Press.

Martin, Gary. 2004. "Sexual Slavery in Texas Cited at D.C. Hearing." *San Antonio Express-News,* July 8, online edition.

Massey, Douglas S. 2007. *Categorically Unequal: The American Stratification System.* New York: Russell Sage Foundation.

Massey, Douglas S., Rafael Alarcón, Jorge Durand, and Humberto González. 1987. *Return to Aztlán: The Social Process of International Migration from Western Mexico.* Berkeley: University of California Press.

Massey, Douglas S., Jorge Durand, and Nolan J. Malone. 2002. *Beyond Smoke and Mirrors: Mexican Immigration in an Era of Economic Integration.* New York: Russell Sage Foundation.

McCaa, Robert. 2003. "Missing Millions: The Demographic Costs of the Mexican Revolution." *Mexican Studies/Estudios Mexicanos* 19 (2): 367–400.

McCay, Robert R. 1981. "The Federal Deportation Campaign in Texas: Mexican Deportation from the Lower Rio Grande Valley during the Great Depression." *Borderlands* 5 (1): 95–120.

———. 2001. "Mexican Americans and Repatriation." *Handbook of Texas Online.* Austin: Texas State Historical Association. http://www.tshaonline.org/handbook/online/articles/MM/pqmyk.html (accessed June 3, 2008).

McGraw, Al. 2003. "The Origins of the Camino Real in Texas." *Texas Almanac,* ed. Mary G. Ramos. http://www.texasalmanac.com/history/highlights/camino/ (accessed January 4, 2009).

McKellar, Sarah S. 1935. "Br'er Coyote." In *Puro mexicano,* ed. J. Frank Dobie, 101–6. Austin: Texas Folk-Lore Society.

McNab, W. Henry, and Peter E. Avers. 1994. *Ecological Subregions of the United States.* Washington, DC: United States Forest Service. http://www.fs.fed.us/land/pubs/ecoregions/ (accessed June 6, 2006).

McWilliams, Carey. 1990 [1948]. *North from Mexico: The Spanish-Speakiing People of the United States.* Westport, CT: Greenwood Press.

Meléndez, Theresa. 1982. "Coyote: Towards a Definition of a Concept." *Aztlán* 13:295–307.

Méndez Martínez, Georgina. 2001. "Los 'migra-pateros' se declaran inocentes." *El Mañana,* June 14, B1.

Mestries Benquet, Francis. 2003. "Crisis cafetalera y migración internacional en Veracruz." *Migraciones Internacionales* 2 (2): 121–48.

Metz, Leon C. 2004. "Rio Grande." In *Handbook of Texas Online,* General Libraries of the University of Texas, Austin, and Texas State Historical Association. Austin: Texas State Historical Association. http://www.tsha.utexas.edu/handbook/online/articles/RR/rnr5.html (accessed June 10, 2006).

Millán, Daniel. 2003. "Denuncian a pollero." *Reforma,* May 20, online edition.

Miller, Mary, and Karl Taube. 1993. *The Gods and Symbols of Ancient Mexico and the Maya: An Illustrated Dictionary of Mesoamerican Religion.* London, UK: Thames and Hudson.

Miller, Tom. 1981. *On the Border: Portraits of America's Southwestern Frontier.* Tucson: University of Arizona Press.

Minaya, Zeke. 2005. "Smuggling Dispute Ends in Men's Death: Fatal Shooting Shows Increasing Violence in Human Trafficking Trade." *Houston Chronicle,* May 21, online edition.

Miró, Ramón. 2003. *Organized Crime and Terrorist Activity in Mexico, 1999–2002.* Washington, DC: Federal Research Division, Library of Congress.

Moctezuma, Miguel. 2000. "El circuito migrante Sain Alto, Zacatecas–Oakland, California." *Comercio Exterior* 50 (5): 396–405.

Montejano, David. 1987. *Anglos and Mexicans in the Making of Texas, 1836–1986.* Austin: University of Texas Press.

Mora Torres, Juan. 2001. *The Making of the Mexican Border: The State, Capitalism, and Society in Nuevo León, 1848–1910.* Austin: University of Texas Press.

Morales, Patricia. 1981, 1987. *Indocumentados mexicanos: Causas y razones de la migración laboral.* Mexico City: Editorial Grijalbo.

Mural. 2005. "Rescate en el desierto." *Mural* (Guadalajara, Jalisco), April 21, 2A.

Negrete Lares, Ángeles. 2001. "Otro inspector del INS acusado de patero." *El Nuevo Heraldo,* June 9, 1.

Nelson, Eugene. 1972. *Bracero.* Culver City, CA: Peace Press.

Nevins, Joseph. 2002. *Operation Gatekeeper: The Rise of the "Illegal Alien" and the Making of the U.S.-Mexico Boundary.* New York: Routledge.

———. 2003. "Thinking Out of Bounds: A Critical Analysis of Academic and Human Rights Writings on Migrant Deaths in the U.S.-Mexico Border Region." *Migraciones Internacionales* 2 (2): 171–90.

———. 2005. "A Beating Worse Than Death: Imagining and Contesting Violence on the U.S.-Mexico Borderlands." *Ameriquests* 2 (2). http://ejournals.library.vanderbilt.edu/ameriquests/index.php (accessed August 25, 2006).

———. 2006. "Boundary Enforcement and National Security in an Age of Global Apartheid." *Dissident Voice,* July 18. http://www.dissidentvoice.org/July06/Nevins18.htm (accessed October 13, 2006).

———. 2008. *Dying to Live: A Story of U.S. Immigration in an Age of Global Apartheid.* San Francisco, CA: City Lights Books.

New York Times. 1954a. "Reds Slip into U.S., Congress Warned: Immigration Service Says 100 Present, Ex-Members Sneak in Daily from Mexico," February 10, 23.

———. 1954b. "Rio Grande Drowns Many of Wetbacks," August 12, 9.

———. 1987. "Excerpts from Regulations to Carry Out New Law on Aliens," January 20, A16.

Newman, Philip M. 1965. "The Law and Its Administration: Profile of an Immigrant's Case. In *Mexican Immigration to the United States: The Record and Its Implications,* by Leo Grebler, 13–16. Los Angeles: Division of Research, Graduate School of Business Administration, University of California, Los Angeles.

Ngai, Mae M. 2007. "A New Green Card Deal." *The Nation,* July 9, 8.

Nordheimer, Jon. 1988. "Aliens Rush to Farmhand's Amnesty." *New York Times,* July 17, 14.

Notimex. 2003a. "Operan en la frontera 80 bandas de 'pateros.'" *El Mañana de Nuevo Laredo,* May 18, online edition.

———. 2003b. "Sobreviviente del tráiler narra el viaje en que murieron 19 migrantes." *La Jornada,* May 18, online edition.

Olea, Nicolás. 1995. "Mercado de futuros del camarón blanco." *Panorama Acuícola* 1 (September–October). http://www.panoramaacuicola.com/noticia.php?art_clave=711 (accessed March 12, 2007).

Olivier, Guilhem. 1999. "Huhuecóyotl, "coyote viejo," el músico transgresor, ¿dios de los otomíes o avatar de Tezcatlipoca?" *Estudios de Cultura Náhuatl* 30:113–32.

———. 2003. *Mockeries and Metamorphoses of an Aztec God: Tezcatlipoca, Lord of the Smoking Mirror.* Boulder: University Press of Colorado.

Orrenius, Pia M. 1999. "The Role of Family Networks, Coyote Prices, and the Rural Economy in Migration from Western Mexico." Federal Reserve Bank of Dallas, Working Paper 99–10.

Paredes, Américo. 1958. *With His Pistol in His Hand: A Border Ballad and Its Hero.* Austin: University of Texas Press.

———. 1993. *Folklore and Culture on the Texas-Mexican Border.* Austin: CMAS Books, Center for Mexican American Studies, University of Texas, Austin.

Passel, Jeffrey S. 2005. *Estimates of the Size and Characteristics of the Undocumented Population.* Washington, DC: Pew Hispanic Center.

———. 2006. *The Size and Characteristics of the Unauthorized Migrant Population in the U.S.: Estimates Based on the March 2005 Current Population Survey.* Washington, DC: Pew Hispanic Center.

Peck, Gunther. 2000. *Reinventing Free Labor: Padrones and Immigrant Workers in the North American West, 1880–1930.* New York: Cambridge University Press.

Peñalosa, Fernando. 1992. "Los cuentos de animales en la tradición oral maya del sur de Mesoamérica: Un análisis preliminar." *Folklore Americano* 54:45–69.

Pérez, Ramón. 1991. *Diary of an Undocumented Immigrant.* Houston, TX: Arte Público Press.

Pew Hispanic Center. 2006. "Estimates of the Unauthorized Migrant Population for States Based on the March 2005 CPS." Fact Sheet. Washington, DC.

Phillips, Julie A., and Douglas S. Massey. 1999. "The New Labor Market: Immigrants and Wages after IRCA." *Demography* 36 (2): 233–46.

———. 2000. "Engines of Immigration: Stocks of Human and Social Capital in Mexico." *Social Science Quarterly* 81 (1): 33–48.

Pinkerton, James. 2005. "Corruption Crosses the Border with Agent Bribes." *Houston Chronicle,* May 30, online edition.

Polaski, Sandra. 2004. "Jobs, Wages, and Household Income." In *NAFTA's Promise and Reality: Lessons from Mexico for the Hemisphere,* ed. John J. Audley, Demetrios G. Papademetriou, Sandra Polaski, and Scott Vaughan, 11–38. Washington, DC: Carnegie Endowment for International Peace.

Pomfret, John. 2006. "Bribery at Border Worries Officials: Mexican Smugglers Intensify Efforts to Entice U.S. Agents." *Washington Post,* July 15, A1.

Portes, Alejandro. 1974. "Return of the Wetback." *Society* 11 (March–April): 40–49.

———. 1994. "The Informal Economy and Its Paradoxes." In *The Handbook of Economic Sociology,* ed. Neal J. Smelser and Richard Swedberg, 426–49. Princeton: Princeton University Press.

———. 1995. "Economic Sociology and the Sociology of Immigration: A Conceptual Overview." In *The Economic Sociology of Immigration: Essays on Networks, Ethnicity, and Entrepreneurship,* ed. Alejandro Portes, 1–41. New York: Russell Sage Foundation.

———. 1996. "Transnational Communities: Their Emergence and Significance in the Contemporary World-System." In *Latin America in the World Economy,* ed. Roberto Patricio Korzeniewicz and William C. Smith, 151–68. Westport, CT: Greenwood Press.

Portes, Alejandro, and Julia Sensenbrenner. 1993. "Embeddedness and Immigration: Notes on the Social Determinants of Economic Action." *American Journal of Sociology* 98 (6): 1320–50.

Pozos, Fernando. 2003. "El laberinto de la política salarial en México." In *La vulnerabilidad laboral del modelo exportador en México,* ed. Fernando Pozos, 191–223. Guadalajara, JA: Universidad de Guadalajara.

Preston, Julia. 2006. "Low Wage Workers from Mexico Dominate Latest Great Wave of Immigrants." *New York Times,* December 19, online edition.

Prieto Pérez, Tomás. 2005. "Capturan a dos 'polleros' a punto de viajar con 36." *Periódico AM* (León, Guanajuato), February 23, online edition.

Raat, W. Dirk. 1996. *Mexico and the United States: Ambivalent Vistas,* Second edition. Athens: University of Georgia Press.

Ramírez, Catherine S. 2005. "Pachucos and Pachucas." *Oxford Encyclopedia of Latinos and Latinas in the United States,* ed. Suzanne Oboler and Deena J. González. New York: Oxford University Press. http://www.oxford-latinos.com/entry?entry=t199.e698 (accessed March 14, 2007).

Ramos, Jorge. 2005. *Morir en el intento: La peor tragedia de inmigrantes en la historia de los Estados Unidos.* New York: HarperCollins

Ramos Aguirre, Francisco. 1994. *Historia del corrido en la frontera tamaulipeca (1844–1994).* Ciudad Victoria, TM: Fondo Nacional para la Cultura y las Artes.

Reisler, Mark. 1976. *By the Sweat of Their Brow: Mexican Immigrant Labor in the United States, 1900–1940.* Westport, CT: Greenwood Press.

Reyes, Belinda I., Hans P. Johnson, and Richard Van Swearingen. 2002. *Holding the Line? The Effect of Recent Border Build-up on Unauthorized Immigration.* San Francisco: Public Policy Institute of California.

Rice, Harvey. 2004. "Officers See More Violence: The Business of Immigrant Smuggling Has New Challenge with Weapons." *Houston Chronicle,* October 29, online edition.

——. 2005. "Judge Won't Allow Smuggler to Change Plea." *Houston Chronicle,* January 28, online edition.

——. 2006a. "Defense Grills Key Witness in Driver's Retrial." *Houston Chronicle,* October 24, online edition.

——. 2006b. "3 Survivors Testify for Defense in Truck Deaths Trial." *Houston Chronicle,* November 15, online edition.

Richardson, Chad, and Rosalva Resendiz. 2006. *On the Edge of the Law: Culture, Labor, and Deviance on the South Texas Border.* Austin: University of Texas Press.

Richmond, Anthony H. 1994. *Global Apartheid: Refugees, Racism, and the New World Order.* Toronto, ON: Oxford University Press.

Robertson, Raymond. 2005. "Has NAFTA Increased Labor Market Integration between the United States and Mexico?" *World Bank Economic Review* 19 (3): 425–48.

Rodríguez, Erik. 2002. "Kyle Clan Accused of Smuggling Migrants." *Austin-American Statesman,* May 24, A1.

Rodríguez, Lori. 1987. "Employers, Illegal Aliens Trapped in a Dilemma." *Houston Chronicle,* March 23, Section 1, 8.

Rodríguez, Néstor. 1996. "The Battle for the Border: Notes on Autonomous Migration, Transnational Communities, and the State." *Social Justice* 23 (3): 21–37.

——. 2004. "Workers Wanted: Employer Recruitment of Immigrant Labor." *Work and Occupations* 31 (4): 453–73.

Rodríguez, Néstor, and Rogelio Núñez. 1986. "An Exploration of Factors That Contribute to Differentiation between Chicanos and Indocumentados." In *Mexican Immigrants and Mexican Americans,* ed. Harley L. Browning and Rodolfo O. de la Garza, 138–56. Austin: CMAS Books, Center for Mexican American Studies, University of Texas, Austin.

Romero, Enrique. 2004. "Tiroteo de policías contra 'polleros.'" *Tabasco Hoy,* November 8, online edition.

Rosenbaum, Robert J. 1998 [1981]. *Mexicano Resistance in the Southwest.* Dallas, TX: Southern Methodist University Press.

Ross, Robert J. S., and Kent Trachte. 1990. *Global Capitalism: The New Leviathan.* Albany: State University of New York Press.

Rothe, Dawn, and Stephen L. Muzzatti. 2004. "Enemies Everywhere: Terrorism, Moral Panic, and U.S. Civil Society." *Critical Criminology* 12:327–50.

Rouse, Roger. 1991. "Mexican Migration and the Social Space of Postmodernism. *Diaspora* 1 (1): 8–24.

Rozemberg, Hernán. 2004. "Public Asked to Fight Slavery." *San Antonio Express-News,* November 30, online edition.

Rumbaut, Rubén, and Walter Ewing. 2007. *The Myth of Immigrant Criminality and the Paradox of Assimilation: Incarceration Rates among Native and Foreign-born Men.* Washington, DC: Immigration Policy Center.

Sahlins, Marshall. 1972. *Stone Age Economics.* Chicago: Aldine.

Salas, Carlos. 2003. "Integración económica, empleo y salarios en México." In *NAFTA y MERCOSUR: Procesos de apertura económica y trabajo,* ed. Enrique de la Garza Toledo and Carlos Salas, 55–75. Buenos Aires, Argentina: Consejo Latinoamericano de Ciencias Sociales.

Salas, Carlos, and Eduardo Zepeda. 2003. "Employment and Wages: Enduring the Costs of Liberalization and Economic Reform." In *Confronting Development: Assessing Mexico's Economic and Social Policy Challenges,* ed. Kevin J. Middlebrook and Eduardo Zepeda, 522–58. Stanford: Stanford University Press.

Saldierna, Georgina. 2003. "Reclaman ayuda a Derbez para detener a *pollero* que causó tragedia." *La Jornada,* May 21, online edition.

Samora, Julian. 1971. *Los Mojados: The Wetback Story.* South Bend, IN: University of Notre Dame Press.

San Antonio Express-News. 2006. "Legal Immigration Set Ludicrously Low," September 9, online edition.

Sánchez Venegas, Adolfo. 2007. "Denuncian que coyotes ocultan 5 millones de toneladas de maíz." *La Crónica de Hoy,* February 7, online edition.

Santamaría, Francisco J. 1983. *Diccionario de mejicanismos, cuarta edición, corregida y aumentada.* Mexico City: Editorial Porrúa.

Santos, Javier, and Gerardo Flores. 2007. "Productores de Jalisco se quejan por el desplome en el precio del frijol," *La Jornada,* February 12, online edition.

Saunders, Lyle, and Olen E. Leonard. 1976 [1951]. "The Wetback in the Lower Rio Grande Valley of Texas. Inter-American Occasional Papers VII." In *Mexican Migration to the United States.* New York: Arno Press.

Schiller, Dane. 1996a. "Smugglers' Shark Boats Thwart Coastline Patrols." *San Antonio Express-News,* July 22, 1A.

———. 1996b. "South Texas Brush Country Immigrants' Deathtrap." *San Antonio Express-News,* June 10, 1A.

———. 1997. "Border Patrol Seizes 290 in Raymondville." *San Antonio Express-News,* January 11, online edition.

———. 1998. "Judge Gives O.K. to Army Border Work." *San Antonio Express-News,* February 14, 1A.

———. 1999a. "Drones Tested for Spotting Smugglers." *San Antonio Express-News,* June 10, 7A.

———. 1999b. "Immigrant Smuggling Lands Couple in Prison." *San Antonio Express-News,* October 16, online edition.

———. 1999c. "Immigrant Smuggling Ring Busted." *San Antonio Express-News,* July 13, online edition.

———. 1999d. "Smuggling Ring Had Been a Raymondville Industry." *San Antonio Express-News,* July 15, online edition.

——. 2006. "A Deadline Is Looming on Passports." *San Antonio Express-News,* October 25, Page 1A.

Schiller, Dane, and Jesse Bogan. 2004. "Nine Dead, Two Survive Crash near Hidalgo." *San Antonio Express-News,* August 10, online edition.

Schlosser, Eric. 2001. *Fast Food Nation: The Dark Side of the All-American Meal.* Boston: Houghton Mifflin.

Schwartz, Marion. 1997. *A History of Dogs in the Early Americas.* New Haven: Yale University Press.

Scott, James C. 1985. *Weapons of the Weak: Everyday Forms of Peasant Resistance.* New Haven: Yale University Press.

——. 1990. *Domination and the Arts of Resistance: Hidden Transcripts.* New Haven: Yale University Press.

Scott, Robert, Carlos Salas, and Bruce Campbell. 2006. "Revisiting NAFTA: Still Not Working for North America's Workers." EPI Briefing Paper No. 173. Washington, DC: Economic Policy Institute.

Scruggs, Otey M. 1960. "The First Mexican Farm Labor Program." *Arizona and the West* 2 (4): 319–26.

——. 1963. "Texas and the Bracero Program, 1942–1947." *Pacific Historical Review* 32 (3): 251–64.

Secretaría de Educación Pública. 1994. *Animales fantásticos y más leyendas.* Mexico City.

Secretaría de Relaciones Exteriores. 2005a. *Guía del migrante mexicano.* Mexico City.

——. 2005b. "México y Estados Unidos establecen el Programa Oasis para proteger a los migrantes y procesar penalmente a traficantes y tratantes de personas." Press release. August 17.

Sedeno, David. 1986. "Living for a Cause: Stacey Merkt Spreads Hope, Help to Refugees." *Houston Chronicle,* June 1, Section 3, 13.

Seltzer, Nate, and George Kourous. 1998. "Immigration Law Enforcement and Human Rights Abuses." *Borderlines* 6 (9), online edition.

Sharma, Nandita. 2005. "Anti-Trafficking Rhetoric and the Making of a Global Apartheid." *NWSA Journal* 17 (3): 88–111.

——. 2006. "White Nationalism, Illegality, and Imperialism: Border Controls as Ideology." In *(En)gendering the War on Terror: War Stories and Camouflaged Politics,* ed. Krista Hunt and Kim Rygiel, 121–44. Aldereshot, UK: Ashgate.

Sharp, John. 1998. *Bordering the Future: Challenge and Opportunity in the Texas Border Region.* Austin: Texas Comptroller of Public Accounts. http://www.cpa.state.tx.us/border/border.html (accessed June 7, 2007).

Singer, Audrey, and Douglas S. Massey. 1998. "The Social Process of Undocumented Border Crossing among Mexican Migrants." *International Migration Review* 32 (3): 561–92.

Sinquin Fueillye, Evelyne. 2006. "La otra cara del dólar." In *Las mujeres en la migración: Testimonios, realidades y denuncias,* ed. Blanca Villaseñor Roca and José Ascensión Moreno Mena, 83–114. Mexicali, Baja California: Albergue del Desierto y Centro de Reintegración Familiar de Menores Migrantes.

Slayden, James L. 1921. "Some Observations on Mexican Immigration." *Annals of the American Academy of Political and Social Science* 93 (January): 121–26.

Spagat, Elliot. 2006. "Border Crackdown Fuels Smugglers' Boom." Associated Press, December 30. http://news.yahoo.com/s/ap/20061230/ap_on_re_us/border_smugglers (accessed January 7, 2007).

Spener, David. 2000. "The Logic and Contradictions of Intensified Border Enforcement in Texas." In *The Wall around the West: State Borders and Immigration Controls in North America and Europe,* ed. Peter Andreas and Timothy Snyder, 115–34. Lanham, MD: Rowman and Littlefield.

———. 2003a. "Controlling the Border in El Paso del Norte: Operation Blockade or Operation Charade?" In *Ethnography at the Border,* ed. Pablo Vila, 182–98. Minneapolis: University of Minnesota Press.

———. 2003b. "Narrativas del mal: El coyote mexicano en el drama del cruce fronterizo." In *Más allá de la ciudad letrada: Crónicas y espacios urbanos,* ed. Boris Muñoz and Silvia Spitta, 379–410. Pittsburgh, PA: Biblioteca de América.

———. 2008a. "El apartheid global, el coyotaje y el discurso de la migración clandestina: Distinciones entre violencia personal, estructural y cultural." *Migración y desarrollo* 10:127–56. English-language version, http://www.migracionydesarrollo.org/.

———. 2008b. "El eslabón perdido de la migración: El coyotaje en la frontera del sur de Texas y el noreste de México." In *Pobreza y migración internacional. El caso de México,* ed. Agustín Escobar Latapí, 365–417. Mexico City: Casa Chata.

Spener, David, and Kathleen Staudt. 1998. "Conclusion: Rebordering." In *The U.S.-Mexico Border: Transcending Divisions, Contesting Identities,* ed. David Spener and Kathleen Staudt, 233–57. Boulder, CO: Lynne Rienner.

Spota, Luis. 1948. *Murieron a mitad del río.* Mexico City: Talleres Gráficos de la Nación.

Stevenson, Mark. 2006. "'Mules' Sneaking More Drugs across Border." Associated Press, May 24, *Yahoo! News.*

Stevenson, Richard W. 1990. "Fight Is Intensified on Fake Documents for Aliens." *New York Times,* August 4, 1.

Taber, Robert. 2002 [1965]. *War of the Flea: The Classic Study of Guerrilla Warfare.* Dulles, VA: Brassey's.

Terán González, Irma. 1998. "Consignan a 'pateros'." *El Mañana de Reynosa,* March 21. Photocopy from news-clip file, Centro de Estudios Fronterizos y Promoción de los Derechos Humanos in Reynosa, Tamaulipas.

Texas Center for Border Economic Enterprise and Development. 2006. "Border Trade." Laredo: Texas A&M International University. http://texascenter.tamiu.edu/texcen_services/border_trade.asp (accessed June 6, 2006).

Texas Parks and Wildlife Department. 2005. "South Texas Wildlife Management: South Texas Vegetation." Austin. http://www.tpwd.state.tx.us/landwater/land/habitats/southtx_plain/vegetation/ (accessed June 9, 2006).

Texas State Historical Association. 2005. *Handbook of Texas On-Line.* Austin. http://www.tsha.utexas.edu/handbook/online/articles /view/PP/rup2.html (accessed March 16, 2005).

Texas Workforce Commission. 2006. "Labor Market Information and Other Data: Unemployment Rates." Austin. http://www.tracer2.com/cgi/dataanalysis/AreaSelection.asp?tableName=Labforce (accessed June 7, 2006).

Thomas, Jeffrey. 2006. "U.S. Determined To Fight Trafficking, Bush Says, Signing New Law." *Washington File of the Bureau of International Information Programs of the U.S. Department of State.* January 10. http://usinfo.state.gov/xarchives/display.html?p=washfile-english&y=2006&m=January&x=200601101742371CJsamohT0.7204553 (accessed May 27, 2007).

Thompson, E. P. 1964. *The Making of the English Working Class.* New York: Pantheon Books.

Torpey, John. 1998. "Coming and Going: On the State Monopolization of the Legitimate 'Means of Movement.'" *Sociological Theory* 16 (3): 239–59.

———. 2000. *The Invention of the Passport: Surveillance, Citizenship, and the State.* New York: Cambridge University Press.

Touraine, Alain. 1990. "The Idea of Revolution." *Theory, Culture, and Society* 7:121–41.

Transactional Records Access Clearinghouse. 2005. *Prosecution of Immigration Cases Surge in U.S. while Sentences Slump.* Syracuse, NY. http://trac.syr.edu/tracins/latest/131/ (accessed March 10, 2007).

Tutt, Bob. 1986. "Immigration: The Golden Door: Validating Who's Legal Is One of Many Problems." *Houston Chronicle,* October 19, Section 1, 24.

United Press International. 1986. "Border Search for 3 Libyans is Stepped-Up." *Houston Chronicle,* January 25, Section 1, 12.

United States Border Patrol. 2003. "Operation Rio Grande: August 25, 1997 to Present." PowerPoint presentation, McAllen sector.

United States Bureau of the Census. 2006. *State and County Quick Facts.* Washington, DC. http://quickfacts.census.gov/qfd/states/48000.html (accessed May 24, 2006).

———. 2008. "Trade in Goods (Imports, Exports and Trade Balance) with Mexico." Washington, DC. http://www.census.gov/foreign-trade/balance/c2010.html (accessed July 18, 2008).

United States Citizenship and Immigration Services. 2004. "Early Immigrant Inspection along the U.S./Mexican Border." Washington, DC. http://uscis.gov/graphics/aboutus/history/articles/MBTEXT.htm (accessed June 27, 2005).

———. n.d. "Historical Immigration and Naturalization Legislation: Legislation from 1981–1996." http://www.uscis.gov/files/nativedocuments/Legislation%20from%20 19811996.Pdf (accessed March 10, 2007).

United States Congress. 1996. *Illegal Immigration Reform and Immigrant Responsibility Act of 1996. Public Law 104–208.* Washington, DC. http://frwebgate.access.gpo.gov/cgi-bin/getdoc.cgi?dbname=104_cong_public_laws&docid=f:publ208.104.pdf (accessed March 10, 2007).

United States Customs and Border Protection. 2005. "Border Safety Initiative." Press release. September 9. http://www.cbp.gov/xp/cgov/border_security/border_patrol/safety_initiative.xml (accessed July 10, 2007).

United States Department of Homeland Security. 2004. *2004 Yearbook of Immigration Statistics.* Washington, DC.

———. 2006. "Defense In-Depth Strategy Applied Permanently in Laredo Sector: Grand Opening of New Checkpoint." *Customs and Border Protection Today* June–July. http://www.customs.gov/xp/CustomsToday/2006/jun_jul/other/new_checkpoint.xml (accessed August 26, 2006).

———. 2008. *2007 Yearbook of Immigration Statistics.* Washington, DC.

United States Department of Labor. 1918. *Annual Report of the Commissioner General of Immigration.* Washington, DC.

United States District Court, Eastern District of Tennessee at Winchester. 2001. "United States of America, Plaintiff, v. Tyson Foods, Inc." Winchester, TN.

United States Drug Enforcement Administration. 2001. "Statement by Donnie R. Marshall, Administrator, Drug Enforcement Administration, before the U.S. House of Representatives Committee on the Judiciary Subcommittee on Crime, March 29, 2001." Washington, DC. http://www.usdoj.gov/dea/pubs/cngrtest/ct032901.htm (accessed April 1, 2006).

United States Government Accountability Office. 2006. *Human Trafficking: Better Data, Strategy, and Reporting Needed to Enhance U.S. Antitrafficking Efforts Abroad.* Washington, DC.

United States Immigration and Naturalization Service. 1954. *1953 Annual Report of the U.S. Immigration and Naturalization Service.* Washington, DC.

——. 1993, 1994. *Statistical Yearbook of the Immigration and Naturalization Service.* Washington, DC.

United States Small Business Administration. 2004. "Small Business Size Standards Matched to North American Industry Classification System." Washington, DC. http://www.sba.gov/size/sizetable2002.html (accessed August 4, 2005).

Urrea, Luis Alberto. 2004. *The Devil's Highway: A True Story.* New York: Little, Brown, and Company.

Urry, John. 2000. "Mobile Sociology." *British Journal of Sociology* 51 (1): 185–203.

Valdez-Suiter, Elisabeth, Nancy Rosas-López, and Nayeli Pagaza. 2007. "Gender Differences." In *Impacts of Border Enforcement on Mexican Migration: The View from Sending Communities,* ed. Wayne A. Cornelius and Jessa M. Lewis, 97–114. San Diego: Center for Comparative Immigration Studies at the University of California, San Diego.

Valley Movement for Human Rights. 2005. *In Our Own Backyard: A Community Report on Human Rights Abuses in Texas' Rio Grande Valley.* Harlingen, TX. http://www.nnirr.org/news/reports/vmhr_report_esp.pdf (accessed July 19, 2006).

Van Schendel, Willem. 2005. "Spaces of Engagement: How Borderlands, Illegal Flows, and Territorial States Interlock." In *Illicit Flows and Criminal Things: States, Borders, and the Other Side of Globalization,* ed. Willem van Schendel and Itty Abraham, 38–65. Bloomington: Indiana University Press.

Vartabedian, Ralph, Richard A. Serrano, and Richard Marosi. 2006. "Rise in Bribery Tests Integrity of U.S. Border: From California to Texas, 200 Officials Indicted since 2004." *Los Angeles Times,* October 23, online edition.

Vásquez, Norberto. 2002. "Bosques, altamente exportables." *Revista Contralínea,* December 2. http://www.contralinea.com.mx/archivo/2002/c9/html/capitales/capitales02dic02.html (accessed June 21, 2005).

Vélez-Ibáñez, Carlos. 1988. "Networks of Exchange among Mexicans in the U.S. and Mexico: Local Level Mediating and International Transformations." *Urban Anthropology* 17 (1): 27–51.

——. 1996. *Border Visions: Mexican Cultures of the Southwest United Status.* Tucson: University of Arizona Press.

Vila, Pablo. 1998. "The Competing Meanings of the Label 'Chicano' in El Paso." In *The U.S.-Mexico Border: Transcending Divisions, Contesting Identities,* ed. David Spener and Kathleen Staudt, 185–211. Boulder, CO: Lynne Rienner.

Villasáez, José. 2003. "Queda en familia muerte de indocumentado." *El Norte,* August 14, online edition.

Warren, Susan, and Judy Wiessler. 1988. "Local Amnesty Flood Hit by Fraud—INS." *Houston Chronicle,* November 23, A1.

Weiner, Tim. 2003. "Wal-Mart Invades, and Mexico Gladly Srrenders." *New York Times,* December 6, online edition.

Wilson, Catherine. 1998. "Women Kept Enslaved in Prostitution." Associated Press. *San Antonio Express-News,* April 24, 10A.

Winingham, Ralph. 1998. "Six Men Are Killed on U.P. Train Tracks." *San Antonio Express-News,* October 13, 1A.

Winkler, Robert. 2002. "Coyotes Now at Home in Eastern United States." *National Geographic News,* August 6. http://news.nationalgeographic.com/news/2002/08/0806_020806_coyote.html (accessed February 27, 2007).

Wolf, Eric R. 1959. *Sons of the Shaking Earth.* Chicago: University of Chicago Press.

——. 1982. *Europe and the People without History.* Berkeley: University of California Press.

Wong, Diana. 2005. "The Rumor of Trafficking: Border Controls, Illegal Migration, and the Sovereignty of the Nation-State." In *Illicit Flows and Criminal Things: States, Borders, and the Other Side of Globalization,* ed. Willem van Schendel and Itty Abraham, 69–100. Bloomington: Indiana University Press.

Woo Morales, Ofelia. 2001. *Las mujeres también nos vamos al Norte.* Guadalajara, JA: Centro Universitario de Ciencias Sociales y Humanidades, Universidad de Guadalajara.

Woodrow, Karen A., and Jeffrey S. Passel. 1990. "Post-IRCA Undocumented Immigration to the United States: An Assessment Based on the June 1988 CPS." In *Undocumented Migration to the United States: IRCA and the Experience of the 1980s,* ed. Frank D. Bean, Barry Edmonston, and Jeffrey S. Passel, 33–75. Washington, DC: Urban Institute Press.

Yardley, Jim. 2000. "Some Texans Say Border Patrol Singles Out Too Many Blameless Latinos." *New York Times,* January 26, A17.

Zamora, Emilio. 1993. *The World of the Mexican Worker in Texas.* College Station: Texas A&M University Press.

Zarazua, Jorge. 2003a. "3 Held in Scheme at U.S. Consulate: Visas, Border Cards Allegedly Sold in Nuevo Laredo." *San Antonio Express-News,* February 1, online edition.

——. 2003b. "Nuevo Laredo Consulate Probe Continues: Most Staffers Put on Paid Leave." *San Antonio Express-News,* January 31, online edition.

——. 2003c. "Nuevo Laredo Consulate Shut in Fraud Probe." *San Antonio Express-News,* January 30, online edition.

——. 2003d. "U.S. Visas Return under Strict Eyes: New Procedures Are in Place at Nuevo Laredo after a Fraud Scheme." *San Antonio Express-News,* May 13, online edition.

——. 2003e. "Visa Dealers Sentenced to Federal Prison: Ex-Consulate Workers, Broker Had Pleaded Guilty to Conspiracy." *San Antonio Express-News,* July 26, online edition.

——. 2006. "281 Is the Road to Death for Immigrants." *San Antonio Express-News,* January 27, online edition.

Zazueta, Carlos H., and César Zazueta. 1980. *En las puertas del paraíso: Observaciones hechas en el levantamiento de la Primera Encuesta a Trabajadores Mexicanos no Documentados Duevueltos de los Estados Unidos, CENIET, Octubre 23–Noviembre 13 de 1977.* Mexico City: Centro Nacional de Información y Estadísticas del Trabajo, Secretaría de Trabajo y Previsión Social.

Zernike, Kate, and Ginger Thompson. 2003. "Deaths of Immigrants Uncover Makeshift World of Smuggling." *New York Times,* June 29, online edition.

Index